AQA GCSE Higher

Anneli McLachlan
Leanda Reeves

www.heinemann.co.uk
✓ Free online support
✓ Useful weblinks
✓ 24 hour online ordering

0845 630 33 33

Part of Pearson

Heinemann is an imprint of Pearson Education Limited, a company incorporated in England and Wales, having its registered office at Edinburgh Gate, Harlow, Essex, CM20 2JE. Registered company number: 872828

www.heinemann.co.uk

Heinemann is a registered trademark of Pearson Education Limited

First published 2009

15
10 9

British Library Cataloguing in Publication Data
A catalogue record for this book is available from the British Library.

ISBN 978 0 435395 93 3

Edited by Ruth Manteca
Designed by Ken Vail Graphic Design, Cambridge
Typeset by Ken Vail Graphic Design, Cambridge
Original illustrations © Pearson Education Ltd.
Illustrated by Beehive Illustration (Mark Ruffle), Stephen Elford, Graham-Cameron Illustration (David Benham), Ken Laidlaw, NB Illustration (Ben Swift), Sylvie Poggio Artists Agency (Rory Walker)
Cover design by Wooden Ark Studio
Picture research by Caitlin Swain and Susi Paz
Cover photo © Masterfile
Printed in China (CTPSC/09)

Acknowledgements
We would like to thank Christopher Lillington, Liliana Acosta da Uribe, Elena Alegre, Iñaki Alegre, Ione Ascanio Green, Nicky Barrett, Clive Bell, Gillian Eades, Clare Farley, Elaine Harnick, Alex Harvey, Ana Machado, Esther Mallol, Ruth Manteca, Philippa McFarland, Judith O'Hare, Susi Paz, Diana Reed, Daniel Reeves, Siobhan Snowden, Caitlin Swain, Carolyn Tabor, Alison Thomas, Ron Wallace, Vicki Whiting and Melissa Wilson for their invaluable help in the development and trialling of this course. We would also like to thank the pupils at the Instituto de Edcuación Secundaria López Neyra (Córdoba) and Isabel Teresa Rubio; the pupils at the Colegio Europa Internacional (Sevilla), Pedro de Lorenzo and Setmaní Valenzuela; Chema Bazán of Lucentum Digital and all those involved with the recordings.

The authors – Anneli Mclachlan and Leanda Reeves (neé Reed) – and publisher would like to thank the following individuals and organisations for permission to reproduce photographs and illustrations:

©PhotoDisc. 1998 p **7**; ©PhotoDisc p **7**; ©Yurchyks/Shutterstock p **7**; ©Photolocation 3/Alamy p **7**; ©Everynight Images/Alamy p **10**; ©Elizabeth Whiting & Associates/Alamy p **10**; ©blickwinkel/Alamy p **10**; ©imagebroker/Alamy p **10**; ©PIxel pusher/Alamy p **10**; ©Johan Furusjö/Alamy p **12**; ©PhotoDisc. 1999 pp **13**, **40**, **110**; ©Ron Buskirk/Alamy p **18**; Philip Lewis/Alamy p **20**; Buzzshotz/Alamy p **20**; ©Headline Photo Agency/Alamy p **26**; ©Barry Mason/Alamy p **26**; ©Pedro Diaz/Alamy p **26**; ©James Goldsmith/Alamy p **28**; ©Kim Karpeles/Alamy p **29**; ©Juan Monino/iStockPhoto p **30**; ©John Warburton-Lee Photography/Alamy p **32**; ©Pearson Education Ltd./Gareth Boden p **36**, **82**; ©Louise Batalla Duran/Alamy p **36**; ©David Young-Wolff/Alamy p **36**; ©Robert Harding Picture Library Ltd./Alamy p **36**; ©Art Kowalsky/Alamy p **40**; ©Stockbyte p **60**; ©Pearson Education Ltd./Jules Selmes pp **66**, **82**, **154**, **176**; ©Nick Hanna/Alamy pp **76**, **78**; ©Pearson Education Ltd./Studio 8. Clark Wiseman p **82**; ©Image Source Ltd. p **82**; ©i love images/Alamy p **87**; ©Iberia p **87**; ©Medical Doctor Nurse Dentist Pharmacist/Alamy p **91**; ©Allstar Picture Library/Alamy p **92**; ©Dimitrios Kambouris/WireImage/GettyImages p **92**; ©James Devaney/WireImage/GettyImages p **92**; ©Dave Hogan/Getty Images Entertainment p **92**; ©Behrouz Mehri/AFP/GettyImages p **92**; ©Kevin Winter/Getty Images Entertainment p **92**; ©Christian Petersen/Getty Images Sport p **95**; ©GettyImages p **95**; ©BWAC Images/Alamy p **98**; ©Robert Fried/Alamy p **108**; ©Alex Livesey/Getty Images Sport p **109**; ©Markus Seidel/iStockPhotos p **110**; ©Philipp Hympendahl/Alamy p **110**; ©Vladimir Piskunov/iStockPhotos p **110**; ©Marco Crisari/iStockPhotos p **110**; ©Bettina Ritter/iStockPhotos p **111**; ©Tequila gang/WB/The Kobal Collection p **114**; ©vario images GmbH & Co.KG/Alamy p **118**; ©Heiko Bennewitz/iStockPhoto p **120**; ©Vera Bogaerts/istockphoto p **128**; ©Ken Welsh/Alamy p **128**; ©Content Mine International/Alamy p **128**; ©One Sotneby's Int Realty p **129**; Igor Marx/istockphoto p **129**; ©Loic Bernard/istockphoto p **130**; ©Nickos/iStockPhoto p **138**; ©Wendell Teodoro/wireimage/GettyImages p **148**; ©Allstar Picture Library/Alamy p **148**; ©Associated Sports Photography/Alamy p **148**; ©Photodisc. Kevin Peterson pp **150**, **159**; ©Jose Manuel Vidal/epa/Corbis p **162**; ©Jon Mikel Duralde/Alamy p **162**; ©Steven May/Alamy p **162**; ©PCL/Alamy p **162**; ©Andrew Reese/istockphoto p **162**; ©Vario Images GmbH & co/Alamy p **162**; ©Mark Eveleigh/Alamy p **162**; ©Jupiter Images/Creatas p **164**; ©AP Photo/Paul White/Empics p **164**; ©Joan Farre/Dorling Kindersley/GettyImages p **164**; ©David Young-Wolff/Alamy p **164**; ©Chris Wayatt/Alamy p **164**; ©Mike Finn-Kelcey/Alamy p **164**; ©Shutterstock/Jan Martin Will p **164**; ©AP Photo/Luis Alvarez/Empics p **164**; ©iStockPhoto p **185**; ©Fernando Botero, Medellín 1932, Una familia 1989, Óleo sobre tela, 241 x 195 cm, Museo Botero, Bogotá, Colección Banco de la República de Colombia, registro 3336 p **192**; ©Photodisc. Photolink p **193**; ©Victoria Sambunaris/Architect Andrew Berman p **194**; ©Lalo Yasky/WireImage/GettyImages p **195**; ©Finca Bellavista p **198**; ©Pat Behnke/Alamy p **217**.
All other photos were provided by **Ione Ascanio Green** (**Mind Studio**) and Pearson Education Ltd.

Every effort has been made to contact copyright holders of material reproduced in this book. Any omissions will be rectified in subsequent printings if notice is given to the publishers.

©El Almadén, www.elalmaden.com p **25**; ©www.sevillaguia.com p **29**; ©Maringa, www.taringa.net p **136**; ©Eroski, www.consumer.es p **149**; ©Pobreza Cero, www.pobrezacero.org p **165**; ©Orienta, www.orienta.org.mx p **191**; ©Greenpeace, www.greenpeace.es p **167**; ©Telecinco, www.informativos.telecinco.es p **173**: ©ComprarCasas, www.comprarcasas.org pp **194**, **198**; ©Solidaridad Internacional, www.solidaridad.org p **199**.

Websites
The websites used in this book were correct and up-to-date at the time of publication. It is essential for tutors to preview each website before using it in class so as to ensure that the URL is still accurate, relevant and appropriate. We suggest that tutors bookmark useful websites and consider enabling students to access them through the school/college intranet.

Contenidos

1 De vacaciones
AQA context: Leisure

2 De paseo por Sevilla
AQA context: Leisure/Home and environment

3 A clase
AQA context: Work and education

Contenidos

4 ¡Perdidos! — AQA context: Lifestyle

5 Los trabajos — AQA context: Work and education

6 Mi tiempo libre — AQA context: Leisure

7 ¡Viva mi barrio!

AQA context: Leisure/Home and environment

8 La salud

AQA context: Lifestyle

9 Nuestro planeta

AQA context: Home and environment

- Talking about where you went
- Using the preterite
- Extending sentences with sequencers

Repaso ¿Adónde fuiste?

Escucha y escribe las letras correctas. (1–5)

***Ejemplo:* 1** b, i,…

¿Cuándo fuiste de vacaciones?	¿Adónde fuiste? Fui a…	¿Con quién fuiste? Fui…	¿Qué hiciste?	¿Qué tal lo pasaste?
a El año pasado…	**f** Grecia	**k** con mis amigos	**p** Escuché música. Tomé el sol.	**u** Lo pasé mal.
b El verano pasado…	**g** Estados Unidos	**l** con mis padres	**q** Fui de excursión y visité monumentos. Conocí a mucha gente.	**v** Lo pasé fenomenal.
c El invierno pasado…	**h** Francia	**m** con mi familia	**r** Mandé mensajes. Esquié.	**w** Lo pasé muy bien.
d Hace dos años…	**i** la República Dominicana	**n** solo	**s** Bailé. Jugué al voleibol.	**x** Lo pasé bien.
e Hace cinco años…	**j** la India	**o** sola	**t** Monté en bicicleta. Saqué fotos.	**y** Lo pasé fatal.

G *The preterite*

➲204

Use the preterite (simple past tense) for completed actions in the past.

	escuchar (*to listen*)	**com**er (*to eat*)	**sal**ir (*to go out*)	ir/ser (*to go/be*)
(yo)	escuch**é**	com**í**	sal**í**	fui
(tú)	escuch**aste**	com**iste**	sal**iste**	fuiste
(él/ella/usted)	escuch**ó**	com**ió**	sal**ió**	fue
(nosotros/as)	escuch**amos**	com**imos**	sal**imos**	fuimos
(vosotros/as)	escuch**asteis**	com**isteis**	sal**isteis**	fuisteis
(ellos/ellas/ustedes)	escuch**aron**	com**ieron**	sal**ieron**	fueron

Some verbs have spelling changes in the 'I' form of the verb:

Infinitive		Preterite	Infinitive		Preterite
jugar	→	ju**gu**é (*I played*)	sacar	→	sa**qu**é (*I took – for photos*)

2 Lee el texto y elige los verbos correctos.

la cordillera = *mountain range*
la catarata = *waterfall*

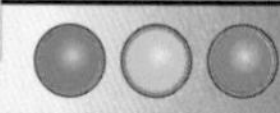

El verano pasado [1]**fui/pasé** a Argentina de vacaciones. [2]**Pasé/Fui** solo, pero lo [3]**fue/pasé** fenomenal. Primero fui a Buenos Aires. Allí [4]**conocí/mandé** a mucha gente, [5]**bailé/saqué** muchas fotos y también [6]**saqué/bailé** tango, que es muy típico allá. Después [7]**fui/comí** a las cataratas de Iguazú, que son preciosas, y luego fui a la cordillera de los Andes, donde finalmente esquié. [8]**Mandé/Fue** una experiencia inolvidable. ¡Viva Argentina!

David

3 Con tu compañero/a, mira las fotos e imagina las vacaciones. Pregunta y contesta.

- ¿Cuándo fuiste de vacaciones?
- ¿Adónde fuiste? (Primero fui a… luego fui a…)
- ¿Con quién fuiste?
- ¿Qué hiciste?
- ¿Qué tal lo pasaste?

In your speaking and writing make sure you add lots of detail to your sentences.

Sequencers and **connectives** will help you to achieve this.

Look at how David used these in his text: **primero**, **después**, **luego**, **también**, **y**, **pero** and **finalmente**.

Include **opinions** too:
Fue un desastre.
Fue una experiencia…
fantástica fenomenal
inolvidable terrible
horrible impresionante

a

La Torre Eiffel en París
Las montañas de los Alpes, cerca de Grenoble

b

La playa de Barbate, en el sur de España
Las ruinas del Anfiteatro de Mérida

4 Escribe un correo sobre tus vacaciones. Contesta a las preguntas del ejercicio 3.

When using the preterite always check that you have included the correct accents. Sometimes you need them and sometimes you don't. Leaving them out if they are needed can change the meaning of the verb!

escuch**o**	*I listen*	esquí**o**	*I ski*
escuch**ó**	*he/she listened*	esqui**ó**	*he/she skied*

- Talking about holidays and weather
- Using irregular verbs in the preterite
- Learning phrases meaning the same thing

1 ¿Qué tal tus vacaciones?

1 Escucha y escribe las letras en el orden mencionado. (1–2)

***Ejemplo:* 1** d, a,...

a Descansé.
b Nadé.
c Hice yoga.
d Fui a clases de baile.
e Di una vuelta en bicicleta.
f Vi lugares de interés.
g Monté a caballo.
h Patiné.
i Esquié.
j Hice alpinismo.
k Hice vela.
l Hice caída libre. No tuve miedo.

2 Listen again. How much did the speakers enjoy their activities? Write a list of the activities in English in order from the most positive to the most negative.

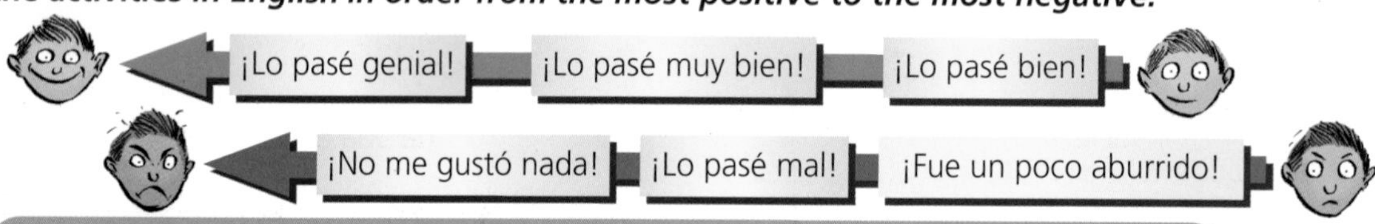
¡Lo pasé genial!
¡Lo pasé muy bien!
¡Lo pasé bien!
¡No me gustó nada!
¡Lo pasé mal!
¡Fue un poco aburrido!

G *The preterite: irregular verbs*

➲204

Some common verbs are irregular in the preterite.
Note that, unlike regular preterite verbs, these don't have any accents!

	hacer *(to do)*	**tener** *(to have)*	**ver** *(to see)*	**dar** *(to give)*
(yo)	hice	tuve	vi	di
(tú)	hiciste	tuviste	viste	diste
(él/ella/usted)	hizo	tuvo	vio	dio
(nosotros/as)	hicimos	tuvimos	vimos	dimos
(vosotros/as)	hicisteis	tuvisteis	visteis	disteis
(ellos/ellas/ustedes)	hicieron	tuvieron	vieron	dieron

3 Read the vocabulary tip and then rewrite these sentences in Spanish.

***Ejemplo:* a** El martes por la tarde hice ciclismo.

a El martes por la tarde di una vuelta en bicicleta.
b Un día fui a la pista de patinaje y luego fui a la piscina.
c Hice natación y también hice equitación.
d Un día monté a caballo y otro día monté en bicicleta.

Keep an eye on words and phrases that mean the same thing. They may be used to test your understanding! Here are some examples:
hacer equitación = montar a caballo
hacer patinaje = patinar = ir a la pista de patinaje
hacer natación = nadar = ir a la piscina
hacer ciclismo = montar en bicicleta = dar una vuelta en bicicleta

Keep a list of these throughout your GCSE course to help you remember them.

Escucha. Copia y completa la tabla. (1–5)

	When?	What?	Weather?	Opinion?
1	*last year*	*rock climbing*		

El año pasado…
El invierno pasado…
El verano pasado…
Hace dos meses…
Hace un año…
hizo buen tiempo.
hizo mal tiempo.
hizo calor.
hizo frío.
hizo sol.
hizo viento.
hubo niebla.
hubo tormenta.
llovió.
nevó.

Con tu compañero/a, pregunta y contesta sobre tus vacaciones.

- ¿Cuándo fuiste de vacaciones?
- ¿Adónde fuiste?
- ¿Qué hiciste?
- ¿Qué tiempo hizo?
- ¿Qué tal lo pasaste? (Lo pasé… Fue una experiencia…)

Lee los textos y escribe la letra correcta para cada texto.

A deportes de invierno
B deportes acuáticos
C vacaciones individuales
D actividades turísticas
E artes marciales

1 El verano pasado fui de crucero por las islas Griegas con mis padres. Lo pasé fenomenal. Hice natación y vela. También hice buceo y esquí acuático. Hizo mucho sol, excepto un día que hubo niebla. ¡Qué raro! Me gustó mucho, lo único malo fue que no pude hacer windsurf. ¡Qué pena! **Juan**

2 El año pasado fui a Argentina de vacaciones y lo pasé fenomenal. Hicimos esquí en Catedral, de allí vienen todos los campeones de esquí de Argentina. Hizo frío y un poco de viento. Nevó mucho, pero también hizo sol. Un día monté en moto de nieve y aunque tuve miedo, fue una experiencia inolvidable. **Alicia**

3 Hace dos años fui a Barcelona de vacaciones con mis amigos. Descansé y nadé en el mar. Un día dimos una vuelta en bicicleta por el puerto y otro día fuimos de excursión a *Tierra Mítica*. Saqué muchas fotos y vi monumentos típicos, pero me aburrí mucho en los museos. Hizo buen tiempo, hizo sol y calor. **Carlos**

Lee los textos otra vez. Contesta a las preguntas.

1 Where was it cold?
2 Where was it foggy?
3 Where was it hot?
4 Who was afraid? Why?
5 Who got bored? Why?
6 Who was disappointed? Why?

- Describing accommodation
- Using the imperfect tense for description
- Giving and justifying opinions

2 ¿Qué tal el hotel?

1 Escucha y apunta los datos en inglés. (1–5)

a type of accommodation **b** country visited **c** description **d** facilities

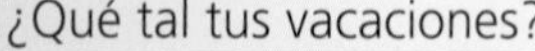

¿Qué tal tus vacaciones?		
Me quedé en… Me alojé en… un hotel de cinco estrellas un albergue juvenil un camping un parador una pensión	Era… No era (nada)… acogedor/ora antiguo/a nuevo/a cómodo/a poco cómodo/a bonito/a feo/a caro/a barato/a animado/a tranquilo/a lujoso/a	Tenía… Había… No tenía… ni… ni… No había… Tampoco había… (un) bar (un) gimnasio (un) restaurante (una) discoteca (una) piscina climatizada (una) sauna (una) cafetería (una) cocina comunitaria
Estaba… en la costa en la montaña en el campo al lado de la playa en el centro de la ciudad		

Understanding and using negatives will help you produce good written and spoken work.

Tampoco… = *not either…* — **Tampoco** tenía sauna.

No… **ni**… **ni** = *neither… nor* — **No** tenía **ni** piscina **ni** gimnasio.

G The imperfect tense

206

The imperfect tense is used to describe what something was like.

El camping **estaba** en la montaña. *The campsite was in the mountains.*
Tenía una piscina impresionante. *It had an impressive swimming pool.*

	estar *(to be)*	**tener** *(to have)*	**vivir** *(to live)*
(yo)	est**aba**	ten**ía**	viv**ía**
(tú)	est**abas**	ten**ías**	viv**ías**
(él/ella/usted)	est**aba**	ten**ía**	viv**ía**
(nosotros/as)	est**ábamos**	ten**íamos**	viv**íamos**
(vosotros/as)	est**abais**	ten**íais**	viv**íais**
(ellos/ellas/ustedes)	est**aban**	ten**ían**	viv**ían**

Only three verbs are irregular in the imperfect tense:

ser *(to be)* → **era** *(it was)*
ir *(to go)* → **iba** *(he/she was going)*
ver *(to see/watch)* → **veía** *(he/she was seeing/watching)*

hay *(there is/there are)* → **había** *(there was/there were)*

2 Con tu compañero/a, haz estos diálogos.

¿Qué tal tus vacaciones?

- Me alojé en…
- Estaba…
- Era…
- Tenía/Había…
- No tenía/había…
- Tampoco tenía/había…

3 Lee los blogs. ¿P (positivo), N (negativo), o P + N (positivo y negativo)?

A Mis vacaciones en Francia fueron horrorosas. Me alojé en un albergue juvenil que era horrible. Estaba en la costa. No era nada cómodo. No había piscina. No había nada. No tenía ni cocina comunitaria, ni sala de desayunos. Lo peor del albergue era que por la noche había mucho ruido.

B El hotel era nuevo y muy cómodo. Estaba en la costa y era muy acogedor, pero no era muy tranquilo. Tenía gimnasio, discoteca y restaurante de comida de todo el mundo. Lo mejor del hotel era que tenía piscina climatizada, aunque lo peor era que había mucha gente.

C Mi hotel en Grecia tenía todo lo que necesitaba. Estaba en la montaña. Tenía discoteca y restaurante. También había una sauna. Era antiguo, pero muy bonito. Mis vacaciones fueron fantásticas. Lo mejor del hotel era que había mucha gente. El hotel era muy animado y no era nada caro.

D Me quedé en un parador en Almagro. Era precioso, muy antiguo y lujoso, pero no era muy animado. No había discoteca. Tampoco tenía piscina. Lo mejor del parador era que tenía un restaurante muy bueno. Fue una experiencia fantástica, pero era un poco caro.

4 *Read the texts again. What was the best or worst thing about each person's holiday?*

Make sure you give opinions in your writing. For a really impressive answer it is important to give opinions but also to extend your sentences by justifying your opinions.

Opinion	**Justification**
Mis vacaciones fueron fantásticas…	porque conocí a mucha gente.

5 Describe tus vacaciones del año pasado.

Me alojé en… en…
Había…
También tenía…
(No) Era…
Lo mejor del hotel era que…
Fue una experiencia fantástica.

Me alojé en…
No había…
Tampoco tenía…
(No) Era…
Lo peor de la pensión era que…
Fue una experiencia horrorosa.

- Talking about holiday activities
- Using the imperfect and the preterite together
- Learning question words

3 Buenas vacaciones

Listen and read the email. Which Spanish title corresponds with each paragraph? (There are two titles too many).

A la historia de la isla	**D** el viaje	**G** la gente
B la vida nocturna	**E** planes para el futuro	**H** el alojamiento
C el tiempo	**F** la flora y la fauna	**I** el deporte

1 ¡Hola Miguel!
¿Qué tal? En febrero **pasé** una semana en Gran Canaria. **Fui** en avión. El vuelo **duró** tres horas y **fue** muy agradable.

2 Mi hotel **estaba** en la costa y **era** muy moderno. **Tenía** un restaurante fantástico y un gimnasio.

3 Casi todos los clientes **eran** ingleses. Los camareros **llevaban** uniforme y **hablaban** un poco de inglés. **Conocí** a muchos españoles que **vivían** cerca del hotel. ¡Todos **eran** muy simpáticos! **Mejoré** mi español gracias a ellos.

4 El primer día **hizo** frío y **llovió** un poco, pero después **hizo** sol toda la semana. A mí me encanta el calor porque ¡en Inglaterra hace tanto frío!

5 **Podías** hacer muchas actividades. **Jugué** al baloncesto e **hice** windsurf y vela. Voy a continuar con la vela en Inglaterra.

6 ¡Por la noche **era** imposible aburrirse! El viernes **bailé** en una discoteca, el sábado **vi** un concurso de fuegos artificiales y el domingo **fui** a una fiesta muy divertida.

7 Para mí Gran Canaria es un lugar de vacaciones ideal. Espero volver el año que viene porque me encanta. **Jorge**

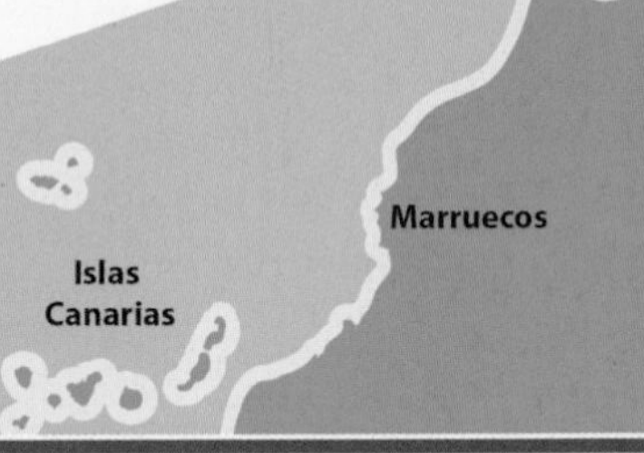

Lee el texto otra vez. Copia y completa la tabla. (Traduce los verbos.)

verbs in the preterite (completed actions)	verbs in the imperfect (descriptions)
pasé – I spent	estaba – it was

G The imperfect tense ➲206

The imperfect is used for *descriptions* in the past, as you saw in the previous unit.

The text above introduces some more verbs in the imperfect tense. Most verbs follow these regular patterns in the imperfect:

	hablar *(to speak)*	poder *(to be able to)*	vivir *(to live)*
(yo)	habl**aba**	pod**ía**	viv**ía**
(tú)	habl**abas**	pod**ías**	viv**ías**
(él/ella/usted)	habl**aba**	pod**ía**	viv**ía**
(nosotros/as)	habl**ábamos**	pod**íamos**	viv**íamos**
(vosotros/as)	habl**abais**	pod**íais**	viv**íais**
(ellos/ellas/ustedes)	habl**aban**	pod**ían**	viv**ían**

G The preterite ➲204

By contrast, the preterite is used for *completed actions* in the past:

Pasé una semana en Gran Canaria.
I spent a week in Gran Canaria.

El primer día **hizo** frío.
On the first day it was cold.

3 ***Use the tip box to help you work out the meaning of these words/phrases from the text in exercise 1.***

1 el vuelo
2 duró
3 agradable
4 mejoré
5 fuegos artificiales

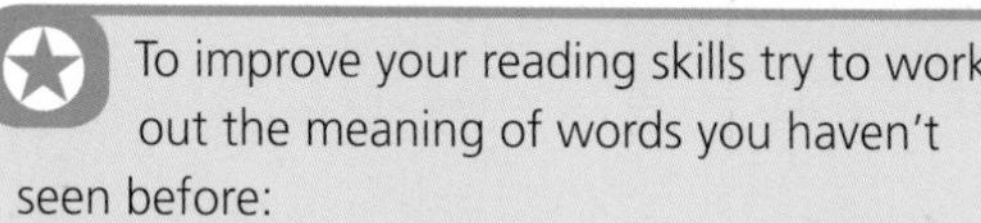

To improve your reading skills try to work out the meaning of words you haven't seen before:

- Is it similar enough to an English word to guess? If not, does it look like an adjective, noun or verb that you already know?
- Can you guess from the context what the word might mean?

4 ***Read the email. Imperfect or preterite? Write the correct verb.***

El invierno pasado [1]**fui/iba** a Nueva York de vacaciones. [2]**Pasé/Pasaba** dos semanas allí. [3]**Me alojé/Me alojaba** en casa de mi amigo Jeremi. Su casa [4]**era/fue** muy lujosa y [5]**tenía/tuvo** unas vistas preciosas de Manhattan. [6]**Fue/Era** una experiencia estupenda porque [7]**hice/hacía** muchísimas cosas. [8]**Vi/Veía** los monumentos más emblemáticos, como la Estatua de la Libertad o el Moma. Un día [9]**patiné/patinaba** en Central Park y otro [10]**comí/comía** una bagel en el Soho. Lo malo fue que [11]**hacía/hizo** frío y un día [12]**nevó/nevaba**. **Íñigo**

las vistas = *views*

5 **Escucha y lee las preguntas. ¿Qué significan?**

1 ¿Cuándo fuiste de vacaciones?
2 ¿Adónde fuiste?
3 ¿Cuánto tiempo pasaste allí?
4 ¿Dónde te alojaste?
5 ¿Cómo era el hotel?
6 ¿Qué había en el hotel?
7 ¿Qué tiempo hizo?
8 ¿Qué hiciste durante tus vacaciones?

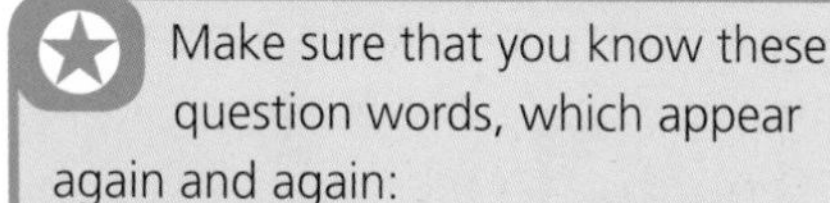

Make sure that you know these question words, which appear again and again:

¿Dónde...?	*Where...?*
¿Adónde...?	*Where to...?*
¿Cuándo...?	*When...?*
¿Cuánto/a...?	*How much...?*
¿Qué...?	*What...? Which...?*
¿Cómo...?	*How...?*

6 **Escucha. Copia y completa la tabla en inglés. (1–4)**

	accommodation/location	facilities	activities	when	weather
1	*wonderful parador, near the sea*				

To make your text as sophisticated as possible:

- use the imperfect to describe things
- use the preterite to express completed actions
- use sequencers: **primero..., luego..., finalmente...**
- use negatives: **no había..., tampoco había...**
- say what the best/worst thing about the holiday was: **lo peor/mejor era...**
- give your opinion about the experience and justify it: **fue una experiencia... porque...**

7 **Eres Jorge. Con tu compañero/a pregunta y contesta. Utiliza las preguntas del ejercicio 5.**

8 **Describe tus vacaciones. Contesta a las preguntas del ejercicio 5.**

- Booking a hotel room
- Using verbs with **usted**
- Dealing with unpredictable questions

4 En el hotel

1 Lee y empareja los correos con las personas correctas.

1

Estimado señor:
Me gustaría reservar una habitación doble y una habitación individual sin minibar. Quisiéramos pasar quince días en el hotel, del 2 al 16 de julio. Somos dos adultos y nuestro hijo de diecisiete años. ¿Está incluido el desayuno? ¿Se admiten perros?
Le saluda atentamente, **Mariana Suárez**

2

Estimado/a señor(a):
Me gustaría pasar dos noches en su hotel. Voy a llegar el 2 de junio y voy a salir el 4 de junio. Quisiera una habitación individual. ¿Cuánto cuestan las habitaciones con vistas al mar? ¿Hay gimnasio en el hotel?
Gracias, **Manuel Ferrer**

3

Estimado/a señor(a):
Me gustaría reservar una habitación individual en su hotel del 8 al 15 de julio. Quisiera una habitación con balcón y con vistas al mar porque quiero sacar fotos de la puesta del sol. ¿Me puede decir si hay conexión a Internet?
Muchas gracias, **Elena Acosta**

4

Estimado señor:
Quisiera reservar una habitación doble con cama de matrimonio. Somos dos adultos.
Vamos a llegar tarde, a las once. ¿Hasta qué hora está abierta la recepción?
Nos gustaría descansar y no hacer nada. ¿Hay servicio de habitaciones?
Quisiéramos pasar ocho noches, del 7 al 15 de agosto.
¿Puede enviarme los precios del alojamiento con pensión completa?
Le saluda atentamente,
Ramón Martínez

quisiera = *I would like*
quisiéramos = *we would like*

a 

b 

c 

d 

2 Busca estas frases en inglés en los correos del ejercicio 1.

1. I would like to reserve a double room.
2. We would like to spend a fortnight at the hotel.
3. Can you tell me if there is Internet access?
4. How much do rooms with sea views cost?
5. We are going to arrive late.
6. Is breakfast included?
7. Until when is reception open?
8. Are dogs allowed?

3 Escucha y escribe las letras de los dibujos mencionados. (1–3)

¿Dígame?		
Me gustaría reservar… Quisiera reservar…	una habitación doble… una habitación individual para… noches/días…	sin/con baño. con balcón. con vistas al mar. con cama de matrimonio.

4 ***Listen again. Which speaker asks about the following? (1–3)***

Room service? ***Internet access?***

Dogs allowed? ***Breakfast times?***

Reception opening times?

¿Hay servicio de habitaciones?
¿Hay conexión a Internet?
¿Hasta qué hora se sirve el desayuno/ la comida/la cena?
¿A qué hora cierra la recepción/el bar?
¿Hasta que hora está abierto/a el restaurante/la recepción?
¿Se admiten perros?

5 Escribe un diálogo, cambiando los datos para a o b.

- ● Hotel Madrid, ¿dígame?
- ■ Quisiera reservar una habitación doble.
- ● ¿Quiere una habitación con balcón o sin balcón?
- ■ Con balcón, por favor.
- ● ¿Para cuántas noches?
- ■ Para 4 noches, del 16 al 20 de agosto.
- ● ¿Su apellido, por favor?
- ■ Watson.
- ● Watson... ¿Cómo se deletrea?
- ■ W-A-T-S-O-N.
- ● Gracias.
- ■ ¿Cuánto es, por favor?
- ● Son 200€.
- ■ ¿Hay conexión a Internet?
- ● Sí, señor.

a

Single room	7–14 September
With sea views	Davies
No breakfast	100€
7 nights	Dogs allowed?

b

Double room
With double bed
5 nights
17–22 July
Simpson
500€
Until what time is breakfast served?

6 ***Listen and write down the questions from the receptionist in Spanish. What do they mean? (1–6)***

The reception desk of a hotel is a place where conversation takes place in a polite way. Writing a letter to a hotel is also a time to use formal language. Use **usted** rather than **tú** in these situations.
The **usted** part of the verb is the third person singular. This is the same as the he/she part of the verb.
Can you find examples of this in the letters in exercise 1?

7 Con tu compañero/a, haz el diálogo del ejercicio 5 delante de la clase.

In your speaking assessment you will have to answer unexpected questions. You will also have the chance to ask a question.
If you are the receptionist try adding one of the questions from exercise 6 at the end of your dialogue. If you are the client:

- listen carefully to the question word
- listen to the verb used – this may help you to form an answer
- if you don't understand the question, ask: **¿Puede repetir, por favor?**
- win time by using short phrases like **A ver...** and **Pues...**

- Making complaints in a hotel
- Using **me hace falta**
- Joining ideas with connectives

5 Reclamaciones

1 Escucha y lee la canción. Escribe las letras en el orden correcto.

a
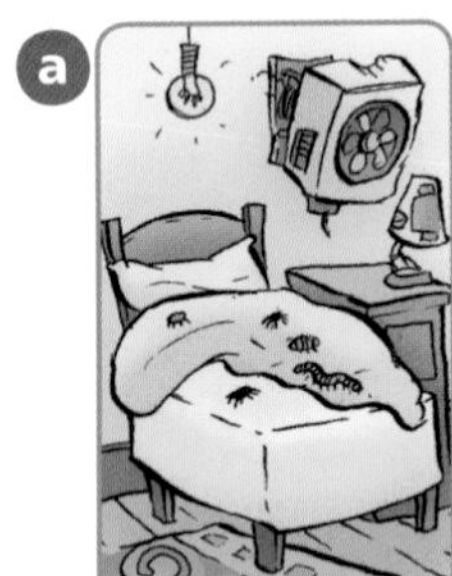

b

c

d

e

Estribillo

¡Ay, este hotel!
Este hotel me vuelve loca.
Quiero quejarme ahora.
¡Quiero un descuento ya!

1
La habitación no está limpia.
Hay insectos en la cama.
El aire acondicionado está roto.
Y la luz no funciona.

[Estribillo]

2
El aseo no está limpio.
No hay papel higiénico.
El baño está sucio.
Y también hay mucho ruido.

[Estribillo]

3
Me hace falta una pastilla de jabón.
¿Qué vamos a hacer Ramón?
Quiero cambiar de habitación.
Esa es mi intención.

[Estribillo]

4
En el suelo hay cucarachas.
En el baño no hay toallas.
El mar, ¿dónde está?
Aquí no hay buenas vistas.

[Estribillo]

5
Necesito un secador.
No funciona el ascensor.
Quiero hablar con el director.
¡Ay! ¡Qué horror! ¡Qué horror!

[Estribillo]

2 Read the statements and write the number for the correct section of the song.

a *Lo siento mucho, señorita. Vamos a limpiar el cuarto de baño en seguida.*

b *Ahora mismo me encargo de su habitación. Voy a llamar al técnico y al servicio de limpieza inmediatamente.*

c *El hotel está casi completo. Un momento… Tengo otra habitación, pero es más cara… A ver…, le puedo hacer un descuento si usted quiere cambiar de habitación…*

d *Lo siento, señorita, pero el director no está.*

e *¡Qué horror! Le voy a dar un bote de insecticida. Voy a ver si hay otra habitación con vistas al mar.*

3 Escucha. Copia y completa la tabla. (1–3)

	problems	desired outcome	reaction of receptionist
1	*dirty toilet,...*		

¿Qué le pasa, señor/señorita?	
El ascensor El aseo La luz La ducha	no funciona.
El baño no está limpio. El aseo está sucio. La habitación no está limpia. La cama está sucia.	

G Me hace falta *(I need)*

A useful phrase to say what you need is **me hace(n) falta...** This behaves like **me gusta(n)**:

Me hace falta	papel higiénico.	*(toilet roll)*
	jabón.	*(soap)*
	un secador.	*(a hair dryer)*
Me hacen falta	toallas.	*(towels)*
	unas aspirinas.	*(aspirins)*

4 Con tu compañero/a, haz dos diálogos.

- ● Ask what is wrong.
- ■ Say what the problem is.
- ● Suggest a solution.
- ■ Say you would like to change rooms.
- ● Say that, unfortunately, the hotel is almost full.
- ■ Ask to speak to the director/demand a discount.

5 Lee el texto y completa las frases en inglés.

El año pasado fui de vacaciones a Barcelona y lo pasé muy mal. Me alojé en una pensión cerca de la Plaza Real. Era barata, pero no era nada acogedora porque estaba sucia y vieja.

No había jabón en el cuarto de baño, tampoco había toallas y por la noche había mucho ruido porque estaba cerca de una calle de mucho tráfico, por eso no dormí mucho.

Lo peor de la pensión eran las cucarachas, había unas cucarachas enormes. ¡Qué asco!

El año que viene voy a ir de camping. Por lo menos allí no hay cucarachas.

1 Jorge had a... time in Barcelona.
2 He stayed...
3 There was no..., no... and a lot of...
4 The worst thing was...
5 Next year Jorge is going to...
6 He thinks that the campsite won't have...

6 Describe unas vacaciones horrorosas. Utiliza las palabras en azul de Jorge.

Use connectives like these to extend your sentences and add opinions to produce really impressive answers.

también	*also*
pero	*but*
por eso	*that's why*
por lo menos	*at least*

Prueba oral

Holidays

You are going to have a conversation with your teacher about holidays. Your teacher could ask you the following:

- Why do people go on holiday?
- What type of holiday do you prefer?
- Describe your last holiday.
- What did you do?
- How was it?

Remember that you will also have to respond to an unexpected question that you have not yet prepared.
The dialogue will last between 4 and 6 minutes.

You are going to listen to Tom, an exam candidate, taking part in the above conversation with his teacher. Listen to part 1 of the conversation (questions 1 and 2 above) and match the beginnings and ends of these sentences.

1 Es importante...
2 Vamos de vacaciones también...
3 A mí me interesan mucho...
4 Cuando voy de vacaciones, ...
5 Además, ...
6 Me encanta...
7 El año que viene...

a vamos a ir a la estación de esquí de Vail...
b para descubrir el mundo, ...
c ir de vacaciones para descansar, ...
d las actividades turísticas...
e hacer esquí.
f me gustan mucho los deportes de invierno.
g me gusta descansar, leer, nadar...

Listen again and note down in English how Tom answers the first two questions.

Listen to part 2 of Tom's conversation and note down the words that fill the gaps.

– Describe tus vacaciones del año pasado.
– El año pasado, (1) _____, fui de vacaciones al sur de España, a Andalucía. Fui con mi familia. (2) _____ vamos de vacaciones todos juntos. Me quedé en una ciudad que se llama Ronda. Está en la montaña. Me alojé en un hotel bastante lujoso de cuatro estrellas. (3) _____ el hotel tenía una piscina climatizada bastante grande y una sala de juegos. (4) _____ no tenía ni restaurante, ni bar. Compartí una habitación doble con mi hermana. (5) _____ porque era demasiado pequeña, pero mis padres tenían una habitación más grande con balcón.

– ¿Qué hiciste durante tus vacaciones?
– Hicimos muchas cosas (6) _____. Fuimos a la playa (7) _____ y (8) _____ jugamos al voleibol. Fue muy divertido e hizo mucho calor. (9) _____ fuimos a una corrida de toros en Ronda, pero (10) _____ porque mi hermana vomitó. ¡Qué horror! A ella le gustan mucho los animales y, por eso la corrida de toros fue demasiado cruel para ella. A mí tampoco me gustó porque es un espectáculo muy cruel.

Look at the words you identified in exercise 3. How would you describe them?

- time expressions
- phrases of opinion

Now listen to part 3 of Tom's conversation and answer the questions.

1 Tom's teacher asks him a question about his holiday in the past tense (*¿Qué tal lo pasaste?*). Which time frames (past, present, future) does he use in his answer?
2 What is the unexpected question that Tom's teacher asks and what does it mean?
3 Listen to his answers to both questions. Find examples of how he talks about the future using ***querer* + infinitive**, ***me gustaría* + infinitive** and ***ir a* + infinitive**.
4 In his answer to the second question, Tom uses two phrases to extend an answer: ***para* + infinitive** and ***por lo menos***. What do these phrases mean?

Now it's your turn! Prepare your answers to the task and then have a conversation with your teacher or partner.

- Use the Grade Studio and Tom's answers to help you plan.
- Adapt what Tom said to talk about yourself but add your own ideas.
- Prepare your answers to the task questions and try to predict what the unexpected question could be. The examiner might base this question on something you have already said, or ask something totally new!
- Record the conversation. Ask a partner to listen to it and say how well you performed.

Award each other one star, two stars or three stars for each of these categories:

- *Pronunciation*
- *Confidence and fluency*
- *Range of tenses*
- *Variety of vocabulary and expressions*
- *Using longer sentences*
- *Taking the initiative*

What do you need to do next time to improve your performance?

GradeStudio

To produce a good answer you need to be able to use a variety of structures.

- Include simple **opinions** and **time expressions**. Select some from exercise 3 that you feel you could use in your own speaking.
- Try to **extend your sentences** in simple ways, using connectives like *y* (and), *pero* (but), *también* (also), *además* (in addition), *porque* (because).
- Referring to the past, present and future will help to show a variety of structures. In part 3, even though he was asked a question about a past holiday, Tom also included some information about hopes for a future holiday.

To go a step further you need to use a wider **variety of tenses**.

- Tom uses the **preterite** and the **imperfect** to talk about his holiday in Spain last year. Find some examples. What does Tom use the preterite for? What does Tom use the imperfect for?
- Try to talk about people other than yourself, so that you use a greater **variety of verbs**. Can you find examples of where Tom does this?
- When giving opinions, use a variety of phrases (things like *lo mejor/peor era* and *no me gustó porque...*).

For a really impressive answer:

- Use **negatives** like *tampoco* and *no..., ni... ni...* See examples of how Tom uses these in exercise 3.
- Use **complex sentences** that contain more than one tense or several ideas joined together in one sentence. Can you find examples of A* sentences in exercise 3?
- Use as great a variety of structures to extend your sentences as possible. Here are some that Tom uses which really add an edge to what he says: *para* + infinitive, *por eso...*, *por lo menos...*

Prueba escrita

Read the text and put these captions in the order they are mentioned.

a ¡Viva el sol! **b** Adiós Dinard **c** No funcionaba nada
d Hizo mal tiempo **e** Un castillo impresionante **f** Mis planes

El verano pasado fui de vacaciones a Francia con mi familia. El viaje fue largo y aburrido. Primero fuimos a un camping cerca de Dinard, donde lo pasamos fatal. ¡Fue un desastre total!

Montamos la tienda en un sitio precioso, pero no hizo buen tiempo. Hizo frío y por la noche tenía mucho frío en el saco de dormir. Un día hizo viento y otro día llovió, y por eso me quedé en la tienda. Jugué a las cartas con mis padres y gané, como siempre.

Carlos

No había agua caliente en el camping. Tampoco había lavandería y eso es imprescindible. Además, los servicios no estaban limpios, pero lo peor era que las duchas no funcionaban. ¡Qué horror! Dos semanas sin ducharse – ¡no gracias! Por eso decidimos cambiar de camping.

Después fuimos a Fougères porque allí el camping era mucho más cómodo. Era caro, pero tranquilo, con duchas que funcionaban y agua caliente. Lo mejor era que había una piscina climatizada. Hizo mucho sol y nadé con mis nuevos amigos. El viernes fui de excursión con mis padres al castillo medieval de Fougères. ¡Es el más grande de Europa! Saqué unas fotos muy chulas. Me gusta mucho sacar fotos.

Al final lo pasamos bien en Francia, pero creo que el año que viene no voy a ir de camping. No me gusta. Prefiero los hoteles. En verano voy a ir de vacaciones con mis amigos. Vamos a hacer un viaje por Europa: España, Italia, Alemania y Francia, y nos vamos a quedar en albergues juveniles. ¡Lo vamos a pasar bomba!

Find the equivalent of these expressions in Spanish in the text. Copy them out under the following headings: preterite, imperfect or near future.

1. First we went to a campsite near Dinard…
2. …where we had a terrible time.
3. One day it was windy… another day it rained…
4. There was no hot water…
5. What's more, the toilets weren't clean…
6. …but the worst thing was that the showers didn't work.
7. …the campsite was much more comfortable…
8. In the end we had a good time in France…
9. In the summer I'm going to go on holiday with my friends.
10. …we are going to stay in youth hostels.

3 ***Look at the text again. Make a list of words and phrases used to do these things:***

- give the text structure
- extend sentences with extra information.

4 ***You might be asked to write about your holidays as a Controlled Assessment task. Use the Grade Studio to help you prepare your account.***

GradeStudio

To produce a good answer you need to use a variety of language and express opinions.

- Find an example of the **present** tense in the text.
- Carlos uses the **preterite** to talk about complete actions in the past. Find three examples.
- Find an example of how Carlos uses the **near future** tense.
- Carlos gives **opinions** throughout. Can you find three examples?

To go a step further you need to use a wider range of language. This might include: other tenses, such as the **imperfect**, verbs referring to a **variety of people** (I, he/she, we, they), **longer sentences** with connectives and time phrases like the ones you listed in exercise 3.

- Find two examples of how Carlos uses the imperfect tense.
- Find examples of where Carlos talks about people other than himself.
- Carlos uses a number of phrases to extend his sentences with extra information and give the text structure. Choose some expressions (not all of them!) that you would like to include in your own text.
- Put some real **exclamations** into your text to make the description more expressive. Where has Carlos done this?

For a really impressive answer:

- Include a **complex sentence** with two tenses in it. For example, use the preterite to talk about what you did, combined with the imperfect to describe what something was like. Can you find an example of this in the fourth paragraph of the text?
- Use **relative pronouns** (*donde* or *cuando*). Look at how Carlos does this.

5 ***Now write a full account of your holidays.***

- Adapt Carlos' text and use language from Module 1. Write at least 200 words.
- Structure your text carefully. Organise what you write in paragraphs.

General summary of the trip

Where? Who with?
How long for?
Details of the journey
In general, how was it?

Main paragraph

Give details of the place where you stayed and what you did (Carlos does this twice for two different places!).
Give details of your hotel/campsite and its facilities (what there was and wasn't)
Talk about the weather.
Describe what you did on different days.
What was the best/worst thing?

Conclusion

Say whether you enjoyed the holiday.
Same again next year? Why/Why not?
Plans for next year.

6 ***Check carefully what you have written.***

- tenses (preterite, imperfect, present, near future?)
- spelling and accents (accents on preterite and imperfect verbs?)
- verb endings (correct for I, he/she, we, they?)

Palabras

¿Adónde fuiste de vacaciones? *Where did you go on holiday?*

Fui a...	*I went to...*
Alemania	*Germany*
Argentina	*Argentina*
Cuba	*Cuba*
Escocia	*Scotland*
España	*Spain*
Francia	*France*
Gales	*Wales*
Grecia	*Greece*
la India	*India*
Inglaterra/Gran Bretaña	*England/Great Britain*
Irlanda	*Ireland*
Italia	*Italy*
México	*Mexico*
Pakistán	*Pakistan*
Portugal	*Portugal*
la República Dominicana	*Dominican Republic*
Estados Unidos	*USA*
¿Cuándo fuiste de vacaciones?	*When did you go on holiday?*
el año pasado	*last year*
el verano pasado	*last summer*
el invierno pasado	*last winter*
hace dos/cinco años	*two/five years ago*
¿Con quién fuiste?	*Who did you go with?*
Fui...	*I went...*
con mi familia	*with my family*
con mis padres	*with my parents*
con mis amigos	*with my friends*
solo/a	*alone*
¿Qué hiciste?	*What did you do?*
Bailé	*I danced*
Conocí a mucha gente	*I met many people*
Escuché música	*I listened to music*
Esquié	*I skied*
Fui de excursión	*I went on a trip*
Jugué al voleibol	*I played volleyball*
Mandé mensajes	*I sent texts*
Monté en bicicleta	*I rode a bike*
Saqué fotos	*I took photos*
Tomé el sol	*I sunbathed*
Visité monumentos	*I visited monuments.*
¿Qué tal lo pasaste?	*How was it?*
Lo pasé...	*It was...*
bien	*good*
muy bien	*very good*
fenomenal	*wonderful*
fatal	*horrible*
guay	*great*
mal	*rubbish*
primero	*first*
después	*after*
luego	*then*
también	*also*
y	*and*
pero	*but*
finalmente	*finally*

¿Qué tal tus vacaciones? *How were your holidays?*

Descansé.	*I rested.*
Monté a caballo.	*I went horse riding.*
Nadé.	*I swam.*
Patiné.	*I skated.*
Esquié.	*I skied.*
Hice yoga.	*I did yoga.*
Hice alpinismo.	*I went climbing.*
Hice vela.	*I went sailing.*
Hice caída libre.	*I went sky diving.*
Fui a clases de baile.	*I went to dance classes.*
Di una vuelta en bicicleta.	*I went for a bike ride.*
Vi lugares de interés.	*I visited places of interest.*
No tuve miedo.	*I wasn't scared.*
¿Qué tiempo hizo?	*What was the weather like?*
Hizo buen tiempo.	*The weather was good.*
Hizo mal tiempo.	*The weather was bad.*
Hizo calor.	*It was hot.*
Hizo frío.	*It was cold.*
Hizo sol.	*It was sunny.*
Hizo viento.	*It was windy.*
Hubo niebla.	*It was foggy.*
Hubo tormenta.	*It was stormy.*
Llovió.	*It rained.*
Nevó.	*It snowed.*

¿Qué tal el hotel? *How was the hotel?*

me alojé en.../me quedé en...	*I stayed in...*
un hotel de cinco estrellas	*a five star hotel*
un albergue juvenil	*a youth hostel*
un camping	*a campsite*
un parador	*a parador*
una pensión	*a B&B*
Estaba...	*It was...*
en la costa	*on the coast*
en la montaña	*in the mountains*
en el campo	*in the countryside*
al lado de la playa	*next to the beach*
en el centro de la ciudad	*in the centre of the city*
Era.../No era (nada)...	*It was.../It wasn't ... at all*
acogedor/a	*welcoming*
antiguo/a	*old*
nuevo/a	*new*
cómodo/a	*comfortable*
poco cómodo/a	*not very comfortable*
bonito/a	*nice*
feo/a	*ugly/horrible*
caro/a	*expensive*
barato/a	*cheap*
animado/a	*lively*
tranquilo/a	*quiet*
lujoso/a	*luxurious*
Tenía...	*It had...*
Había...	*There were...*
No tenía... ni... ni...	*It had neither... nor...*
No había... tampoco había...	*There were no... nor...*
(un) bar	*a bar*
(un) gimnasio	*a gym*
(un) restaurante	*a restaurant*
(una) discoteca	*a disco*
(una) piscina climatizada	*a heated pool*
(una) cafetería	*a café*
(una) sauna	*a sauna*
(una) cocina comunitaria	*a shared kitchen*
¿Qué era lo mejor o lo peor del hotel?	*What was the best or worst thing about the ... hotel?*
Lo mejor/peor era que...	*The best/worst thing was that...*

Buenas vacaciones *A good holiday*

Pasé una semana.	*I spent a week.*
Fui en avión.	*I went by plane.*
El vuelo duró…	*The flight lasted…*
Mi hotel estaba en la costa.	*My hotel was on the coast.*
Era muy moderno.	*It was very modern.*
Tenía un restaurante fantástico.	*It had a fantastic restaurant.*
Los clientes eran ingleses.	*The clients were English.*
Los camareros llevaban uniforme.	*The waiters wore a uniform.*
Hablaban inglés.	*They spoke English.*
Conocí a muchos jóvenes.	*I met a lot of young people.*
Eran muy simpáticos.	*They were very nice.*
Mejoré mi español.	*I improved my Spanish.*
Hizo sol toda la semana.	*It was sunny all the week.*
Podías hacer…	*You could do…*
¿Cuándo fuiste de vacaciones?	*When did you go on holiday?*
¿Adónde fuiste?	*Where did you go?*
¿Cuánto tiempo pasaste allí?	*How long did you stay there?*
¿Dónde te alojaste?	*Where did you stay?*
¿Cómo era el hotel?	*How was the hotel?*
¿Qué había en el hotel?	*What facilities did the hotel have?*
¿Qué hiciste durante tus vacaciones?	*What did you do on your holiday?*

En el hotel *At the hotel*

¿Dígame?	*¿Could you please tell me?*
Estimado/a Señor(a)	*Dear Sir/Madam*
Me gustaría/Quisiera reservar…	*I would like to reserve*
una habitación individual	*a single room*
una habitación doble	*a double room*
para… noches	*for… nights*
para… días	*for… days*
sin/con balcón	*with/without a balcony*
con vistas al mar	*with sea views*
con baño	*with a bath*
con cama de matrimonio	*with double bed*
¿Para cuántos días?	*For how many days?*
¿Para cuántas noches?	*For how many nights?*
Voy/vamos a llegar el…	*I/We will arrive on …*
del… hasta…	*from the… to the…*
una semana/quince días	*a week/fortnight*
¿Quiere una habitación con baño o sin baño?	*Would you like a room with or without a bath?*
¿Cuánto es?	*How much is it?*
¿Hay servicio de habitaciones?	*Is there room service?*
¿Hay conexión a Internet?	*Is there Internet access?*
¿Hasta qué hora se sirve el desayuno/la comida/ la cena?	*Until what time do you serve breakfast/lunch/dinner?*
¿A qué hora cierra la recepción/el bar?	*What time does the reception/bar close?*
¿Hasta qué hora está abierto el restaurante?	*Until what time is the restaurant open?*
¿Se admiten perros?	*Are dogs allowed?*

Reclamaciones *Complaints*

¿Qué le pasa señor/señorita?	*What is the matter Sir/Madam?*
Me hace(n) falta…	*I need…*
Necesito…	*I need…*
papel higiénico	*toilet paper*
jabón	*soap*
toallas	*towels*
un secador	*a hairdryer*
aspirinas	*aspirins*
(no) está…	*it is (not)*
no funciona…	*the… doesn't work*
no hay…	*there are no…*
el ascensor	*the lift*
el aseo	*the toilet*
la luz	*the light*
la ducha	*the shower*
La habitación/la cama está sucia/no está limpia.	*The room/bed is dirty/isn't clean.*
El baño/el aseo está sucio/no está limpio.	*The bath/toilet is dirty/isn't clean.*
Hay mucho ruido.	*There's a lot of noise.*
Quiero quejarme ahora.	*I want to complain now.*
Quiero un descuento.	*I want a discount.*
Quiero cambiar de habitación.	*I want to change room.*
Quiero hablar con el director.	*I want to speak to the manager.*
Me vuelve loco/a.	*It drives me mad.*
El año que viene voy a…	*Next year I'm going to…*
Va a ser…	*It's going to be…*

- Giving personal information
- Using the present tense
- Extending sentences with **cuando...**

Repaso 1 *Mi vida*

Escucha y lee los textos. Copia y completa la tabla.

	personality	interests
1	*patient,...*	*ICT, chats, reads/writes emails,...*

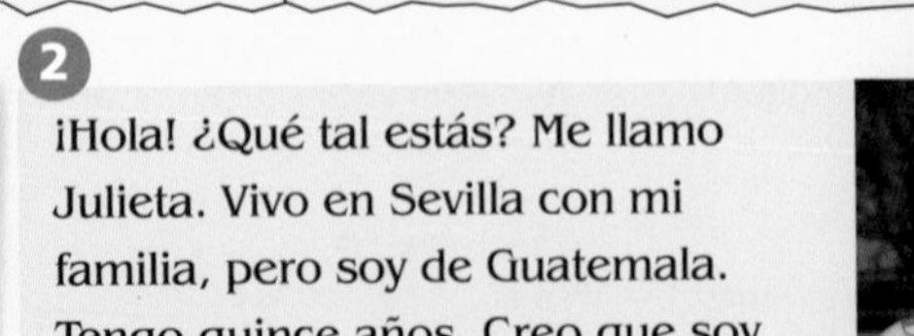

1 Me llamo Antonio y vivo en Salamanca. Tengo diecisiete años. Mis amigos dicen que soy paciente, inteligente y creativo. Me encanta la informática. **Todos los días** chateo con mis amigos y navego por Internet. **A veces** leo y escribo correos. Descargo música por las tardes. El rock es mi vida, y **los fines de semana** escribo un blog de música rock. **De vez en cuando** juego con el ordenador o con la Wii. **Siempre** voy de vacaciones a la playa. Me encanta tomar el sol.

2 ¡Hola! ¿Qué tal estás? Me llamo Julieta. Vivo en Sevilla con mi familia, pero soy de Guatemala. Tengo quince años. Creo que soy una persona dinámica y bastante ambiciosa. **Los sábados** salgo con mis amigas y vamos de compras. **Normalmente** compro maquillaje y ropa. Voy al cine **una vez a la semana**. Sobre todo veo dramas o comedias. **Nunca** veo películas de terror. En el futuro quiero ser actriz. **En verano** hago cursos de arte dramático y voy de compras.

Read the texts again. Translate the adverbs of frequency (in red) into English.

Con tu compañero/a, pregunta y contesta en lugar de Antonio o Julieta. *Use the adverbs of frequency from exercise 1.*

- ¿Cuántos años tienes?
- ¿De dónde eres?
- ¿Dónde vives?
- ¿Cómo eres?
- ¿Qué haces en tu tiempo libre? (Todos los días..., de vez en cuando...)

leo...	escribo...
navego...	chateo...
descargo...	juego...
salgo...	voy...
compro...	veo...
hago...	

G *The present tense* ➲200, 202

For the present tense you change the endings like this:

	escuchar *(to listen)*	**leer** *(to read)*	**vivir** *(to live)*
(yo)	escucho	leo	vivo
(tú)	escuchas	lees	vives
(él/ella/usted)	escucha	lee	vive
(nosotros/as)	escuchamos	leemos	vivimos
(vosotros/as)	escucháis	leéis	vivís
(ellos/ellas/ustedes)	escuchan	leen	viven

Some verbs are stem-changing, like **jugar** (**u → ue**) and **tener** (**e → ie**).

Some verbs, like **hacer** and **tener**, are irregular in the first person ('I' form) only.
Others, like **ser**, are more irregular.

	hacer *(to do/make)*	**ser** *(to be)*	**tener** *(to have)*
(yo)	hago	soy	tengo
(tú)	haces	eres	tienes
(él/ella/usted)	hace	es	tiene
(nosotros/as)	hacemos	somos	tenemos
(vosotros/as)	hacéis	sois	tenéis
(ellos/ellas/ustedes)	hacen	son	tienen

4 ***Read the holiday ads and decide which one would be suitable for each person from exercise 1. There is one ad too many.***

a

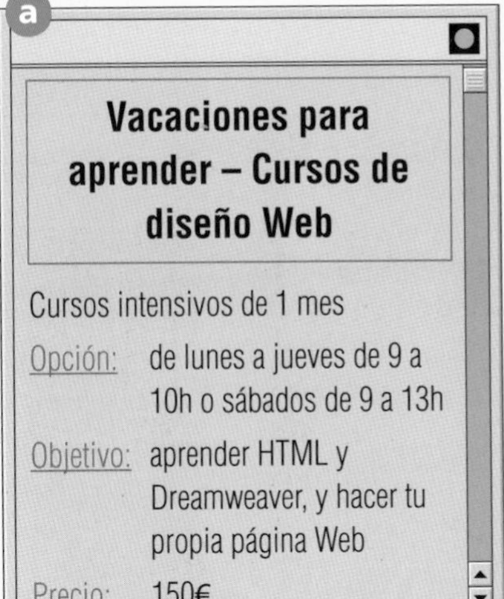

Vacaciones para aprender – Cursos de diseño Web

Cursos intensivos de 1 mes

Opción: de lunes a jueves de 9 a 10h o sábados de 9 a 13h

Objetivo: aprender HTML y Dreamweaver, y hacer tu propia página Web

Precio: 150€

b

Vacaciones de invierno – Viajes a la nieve

¿Quieres mejorar tu técnica o pasártelo bien en compañía de amigos?

Te garantizamos una estancia muy divertida.

Las clases tienen lugar por las mañanas o por las tardes, en grupos pequeños de 4 a 12 participantes.

Precio: 300€ (una semana)

c

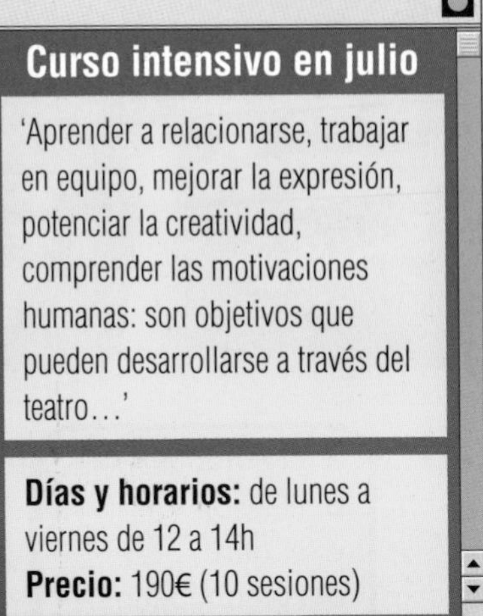

Curso intensivo en julio

'Aprender a relacionarse, trabajar en equipo, mejorar la expresión, potenciar la creatividad, comprender las motivaciones humanas: son objetivos que pueden desarrollarse a través del teatro…'

Días y horarios: de lunes a viernes de 12 a 14h
Precio: 190€ (10 sesiones)

5 **Escucha. ¿Qué tiempo hace? Escribe las letras correctas. (1–4)**

Ejemplo: **1** b, e,…

¿Qué tiempo hace?
Hace buen tiempo.
Hace mal tiempo.
Hace calor.
Hace frío.
Hace sol.
Hace viento.
Hay niebla.
Hay tormenta.
Está nublado.
Está despejado.
Llueve.
Nieva.

6 **Escucha otra vez. ¿Qué país se describe?**
(There is one country too many.)

Jamaica
Irlanda
Islandia
España
Alemania

7 **Describe la rutina de Pepe.**

1 Cuando 

2 En invierno, cuando 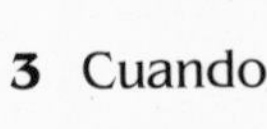, 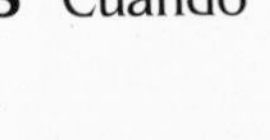

3 Cuando , ; pero cuando ,

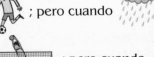

4 Cuando , ; pero cuando , 

Cuando… *When…*
Cuando hace sol, voy a la piscina.
When it's sunny, I go to the swimming pool.
Use expressions like **cuando** to combine phrases and extend your sentences. This will produce impressive answers in your speaking and writing.

- Talking about means of transport
- Using adverbs
- Listening for the 24-hour clock

Repaso 2 *En ruta*

1 Lee y empareja las fotos con los medios de transporte. (Sobra una palabra.)

- **a** el autobús
- **b** el avión
- **c** el tren
- **d** el monopatín
- **e** la bicicleta
- **f** el barco
- **g** a pie
- **h** el autocar
- **i** el coche
- **j** el metro
- **k** la moto
- **l** el tranvía

2 Escucha y lee. Copia y completa la tabla. (1–9)

	mode of transport	reason
1	*bus*	*not expensive*

1 A veces cojo el autobús porque **no es caro** y porque **puedo leer**.

2 Prefiero ir a pie porque **me gusta hacer ejercicio**.

3 Normalmente cojo un taxi porque es **lo más rápido**.

4 Generalmente voy en monopatín porque **me da independencia**.

5 No me gusta nada viajar en autobús, especialmente porque **la gente me molesta** y **odio esperar en la parada de autobús**.

6 Voy siempre en moto porque **llego rápidamente** a todos los sitios.

7 Principalmente cojo la bici porque **no contamina**. Creo que **hay demasiada contaminación**.

8 Utilizo frecuentemente el transporte público, como el autobús y el metro, porque **es barato**, pero sobre todo porque **hay que pensar en el medio ambiente**.

9 **Para distancias largas** solamente cojo el avión.

> When you use **en** (by) to say how you travel e.g. *Voy en autobús.* (I go by bus.), remember to leave out the definite article **el** or **la**.

¿Cómo prefieres viajar? Escribe un párrafo.
*Use some of the expressions in **purple** in exercise 2 to make your paragraph interesting.*

Ejemplo: Normalmente prefiero ir en autobús porque es barato y porque hay que pensar en el medio ambiente. A veces cojo un taxi porque es más rápido…

Normalmente… Frecuentemente… Solamente… A veces… Nunca…	prefiero ir… voy…	en … a pie…
porque…	es limpio. es cómodo. es rápido. es lento. es barato. es caro. es ecológico.	

G Adverbs

➲219

Adverbs describe actions. Many adverbs are formed by adding **-mente** to the feminine form of the adjective.

rápidamente *quickly*
lentamente *slowly*
generalmente *usually*
normalmente *normally*
frecuentemente *frequently*
solamente *only*

Use these adverbs in your speaking and writing to make your language more varied.

Escucha. Copia y completa la tabla (1–5). Lee el primer diálogo como modelo.

- Buenos días. ¿Qué quería?
- Quiero cuatro billetes para Madrid, por favor.
- ¿Sólo de ida o de ida y vuelta?
- De ida y vuelta, por favor. ¿A qué hora sale el tren?
- Sale a las ocho diez.
- ¿De qué andén sale?
- Sale del andén 7.
- ¿Y a qué hora llega?
- Llega a las trece veintisiete.
- ¿Es directo?
- No, hay que cambiar.

	destino	salida	andén	llegada	directo
1	Madrid	08:10am	7	13:27pm	✗

Sometimes, when you hear clock times, they will be in the 24-hour clock. From 1 pm onwards you'll need to listen for numbers higher than 12!

las trece	13:00
las catorce cero tres	14:03
las quince treinta y cuatro	15:34
las dieciséis treinta	16:30

Con tu compañero/a, haz tres diálogos. Cambia los datos del ejercicio 4.

destino	¿cuántas personas?	→ →←	salida	llegada	andén	directo
Sevilla	2	→←	13:21	15:05	3	✓
Málaga	1	→	10:20	12:25	6	✗
Granada	3	→←	18:06	20:10	4	✓

Read these words that you might see around a Spanish train station. What would you be doing in each of these places? Use a dictionary to help you.

a Tienda de regalos
b Paso subterráneo
c Sala de espera
d Salidas
e Llegadas
f Salida de emergencia
g Cafetería
h Taquilla
I Trenes AVE
j Venta de billetes
k Horarios
l Consigna automática

- Planning a day out
- Using the near future
- Understanding questions

1 La oficina de turismo

España
• Sevilla

Escucha y escribe la letra correcta. (1–8)

Ejemplo: **1** f

a el Alcázar

b el barrio de Santa Cruz

c la catedral y la Giralda

d la Torre del Oro

e la plaza de España

f el parque de María Luisa

g la plaza de toros

h el centro comercial Plaza de Armas

Escucha otra vez. Escribe la actividad que se menciona. (1–8)

Ejemplo: **1** dar un paseo por…

sacar fotos
comprar recuerdos
ver lugares de interés
disfrutar de unas vistas espléndidas
dar un paseo por…
comer algo
descubrir todo sobre las corridas
subir a la torre

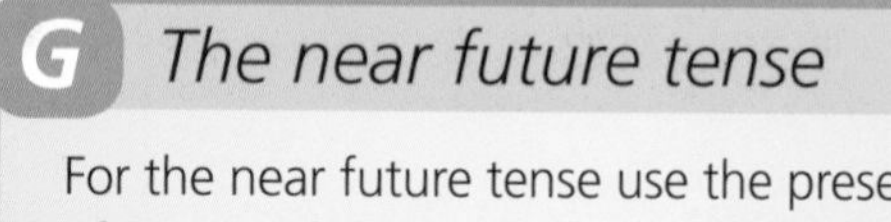

G *The near future tense* ➲208

For the near future tense use the present tense of **ir + a + infinitive**:

(yo)	voy		
(tú)	vas		comprar
(él/ella/usted)	va	a	comer
(nosotros/as)	vamos		subir
(vosotros/as)	vais		
(ellos/ellas/ustedes)	van		

Escucha y completa las preguntas. ¿Qué significan? (1–5)

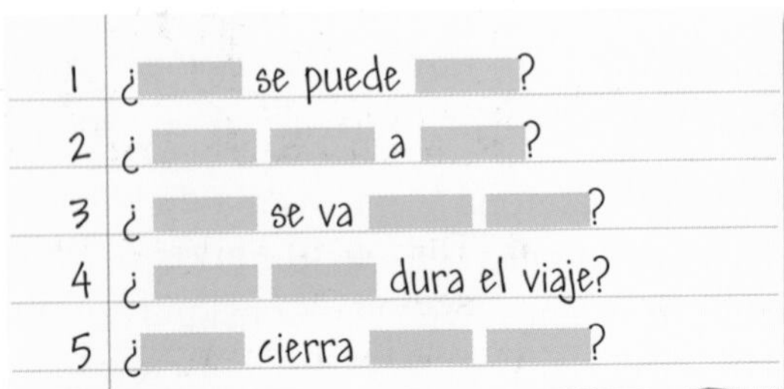

1 ¿ se puede ?
2 ¿ a ?
3 ¿ se va ?
4 ¿ dura el viaje?
5 ¿ cierra ?

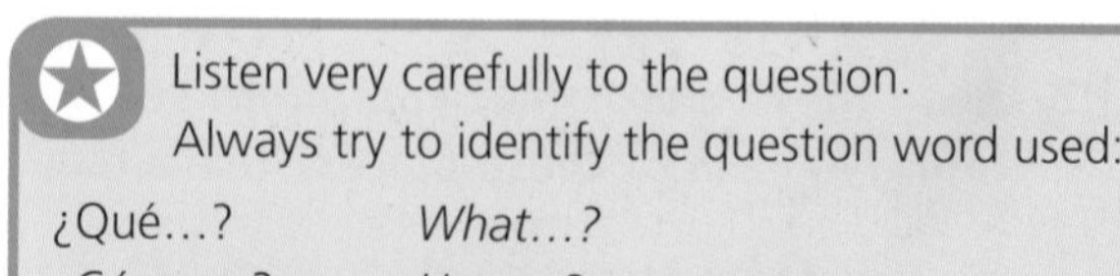

Listen very carefully to the question.
Always try to identify the question word used:

¿Qué…?	*What…?*
¿Cómo…?	*How…?*
¿Cuánto…?	*How much…?*
¿Cuándo…?	*When…?*

4 Con tu compañero/a, pregunta y contesta.

- ¿Qué se puede ver en Sevilla?
- ¿Qué vas a hacer en Sevilla?
- ¿Cómo va a ser?
- ¿Cómo se va al…/a la…?
- ¿Cuánto tiempo dura?
- ¿A qué hora abre/cierra el/la…?

- Se puede ver…
- Voy a…/Vamos a…
- Va a ser estupendo/fascinante…
- Se va en/a…
- Si vas en/a…, dura…
- Abre/Cierra a la/a las…

5 Planea un día de actividades turísticas para un grupo de amigos en Sevilla.

Primero… Por la mañana… Luego… Por la tarde… Por la noche…	vamos a… voy a…	ir a…/al… ver lugares de interés. disfrutar de vistas espléndidas. dar un paseo por… comer algo. subir a la torre. comprar recuerdos. sacar fotos.	Va a ser… guay. interesante. fascinante. maravilloso. increíble. impresionante.
También vamos a… porque me encanta/me gusta mucho…			

6 Lee el texto y completa las frases en inglés.

Disfruta de una manera diferente y divertida de hacer turismo.

¿Tienes ganas de visitar el parque de María Luisa de Sevilla en nuestros originales cuadriciclos a pedales?

Sevilla posee un clima excepcional con más de 300 días de sol al año, perfecto para pasear en bicicleta tranquilamente.

Los cuadriciclos son muy cómodos y fáciles de llevar, son seguros y aptos para cualquier edad. Además, todos llevan un asiento delantero especial para niños con cinturón de seguridad.

Sin duda es la mejor manera de conocer el lugar más romántico y emblemático de la ciudad de Sevilla.

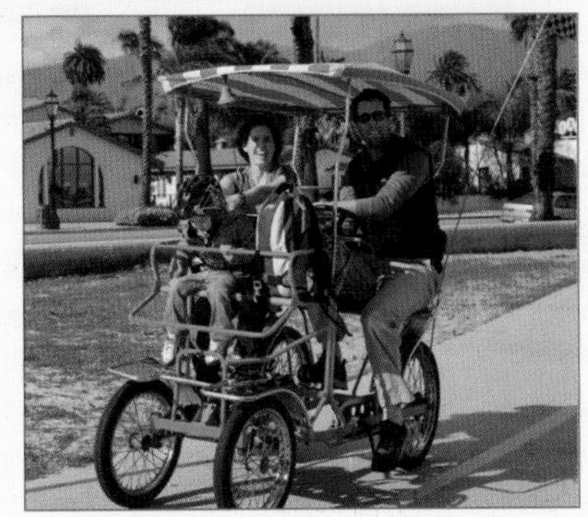

a This form of tourism is…
b Seville has an exceptional climate with more than…
c The 'bikes' are very…
d They have a special children's seat with…
e It is the best way to…

- Asking for and understanding directions
- Using imperatives
- Using sequencers (**primero…, después…**)

2 Comprando recuerdos

Escucha y escribe la letra correcta y el precio correcto. (1–9)

Ejemplo: **1** e – 20€

Con tu compañero/a, pregunta y contesta por los objetos del ejercicio 1.

● ¿Dónde se puede comprar un collar? ■ En la joyería.

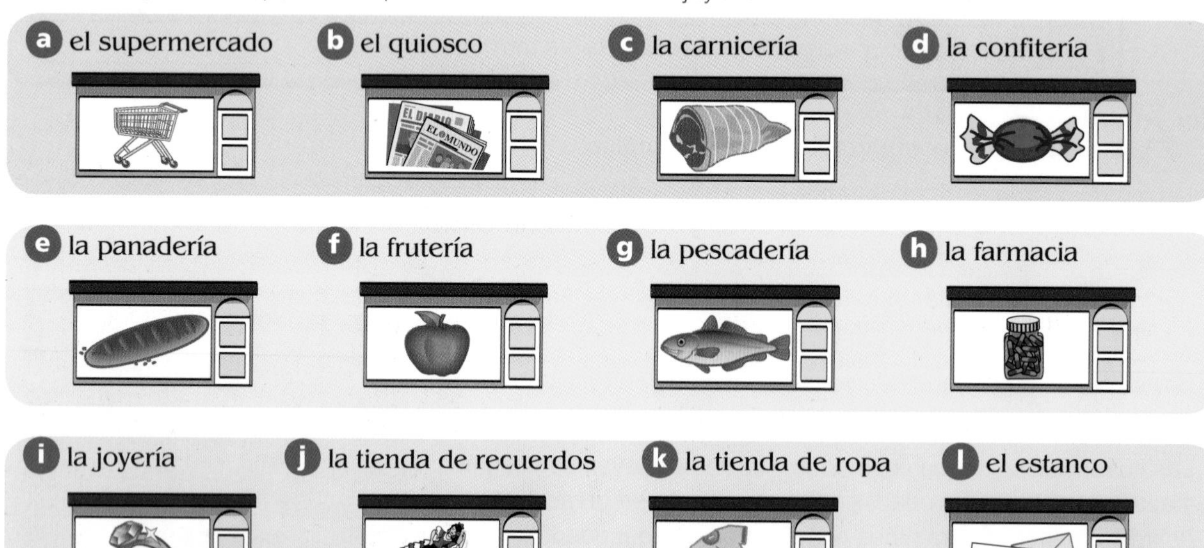

Choose four shops from the list above. Write a short text in Spanish about what you can buy there. Look up words in your dictionary if necessary.

Ejemplo: En el supermercado se puede comprar chorizo,…

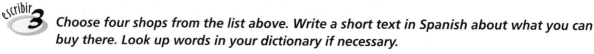

Lee las frases. Empareja las frases en inglés con el español. Escucha y verifica tus respuestas.

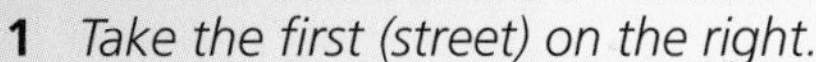

1	*Take the first (street) on the right.*	**a**	Cruza la plaza.
2	*Take the second (street) on the left.*	**b**	Gira en la esquina.
3	*Go past the lights.*	**c**	Cruza el puente.
4	*It's nearby.*	**d**	Pasa los semáforos.
5	*Cross the bridge.*	**e**	Está cerca.
6	*Go straight on.*	**f**	Está lejos.
7	*It's on the left-hand side.*	**g**	Sigue todo recto.
8	*Cross the square.*	**h**	Está a mano izquierda.
9	*It's far away.*	**i**	Está a mano derecha.
10	*Turn the corner.*	**j**	Está al final de la calle.
11	*It's on the right-hand side.*	**k**	Está al lado del/de la…
12	*It's at the end of the street.*	**l**	Está enfrente del/de la…
13	*It's next to…*	**m**	Toma la primera calle a la derecha.
14	*It's opposite…*	**n**	Toma la segunda calle a la izquierda.

G *Imperatives*

➲230

Imperatives are used to give commands.

	tú (you, singular, informal)	vosotros/as (you, plural, informal)
-ar	cruz**a**	cruz**ad**
-er	com**e**	com**ed**
-ir	viv**e**	viv**id**

Cruz**a** la plaza. *Cross the square.*
Gir**a** a la derecha. *Turn right.*

These verbs are irregular in the **tú** form:

decir	**di**
hacer	**haz**
ir	**ve**
poner	**pon**
venir	**ven**

Escucha las direcciones y mira el mapa. Escribe el nombre de la tienda correcta. (1–3)

Con tu compañero/a haz diálogos. Utiliza el mapa del ejercicio 5.

¿Por dónde se va al…/a la…?
A ver…
Pues…
Entonces…
Primero…
Después…
Luego…
Ahora estás en…
Un poco más lejos…

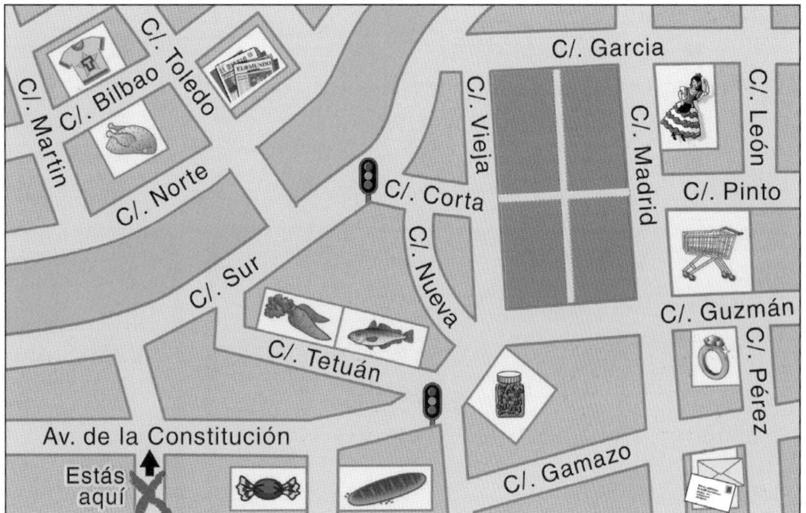

- Ordering in a restaurant
- Using **me gusta** + article, **como** without article
- Working with distractors while listening and reading

3 Tomando tapas

1 Escucha y lee. ¿Qué significa?

Ejemplo: *gazpacho* = gazpacho soup,…

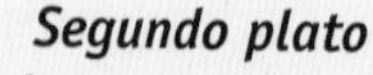

Restaurante La Alhambra

Menú del día – 15€

Primer plato

gazpacho
lentejas con chorizo
jamón serrano
sopa de ajo
tortilla de patatas

Segundo plato

merluza en salsa verde
paella
chuleta de cerdo con verduras
filete de ternera
calamares

Las especialidades de la casa

gambas al ajillo
judías verdes con jamón
pescaito frito

Postres

flan
helados de fresa, vainilla y chocolate
tarta de queso

+ pan + bebida

2 Escucha y escribe los platos mencionados. (1–8)
Escucha otra vez. ¿Les gusta ♥ o no les gusta 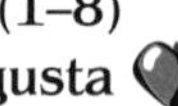**?**

Ejemplo: **1** paella – ♥

3 Con tu compañero/a, pregunta y contesta.

- ¿Qué te gusta comer?
- ¿Qué no te gusta comer?
- ¿Qué comes normalmente?
- ¿Qué tal está(n) el…/la…/los…/las…?

- Me gusta(n) el… /la… /los… /las …
- No me gusta(n) el… /la… /los… /las…
- Normalmente como…, pero no como nunca…
- Está(n) buenísimo/a(s) / riquísimo/a(s).
- Está(n) asqueroso/a(s). ¡Qué asco!

Practise these sounds and then pay attention to your pronunciation as you do exercise 3:

ga**z**pacho	'th'
espe**c**ialidad	'th'
torti**ll**a	'y'
lente**j**as	'h' (back of throat!)

Listen and repeat:
Nuestras espe**c**ialidades son el ga**z**pacho, la torti**ll**a y las lente**j**as con chori**z**o.

G *The definite article* ➲212

When **me gusta** is used with a noun you need the definite article.

(No) Me gusta **el** jamón/**la** paella.
(No) Me gustan **los** calamares/**las** sardinas.

With verbs like **comer**, **tomar** and **beber** no article is used:
Bebo vino y no como pescado.

4 ***Listen and read carefully. Francisco and Valeria mention lots of different dishes, but what do they actually order?***

Camarero: ¿Qué van a tomar?
Valeria: Vamos a tomar tapas: una ración de jamón, unas gambas al ajillo y tortilla, por favor.
Francisco: Yo tengo hambre. La especialidad de la casa, el pescaito frito, ¿está bueno?
Camarero: Sí, está muy bueno, señor.
Francisco: ¿Te gusta el pescaito frito, Valeria?
Valeria: ¿El pescaito frito? No, a mí no me gusta mucho. Prefiero la carne.
Francisco: A ver, ¿te gusta el filete de ternera?
Valeria: No, para mí la chuleta de cerdo con verduras.
Camarero: Muy bien. ¿Y para beber...?
Valeria: Tengo sed. Voy a tomar agua mineral, pero sin gas.
Francisco: A mí me pone una cerveza, por favor.
Camarero: Muy bien, ¡qué aproveche!
Valeria: Las gambas, ¡qué ricas! Todo está muy bueno.
Francisco: Sí, pero me falta el cuchillo y tampoco hay sal.
Camarero: Lo siento, señor. En seguida se lo traigo. ¿Algo más?
Francisco: No, nada más. ¿Me trae la cuenta, por favor?...

Often listening and reading questions will include *distractors*. These are extra bits of information that may make you jump to the wrong conclusion. For example, two people may discuss options on a menu but then order something different. The key is to listen or read to the end of the passage rather than jumping to conclusions.

ZONA CULTURA

¿El servicio está incluido?

In Spain, service is normally included. You don't need to ask.

You may wish to leave a tip, **una propina**, even so.

5 **Escribe las frases en español.**

a I am hungry.
b She is thirsty.
c Have a good meal.
d I am going to have...
e But there is no salt.
f I don't have a knife.
g Anything else?

6 **Escucha. Copia y completa la tabla en inglés. (1–2)**

	1	2
1st course		
2nd course		
dessert		
problems		

De primer plato De segundo plato De postre	voy a tomar...	Me falta	el tenedor. el cuchillo. la cuchara.
No hay	sal. aceite. vinagre.	El plato El vaso	está sucio.
Está muy salado/a.		El vino está malo.	

7 **Con tus compañeros/as, escribe un diálogo en el restaurante. Usa el diálogo del ejercicio 4 como ejemplo.**

- Describing a day out
- More of the preterite and the imperfect
- Recognising and expressing mixed opinions

4 En Sevilla

Escucha y lee. Luego escribe las letras de las cinco frases correctas.

1 Ricardo: ¿Qué tal tu visita a Sevilla, Lola?	**Lola:** ¡Genial! Me encantó la ciudad. Vi monumentos maravillosos como el Alcázar, la Torre del Oro y la Giralda. Desde allí [1] **las vistas eran preciosas, pero había muchos turistas**.
2 Ricardo: ¿Visitaste la ciudad a pie?	**Lola:** [2] Sí, **recorrí a pie todo** el Barrio de Santa Cruz. Hay tiendas muy interesantes por allí y compré muchos recuerdos. El jueves [3] **estaba muy cansada**, así que cogí un autobús turístico y [4] **vimos unos lugares muy interesantes**. Había un guía que explicaba todo, la historia, la arquitectura…
3 Ricardo: ¿Qué tiempo hizo?	**Lola:** Hizo sol y muchísimo calor, ¡demasiado calor!, pero eso es normal en Sevilla.
4 Ricardo: ¿Qué tal la comida?	**Lola:** A ver…, la comida estaba muy buena. Por lo general, comí tapas, bocadillos de jamón y perritos calientes. Una noche fui a un restaurante con mi padre y [5] **me encantó el ambiente**. Comí sopa de ajo y paella. Mi padre comió pescaito frito.
5 Ricardo: ¿Qué es lo que más te gustó, Lola?	**Lola:** A ver…, [6] **lo que más me gustó** fue la catedral y también los sevillanos, que son muy simpáticos. [7] **Lo que menos me gustó**… ¡el calor! Hizo mucho calor.
6 Ricardo: ¿Vas a volver?	**Lola:** Claro que sí. [8] **Mis vacaciones fueron superdivertidas, y por eso creo que voy a volver en julio**.

a Lola was impressed by the buildings.
b She saw some of the city on foot.
c On Wednesday she took a tour bus.
d There was no guide on the tour bus.
e The weather was too hot.
f Lola ate snacks generally.
g Lola is a vegetarian.
h Lola's father ate pork.
i She found people in Seville very nice.

La Giralda

The phrases in red could be useful for your work later on. Write them out and translate them into English.

G The preterite and the imperfect ➲204–206

The preterite is used for a completed action in the past.

Comí sopa de ajo y sardinas.	*I ate garlic soup and sardines.*
El jueves **cogí** un autobús turístico.	*On Thursday I took a tour bus.*

The imperfect tense is used to describe what something was like.

La Giralda **era** increíble.	*The Giralda was incredible.*
Había muchos turistas.	*There were lots of tourists.*

3 Con tu compañero/a, pregunta y contesta sobre una visita a Londres o a otra ciudad.

● ¿Adónde fuiste?	■ Fui a…
● ¿Cuánto tiempo pasaste allí?	■ Pasé…
● ¿Qué tal tu visita a Londres?	■ Lo pasé guay/fenomenal. Vi…, fui a/al…, saqué…, di un paseo por… , compré…, subí a la torre…, disfruté de vistas…
	■ El Big Ben/Madame Tussauds era… Había…
● ¿Visitaste la ciudad a pie?	■ Visité la ciudad a pie/en…
● ¿Qué tiempo hizo?	■ Hizo…
● ¿Qué tal la comida?	■ La comida estaba…
● ¿Qué es lo que más te gustó?	■ Lo que más me gustó fue/fueron… Pero no me gustó…
● ¿Vas a volver?	■ …

Think about how you would improve this.

- Think about whether you need to use the preterite or the imperfect tense.
- Use impressive phrases like: **Lo que más me gustó…**
- Think about extra details you could add to make your Spanish stand out. Some of the phrases in red in exercise 1 could help you.

4 Escucha y escribe P (positivo), N (negativo), P+N (positivo + negativo). (1–3)

With questions where you are looking for positive and negative opinions, it is important to keep an open mind right to the end of the sentence. Sometimes what looks like a negative opinion can actually be both positive and negative.

Often sentences containing a mixed opinion will contain words and phrases like:

pero *but*
por un lado… **por otro lado**… *on one hand… on the other hand…*
lo que mas me gustó… **lo que menos me gustó**… *what I liked most… what I liked least…*

5 Escucha otra vez. Escribe la letra correcta. (1–3)

1 Pablo thinks Seville is
- **a** pretty but dirty.
- **b** historic but too crowded.
- **c** historic but dirty.

2 The thing that Carlos liked least was
- **a** the food.
- **b** the people.
- **c** the museums.

3 The thing that Isabel liked best was
- **a** the Giralda.
- **b** the museums.
- **c** the atmosphere.

6 Describe unas vacaciones en una ciudad.

Ejemplo: El año pasado pasé cinco días en Londres. Lo pasé…

- Use the questions in exercise 3 to help you.
- Add extra details like the red phrases in exercise 1 to make your knowledge of Spanish stand out.

- Talking about festivals
- Understanding three time frames
- Using **para** to extend sentences

5 Las fiestas

Escucha y lee. Apunta los siguientes datos en inglés.

- Which festival is mentioned?
- What does it involve?

Marcelo

El Diwali es una fiesta religiosa hindú conocida como el festival de las luces. Es la entrada del nuevo año hindú, y una de las noches más importantes del año. Simboliza la necesidad del hombre de avanzar hacia la Verdad.

Durante la fiesta decoramos las casas con lámparas de colores y guirnaldas. Viene mucha gente, y por eso preparamos comida para todo el mundo. Cocinamos unos platos muy ricos y unos dulces buenísimos. Hacemos regalos a la familia y a los amigos. La gente lleva su ropa nueva y hace explotar petardos y fuegos artificiales.

El año pasado lo pasamos muy bien porque vinieron mis primos de Delhi para celebrarlo con mi familia. Trajeron unos dulces riquísimos. En 2012 vamos a ir a Delhi para celebrar el Diwali con ellos. Tengo muchas ganas de ver cómo lo celebran allí.

María

Para nosotros la Navidad es una fiesta importante y la celebramos el veinticuatro de diciembre. En casa decoramos un árbol de navidad y ponemos un belén. Asistimos a la Misa de Navidad, luego nuestros amigos vienen y cenamos pavo.

El año que viene vamos a celebrar la Navidad en México. Allí la Navidad es una fiesta muy religiosa. Los mexicanos decoran las casas con muchos colores. Me gustaría romper una piñata, pero no sé si eso es típico en Navidad.

Lía

La Feria de Abril es la fiesta de los sevillanos. Hay un ambiente muy especial. La gente lleva trajes tradicionales de flamenco, baila, canta, come, bebe y ríe. Hay coches de caballos y todas las casetas están iluminadas, ¡me encanta!

En la Feria es típico comer el pescaito con una copa de fino. Además, todas las tardes hay corridas de toros. El año pasado fui con unos amigos y lo pasamos bomba.

El año que viene voy a ir a la Feria con mi amiga francesa Élodie. También van a venir mis primos. Vamos a bailar sevillanas y vamos a ir al parque de atracciones, pero no vamos a ir a una corrida porque Élodie es anti-corridas y odia el maltrato de animales.

Use these phrases to extend and add extra information to sentences:

para + person	**Para** la familia (**for** the family)
para + infinitive	**Para** recibir regalos (**in order to** receive presents)

2 ***Which examples of the following verbs can you find in exercise 1?***

1 decorar *(to decorate)*
2 venir *(to come)*
3 simbolizar *(to symbolise)*
4 celebrar *(to celebrate)*
5 llevar *(to wear)*
6 traer *(to bring)*

G *Three tenses: the present, the preterite and the near future* ➲ 200, 204, 208

The texts above contain information about the past, present and future. A useful verb for festivals where lots of people visit each other is: venir *(to come)*.

	present	**preterite**	**near future**
(yo)	vengo	vine	voy a venir
(tú)	vienes	viniste	vas a venir
(el/ella/usted)	viene	vino	va a venir
(nosotros/as)	venimos	vinimos	vamos a venir
(vosotros/as)	venís	vinisteis	vais a venir
(ellos/ellas/ustedes)	vienen	vinieron	van a venir

3 Lee los textos otra vez. Contesta a las preguntas.
Who...(careful: it might be someone other than Marcelo, María and Lía)

a goes to Mass?
b will dance at the Feria?
c lights lanterns?
d doesn't like bullfights?
e eats fish?
f drinks Sherry?
g sets off fireworks?
h came from Delhi?
i went with Lía to the Feria last year?

4 Elige un texto. Copia y completa la tabla con los verbos.

Pasado	Presente	Futuro	Inglés
	es		is

5 Escucha y apunta los datos en inglés. (1–3)

- Which festival are they talking about?
- What does it involve?
- Are they talking about the past (Pa), the present (Pr) or the future (F)?

a 
San Fermines

b 
El día de los Muertos

c 
Ramadán

d 
Nochevieja

6 Completa el texto con las palabras del recuadro.

Eid al Fitr es una fiesta musulmana muy importante. En el mes de Ramadán no (1) ______ ni bebemos durante el día. Al terminar el Ramadán (2) ______ la festividad del Eid al Fitr. Antes de la fiesta, la gente (3) ______ dulces y regalos para la familia. (4) ______ vinieron mis tíos y mis primos. Mi madre (5) ______ una cena muy rica.
Un día (6) ______ a Kaaba para celebrar Eid con mis padres.
Mi hermana también (7) ______ conmigo.
Khaled

compra · voy a ir · cocinó · va a venir · el año pasado · comienza · comemos

Prueba oral

Travelling abroad

You are going to play the role of a tourist who is being interviewed about their experiences of visiting a popular city and your teacher is going to play the role of the interviewer. Your teacher could ask you the following:

- Which city did you visit?
- What is it like?
- What did you visit?
- How did you get around?
- What did you like best? Why?
- What was the food like?
- Will you return to Seville? What will you go and see?

Remember that you will have to respond to an unexpected question that you have not yet prepared.
The dialogue will last between 4 and 6 minutes.

You are going to listen to Barney, an exam candidate, taking part in the above interview with his teacher. Listen to part 1 of the interview. Listen out for the phrases below and put them in the order in which he says them.

1 ...tiene muchos lugares de interés...
2 La plaza de toros era impresionante...
3 Sevilla es una ciudad maravillosa.
4 ...allí se puede ir de compras...
5 ¡Qué bonito!
6 Disfruté de vistas espléndidas.
7 Me encantó...
8 ...es muy diferente de Inglaterra.

Listen again and note down in English how Barney answers the first three questions.

Listen to part 2 of Barney's conversation and note down the words that fill the gaps.

– ¿Cómo visitaste la ciudad?
– (1) ______ la ciudad a pie, pero el viernes (2) ______ un autobús turístico panorámico para ver unos lugares muy interesantes. Normalmente no me gusta nada viajar en autobús, pero este (3) ______ muy limpio y (4) ______ muy cómodo.
– ¿Qué fue lo que más te gustó?
– A ver, lo que más me gustó fueron los monumentos. El primer día fui de excursión a las ruinas de Itálica, a siete kilómetros de Sevilla. ¡Lo (5) ______ bomba! Itálica es una antigua ciudad romana. (6) ______ increíble. ¿Qué más? El tiempo me gustó mucho porque (7) ______ sol y ¡me encanta el sol! Lo que menos me gustó... a ver... (8) ______ muchos turistas y por eso no era muy tranquilo.
– ¿Qué tal la comida?
– Por lo general la comida (9) ______ muy rica. El sábado fui a un restaurante y (10) ______ mucho el ambiente. Comí pescado, estaba delicioso.

Look at the verbs you identified in exercise 3. Which tense are they in? Can you explain why?

- preterite
- imperfect

5 ***Now listen to part 3 of Barney's interview and answer the questions.***

1 Barney says that he would like to go back to Seville *para ir de compras*. What does the structure *para* + infinitive mean?
2 What is the unexpected question that the examiner asks and what does it mean?
3 Barney talks about what he would like to do in the future using *querer* + infinitive (to want to), *ir a* + infinitive (going to) and *me gustaría* + infinitive (I would like to). Can you note down one example of each from the second question?

6 ***Now it's your turn! Prepare your answers to the task and then have an interview with your teacher or partner.***

- Use the Grade Studio and Barney's answers to help you plan.
- Adapt what Barney said to talk about yourself but add your own ideas.
- Prepare your answers to the task questions and try to predict what the unexpected question could be. The examiner might base this question on something you have already said, or ask something totally new!
- Record the conversation. Ask a partner to listen to it and say how well you performed.

Award each other one star, two stars or three stars for each of these categories:
- *Pronunciation*
- *Confidence and fluency*
- *Range of tenses*
- *Variety of vocabulary and expressions*
- *Using longer sentences*
- *Taking the initiative*

What do you need to do next time to improve your performance?

GradeStudio

To produce a good answer you need to be able to use a variety of structures.
- Show how you can use more than one tense like the **preterite** to refer to the past, the **present tense** to refer to your feelings or opinions in general, and the **near future** (*ir a* + infinitive).
- Give **simple opinions**. Use phrases like *me encantó* (I loved...) and *me gustó* (I liked...).
- Use **adjectives** to describe things. Can you find examples of where Barney does this?

To go a step further you need to use a wider variety of language.
- Use the **preterite** and the **imperfect** when talking about the past. Look back to see how each of these tenses was used in exercise 3.
- Use a **variety of structures** to refer to the future like *quiero* + infinitive (I want to), *voy a* + infinitive (I am going to) and *me gustaría* + infinitive (I would like to).
- Express **more detailed opinions** like *lo que más me gusto...* (what I liked most was...) and *lo que menos me gusto...* (what I liked least was...). Can you find examples of these in Barney's conversation?

For a really impressive answer:
- **Express points of view** and make sure you **justify them in detail**. Can you find examples of where Barney does this?
- Extend your **connectives** that take an **infinitive** like *para* (in order to). Can you find an example in exercise 3?

1 ***Read the text and find these words in Spanish:***

Easter **is celebrated** **symbol** **a religious festival** **celebrations** **Catholics** **religious processions** **people from Seville** **fireworks**

La Semana Santa

Naomi

En Inglaterra normalmente se regalan huevos de chocolate en Semana Santa, y a veces también se regalan huevos de gallina pintados. ¡Me encanta el chocolate! La Semana Santa se celebra después de la Cuaresma (40 días de ayuno). La gente come huevos para celebrar el fin del ayuno. El huevo también es símbolo de nueva vida y de la resurrección de Jesús.

En España la Semana Santa es una fiesta religiosa muy importante. Comienza el Domingo de Ramos y termina el Domingo de Resurrección. En las celebraciones, los católicos expresan su tristeza por la muerte de Jesús y luego su alegría por su resurrección.

El año pasado pasé la Semana Santa en Sevilla con la familia de mi amiga Sonia. Sus padres son católicos, por eso fuimos a ver las procesiones religiosas. Los sevillanos llevaban ropa de nazarenos y acompañaban las procesiones con cirios y cruces. Al principio tenía un poco miedo, pero luego entendí que eso forma parte de la tradición de la Semana Santa.

El Domingo de Resurrección, para concluir las celebraciones, es tradicional disfrutar de una cena especial. En casa de mi amiga Sonia, comimos cordero, y de postre, un pastel muy rico. Después de la cena vinieron unos amigos de la familia y fuimos a ver los fuegos artificiales.

Esta experiencia, desde un punto de vista cultural, fue fascinante. Lo bueno fue que aprendí muchas cosas y hablé español. Lo que más me gustó fue la cena tradicional. Creo que es importante viajar para conocer la cultura de otros países.

El año que viene voy a visitar Perú con Sonia. Sus padres también van a venir. Vamos a ver cómo celebran la Semana Santa allí. Vamos a ir a Ayacucho. ¡Va a ser genial!

2 ***Answer the questions in English.***

1. According to the text, what do eggs symbolise at Easter?
2. Which days mark the start and end of Easter week?
3. What did the people of Seville carry in the processions?
4. How did Naomi feel at first?
5. What did Naomi eat at the traditional meal?
6. Why does she think travel is important?
7. What is Naomi going to do next year?
8. Who will she go with?

la Cuaresma = *Lent*
el ayuno = *fasting*
el Domingo de Ramos = *Palm Sunday*
el Domingo de Resurrección = *Easter Sunday*
los nazarenos = *penitents (sinners seeking pardon)*
los cirios = *candles*
las cruces = *crosses*

3 *Find these expressions in the text.*

1 it is a symbol of
2 a very important religious festival
3 it starts on… and finishes on…
4 last year
5 at first… but then…
6 to conclude the celebrations
7 it is traditional to enjoy a special dinner
8 this experience was fascinating from a cultural point of view
9 the good thing was that
10 what I liked most was
11 I think it's important
12 next year

4 *The expressions you have found could be useful for your own writing to help with the following. Which category applies for each of the phrases in exercise 3?*

- giving facts
- extending sentences with time expressions
- giving opinions

5 *You might be asked to write about a celebration as a Controlled Assessment task. Use the Grade Studio to help you prepare your account.*

GradeStudio

To produce a good answer you need to use a variety of language and express opinions.

- Find three examples of how Naomi uses the **present** tense in her text.
- Find three examples of how Naomi uses the **preterite**.
- Find three examples of how Naomi uses the **near future** tense.
- Find two examples of how Naomi expresses **opinions** in her account.

To go a step further you should use a wider range of language. This might include other tenses, such as the imperfect, and verbs referring to a variety of people (I, he/she, we, they).

- Find two examples of how Naomi uses the **imperfect** tense to describe things in the past.
- Find examples of verbs that **refer to other people**, e.g. 'we' or 'they'.

For a really impressive answer:

- Include **complex sentences** which combine more than one tense. Look at how Naomi does this using the phrase '*Al principio… pero luego…*'
- Give and **justify your opinions**. Look at how Naomi does this here: '*Creo que es importante viajar para conocer la cultura de otros países.*'
- Naomi uses some **adverbs** in her account. Which other adverbs could you use?

6 *Now write a full account of a celebration.*

- Use Naomi's text and language from Module 2 to help you. Write at least 200 words.
- Structure your text carefully. Organise what you write in paragraphs.

Introduction

General summary of the celebration
What normally happens? When?

Main paragraph

Give details of what you did at this particular celebration.
Describe what you saw and how you felt.
Give details about clothes, food and traditions.
What was the best/worst thing?

Conclusion

Say whether you enjoyed the celebration.
Talk about plans for next year.

7 *Check what you have written carefully. Check:*

- spelling and accents
- tenses
- verb endings

Leer y escuchar

***Read the young people's comments on their home town, Seville. What is each person's opinion of Seville? Write each person's name followed by P (positive), N (negative) or P+N (positive and negative).* (4 marks)**

El transporte público es un poco lento, sobre todo en las horas punta. Los monumentos históricos son muy interesantes y están bien mantenidos. ***Sergio***

La industria hotelera nos da muchas oportunidades de trabajo. Lo malo es que muy pocos turistas hablan español. ***Diego***

La vida nocturna es divertida y animada para los jóvenes. Los teatros y los centros comerciales son modernos y muy populares entre los adultos y los turistas. ***Jessica***

Los hoteles son feos y muy caros. Hay muy pocos lugares de interés y las instalaciones deportivas están muy sucias. ***Marisol***

Remember, negative opinions don't always contain the word 'no'. Look for other clues, such as the adjectives each person uses.

Read Teresa's text about her visit to Seville and answer the questions.

1 Do you think Teresa had been looking forward to going to Seville? Write yes or no and give a reason for your answer. (1 mark)
2 What exactly surprised her about the city? (1 mark)
3 How did she go to the Monastery? (1 mark)
4 Why would she like to go back to Seville? (1 mark)
5 In the end what was her overall view of the city? (1 mark)
a quite unusual **b** plenty of variety **c** very friendly

You may find questions of different degrees of difficulty about the same text. The first question will not necessarily be the easiest one, so don't give up if you can't answer it: look at the other questions, too.

There might be a 'deductive' question, in which you have to draw your own conclusions, based on evidence from the whole passage.

Antes de ir a Sevilla me interesaba muy poco esa ciudad porque mi amiga me dijo que era vieja y aburrida. En realidad, me impresionó la arquitectura magnífica cuando llegué allí.
Vi fotos en Internet de las partes modernas e industriales de la ciudad y pensé que no había ni zonas verdes ni barrios antiguos. ¡Qué sorpresa!
Un día hicimos una excursión al Monasterio de San Isidro. Normalmente los turistas van allí en autocar. Nosotros decidimos ir en bicicleta y fue mucho más interesante.
Se dice que la historia y la cultura son las razones principales para volver a Sevilla, pero a mí lo que me interesa es la posibilidad de ir al museo de baile flamenco durante mi próxima visita.
En resumen Sevilla es una de las ciudades más variadas del mundo. ¡Vale la pena visitarla!

Listen to the weather forecast for Seville and answer the questions. (1–3)

1 What is the weather like at the moment? (1 mark)

a 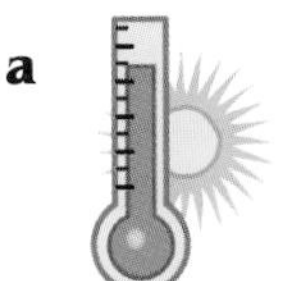 **b** 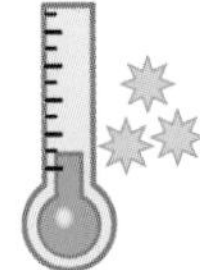 **c** 

2 What was the weather like yesterday? (1 mark)

a  **b** **c** 

3 What will the weather be like tomorrow? (1 mark)

a  **b**  **c** 

Look at the question and decide what key words you need to listen for. In this task, it's not just the weather, but the **time expressions** which are important.

Every question will contain 'distractors'. In this question, you will hear more than one weather phrase each time. So listen carefully for other small words which will give you the right answer. The correct answer might be at the start or at the end of the recording!

Listen to the conversations and answer the questions. (1–2)

1 Do you think Pedro and María are going to go on a bus tour of the city? Write yes or no and give a reason for your answer. (1 mark)
2 Do you think they are looking forward to eating out tonight? Write yes or no and give a reason for your answer. (1 mark)

Beware of unnecessary language or information in the recording, which might mislead you. Always listen to the whole of the recording before answering the question. In this question, the mark is awarded for getting the yes/no part and the reason correct. If you just write 'yes' or 'no' or just give a reason, you won't get a mark.

Why did each person visit Seville? Listen and write the correct letter for each name. (2 marks)

Example: Tomás **c**

1 Sofía
2 Fernando

Reasons for going to Seville

a to experience the nightlife
b to see a bullfight
c to sample the local food
d to meet some relatives
e to visit monuments

Study the example carefully as it's usually there to help! There is often more than one 'clue' in the recording, to help you get the answer, but, as always, beware of distractors.

Palabras

Mi vida *My life*

¿Cómo eres?	*What are you like?*
¿Cómo te llamas?	*What's your name?*
Me llamo…	*My name is…*
¿Cuántos años tienes?	*How old are you?*
Tengo… años.	*I'm… years old*
¿De dónde eres?	*Where are you from?*
Soy de…	*I'm from…*
¿Dónde vives?	*Where do you live?*
Vivo en…	*I live in…*
¿Cómo eres?	*What are you like?*
Soy…	*I'm…*
¿Qué haces en tu tiempo libre?	*What do you do in your free time?*
leo y escribo correos/mi blog	*I read and write emails/my blog*
navego por Internet	*I surf the net*
descargo música	*I download music*
juego con el ordenador	*I play on my computer*
chateo	*I chat (online)*
salgo con mis amigos	*I go out with my friends*
voy de compras	*I go shopping*
compro maquillaje y ropa	*I buy make-up and clothes*
veo la televisión	*I watch TV*
voy al cine/teatro	*I go to the cinema/theatre*

¿Qué tiempo hace? What's the weather like?

Hace buen tiempo.	*The weather's good.*
Hace mal tiempo.	*The weather's bad.*
Hace calor.	*It's hot.*
Hace frío.	*It's cold.*
Hace sol.	*It's sunny.*
Hace viento.	*It's windy.*
Hay niebla.	*It's foggy.*
Hay tormenta.	*It's stormy.*
Está nublado.	*It's cloudy.*
Está despejado.	*It's clear.*
Llueve.	*It's raining.*
Nieva.	*It's snowing.*
Cuando… pero cuando…	*When… but when…*

En ruta *En route*

el autobús	*bus*
el autocar	*coach*
el avión	*plane*
el barco	*boat*
el coche	*car*
el metro	*underground*
el monopatín	*skateboard*
el tren	*train*
la bicicleta	*bicycle*
la moto	*scooter*
el tranvía	*tram*
a pie	*on foot*
la parada	*(bus) stop*
a veces	*sometimes*
frecuentemente	*frequently*
generalmente	*generally*
normalmente	*usually*
solamente	*only*
prefiero ir/voy…	*I prefer to go/I go…*
porque es…	*because it is…*
La gente me molesta.	*People annoy me.*
Me da independencia.	*It gives me independence.*
Me gusta leer/escuchar música en…	*I like to read/listen to music on…*
Odio esperar.	*I hate waiting.*
¿A qué hora sale el primer/último/próximo tren?	*What time does the first/last/next train go?*
¿De qué andén sale?	*Which platform does it leave from?*
¿A qué hora llega?	*What time does it arrive?*
¿Es directo?	*Is it direct?*
el billete de ida y vuelta	*return ticket*
la llegada	*arrival*
la sala de espera	*waiting room*
la salida	*exit*
la taquilla	*ticket booth*

La oficina de turismo *The tourist office*

¿Qué se puede hacer/ver/visitar?	*What can you do/see/visit?*
¿Qué vas a hacer en…?	*What are you going to do in…?*
¿Cómo va a ser?	*What's it going to be like?*
¿Cómo se va al/a la…?	*How do you get to…?*
¿Cuánto tiempo dura?	*How long does it last?*
¿Cuándo abre/cierra…?	*When does… open/close?*
¿A qué hora abre/cierra…?	*What time does… open/close?*
el centro comercial	*shopping centre*
primero	*first*
por la mañana	*in the morning*
luego	*then*
por la tarde	*in the afternoon*
por la noche	*at night*
vamos a…	*we're going to…*
voy a…	*I'm going to…*
comprar recuerdos	*buy souvenirs*
comer algo	*eat something*
dar un paseo por…	*walk around…*
descubrir todo sobre las corridas	*find out all about bullfighting*
disfrutar de unas vistas espléndidas	*enjoy some splendid views*
sacar fotos	*take photos*
subir a la torre	*go up the tower*
ver lugares de interés	*see places of interest*
Va a ser…	*It's going to be…*
También vamos a…	*We're also going to…*
porque me encanta/me gusta mucho…	*because I love/like it a lot…*

Comprando recuerdos *Buying souvenirs*

¿Dónde se puede comprar un collar?	*Where can you buy a necklace?*
un abanico	*a fan*
una camiseta	*a t-shirt*
un chorizo	*a Spanish sausage*
una gorra	*a cap*
una muñeca	*a doll*
unos pendientes	*earrings*
unas postales	*some postcards*
una taza	*a mug*
el estanco	*tobacconist's*
el quiosco	*kiosk*

el supermercado	*supermarket*
la carnicería	*butcher's*
la confitería	*sweet shop*
la farmacia	*chemist's*
la frutería	*greengrocer's*

la joyería	*jeweller's*
la panadería	*baker's*
la pescadería	*fishmonger's*
la tienda de recuerdos	*souvenir shop*
la tienda de ropa	*clothes shop*

¿Por dónde se va al/a la…? *How do you get to…?*

Cruza la plaza.	*Cross the square.*
Gira en la esquina.	*Turn the corner.*
Cruza el puente.	*Cross the bridge.*
Pasa los semáforos.	*Pass the traffic lights.*
Toma la primera calle a la derecha.	*Take the first street on the right.*
Toma la segunda calle a la izquierda.	*Take the second street on the left.*
Sigue todo recto.	*Go straight ahead.*
Está a mano izquierda/derecha.	*It's on the left/right-hand side.*
Está al final de la calle.	*It's at the end of the street.*

Está al lado del/de la…	*It's next to…*
Está enfrente del/de la…	*It's opposite…*
Está cerca.	*It's near.*
Está lejos.	*It's far.*
A ver…/Pues…/Entonces…	*Let's see…/Next…/Then…*
Primero…	*First…*
Después…	*After…*
Luego…	*Then…*
Ahora estás en…	*Now you're at…*
Un poco más lejos…	*A little further…*

Tomando tapas *Eating tapas*

tener hambre/sed	*to be hungry/thirsty*
Me gusta…	*I like…*
el gazpacho	*gazpacho (chilled soup)*
las lentejas con chorizo	*lentils with sausage*
el jamón serrano	*Serrano ham*
la sopa de ajo	*garlic soup*
la tortilla de patatas	*potato omelette*
la merluza en salsa verde	*hake in a parsley and wine sauce*
la paella	*paella*
la chuleta de cerdo con verduras	*pork chop with vegetables*
el filete de ternera	*fillet of veal*
los calamares	*squid*
las gambas al ajillo	*prawns with garlic*
judías verdes con jamón	*broad beans with ham*
pescaito frito	*fried fish*
los postres	*dessert*
el flan	*crème caramel*
Helados de…	*…ice-cream*
la tarta de queso	*cheesecake*
el agua mineral con gas/sin gas	*sparkling/still mineral water*
De primer/segundo plato	*For starter/main course/*

De postre	*For dessert*
Voy a tomar…	*I'm going to have…*
No hay sal/aceite/vinagre.	*There's no salt/oil/vinegar.*
Está muy salado/a.	*It's very salty.*
El plato/vaso está sucio.	*The plate/glass is dirty.*
El vino está malo.	*The wine is off.*
Me falta el cuchillo.	*I haven't got a knife.*
Me falta la cuchara.	*I haven't got a spoon.*
Me falta el tenedor.	*I haven't got a fork.*
¿Me pone…?	*Could I have…?*
¿Y para beber?	*And to drink?*
¿Algo más?	*Anything else?*
Nada más.	*Nothing else.*
La cuenta por favor.	*The bill, please.*
¡Que aproveche!	*Enjoy your meal.*
la especialidad de la casa	*house speciality*
el menú	*the menu*
rico	*delicious*
¿El servicio está incluido?	*Is service included?*
la propina	*tip*

En Sevilla *In Seville*

¿Adónde fuiste?	*Where did you go?*
Fui a…	*I went to…*
¿Cuánto tiempo pasaste allí?	*How much time did you spend there?*
Pasé…	*I spent…*
¿Qué tal tu visita a (Londres)?	*How was your visit to (London)?*
Lo pasé guay/fenomenal.	*It was great/wonderful.*
Compré…	*I bought…*
Di un paseo por…	*I had a walk round…*
Disfruté de vistas…	*I enjoyed… views*
Fui a…	*I went to…*
Saqué…	*I took…*
Subí a la torre…	*I went up the…tower*
Vi…	*I saw…*
La Giralda era…	*Giralda was…*

Había…	*There was/were…*
¿Visitaste la ciudad a pie?	*Did you visit the city on foot?*
Visité la cuidad a pie/en…	*I visited the city on foot/by…*
¿Qué tiempo hizo?	*What was the weather like?*
Hizo…	*It was…*
¿Qué tal la comida?	*How was the food?*
La comida estaba…	*The food was…*
¿Qué es lo que más te gustó?	*What did you like best?*
Lo que más/menos me gustó fue/fueron…	*What I liked best/least was/were…*
Pero no me gustó…	*But I didn't like…*
¿Vas a volver?	*Will you go back?*
Por un lado… por otro lado…	*On one hand… on the other hand…*

Las fiestas *Festivals*

Es una fiesta…	*It's a… festival*
Decoramos las casas/un árbol de navidad.	*We decorate the houses/a Christmas tree.*
Viene mucha gente.	*A lot of people come.*
Preparamos comida para todo el mundo.	*We prepare food for everyone.*

Hacemos regalos.	*We give presents.*
Cocinamos.	*We cook.*
Cenamos…	*We eat… for dinner.*
celebramos	*we celebrate*
Hay un ambiente muy especial.	*There's a very special atmosphere.*
los fuegos artificiales	*fireworks*

- Giving opinions on school subjects
- Using **me gusta, me encanta**, etc.
- Revising basic vocabulary

Repaso 1 *Las asignaturas*

Empareja las frases con los dibujos. Identifica si la opinión es positiva (P) o negativa (N).

Ejemplo: **1** j – (P)

1 Me gusta el español porque es entretenido.
2 Odio la geografía porque es aburrida.
3 No me gustan las ciencias porque son complicadas.
4 Me encantan las matemáticas porque no son difíciles.
5 Me gusta mucho el comercio porque es muy práctico.
6 Me encanta el teatro porque es divertido.
7 No me gusta nada la informática porque no es fácil.
8 Me gusta el dibujo porque es muy útil.

me encanta me gusta mucho me gusta no me gusta no me gusta nada odio	el francés el dibujo la educación física la informática la música la tecnología la religión
me encanta**n** me gusta**n** mucho me gusta**n** no me gusta**n** no me gusta**n** nada odio	las matemáticas las ciencias los idiomas la geografía **y** la historia el teatro **y** el español

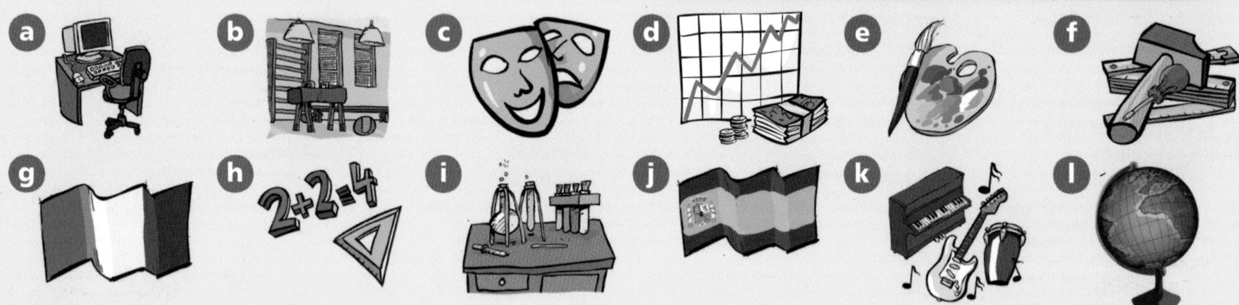

Escucha. Copia y completa la tabla. (1–5)

	subject	day(s)	opinions (x2)
1	*maths*	*Tuesday*	*boring/difficult*

lunes	viernes
martes	sábado
miércoles	domingo
jueves	

Con tu compañero/a, pregunta y contesta.

- ● ¿Cuándo tienes tecnología?
- ■ Tengo tecnología los miércoles. Me gust**a** la tecnología porque **es** divertid**a** y además **es** útil.
- ● ¿Qué días tienes matemáticas?
- ■ Tengo matemáticas los martes y los jueves. No me gusta**n** las matemáticas porque **son** aburrid**as** y también **son** difícil**es**.

While speaking concentrate on being accurate!
School subjects and opinions are easy to understand, but make sure you use the *correct endings*.

4 Lee el correo de Luis. ¿Qué le gusta o no le gusta estudiar? ¿Y a Rafa? Apunta los datos en inglés.

¡Hola! Me llamo Luis y mi mejor amigo del instituto se llama Rafa. Mi asignatura preferida es la biología porque es interesante y porque me encanta el mundo animal, pero a Rafa no le interesan demasiado las ciencias. Él prefiere las asignaturas artísticas, como el dibujo o la música. La asignatura que menos le gusta es la historia porque odia memorizar datos y fechas. A los dos nos gustan los idiomas porque nos interesa viajar y aprender cosas sobre otras culturas.

G Pronouns + verbs of opinion

➲214

In Spanish, some verbs of opinion are preceded by a pronoun, e.g.: **gustar**, **encantar** and **interesar**. You use these in a similar way to the English verbs like *to interest*, with the verb in the *third person* and a *pronoun* with it (*it interests me*).

me gusta(n)	*I like*	**nos** gusta(n)	*we like*
te gusta(n)	*you (sing.) like*	**os** gusta(n)	*you (pl.) like*
le gusta(n)	*he/she likes*	**les** gusta(n)	*they like*

Me gusta **el** español. *I like Spanish.*
Remember to use the definite article that agrees with the following noun.

Not all verbs of opinion need a pronoun, e.g.: **odiar** and **preferir**.
Odio las matemáticas. *I hate maths.* Prefiero el francés. *I prefer French.*

Nico el Gamberro

5 Escucha y completa los espacios del horario de Nico el Gamberro. (1–5)

hora	lunes	martes	miércoles	jueves	viernes
8.45	matemáticas	c	informática	inglés	física
9.45	inglés	d	historia	biología	lengua
10.45			recreo		
11.00	lengua	teatro	e	lengua	informática
12.00	a	matemáticas	f	i	j
13.00			comida		
15.45	geografía	religión	g	tecnología	geografía
16.45	b	lengua	h	inglés	k

6 Habla del horario de Nico el Gamberro con tu compañero/a.

- ● ¿A qué hora tiene Nico… los lunes/martes/etc.?
- ■ Tiene… a la(s)…

7 Escribe un correo. Incluye información sobre tus asignaturas y tu horario.

★ Don't ignore the basics when revising language you've seen before. You need to know your numbers and how to tell the time.

★ When answering the question ¿A qué hora…? remember to say the time using:
Tengo ciencias **a la** una y dibujo **a las** dos/tres/etc.

- Describing your school routine
- Using the present tense with time expressions
- Improving your spoken and written texts

Repaso 2 *En clase*

Lee el texto y completa las frases.

1 Catarina usually goes to school by...
2 She walks to school in...
3 She does not like going by...
4 She goes by train with her friend Felipe in...
5 Her sister often goes to school by...
6 Her sister goes by bus in...

Por la mañana voy al instituto en autobús, pero **en verano** voy andando porque hace buen tiempo. **Nunca** voy en metro porque no me gusta. **Por la tarde** vuelvo a casa en tren con mi amigo Felipe. Él **siempre** coge el tren y es divertido. Mi hermana va al instituto en bicicleta **a menudo**, pero **en invierno** va conmigo en autobús.

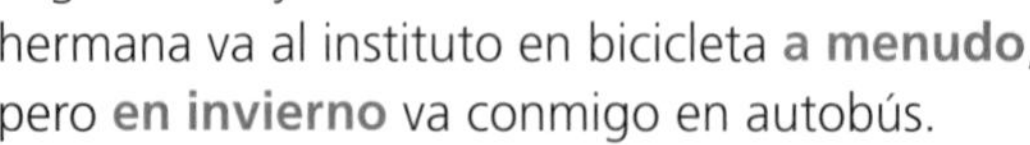

Las estaciones
la primavera
el verano
el otoño
el invierno

Con tu compañero/a, haz estos diálogos.

● ¿Cómo vas al colegio?	■ Normalmente voy..., pero mi hermano/a va...
● ¿Cómo vuelves del colegio?	■ Vuelvo...
● ¿Coges el autobús a diario?	■ Sí, cojo.../No, no cojo... Cojo...
● ¿Vas andando alguna vez?	■ Sí, voy.../No, no voy... Voy...
● ¿Te gusta ir en bici?	■ Sí/No, me gusta/encanta ir...
● ¿Cómo vas al colegio en verano/invierno/otoño/primavera?	■ En... voy...
● ¿Qué medio de transporte prefieres para ir al insti?	■ Prefiero ir...

Adding time expressions (such as seasons, time of day, etc.) to your speaking and writing will add length and complexity to your sentences.

G The present tense

➲200–202

	(-**er** verbs)	(-**ir** verbs)
	coger *(to take)*	**preferir** *(to prefer)*
(yo)	coj**o**	prefi**e**r**o**
(tú)	cog**es**	prefi**eres**
(él/ella/usted)	cog**e**	prefi**ere**
(nosotros/as)	cog**emos**	prefer**imos**
(vosotros/as)	cog**éis**	prefer**ís**
(ellos/ellas/ustedes)	cog**en**	prefi**eren**

To say that you walk somewhere you can use **ir andando** or **ir a pie**:
Van andando/a pie al cole.
They walk to school.

Some verbs like **coger** are irregular in the first person and other verbs like **preferir** are stem changing (e → ie), but they have regular endings.

Cojo el tren, pero tú **coges** el autobús. *I take the train but you take the bus.*

Escucha y escribe las letras correctas. (1–4)

Escucha y rellena los espacios en blanco.

Pablo: ¿A qué hora empiezan tus clases?
María: Muy temprano… Empiezan a las (1) _____ de la mañana.
Pablo: ¿Qué (2) _____ en clase normalmente?
María: (3) _____ escucho al profe, pero también hablo con mis amigos.
Pablo: ¿Qué tienes que llevar a clase?
María: Siempre llevo mi (4) _____, unos bolígrafos y una regla. También necesito mis cuadernos y mis (5) _____.
Pablo: ¡Claro! ¿Qué haces a la hora de comer?
María: Todos los (6) _____ voy al club de ajedrez y a veces juego al fútbol en el patio.
Pablo: ¿Qué haces después del (7) _____?
María: De vez en cuando voy al club de (8) _____ y hago mis deberes.

Con tu compañero/a, contesta a las preguntas de ejercicio 4.

En clase…	escucho al/a la profe. hablo, leo y uso el diccionario.
A la hora de comer… En el recreo/verano/invierno… Después del colegio…	juego al tenis y hago natación. voy al club de ajedrez/idiomas. canto en el coro y toco en la orquesta.

See how many of the underlined verbs from exercise 4 you can use in your own speaking or writing on school routine.

Mira la historia de Tomás Tontorrón. Describe su día.

When describing Tomás' day use all the information from exercises 2 and 5. Don't forget to include:

- different time expressions
- a variety of verbs
- descriptions of activities
- opinions
- use a dictionary if you need to

COLEGIO
En invierno, normalmente los jueves Tomás Tontorrón va a...

- Producing descriptions of school life
- Using the imperfect and present tenses
- Giving a range of opinions

1 ¿Cómo es tu insti?

Mira el plano del colegio. Escribe las letras correctas. (Sobran dos palabras.)

Ejemplo: **1** h

a unos laboratorios
b unos vestuarios
c unas aulas
d un comedor
e un gimnasio
f una biblioteca
g una sala de profesores
h un campo de fútbol
i una piscina
j una pista de atletismo
k un salón de actos
l un patio

¿Qué **hay** en el colegio? Escucha e identifica las tres letras correctas. (1–4)

Escucha otra vez. ¿Las opiniones sobre las instalaciones son positivas (P), negativas (N) o positivas y negativas (P+N)? (1–4)

Ejemplo: **1** P + N

Lo bueno es que…	hay…	campo de fútbol.
Lo malo es que…	no hay…	piscina.
Lo que más me gusta es que…	tenemos…	gimnasio.
Lo que menos me gusta es que…	no tenemos…	comedor.
Por un lado/por otro lado…		patio.

Read Mónica's webpage. Decide if the statements are true (T), false (F) or not mentioned (NM).

1 There is an indoor swimming pool and an athletics track.
2 It is a specialist school with modern classrooms.
3 There are too many school rules.
4 Mónica does not like wearing uniform.
5 It's a mixed state school.
6 The lessons start at nine and end at four in the afternoon.

Voy a un colegio femenino privado. Hay cuatrocientas alumnas aproximadamente. En mi cole **hay** buenas instalaciones, **por ejemplo**, los laboratorios son grandes y las aulas modernas. Sin embargo, **no tenemos ni** piscina **ni** pista de atletismo. **Tampoco** tenemos una pista de tenis, ¡es una lástima!
Estoy en cuarto de la ESO, y las clases **empiezan** a las nueve y **terminan** a las cuatro. **Lo bueno es que** mi colegio es una "ecoescuela" y para proteger al medioambiente reciclamos toda la basura. **Lo malo es que** llevamos uniforme, ¡qué lata!

5 Haz una conversación.

- ¿Cómo es tu instituto?
- ¿A qué hora empiezan/terminan las clases?
- ¿Qué hay en tu instituto?
- ¿Te gusta tu instituto? ¿Por qué (no)?

Voy a un colegio femenino / masculino / mixto / privado / público / especializado en…
Las clases empiezan a… y terminan a…
Hay…/No hay…
También tenemos… y…, pero no tenemos… ni… ni…
Tampoco hay…
Lo bueno/malo es que…
Lo que más/menos me gusta…

Some Spanish words are the same in English (cognates) or very similar but they are pronounced very differently. Remember to pronounce these words using Spanish letter sounds:

gimnasio	*him – nass – ee – yoh*
hora	*or – ra*
atletismo	*at – let – ees – moh*

6 Lee el blog. Contesta a las preguntas en inglés.

¡Bienvenid@ a mi blog!

¿Qué tal, colega? Me llamo Raquel y estás leyendo mi blog sobre el insti. Estoy en tercero de la ESO en el instituto Santa Bárbara. Es un colegio mixto con quinientos alumnos y sesenta profesores. Mi insti es bastante moderno. Es un edificio de tres pisos y fue construido en los años setenta. Hay buenas instalaciones y cada aula tiene cuatro ordenadores y una pizarra interactiva. Antes no había ni ordenadores ni pizarras interactivas.

El sistema escolar también era diferente. Antes era obligatorio estudiar religión y latín, ahora no. El edificio también era más pequeño porque no teníamos todavía la gran biblioteca que tenemos hoy. En general los profesores son amables y tolerantes. Antes eran más severos y estrictos, y nunca llegaban tarde. Los estudiantes eran más tranquilos. Lo que más me gusta de mi insti es la comida. Está muy buena y siempre hay una gran variedad de platos, pero en los años setenta la comida era muy mala.

1 What type of school does Raquel attend?
2 How does she describe the school building? (2 details)
3 Describe the facilities in the classrooms. (2 details).
4 How does the school building compare now to how it was in the 1970s?
5 What are the teachers like today and how were they in the 1970s?
6 Are the students better behaved nowadays?
7 What does Raquel like most about her school and why?

7 Escribe un blog sobre tu colegio.

Present	Imperfect
Mi colegio **es**…	Mi colegio **era**…
El edificio **es**…	El edificio **era**…
(No) **hay**…	(No) **había**…
Los estudiantes **son**…	Los estudiantes **eran**…
Estudian…	**Estudiaban**…
Los profesores **son**…	Los profesores **eran**…
La comida **es**…	La comida **era**…

- Describing school uniform and rules
- Using phrases followed by an infinitive
- Giving and justifying opinions

2 Las normas del insti

1 Lee los textos y escribe el nombre correcto. ¿Quién es?

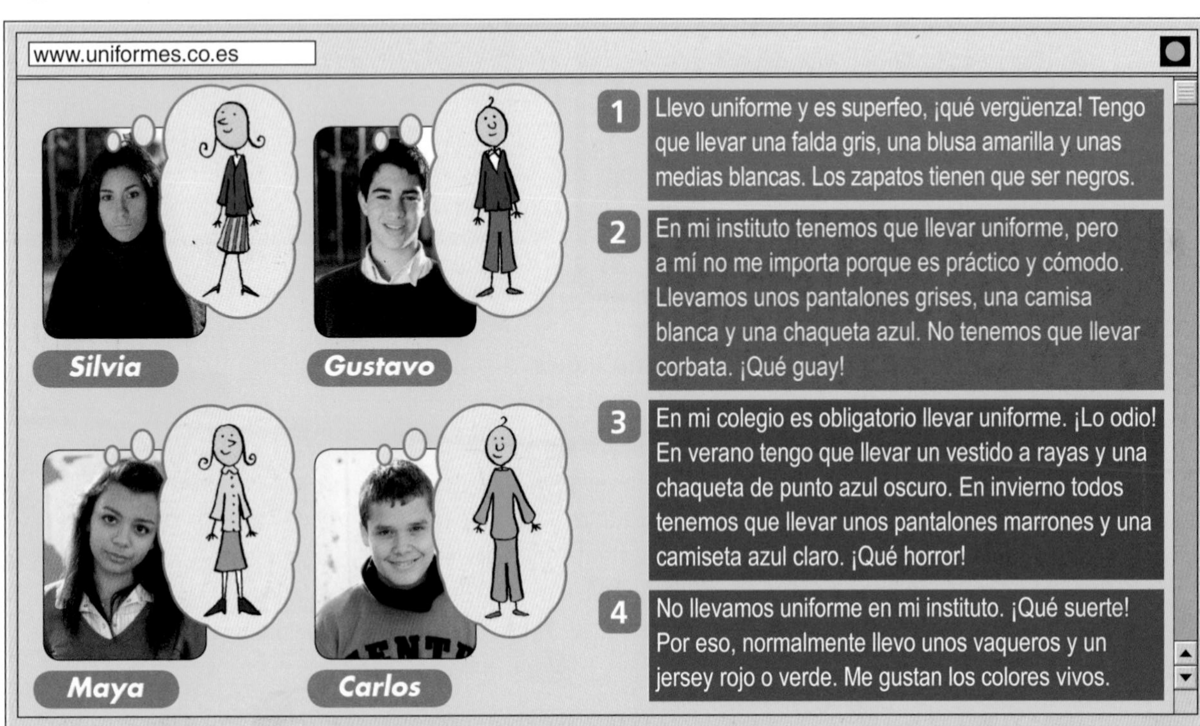

1 Llevo uniforme y es superfeo, ¡qué vergüenza! Tengo que llevar una falda gris, una blusa amarilla y unas medias blancas. Los zapatos tienen que ser negros.

2 En mi instituto tenemos que llevar uniforme, pero a mí no me importa porque es práctico y cómodo. Llevamos unos pantalones grises, una camisa blanca y una chaqueta azul. No tenemos que llevar corbata. ¡Qué guay!

3 En mi colegio es obligatorio llevar uniforme. ¡Lo odio! En verano tengo que llevar un vestido a rayas y una chaqueta de punto azul oscuro. En invierno todos tenemos que llevar unos pantalones marrones y una camiseta azul claro. ¡Qué horror!

4 No llevamos uniforme en mi instituto. ¡Qué suerte! Por eso, normalmente llevo unos vaqueros y un jersey rojo o verde. Me gustan los colores vivos.

2 Escucha. ¿Quién habla? ¿Silvia, Gustavo, Maya o Carlos? Escribe S, G, M ó C. (1–4)

(No…)	un jersey	un vestido	rojo	negro
Llevo…	una falda	una camisa	blanco	morado
Llevamos…	una camiseta	una corbata	amarillo	verde
Tengo que llevar…	unos pantalones	unos vaqueros	gris	marrón
	unos calcetines	unos zapatos	naranja	rosa
Tenemos que llevar…	una chaqueta (de punto)		azul	
	unas medias		claro/oscuro	

Use the correct endings!

G Adjectives of colour

➲216

Remember to make your adjectives of colour agree with the noun they describe.

Ending in:	Masc Sing.	Fem. Sing.	Masc. Pl.	Fem. Pl.
-o	amarillo	amarilla	amarillos	amarillas
-e/-a	verde	verde	verdes	verdes
consonant	azul	azul	azules	azules

Adjectives like **rosa** or **naranja** *can* take an –s with the plural noun.

A colour adjective followed by **claro** (light) and **oscuro** (dark) takes the masculine form even if describing a feminine or plural noun, e.g.: unos zapatos azul claro, unas medias azul claro.

hablar 3 **Haz diálogos para las personas del ejercicio 1.**

- ● ¿Llevas uniforme, Silvia?
- ■ Sí, tengo que llevar uniforme.
- ● ¿Cómo es?
- ■ En verano llevo un vestido de rayas y una chaqueta de punto azul oscuro. ¡Qué horror! No me gusta nada mi uniforme. En invierno…

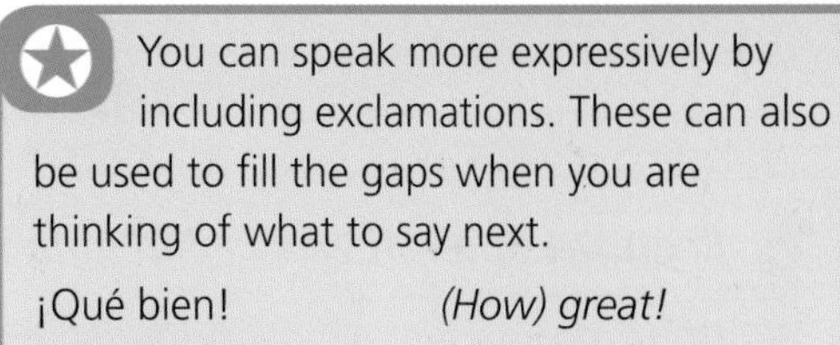

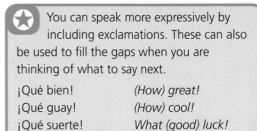

You can speak more expressively by including exclamations. These can also be used to fill the gaps when you are thinking of what to say next.

¡Qué bien!	*(How) great!*
¡Qué guay!	*(How) cool!*
¡Qué suerte!	*What (good) luck!*
¡Qué horror!	*How awful!*
¡Qué vergüenza!	*How embarrasing!*
¡Qué lío!	*What a mess!*
¡Qué va!	*No way!*

escribir 4 **Describe tu uniforme o tu ropa para ir al colegio. Incluye colores y otros adjetivos.**

bonito elegante guay cómodo práctico feo anticuado

leer 5 **Lee las normas del instituto. ¿Existen estas normas en tu instituto? Escribe ✔ o ✘ para cada frase. Usa el diccionario.**

a Está prohibido llevar maquillaje.
b Está prohibido llevar joyas y piercings.
c Está prohibido escuchar tu MP3 en clase.
d No se permite usar el móvil o mandar mensajes en clase.
e No se permite comer chicle en clase.
f No se debe correr por los pasillos.
g No se debe salir del instituto durante la jornada escolar.
h Los alumnos tienen que ser puntuales y amables.
i Los alumnos no deben ser ni desobedientes ni groseros.

escuchar 6 **Escucha e identifica las normas mencionadas. Escucha otra vez y escribe positivo (P) o negativo (N). (1–4)**

Ejemplo: **1** a, f, g – N

G *The infinitive*

When describing rules, there a several structures which take the **infinitive**:

Está prohibido
No se permite
No se debe
(No) tiene(n) que
\+ llevar / usar / mandar / comer

escribir 7 **Escribe las normas de tu instituto.**

Rule	**Opinion**	**Justify opinion**
En el cole tengo que llevar uniforme.	¡Qué horror! Odio el uniforme.	Es feo y además es bastante incómodo.

- Describing teachers
- Using comparatives and superlatives
- Agreeing and disagreeing

3 ¡Los profesores!

1 ***Read the Spanish words and note pairs of opposites. What do they mean?***

Ejemplo: paciente/impaciente *(patient/impatient)*

paciente · antipático/a · listo/a · trabajador(a) · impaciente · raro/a · normal · pesimista · perezoso/a · simpático/a · tolerante · aburrido/a · severo/a · divertido/a · optimista · tonto/a

2 Escucha y escribe las asignaturas y la descripción del/de la profesor(a). (1–6)

***Ejemplo:* 1** matemáticas/paciente

3 Escucha y rellena las frases. (1–6)

1. Mi profesor de inglés es más ____ que mi profesor de matemáticas.
2. Mi tutor es más ____ que mi profesor de ciencias.
3. Mi profe de matemáticas es menos ____ que mi profe de inglés.
4. Mi profe de español es tan ____ como mi profe de francés.
5. Mi profesor de ____ es el mejor.
6. Mi profesora de ____ es la peor.

4 Rellena las frases del ejercicio 3 con tus opiniones.

G *Comparatives*

➲218

más… que	*more… than*
menos… que	*less… than*
mejor que…	*better than…*
peor que…	*worse than…*
tan… como…	*as… as…*

Mi profe de inglés es **más** severo **que** mi profe de teatro.
Mi profesora de dibujo es **tan** simpática **como** mi profe de música.

Superlatives

el/la más…	*the most…*
el/la menos…	*the least…*
el/la mejor…	*the best…*
el/la peor…	*the worst…*

El profesor de historia es **el más** simpático.
La profesora de religión es **la peor** del instituto.

For more than one person use **los** (males or mixed group) or **las** (females):
Los profesores jóvenes son **los más** impacientes.

5 Lee el texto y contesta a las preguntas.

Jorge: Hola, Jade. ¿Qué tal tu colegio en Inglaterra? Yo no estoy muy contento este curso aquí en Madrid porque tenemos una profesora nueva de ciencias, la señora Torres. Me cae fatal. **Me parece** que es una pesada y es demasiado severa. **No estoy de acuerdo** con su manera de enseñar. Por ejemplo, el martes pasado hablé con mi compañero porque no entendía sus explicaciones y se enfadó conmigo. **Para mí** que está loca. Después me quedé sin recreo porque no terminé el ejercicio. ¡No es justo! **Creo que** la señora Torres es mucho más exigente que el señor López (el profesor de ciencias de antes). También nos pone demasiados deberes. Ayer en clase no nos dejó hablar, ni trabajar en equipo. ¡Tuvimos que escribir una lista con las normas del instituto! Estoy harto de sus clases porque la señora Torres es realmente una tía paliza.

1. Who is Señora Torres?
2. How does Jorge describe señora Torres? (2 details)
3. Why did señora Torres get cross with Jorge last Tuesday?
4. What punishment did Jorge get?
5. How does señora Torres compare to their old teacher?
6. What were they not allowed to do in science class yesterday? (2 details)

Me cae fatal. = *I can't stand him/her.*
enseñar = *to teach*
enfadarse = *to get angry*
quedarse sin = *to go without/to miss*
exigente = *demanding*
estoy harto de = *I am fed up with*
un tío paliza/una tía paliza = *an annoying man/woman*

6 Escucha. Copia y completa la tabla. (1–5)

	Who are the teachers talking about?	Debate phrases used	Do they agree or disagree? (A or D)
1	Geography teacher	Creo que... Estoy de acuerdo...	A

Keep a *useful phrases* list and remember to add to it frequently when you come across new language that can be used for lots of different topics. The phrases of debate in bold in the text above can be used over and over again and will really help to take your speaking and writing up a level!

7 ¡A debate! Habla con tu compañero/a de tus profesores.

¡A debate!		
¿Qué opinas del profesor de…? ¿Qué te parece la profesora de…?		
Creo que… Pienso que… Para mí… Me parece que… Por ejemplo…	Estoy de acuerdo (con)… No estoy de acuerdo (con)… Estoy a favor (de)… Estoy en contra (de)… ¿Y tú? ¿Y usted?	¡Por supuesto! ¡Claro! Es verdad. …pero… …sin embargo…

- Describing school pressures and problems
- Using quantifiers (**muy…, un poco…**)
- Improving your listening skills

4 El acoso escolar

Read the phrases in the blue box below and look at the photos. Write an appropriate phrase in Spanish for each photo.

***Ejemplo:* a** En mi opinión, el estrés de los exámenes es normal.

a

b

c

d

e

Escucha y escribe la letra correcta del ejercicio 1. (1–5)

Don't panic if you don't understand some words in a listening exercise. Think about the key language you are listening for. For exercise 2 have in your head the key phrases for each of the images a–e whilst you listen.

En mi opinión…	el acoso escolar el ataque físico el fracaso escolar el estrés de los exámenes la presión del grupo hacer novillos	es un problema serio. es el mayor problema. es una tontería. ocurre frecuentemente. ocurre raras veces. es normal.
Es difícil… No es fácil…	sacar buenas notas todo el tiempo. prepararse para las presentaciones orales. repasar los apuntes para los exámenes.	
Se debería… No se debería…	respetar maltratar insultar golpear intimidar	a los demás.

Contesta a las preguntas.

- ¿Cuál es el mayor problema de tu instituto?
- ¿Ocurre frecuentemente el acoso escolar?
- En tu opinión, ¿qué es difícil para los alumnos?
- En tu opinión, ¿qué no se debería hacer a los demás?

Creo que…
Para mí…
En mi opinión…
Por ejemplo…
Hay… Existe(n)… Tenemos…

4 Lee el correo electrónico e identifica las fotos apropiadas del ejercicio 1.

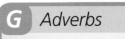

Hola, ¿qué tal? Estoy mal en mi instituto porque lo odio y además estoy **muy** estresada. Tengo muchos exámenes el mes que viene y lo peor es que tengo que hacer un examen oral de francés. No hablo bien francés porque es **demasiado** difícil. ¡No soy francesa! Todos los días después del instituto preparo **un poco** mi presentación oral en casa. Tengo que hablar de mis últimas vacaciones, pero no sé cómo hablar en pasado. ¡Los verbos son **tan** difíciles! Tengo otro problema. Mi mejor amigo, que se llama Juan, tiene un móvil nuevo y siempre está grabando lo que pasa en las aulas o en el comedor. Ayer Juan grabó en el patio una pelea entre dos chicos, y ahora el chico menor piensa que es una víctima del "happy slapping", así que Juan tiene que ir a hablar con el director del instituto. Juan no es un joven agresivo y odia el acoso escolar. Por lo general es una persona **bastante** amable y simpática, pero debe pensar más antes de actuar. En mi opinión, no es bueno usar el móvil para grabar a otros sin pedir permiso. *Carolina*

grabar = *to film*

5 Lee el texto otra vez. Contesta a las preguntas.

1 How is Carolina feeling? (2 details)
2 Why is she feeling like this?
3 How is she preparing herself for next month's exam?
4 What does her best friend do all the time at the moment?
5 Who does Juan have to speak with and why?
6 What kind of person is Juan? (2 details)
7 Does Carolina think Juan's behaviour is acceptable?

G Adverbs ➲219

Adverbs are important in extending your sentences.
You can use these to describe verbs (estudio **demasiado**) or to enhance adjectives (**demasiado** fácil).

bastante	*quite*
un poco	*a bit*
poco	*not very/not very much*
demasiado	*too (much)*

These adverbs are used only with adjectives:

muy	*very*
tan	*so*

6 Lee de nuevo y escribe las frases azules en inglés.

7 Escribe las siguientes frases en español.

1 I hate my school. I'm so stressed!
2 Next month I have to do an oral presentation and it's not easy to revise.
3 In my school bullying is also a very serious problem.
4 People shouldn't intimidate or insult others.
5 I'm quite a nice person and in my opinion we need to respect other people.

8 Escribe un correo electrónico a Carolina. Escribe sobre los problemas que existen en tu colegio.

Yo también estoy mal en el instituto.
...es un problema serio en mi colegio.
Lo peor es que... y todos los días...
Tengo otro problema...

En mi opinión...
Es difícil...
No se debería...

- Describing the schools of the future
- Using the future tense
- Using questions to form answers

5 El cole del futuro

Escucha y escribe la letra correcta. (1–6)

Ejemplo: **1** c

Lee las frases. Identifica los verbos. ¿Presente o futuro? Escribe P o F. Traduce las frases al inglés.

1. En mi colegio tenemos una biblioteca enorme.
2. No será obligatorio llevar uniforme.
3. En la biblioteca no habrá tantos libros. Habrá tecnología punta y muchos ordenadores.
4. Los alumnos van a clase de lunes a viernes.
5. En el instituto nos enseñan música rock. ¡Es guay!
6. Los alumnos tendrán la oportunidad de hacer viajes de estudios por todo el mundo.
7. Los alumnos aprenderán a esquíar en el cole.
8. En el colegio hay un salón de actos fantástico y todos aprenden a bailar.

Escribe cuatro frases sobre los colegios del futuro.

En el colegio del futuro (no) habrá… (no) tendremos…	aulas grandísimas. una sala de juegos interactiva. una piscina olímpica. una pista de esquí. un gimnasio supergrande. alumnos de todo el mundo. robots en vez de profes. tecnología punta. ordenadores. cuadernos y libros. viajes de estudios en…/por todo el mundo.
El colegio del futuro (no) tendrá…	
En el colegio del futuro (no) podrás… (no) deberás… (no) será obligatorio…	llevar uniforme. escuchar podcasts de las clases.
Los alumnos irán al cole…	todos los días. solamente tres días a la semana.

G The Future tense

➲208

The future tense is used to convey a very definite future or a prediction: what **will** happen or what you think **will** happen.

To form the future tense, add the following endings to the **infinitive** of all regular verbs. Be careful with stem changing verbs or irregular verbs that you get the infinitive right (e.g.: jugar, ir, etc.).

(yo)	**-é**
(tú)	**-ás**
(él/ella/usted)	**-á**
(nosotros/as)	**-emos**
(vosotros/as)	**-eis**
(ellos/ellas/ustedes)	**-án**

Some verbs have an irregular future stem but take the same endings:

hacer	→	**har**é, **har**ás, etc.
tener	→	**tendr**é, **tendr**ás, etc.
poder	→	**podr**é, **podr**ás, etc.
querer	→	**querr**é, **querr**ás, etc.
haber	→	**habr**á

Escucha y lee. ¿Qué se menciona? Escribe las letras correctas.

Juan: En tu opinión, Nuria, ¿cómo **será** el colegio del futuro?
Nuria: El colegio del futuro **será** distinto y mejor, ¡claro!
J: ¿Cuántos alumnos **habrá** en el colegio?
N: El colegio **tendrá** muchos alumnos porque nuestra población **será** mayor. **Tendrá** por lo menos dos mil alumnos.
J: ¿A qué hora **empezará** el colegio y a qué hora **terminará**?
N: **Empezará** a las ocho de la mañana y **terminará** a las ocho de la tarde.
J: ¿Qué **estudiarás** tú en el colegio?
N: **Estudiaré** bachillerato, pero otros jóvenes **harán** ciclos formativos para aprender un oficio, por ejemplo mecánico.
J: ¿Qué **harán** los profesores?
N: Los profesores **enseñarán** a los alumnos de la misma manera, pero no **habrá** cuadernos para corregir porque los deberes no **existirán.**
J: ¡Vaya! Y, ¿cómo **serán** las aulas?
N: Las aulas **serán** muy modernas y cada alumno **tendrá** su propio portátil.
J: ¡Qué guay! Aunque al ser tan grande, ¿**será** peligroso?
N: ¡No te preocupes! El colegio del futuro **estará** muy bien organizado y **habrá** un sistema de seguridad muy efectivo. No **habrá** violencia entre los estudiantes. Todos **estudiaremos** juntos sin problemas.

- **a** biblioteca
- **b** piscina cubierta
- **c** campo de fútbol
- **d** ordenadores portátiles
- **e** tecnología interactiva
- **f** cuadernos tradicionales
- **g** sala de juegos
- **h** seguridad
- **i** horarios
- **j** comida sana

Question words – yes, you've heard it before! They are particularly important for listening and speaking exams. Make sure you know them. Here are the ones from Escuchar 4. Can you think of any others?

¿Qué?	*What?*
¿Cómo?	*How?/What… like?*
¿Cuántos/as?	*How many?*
¿A qué hora?	*At what time?*

Lee el diálogo otra vez. ¿Verdadero (V), falso (F) o no se menciona (NM)?

1. According to Nuria, the future school will be better.
2. The future school will not have more than one thousand pupils.
3. The future school will be open twelve hours a day.
4. There will be no cars allowed in the road by the school.
5. You will be able to study for an apprenticeship at the school.
6. The teachers will still have lots of notebooks to mark.
7. There will be interactive whiteboards in each classroom.
8. The school could have problems with violence from pupils.

Look at the verbs in purple in the dialogue in exercise 4. What do they mean in English?

Habla de un colegio del futuro. Contesta a las preguntas del ejercicio 4.

- ¿Cómo será el colegio del futuro? (Creo que el colegio del futuro será…)
- ¿Cuántos alumnos habrá? (Habrá…)
- ¿Qué harán los profesores? (Los profesores…)

When answering questions in Spanish you can re-use the verbs in the questions to help form your answers. Remember that if the verbs are addressed directly to you, you will need to change the endings (from **tú** to **yo**):

¿Qué idiomas hablar**ás** en el futuro?
Hablar**é** inglés, chino y español.

However, if the verbs are asking about something or someone else you can use them exactly in the same form:

¿Cómo **será** el colegio del futuro?
El colegio del futuro **será** extraordinario.

Prueba oral

School

You are going to have a conversation with your teacher about your school. Your teacher could ask you the following:

- What do you study at school?
- What subjects do you like or dislike?
- What do you do during lunch or after school?
- What was your favourite club or activity last year? Why?
- What rules are there in your school?
- What do you think schools will be like in the future?

Remember that you will have to respond to an unexpected question that you have not yet prepared.
The dialogue will last for between 4 and 6 minutes.

You are going to listen to Jason, an exam candidate, taking part in the above conversation with his teacher. Predict which of the first two questions above he will use each of the following phrases to answer. Then listen to part 1 of the conversation to check whether you were right.

1. ...es mi asignatura preferida...
2. ...estudio ocho asignaturas en total...
3. ...me interesa mucho aprender...
4. El año que viene voy a hacer...
5. Tampoco me gustan...
6. ...porque es demasiado fácil.
7. No estudio religión o francés porque...

Listen again and note down in English the main points of Jason's answers for these first two questions.

Listen to part 2 of Jason's conversation and note down the words that fill the gaps.

– ¿Qué haces a la hora de comer y después del colegio?
– Pues… hago muchas actividades diferentes. (1) ______, (2) ______ voy al club de ajedrez y (3) ______ del colegio voy al club de teatro. Me encanta el teatro porque es muy creativo. (4) ______ me gusta bastante jugar al tenis. Para mí el tenis es más divertido que el baloncesto. Si no tengo ni club ni deporte, prefiero charlar con mis amigos en el parque cerca del instituto.

– ¿Cuál fue tu actividad preferida el año pasado?
– A ver… (5) ______ aprendí mucho porque toqué la flauta en la orquesta y lo pasé bomba. (6) ______ fue un poco difícil tocar bien en un grupo tan grande (7) ______ después de unas semanas fue más fácil. Tocaba en la orquesta los miércoles (8) ______ del colegio. El (9) ______ aprenderé a tocar la guitarra (10) ______ porque quiero formar parte de un grupo.

Look at the words you identified in exercise 3. How would you describe them?

- time expressions
- connectives for adding information

5 Now listen to part 3 of Jason's conversation and answer the questions.

1 Listen to Jason's answer to the first question. Can you find examples of negatives that he uses?
2 In his answer to the second question Jason uses four future tense verbs. What are they?
3 Can you spot the comparative that he uses in his response to the second question?
4 What is the unexpected question that the examiner asks, and what does it mean?
5 Which two adverbs does Jason use in his third answer?

6 Now it's your turn! Prepare your answers to the task and then have a conversation with your teacher or partner.

- Use the Grade Studio and your answers to exercises 1–5 to help you plan.
- Adapt what Jason said to talk about yourself but add your own ideas.
- Prepare your answers to the questions and try to predict what the unexpected question could be. The examiner might base this question on something you have already said, or ask something totally new!
- Record the conversation. Ask a partner to listen to it and say how well you performed.

Award each other one star, two stars or three stars for each of these categories:

- *Pronunciation*
- *Confidence and fluency*
- *Range of tenses*
- *Variety of vocabulary and expressions*
- *Using longer sentences*
- *Taking the initiative*

What do you need to do next time to improve your performance?

GradeStudio

To produce a good answer you need to be able to use a variety of structures.

- Use a **variety of verb tenses**. Find one example in exercise 3 where Jason uses the **present tense**, the **preterite** and the **future tense**.
- Use simple **connectives** to extend your sentences like *y* (and), *pero* (but), *también* (also) and *porque* (because).
- Include **simple opinions**, for example in part 1 where Jason says *'No me interesa la informática.'* (Information Technology doesn't interest me).

To go a step further you need to use a wider variety of language.

- Use **qualifiers**, for example *bastante* (quite), *demasiado* (too), *un poco* (a bit), *muy* (very). Can you find examples of these in exercise 3?
- Include **time expressions** like the ones you identified in exercise 4.
- Express **points of view** using expressions like Jason uses, *Para mí...* (for me), *Creo que...* (I believe that), *Pienso que...* (I think that).
- Use **exclamations**, for example Jason uses, *¡Qué rollo!* (What a drag!) and *¡Qué horror!* (How horrible!).

For a really impressive answer:

- Use more **complex sentences** that contain more than one tense. Jason uses this sentence in part 1, *'La historia es mi asignatura preferida porque me interesa mucho aprender como vivía la gente en el pasado'.* Which tenses is he using here?
- Include a **comparative** or the **superlative** in your conversation. Can you find any examples in exercise 3?
- Use **negatives** like *tampoco* (not either) and *no... ni...* (neither... nor...).

Prueba escrita

1 *Read the text and choose the correct title for each paragraph.*

a *Las actividades físicas* **b *El teatro*** **c *Mi cole y los profes***
d *Los idiomas* **e *Mi familia y yo***

Julio

1 Me llamo Julio y tengo quince años. Vivo con mis padres y mi hermano en el centro de Madrid. Mi colegio está bastante cerca, y por eso normalmente voy a pie o en bicicleta. Cuando hace mal tiempo, voy en autobús. ¡Mi hermano es más perezoso que yo, y siempre va en autobús!

2 Mi cole es masculino y privado. Somos seiscientos alumnos y hay por lo menos sesenta profesores. A mi parecer los profesores son muy simpáticos, aunque hay algunos que son muy severos.

3 El colegio tiene unas instalaciones impresionantes. Por ejemplo, hay dos piscinas y ocho pistas de tenis. También hay una pista de atletismo y varios campos de fútbol y de rugby. A mí me interesan los deportes, pero no juego en ningún equipo, aunque la semana pasada participé en una competición de natación. A mi hermano no le gusta nada jugar al fútbol. ¡Prefiere jugar con el ordenador!

4 Lo que más me gusta del colegio es el salón de actos porque es muy grande, ¡como un centro comercial! Mi asignatura preferida es el teatro porque es muy divertido y soy una persona muy creativa. Hace seis meses fuimos un fin de semana a Inglaterra con el colegio. El sábado por la noche un grupo de alumnos fue al cine, pero yo fui con otro grupo a ver una obra de Shakespeare en Stratford. El teatro era muy grande y fue una experiencia impresionante, pero como no hablo muy bien inglés, no entendí mucho.

5 La verdad es que no me gustan demasiado los idiomas. En marzo del año que viene iré a Francia con el colegio. Pasaré una semana con una familia francesa y tendré que hablar francés. ¡Tengo mucho miedo!

2 *Read the text again and answer the questions in English.*

1 How does Julio normally get to school? Why?
2 How many teachers are there at Julio's school?
3 What did Julio do last week?
4 How does Julio describe his school hall?
5 Why does Julio like drama?
6 When did Julio go to England?
7 What did Julio do while other students went to the cinema?
8 When is Julio going to France?
9 How does Julio feel about his trip to France?

3 *Find the equivalent of these expressions in Spanish in the text.*

1. My school is... (location)
2. When the weather is bad...
3. My school is... (description)
4. there are at least
5. although
6. The school has...
7. I am interested in...
8. What I like most...
9. My favorite subject is...
10. In March next year...

4 *Look at the text again. Make a list of words and phrases used to do these things:*

- give opinions
- extend sentences with extra information

5 *You might be asked to write about your school as a Controlled Assessment task. Use the Grade Studio to help you prepare your account.*

To produce a good answer you need to use a variety of structures and express opinions.

- Julio uses the **present tense** to talk about what sports facilities his school **has**.
- He uses the **preterite** to talk about when he **went** to England.
- Look at how Julio uses the **future tense** to say what he **will do** next year.
- Can you find an example of where Julio uses the following **connectives** in his text: *y, pero, porque, también, aunque?*
- Can you find three examples of how Julio gives his **opinion** in his text?

To go a step further you need to use a wider range of language. This might include: other tenses, such as the **imperfect** and **longer sentences** with connectives and time phrases.

- Look at how Julio uses the **imperfect** tense to describe the theatre.
- Look at the expressions that Julio uses to **extend his sentences** that you identified in exercise 4. Which expressions could you include in your own text?

For a really impressive answer:

- Use **comparatives**. Can you find an example of how Julio uses a **comparative** in paragraph 1?
- Include a **complex sentence** with more than one tense in it. Can you find a sentence where Julio has combined the present tense, the preterite and the imperfect tense?
- **Give and justify your opinions**. Look at how Julio does this when he is talking about his school hall.

6 *Now write a full account of your school.*

- Adapt Julio's text and use language from Module 3. Write at least 200 words.
- Think about what you can say in an accurate and interesting way. This is more important than being completely truthful about your school!
- Structure your text carefully. Organise what you write in paragraphs.

General summary of your school

Introduce yourself and your school

Main paragraph

What type of school is it? What facilities are there?
Talk about the subjects and activities that you like/don't like.
What are the teachers like?
Talk about an event that happened, e.g.: a school trip or a competition.

Conclusion

What are your plans for next year?

7 *Check carefully what you have written.*

- tenses (imperfect to describe things in the past, preterite to express completed actions in the past)
- verb endings
- spelling and accents (correct accented endings for preterite and future verbs)

Palabras

Las asignaturas *Subjects*

las asignaturas	*subjects*
el comercio	*business studies*
el dibujo	*art*
el español	*Spanish*
el francés	*French*
el inglés	*English*
el teatro	*drama*
la educación física	*PE*
la geografía	*geography*
la historia	*history*
la informática	*ICT*
la música	*music*
la religión	*RE*
la tecnología	*D&T*
los idiomas	*languages*
las ciencias	*science*
las matemáticas	*maths*
(No) me gusta(n)	*I (don't) like*
Me encanta(n)	*I love*
Me gusta(n) mucho	*I like… very much*
No me gusta(n) nada	*I don't like… at all*
Odio	*I hate*
Mi asignatura preferida es…	*My favourite subject is…*
porque es…/son…	*because it is/they are…*
A el/ella (no) le gusta la música porque es…	*He/she (doesn't like) likes music because…*
mi horario	*my timetable*
el lunes	*on Monday*
el martes	*on Tuesday*
el miércoles	*on Wednesday*
el jueves	*on Thursday*
el viernes	*on Friday*
el sábado	*on Saturday*
el domingo	*on Sunday*
¿Cuándo tienes…?	*When do you have…?*
¿Qué día tienes (inglés)?	*What day do you have (English)?*
Tengo inglés los martes	*I have English on Tuesdays.*
¿A qué hora tienes…?	*What time do you have…?*
A la una/A las dos	*At one o'clock/At two o'clock*
…y/menos cuarto	*quarter past/to…*
…y/menos cinco	*five past/to…*
…y media	*half past…*
¿Qué hora es?	*What time is it?*
Es la una.	*It's one o'clock.*
Son las…	*It's… o'clock.*

En clase *In class*

la primavera	*spring*
el verano	*summer*
el otoño	*autumn*
el invierno	*winter*
¿Cómo vas al colegio?	*How do you go to school?*
Voy andando/a pie.	*I walk.*
Voy en…	*I go by…*
¿Cómo vuelves del colegio?	*How do you come back from school?*
vuelvo…	*I come back…*
¿A qué hora empiezan tus clases?	*What time do your classes start?*
Empiezan a las…	*They start at…*
¿A qué hora terminan tus clases?	*What time do your classes finish?*
Terminan a las…	*They finish at…*
¿A qué hora es el recreo/ la hora de comer?	*What time is break/lunchtime?*
Es a las…	*It's at…*
¿Qué haces en clase?	*What do you do in class?*
¿Qué tienes que llevar a clase?	*What do you need to take to class?*

¿Cómo es tu insti? *What's your school like?*

un campo de fútbol	*a football pitch*
un comedor	*a canteen*
un gimnasio	*a gym*
un patio	*a playground*
un salón de actos	*a drama studio*
una biblioteca	*a library*
una piscina	*a swimming pool*
una pista de atletismo	*an athletics track*
una sala de profesores	*a staffroom*
unos laboratorios	*science labs*
unos vestuarios	*cloakrooms*
unas aulas	*classrooms*
Lo bueno/malo es que…	*The good/bad thing is that…*
Lo que más/menos me gusta…	*What I like most/least is…*
Por un lado/por otro lado…	*On one hand/on the other hand…*
Voy a…	*I go to…*
Es un colegio…	*It is a… school*
femenino/masculino/mixto	*girls/boys/mixed*
privado/público	*private/public*
un colegio especializado en…	*a school that specialises in…*
Las clases empiezan a las… y terminan a las…	*Classes start at… and finish at…*
pero no tenemos… ni… ni…	*but we don't have either… or…*
Tampoco hay…	*There isn't/aren't… either*
Estoy en segundo de la ESO.	*I'm in the second year of school. (Y9 equivalent)*
tercero de la ESO	*third year of school. (Y10 equivalent)*
cuarto de la ESO	*fourth year of school. (Y11 equivalent)*
Hay quinientos alumnos.	*There are 500 pupils.*
Hay setenta profesores.	*There are 70 teachers.*
(No) llevamos uniforme.	*We (don't) wear uniform.*
En mi cole hay/no hay…	*My school has/doesn't have…*
unas instalaciones buenas/malas	*good/bad facilities*
Antes había…	*Before, there was/were…*
más/menos…	*more/fewer*
No teníamos…	*We didn't have…*
ordenadores	*computers*
pizarras interactivas	*interactive whiteboards*
En las aulas había pizarras.	*The classrooms had blackboards.*
Todos estudiaban…	*Everyone studied…*
El colegio/el edificio era más grande/pequeño.	*The school/building was bigger/smaller.*
Los profesores eran más/menos…	*The teachers were more/less…*

Las normas del insti *School rules*

Normalmente	*Usually*
Tengo que llevar…	*I have to wear…*
Tenemos que llevar…	*We have to wear…*
(No) llevo…	*I (don't) wear…*
(No) llevamos…	*We (don't) wear…*
Es obligatorio.	*It's compulsory.*
un jersey	*a sweater*
un vestido	*a dress*
una camisa	*a shirt*
una camiseta	*a t-shirt*
una chaqueta (de punto)	*a jacket (blazer)*
una corbata	*a tie*
unos calcetines	*socks*
una falda	*a skirt*
unos pantalones	*trousers*
unos vaqueros	*jeans*
unos zapatos	*shoes*
unas medias	*tights*
amarillo	*yellow*
azul	*blue*
blanco	*white*
gris	*grey*
negro	*black*
marrón	*brown*
morado	*purple*
naranja	*orange*
rojo	*red*
rosa	*pink*
verde	*green*
oscuro/claro	*dark/light*
de rayas	*striped*
Los alumnos tienen que ser…	*Pupils have to be…*
Los alumnos no deben ser…	*Pupils shouldn't be…*
Está prohibido…	*… is not allowed.*
No se permite…	*… is not permitted.*
No se debe…	*You shouldn't…*

Los profesores *Teachers*

Es…	*He/She is…*
Mi profe de… es más/menos… que…	*My… teacher is more/less… than…*
Mi profe de… es mejor/peor que…	*My… teacher is better/worse than…*
tan….como	*as… as…*
el/la más	*the most*
el/la menos	*the least*
el/la mejor	*the best*
el/la peor	*the worst*
¿Qué opinas del profesor de (ciencias)?	*What do you think of the (science) teacher?*
¿Qué te parece la profesora de (inglés)?	*What do you think of the (English) teacher?*
Creo que mi profesor de…	*I think that my… teacher*
Me parece que…	*It seems to me that…*
Para mí…	*As for me…*
Pienso que/Creo que…	*I think that…*
Por ejemplo…	*For example…*
(No) estoy de acuerdo con…	*I (don't) agree with…*
Estoy a favor de…	*I'm in favour of…*
Estoy en contra de…	*I'm against…*
Estoy harto de…	*I'm fed up with…*
¿Y tú?/¿Y usted?	*And you?*
¡Claro!	*Indeed!*
Es verdad.	*That's true.*
Pero…	*But…*
¡Por supuesto!	*Of course!*
Sin embargo…	*Nevertheless…*
enseñar bien/mal	*to teach well/badly*
Nos pone demasiado deberes.	*He/She gives us too much homework.*

El acoso escolar *School bullying*

En mi opinión…	*In my opinion…*
el acoso escolar	*bullying*
el ataque físico	*physical attack*
el fracaso escolar	*failure at school*
el estrés de los exámenes	*exam stress*
la presión del grupo	*peer pressure*
hacer novillos	*to skip a class*
…es un problema serio	*…is a serious problem*
…es el peor problema	*…is the worst problem*
…es una tontería	*…is ridiculous*
…ocurre frecuentemente	*…happens frequently*
…ocurre raras veces	*…rarely happens*
…es normal	*…is normal*
Es difícil…	*It is difficult…*
No es fácil…	*It isn't easy to…*
sacar buenas notas	*to get good grades*
prepararse para las presentaciones orales	*to prepare yourself for oral presentations*
repasar los apuntes para los exámenes	*to revise for exams*
(No) se debería…	*You should (not)…*
respetar	*to respect*
maltratar	*to ill-treat*
insultar	*to insult*
golpear	*to hit*
intimidar	*to intimidate*
a los demás	*others*
Hay…/Existe(n)…/Tenemos…	*There is/are…/We have…*

El cole del futuro *The school of the future*

¿Cómo será el cole del futuro?	*What will the school of the future be like?*
¿Qué harán los profesores?	*What will the teachers do?*
¿A qué hora empezará/terminará el colegio?	*What time will school start/ finish?*
¿Cuántos alumnos habrá en el colegio?	*How many pupils will there be in school?*
En el colegio del futuro (no) habrá…	*In the school of the future there will (not) be…*
El colegio del futuro (no) tendrá…	*The school of the future will (not) have…*
En el colegio del futuro…	*In the school of the future…*
(no) podrás…	*you will (not) be able to…*
(no) deberás…	*you will (not) have to…*
(no) será obligatorio…	*It will (not) be compulsory to…*
Los alumnos irán al cole…	*Pupils will go to school…*

- Talking about your family
- Using possessive adjectives
- Saying numbers and dates

Repaso *Mi familia*

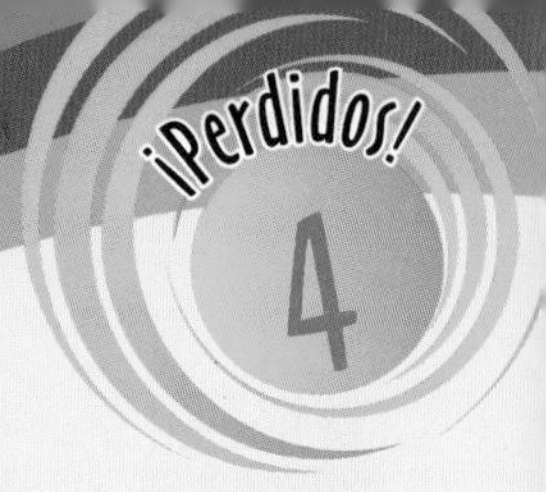

1 Lee el diálogo y rellena los espacios en blanco con las palabras del cuadro.

Nico: ¿(1) ______ es tu cumpleaños, Tina?
Tina: Mi cumpleaños es el 13 de febrero. ¿Y el tuyo?
Nico: El ocho de agosto.
Tina: ¿(2) ______ años tienes?
Nico: Tengo quince años.
Tina: ¿(3) ______ eres?
Nico: Soy alto y delgado.
Tina: ¿Cómo es tu pelo?
Nico Tengo el pelo corto y negro. ¿(4) ______ son tus ojos?
Tina: Tengo los ojos azules.

De qué color
Cómo
Cuántos
Cuándo

2 ¿Qué significan estas palabras? Utiliza el diccionario.

padre · madre · padrastro · marido · mujer · hermano mayor/menor
hijo · abuelo · tío · hermanastro · primo · nieto · bebé · sobrino

3 Try to work out how you would say these in Spanish.

1 stepmother
2 older sister
3 half sister
4 aunt
5 grandmother
6 granddaughter
7 daughter
8 niece

4 You are Pedro. Listen and write down which member of your family is being described. (1–10)

Example: **1** Mi padre, Alejandro

Sabrina Machado Gil 27/1/2000

David Machado Gil 12/11/1994

Leandro García Machado 31/1/1978

Viviana García Machado 17/12/1994

Me llamo Pedro. Nací el 16 de septiembre de 1995.

Pedro García Machado 16/9/1995

Rosana Gil Milá 18/4/1971

Federico Machado Pérez 28/7/1968

Juliana Machado Pérez 21/2/1955

Alejandro García Cid 15/6/1953

Luisa Pérez Cía 06/08/1935

Martín Machado Villa 11/12/1933

When you are listening to higher numbers don't panic! Break them down into their elements.
1945 mil novecientos cuarenta y cinco

5 Piensa en alguien y mira el árbol genealógico. ¡Juega con tu compañero/a!

- ¿De qué color son sus ojos?
- ¿Cómo es su pelo?
- ¿Cuándo es su cumpleaños?
- ¿Es…?

- Tiene los ojos…
- Tiene el pelo… y…
- Su cumpleaños es el…

Me llamo… Mi padre se llama…	Nací el… de… Nació el… de…	
enero febrero marzo abril mayo junio julio agosto septiembre octubre noviembre diciembre		
Tiene los ojos… azules marrones grises verdes	Tiene el pelo… blanco largo castaño corto gris liso negro rizado pelirrojo ondulado rubio moreno	Es calvo. Tiene barba. Tiene bigote. Lleva gafas. Tiene pecas.

6 Empareja los contrarios. Luego escribe una frase con cada palabra.

Ejemplo: Mi padre es alto pero gordo.

a joven
b bajo/a
c viejo/a
d alto/a
e gordo/a
f feo/a
g delgado/a
h guapo/a

G *Possessive adjectives*

	singular	**plural**
my	mi	mis
your (singular)	tu	tus
his/her/its	su	sus
our	nuestro/nuestra	nuestros/nuestras
your (plural)	vuestro/vuestra	vuestros/vuestras
their	su	sus

The possessive adjective must agree depending on whether it describes one or more things or people:
mi herman**a** *my sister*
mis herman**as** *my sisters*

Nuestro *(our)* and **vuestro** (*your* – more than one person) must also change depending on whether the noun is masculine or feminine:
nuestr**as** herman**as** *our sisters*
nuestr**os** herman**os** *our brothers*

7 Escribe estas frases en español.

1. My sister is called Marga.
2. My brothers have blue eyes.
3. Her grandmother is quite old.
4. Their son is 5 years old.
5. My dad is bald.
6. Your brother is good-looking.

8 Escribe un texto sobre 4 personas de tu familia.

- *Include information on who they are, their birthday and what they look like.*
- *Make sure you extend your sentences as much as possible with connectives:* Es calvo **pero** tiene bigote. **También** tiene pecas **y** lleva gafas.

- Talking about relationships
- Using **ser** and **estar**
- Talking about the present and the past

1 Los supervivientes

Catástrofe aérea

Un avión de pasajeros de la aerolínea Mundial se estrelló el jueves 15 de octubre en una isla desierta. No se conocen las causas del accidente y no se sabe si hay supervivientes…

1 ***Listen and read the texts on the survivors of the plane crash. Note down details of each person's nationality and character.***

Leonora Paraíso

Soy española. Soy una persona creativa y paciente. Me parezco mucho a mi padre, que murió el año pasado. Antes del accidente era diseñadora gráfica. Me casé cuando era demasiado joven. Tuve muchos problemas y me divorcié tres meses después.

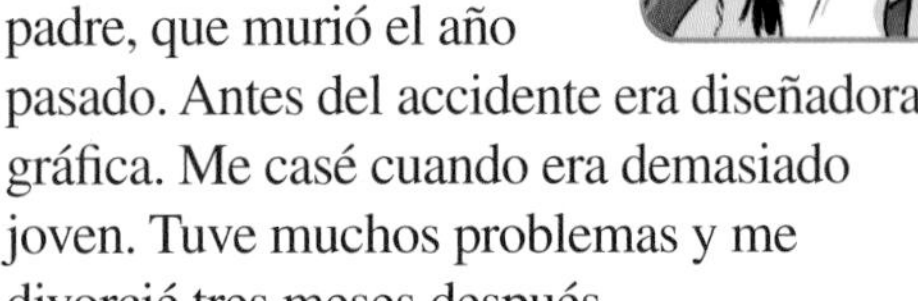

Inmaculada Barallo

Soy colombiana. Antes del accidente era abogada. Soy una persona enérgica y honesta. Antes tenía una relación problemática con mi madre. Ahora que está jubilada nos llevamos mucho mejor. Estoy separada. Me separé de mi marido recientemente.

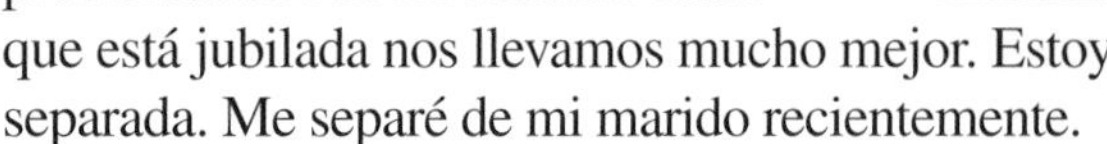

Benedicto Manzanal

Soy peruano. Antes del accidente era estudiante de medicina. Tengo mucho sentido del humor y soy tolerante y optimista. No soy nada serio. Vivía con mi mamá y mi hermana en Lima. Tenía una relación de amor y odio con mi mamá. Es una persona difícil porque es alcohólica. De momento estoy soltero, pero espero encontrar pronto a mi chica ideal.

Eugenio Luna

Soy estadounidense, de Los Ángeles. Antes era mecánico y me encantaba mi trabajo. Soy honesto y trabajador. No soy nada perezoso. Estoy casado con una mujer maravillosa. La quiero mucho y la echo de menos.

Alicia Manzanal

Soy peruana y soy la hermana menor de Benedicto. Antes estudiaba bachillerato y quería ir a la universidad. Aquí en la isla estudiar me da igual. Soy ambiciosa y alegre. Afortunadamente me llevo bien con mi hermano.

2 ***Read the texts again.***

Who… **1** …got divorced after three months?
2 …separated from their husband?
3 …looks like their father?
4 …married too young?
5 …gets on well with their brother?
6 …misses his wife?

G *Reflexive verbs: to express relationships*

➲202

Verbs which express relationships are often reflexive verbs:

casar**se**	*to get married*
divorciar**se**	*to get divorced*
llevar**se** bien/mal con	*to get on well/badly with*
separar**se**	*to separate*
parecer**se**	*to look like*

Can you spot these types of verbs in the texts?

Present tense

	llevarse *(to get on with)*	
(yo)	**me** llev**o**	bien/mal con…
(tú)	**te** llev**as**	
(él/ella/usted)	**se** llev**a**	
(nosotros/as)	**nos** llev**amos**	
(vosotros/as)	**os** llev**áis**	
(ellos/ellas/ustedes)	**se** llev**an**	

Look for the following phrases in the texts in exercise 1. Identify which tense has been used in Spanish for each one.

1 I get on well with my brother.
2 We get on much better.
3 I separated.
4 I got divorced.
5 I got married.
6 I miss her.
7 I look like my father.
8 I love her very much.

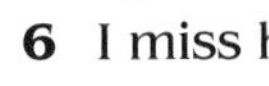

Busca el equivalente de estas expresiones en español en el texto.

1 She's retired. 2 I'm single. 3 I'm married. 4 I'm separated.

Con tu compañero/a, mira este perfil. Pregunta y contesta.

- ¿Cómo se llama usted?
- ¿De dónde es?
- ¿Está casada?
- ¿Cuándo se casó?
- ¿Cuándo se separó?
- ¿Tiene hijos?
- ¿Se lleva bien con su familia?
- ¿A quién se parece?

Nombre: Rigoberta
Apellido: Manzanal
Nacionalidad: peruana
Estado civil: separada en 1996, (me casé en 1986)
Hijos: Benedicto – 23 años, Alicia – 17 años
Comentarios: Me parezco a mi padre, me llevo bien con mis hermanas y con mis hijos.

G Ser *and* estar

202

Ser is used to describe a profession or an essential quality, which won't change:
Soy abogada. *I'm a lawyer.*
Soy inteligente. *I'm intelligent.*

Estar is used to describe a temporary situation and marital state (single, married, divorced, etc.):
Hoy estoy triste. *Today I'm sad.*
Estoy divorciado. *I'm divorced.*

	ser *(to be)*	**estar** *(to be)*
(yo)	soy	estoy
(tú)	eres	estás
(él/ella/usted)	es	está
(nosotros/as)	somos	estamos
(vosotros/as)	sois	estáis
(ellos/ellas/ustedes)	son	están

Escucha. Copia y completa la tabla en inglés. (1–3)

	name	personality	marital status	relations with others
1	Juan	sense of humour,...		

Present
Soy creativo/a, gracioso/a, optimista, enérgico/a, serio/a, ambicioso/a, honesto/a, alegre, tolerante, paciente, feliz.
Me parezco a...
Me llevo bien/mal con...
Tenemos una relación problemática...
Estoy soltero/a, casado/a, divorciado/a, separado/a.

Past
Antes del accidente era...
Me llevaba bien/mal con...
Teníamos una relación de amor y odio...
Me casé con... en...
Me divorcié/separé... años después.

Write a description of another character that has been stranded on the island. Use your knowledge of verbs to talk about them and their relationships in the present and the past.

- Talking about daily routine
- Using reflexive verbs
- Using **desde hace** (for...)

2 La vida cotidiana

1 Escucha a Eugenio y escribe las letras correctas. (1–6)

Me despierto temprano.
Me levanto.
Me ducho.
Me lavo los dientes.
Me baño en el mar.
No me peino.
No me afeito nunca.
Me visto.
Desayuno fruta.
Meriendo a las cuatro.
Ceno pescado.
Me acuesto tarde.

Be careful when pronouncing two vowels in a word in Spanish.

Listen and repeat these phrases:

Me desp**ie**rto. L**ue**go me af**ei**to, me p**ei**no y desp**ué**s me lavo los d**ie**ntes.

G *Reflexive verbs*

202

In the previous unit you saw reflexive verbs connected with relationships.
Reflexive verbs also often describe an action you do *to yourself*.

me lavo — *I wash* ***myself***

Present tense

Lavarse *(to wash yourself)* is a reflexive -ar verb:

	lavarse
(yo)	**me** lav**o**
(tú)	**te** lav**as**
(él/ella/usted)	**se** lav**a**
(nosotros/as)	**nos** lav**amos**
(vosotros/as)	**os** lav**áis**
(ellos/ellas/ustedes)	**se** lav**an**

Some of the reflexive verbs in this unit are also stem-changing:

desp**e**rtarse *(to wake up)* → me desp**ie**rto
ac**o**starse *(to go to sleep)* → me ac**ue**sto
v**e**stirse *(to get dressed)* → me v**i**sto

2 Write some questions to ask a person on the island about their routine. Use the tú form and remember, some verbs are reflexive and others are not.

Ejemplo: ¿A qué hora **te** levantas?
¿Qué cenas?

¿Dónde? ¿Qué? ¿Cuándo? ¿A qué hora? ¿Con quién?

3 **Eres una persona de la isla. Con tu compañero/a pregunta y contesta a las preguntas del ejercicio 2.**

4 Escucha la canción y rellena los espacios en blanco con las palabras del cuadro.

Vivo en esta isla (1) ______.
Esto es muy raro. Todo es muy extraño.
Desde hace un año (2) ______ la misma ropa
y todos los días como (3) ______ en la sopa.
Desde hace un año desayuno piña…
Ni (4) ______, ni me afeito. ¡Ay, ay, ay mi niña!
Durante la noche tengo frío, durante el día (5) ______.
En la isla no hay aseo… ¡Buagh, qué olor!
Desde hace un año bebo (6) ______.
Esta isla me vuelve loco.
Y hace poco me he enamorado,
de una mujer madura, es muy complicado…

pescado leche de coco desde hace un año
me pongo tengo calor me peino

To say *how long* you've been doing something use the phrase **desde hace** and the *present tense* of the verb. (This is different from English!)

¿**Desde hace** cuánto tiempo **vives** en la isla?
***How long have you been living** on the island?*

Vivo en la isla **desde hace** un año.
*I've been living on the island **for** a year.*

5 Escucha. Copia y completa la tabla en inglés. (1–3)

	Activity mentioned?	How long?	Opinion of it?
1	eat fruit for breakfast		

6 Lee el diario de Alicia y contesta a las preguntas.

In which season does Alicia:

1 get the worst rains?
2 enjoy the wildlife around her?
3 feel most fearful?
4 find it easiest to get food?
5 get up early?

Querido diario:
Estoy en esta isla desde hace un año. Ahora en verano hace mucho calor, por eso me levanto temprano para hacer mis tareas y luego descansar. En verano es más fácil encontrar comida que el resto del año. Hay fruta, huevos y pescado en abundancia. Lo que más me gusta es la primavera porque hay pájaros exóticos y tortugas gigantes. El otoño es aburrido. En invierno llueve con mucha intensidad, ¡odio la lluvia! Paso todo el tiempo en la cabaña porque las tormentas me dan mucho miedo.

7 Describe la rutina diaria de una persona perdida en una isla. Utiliza estas frases.

Vivo en la isla desde hace…
Todos los días… (include details of your personal routine)
En primavera/verano/otoño/invierno… (include details specific to the season)
Lo que más me gusta es…
Me encanta(n)…
Lo que menos me gusta es…
Odio…

- Talking about chores
- Using the present, preterite and imperfect tenses
- Using negatives

3 Las tareas

1 Escucha. ¿Qué tareas hacen Leonora y Eugenio? Escribe las letras correctas. (1–3)

Tareas en la isla

a Lavo los platos.

b Hago la cama.

c Limpio mi dormitorio.

d Arreglo mis cosas.

e Cocino.

f Pongo la mesa.

g Quito la mesa.

h Pesco.

i Trabajo en el jardín.

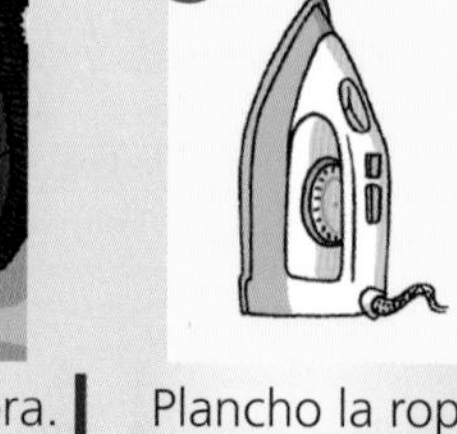

Tareas en casa

j Paso la aspiradora.

k Plancho la ropa.

2 Escucha a Benedicto e Inma. ¿Qué tareas **no** hacen? Escribe las letras del ejercicio 1. (1–3)

Listen out for negatives in listening texts. They can alter the meaning completely. Sometimes the negative is two-part, sometimes it isn't.

Nunca plancho mis camisas.
No plancho **nunca** mis camisas. } *I never iron my shirts.*

Tampoco tenemos aspiradora.
No tenemos aspiradora **tampoco**. } *We don't have a vacuum cleaner either.*

G *Negatives*

➲220

Put **no** before the verb to make it negative.

No limpio. *I don't clean.* **No** hago la cama. *I don't do my bed.*

Here are some others:

nada	*nothing*
No hago **nada**.	*I do nothing.*
nadie	*no one*
Nadie se queja.	*No one complains.*
tampoco	*not either*
Tampoco pongo la mesa.	*I don't lay the table either.*

nunca	*never*
Nunca lavo los platos.	*I never wash the dishes.*
ningún, **ninguna**	no/none at all
No tengo **ningún** mensaje.	*I have no messages at all.*
ni… ni…	*neither… nor…*
Ni paso la aspiradora **ni** plancho.	*I neither vacuum nor iron.*

Write a paragraph in Spanish about jobs you don't do at home. Answer these questions and try to use all of the negative expressions in the grammar box.

- *What don't you do?* (No…, ni… ni…, tampoco…)
- *What don't you like doing?* (No me gusta…, no me gusta nada…, nunca tengo ganas de… + **infinitive**)
- *Which jobs does no one do?* (Nadie…)

Lee el texto y elige el verbo correcto.

Intento ser organizada en la isla. Hay que tener una rutina. Todos los días (1) **arreglo/arreglé/arreglaba** mis cosas y luego (2) **trabajo/trabajé/trabajaba** en el jardín. Me gusta la tranquilidad del jardín. Ayer por ejemplo (3) **paso/pasé/pasaba** el día entero aquí. Más tarde (4) **pongo/puse/ponía** y (5) **quito/quité/quitaba** la mesa y también (6) **lavo/lavé/lavaba** los platos. Normalmente no (7) **hago/hice/hacía** esta tarea, pero ayer Benedicto no quiso hacerla porque estaba de mal humor. Creo que está deprimido. Antes, cuando (8) **soy/fui/era** abogada, (9) **tengo/tuve/tenía** que planchar mi ropa todos los días, pero ahora en la isla la ropa planchada no es nada útil. Antes nunca (10) **trabajo/trabajé/trabajaba** en el jardín, pero ahora es un placer. 

Look for time markers to help you:

todos los días/normalmente → present tense
ayer *(yesterday)* → preterite tense
antes *(in the past)* → imperfect tense

G *Three tenses: present, preterite and imperfect*

➲200–206

In order to produce accurate Spanish, you need to use different tenses correctly.
The *present* is used for something you do every day.
The *preterite* is used for a completed action in the past.
The *imperfect* is used to say what you used to do.

present	*preterite*	*imperfect*
trabajo *(I work)*	trabajé *(I worked)*	trabajaba *(I used to work)*
voy *(I go)*	fui *(I went)*	iba *(I used to go)*
hago *(I do/make)*	hice *(I did/made)*	hacía *(I used to do/make)*
tengo *(I have)*	tuve *(I had)*	tenía *(I used to have)*

Lee el texto otra vez. Copia y completa la tabla en inglés.

	every day	recently/yesterday	before the accident
chores/activities	I tidy up my things		

Con tu compañero/a, imagina que eres otra persona de la isla. Pregunta y contesta.

- ¿Qué haces normalmente para ayudar en la isla?
- ¿Qué **no** haces?
- ¿Qué hiciste ayer? ¿Y la semana pasada?
- ¿Qué hacías en casa antes del accidente?

- Describing people's personalities
- Talking about relationships in the past and present
- Making deductions while listening

4 Otro accidente

1 Empareja el español con el inglés.

Ejemplo: **1** agresivo/a – **e** aggressive

1 agresivo/a	**a** quiet
2 callado/a	**b** tolerant
3 egoísta	**c** pessimistic
4 amable	**d** respectful
5 maleducado/a	**e** aggressive
6 simpático/a	**f** optimistic
7 introvertido/a	**g** cheerful
8 maduro/a	**h** selfish
9 optimista	**i** sincere
10 pesimista	**j** friendly
11 sincero/a	**k** impolite
12 respetuoso/a	**l** kind
13 tolerante	**m** mature
14 alegre	**n** introverted
15 valiente	**o** brave

In this exercise, first identify cognates and near cognates, and then see what is left in the list. Beware of false friends that can be misleading, for example: **simpático** = friendly, not sympathetic.

2 Escucha y escribe la persona y un adjetivo en español del ejercicio 1. (1–8)

Ejemplo: **1** hijo – maduro

When listening try to think laterally!

- Listen and try to deduce what the person is like from the description. But be careful – you won't hear the adjectives above mentioned.
- Pay attention to negatives as they change the meaning of the sentence completely.

3 Describe tu relación con otra persona ahora y antes. ¡Atención a los verbos!

Present

Mi hermano/a, tío/a, primo/a, madrastra… **se llama**…
Me llevo bien/mal con él/ella.
Normalmente **es**… porque…, pero **puede** ser un poco/bastante/muy…
Tiene mucho/poco sentido de humor.
A veces me **vuelve** loco/a porque…

Past

Antes **me llevaba**… con él/ella.
Normalmente **era**… porque…
Podía ser un poco/bastante/muy…
Tenía mucho/poco…
A veces me **volvía** loco/a…

4 Escucha y lee.

a El día del accidente hacía sol y nos levantamos temprano. Hacía buen día y estábamos de muy buen humor.

b Fuimos a la playa. Eugenio fue a pescar y nosotras fuimos a buscar conchas. Benedicto quería estar solo y no vino con nosotros. Estaba nervioso y no hablaba mucho.

c Una hora después, Inma fue a buscar a Benedicto para saber si todo estaba bien.

d Normalmente Alicia no suele nadar en el mar, pero esa mañana el mar estaba precioso, así que decidió bañarse conmigo.

e Mientras tanto, en la casita, Benedicto hablaba con Inma. Por fin, Benedicto le declaró a Inma su amor, y le dio un gran beso.

f De repente, Eugenio vio algo en el agua y empezó a gritar: '¡Tiburón, tiburón! ¡Alicia, Leonora, salid inmediatamente! ¡Hay un tiburón!'

g Yo salí enseguida, pero Alicia se quedó en el agua. Vimos una forma oscura y luego el agua se llenó de sangre. Era la sangre de Alicia. El tiburón había mordido a Alicia en la pierna.

h Benedicto e Inma vinieron corriendo. Benedicto fue a socorrer a Alicia, que estaba inconsciente.

i Benedicto limpió y curó la herida de su hermana. Benedicto era estudiante de medicina antes del accidente. Alicia tenía fiebre. Teníamos miedo por ella. Eugenio dijo: '¡Va a morir, va a morir!'

5 Con tu compañero/a describe a las personas de la historia. Utiliza los adjetivos del ejercicio 1.

…era muy/poco…
No era muy…

6 Con tu compañero/a, habla. ¿Qué va a pasar?

En mi opinión…	va a ser una tragedia.
Pienso que…	va a ser una historia alegre.
Estoy de acuerdo con que…	Alicia va a morir.
No estoy de acuerdo con que…	Benedicto va a casarse con Inma.
A mí me parece que…	Alicia va a sobrevivir.
Creo que…	…va a enamorarse de…
	un equipo de rescate va a venir.

7 Escucha y escribe qué pasó en inglés.

- Talking about experiences and hopes
- Using three time frames
- Extending answers

5 Un año después

Encuentran cinco supervivientes del avión desaparecido de la compañía 'Mundial'

El País, 9 de noviembre

Se han encontrado 5 personas en una isla desierta en el océano Pacífico.
'Muchas personas no lograron salir del avión a tiempo' declaró Leonora Paraíso.

Más de 200 personas viajaban en el avión 737 que desapareció el otoño pasado. Todavía no se han encontrado los restos del accidente.

1 Escucha y lee el texto. Empareja los párrafos con los títulos en inglés. *(There are two titles too many).*

a qualities I didn't know I had
b how I have changed
c making up for lost time
d peace at last
e therapy for others
f a future with a family
g the person I was

1 **A ver…**, antes del accidente **creo que** era egoísta y poco maduro. No me preocupaba mucho por los sentimientos de los demás. Tampoco sabía expresar bien mis propios sentimientos.
2 **Sin embargo, en mi opinión, ahora** soy **mucho más** tolerante. **También** soy más abierto y menos introvertido. Vivo con Inma y hablamos todo el rato. Charlamos sobre nuestros problemas y también sobre nuestras alegrías.
3 La experiencia en la isla me enseñó muchas cosas, **por ejemplo**, que soy una persona fuerte. Aprendí que puedo sobrevivir, ser independiente, y **sobre todo me di cuenta** de que hay que disfrutar y vivir el momento.
4 En el futuro me gustaría tener una familia **porque** me encantan los niños. Inma y yo nos vamos a casar el año que viene y vamos a trabajar juntos.
5 Tenemos experiencia en esto, y **por eso** queremos ayudar a las personas que han sufrido un trauma como el nuestro. Podemos explicar que la vida continúa…

Benedicto

preocuparse = *to worry about*
darse cuenta de que = *to realise that*

2 Lee el texto otra vez. ¿Qué significan las palabras en rojo?

You can use the phrases in red to extend your sentences and make them sound much more sophisticated. Look at the difference between these two sentences:

Ahora soy tolerante.
Sin embargo, en mi opinión, ahora soy mucho más tolerante.

3 Escucha. Apunta los siguientes datos en inglés. (1–4)

1 What was she like before? (mention 2 things)
2 What is she like now?
3 What does she plan for the future?
4 What did she learn on the island?

4 Pregunta y contesta en lugar de Eugenio. Utiliza el tiempo verbal correcto.

● ¿Qué tipo de persona eras antes de vivir en esta isla?
■ En mi opinión (**ser**) una persona honesta y trabajadora. (**ser**) mecánico y (**trabajar**) mucho. Además, creo que (**ser**) un poco egoísta.
● ¿Qué tipo de persona eres ahora?
■ A ver… Ahora (**ser**) diferente, (**ser**) más generoso. He cambiado mucho. (**ser**) más optimista y (**vivir**) al día. No (**malgastar**) el tiempo en tonterías.
● ¿Qué aprendiste en la isla?
■ En la isla (**aprender**) que la gente (**poder**) sobrevivir con pocas cosas. También (**aprender**) a ser generoso y a compartir con los demás.
● ¿Y que vas a hacer en el futuro?
■ (**hacer**) muchas cosas. (**trabajar**) como mecánico para una compañía aérea, sobre todo para (**prevenir**) este tipo de accidentes.

prevenir = *to prevent*

As you work through the questions in exercise 4 pay special attention to the tenses you use:

Preterite: for completed actions in the past.

En la isla **aprendí** muchas cosas.	*On the island I learnt many things.*

Imperfect: for descriptions in the past or to say how things used to be.

Antes **era** egoísta.	*Before, I used to be selfish.*
No me preocupaba mucho.	*I didn't use to worry much.*

Present: to describe general situations.

Soy una persona fuerte.	*I am a strong person.*

Near future or *me gustaría + an infinitive*: to talk about the future.

Vamos a trabajar juntos.	*We are going to work together.*
Me gustaría viajar.	*I would like to travel.*

5 Escribe una entrevista con una persona perdida en una isla desierta. Utiliza las preguntas del ejercicio 4.

¿Qué tipo de persona eras antes? ¿Qué tipo de persona eres ahora? ¿Qué aprendiste en la isla?	Antes del accidente era… Ahora soy mucho más/menos… Esta experiencia me enseñó… Me di cuenta de que… Aprendí que…	
¿Qué quieres hacer en el futuro?	En el futuro voy a… Me gustaría… …por eso quiero…	viajar. casarme. tener niños. trabajar.

Use the expressions from exercise 1 to extend your answers as much as you can.

Be aware of the tenses you are using: imperfect, preterite, present and near future.

Prueba oral

Describing yourself

You are being interviewed by your teacher. You will play the role of someone who was stranded on a desert island and your teacher will play the role of the interviewer. Your teacher could ask you the following:

- Can you describe yourself and your family?
- What were you like before living on the island?
- What are you like now?
- What did you learn on the island?
- Do you get on well with your family and friends now?
- What do you want to do in the future?

Remember that you will have to respond to an unexpected question that you have not yet prepared.
The dialogue will last between 4 and 6 minutes.

You are going to listen to Lyra, an exam candidate, taking part in the above interview with her teacher. Read the following phrases to check you understand them. Which phrase will she use to answer each of the first three questions? Write 1, 2 or 3. Then listen to part 1 to check whether you were right.

1 Nací el nueve de mayo…
2 Ahora… soy más tolerante.
3 …antes del accidente…
4 Además, soy menos seria…
5 No me preocupaba nada por los demás…
6 Mi hermana tiene…
7 …era un poco egoísta…
8 …no era muy simpática.
9 …soy inglesa.
10 …me parezco a ella.

Listen to part 1 again. Which of the following adjectives does she use to describe herself?

1 celosa
2 egoísta
3 madura
4 sensible
5 traviesa
6 inmadura
7 tolerante
8 paciente
9 ambiciosa
10 alegre
11 seria
12 simpática

Listen to part 2 of Lyra's interview and note down the words that fill the gaps.

– ¿Qué aprendiste en la isla?
– Lo cierto es que (1) ______ mucho tiempo para pensar en la isla y mi experiencia me enseñó que hay que disfrutar de la vida. (2) ______ que el estrés no vale la pena. No (3) ______ ganas de trabajar como antes. Ahora (4) ______ que mi familia y mis amigos (5) ______ mucho más importantes que el dinero y el trabajo.
– ¿(6) ______ bien con tu familia y tus amigos ahora?
– Antes (7) ______ una relación conflictiva con mi padre, pero ahora (8) ______ muy bien con él. Nunca tenemos problemas. Antes tenía una buena relación con mi madre, pero ahora (9) ______ mucho mejor. También (10) ______ más tiempo para mis amigos y tengo una buena relación con ellos.

Look at the words you identified in exercise 3. Which tense are they in?

- present
- preterite
- imperfect

Now listen to part 3 of Lyra's interview and answer the questions.

1 In her answer to the first question Lyra uses *me gustaría* + infinitive, *quiero* + infinitive and the future tense to talk about the future. Can you spot an example of each?
2 What is the unexpected question that the examiner asks and what does it mean?
3 How does Lyra use a superlative in her answer to the second question?

Now it's your turn! Prepare your answers to the task and then have a conversation with your teacher or partner.

- Use the Grade Studio and your answers to exercises 1–5 to help you plan.
- Adapt what Lyra said to talk about yourself but add your own ideas.
- Prepare your answers to the task questions and try to predict what the unexpected question could be. The examiner might base this question on something you have already said, or ask something totally new!
- Record the conversation. Ask a partner to listen to it and say how well you performed.

Award each other one star, two stars or three stars for each of these categories:

- *Pronunciation*
- *Confidence and fluency*
- *Range of tenses*
- *Variety of vocabulary and expressions*
- *Using longer sentences*
- *Taking the initiative*

What do you need to do next time to improve your performance?

GradeStudio

To produce a good answer you need to be able to use a variety of structures.

- Use a variety of tenses, for example the **present tense** to describe yourself and your family, the **preterite** to describe what you learnt on the island and the ***quiero* + infinitive** (I want to…) to describe what you would like to do in the future.
- Use simple **connectives** to extend your sentences such as *y* (and), *pero* (but), *también* (also) and *porque* (because).
- Use **adjectives** to describe yourself and others. Lyra used these adjectives to describe herself, for example *egoísta, inmadura, seria…* Was she like that before or after being on the island?

To go a step further you need to use a wider variety of language.

- Use the **preterite** and the **imperfect tense** to talk about yourself in the past. Look back at the variety of verbs that you identified in exercise 3.
- Use a **variety of structures** to talk about the future. Lyra uses *me gustaría* + infinitive (I would like to), *quiero* + infinitive (I want to) and the future tense (I will).
- Use **reflexive verbs** to talk about your relationships with your family and friends. Can you remember any that Lyra used?
- A variety of **time expressions** will help you to gain higher marks. Lyra uses *antes* (before), *ahora* (now) and *en el futuro* (in the future).

For a really impressive answer:

- Use **more complex sentences** that contain more than one tense. Can you find where Lyra does this in exercise 3?
- Use **comparatives**, for example Lyra says *'… soy más tolerante y menos ambiciosa'*.
- Use a **variety of negatives**, for example Lyra says ***'Nunca** tenemos problemas'*, ***'No** me preocupaba **nada** por los demás…'* and ***'No** tengo ganas de…'*.
- Use **sophisticated phrases** such as those Lyra uses *'La verdad es que…'* (The truth is that…), *'Lo cierto es que…'* (What's certain is that…).

1 Read the text and choose the correct title for each paragraph. What words/phrases support your decisions?

a Positive relationships with parents
b Romantic relationships
c Brothers and sisters
d Negative relationships with parents

Juanita Cruz

1 Me llamo Juanita Cruz. Tengo quince años y soy española. Soy hija única. A veces me gustaría tener hermanos, pero ser hija única tiene muchas ventajas también. Por ejemplo, tengo mucha independencia y no tengo que compartir mis cosas.

2 Mis padres están divorciados desde hace ocho años. Creo que me parezco mucho a mi madre y por lo general me llevo muy bien con ella. Lo mejor es que tiene mucho sentido del humor. Mi madre es tan alta como yo y es bastante delgada. Tiene los ojos azules y el pelo rubio. Le encanta cocinar y reír. Tenemos muy buena relación, y por eso vivo con ella.

3 Antes también tenía una buena relación con mi padre, pero ahora no nos llevamos bien. Tenemos una relación muy conflictiva porque él es muy egoísta. Además, lo peor es que puede ser agresivo y violento. Siempre hay mucha tensión entre nosotros. Tampoco me llevo bien con mi madrastra. No sé si nuestra relación mejorará. Hace dos años fui de vacaciones con ellos a la República Dominicana. El hotel era lujoso y la playa era preciosa, pero fue un desastre total porque mi padre me ponía verde todo el tiempo. En mi opinión es una persona muy insegura.

poner verde a alguien = *to talk about someone behind their back*

4 Ahora tengo novio. Es muy guapo, pero para mí lo más importante es que es una persona sincera. Tenemos una química muy especial y por eso estamos bien juntos. En el futuro me gustaría viajar con él, pero yo nunca me casaré porque creo que el amor es más importante que el matrimonio. Sé que cuando dos personas se casan, nadie sabe qué pasará…

2 Complete the statements in English.

1 According to Juanita, being an only child has many…
2 Juanita's parents have been divorced…
3 Juanita's mother loves… and…
4 Juanita's father can be… and…
5 According to Juanita, on holiday her father…
6 Juanita's boyfriend is…
7 According to Juanita, love…

3 Find the equivalent of these expressions in Spanish in the text.

1 For example, I have a lot of independence…
2 In general I get on very well with…
3 We have a very good relationship…
4 …for this reason I live with…
5 I used to have a good relationship with…
6 I don't know if our relationship will improve.
7 We have a very special chemistry…
8 I will never get married…

4 ***Look at the expressions you found in exercise 3. Which of these phrases can you use in your own account? Could you adapt or complete some of the phrases to make them relevant to you?***

Ser hija única tiene muchas ventajas. → *Ser el hijo mayor tiene muchas ventajas.*

5 ***You might be asked to write about your family as a Controlled Assessment task. Use the Grade Studio to help you prepare your account.***

GradeStudio

To produce a good answer you need to use a variety of structures and express opinions.

- Juanita uses the **present tense** to describe her mother and her father, the **preterite** to talk about when she went on holiday with her father and the **future** to say that she won't get married.
- Find the sentence where Juanita gives her opinion about her father.
- Find four simple **connectives** in Juanita's text (words like *y*, *también*...).

To go a step further you need to use a wider range of language.
This might include: other tenses such as the **imperfect**, verbs referring to a **variety of people** (I, he/she, we, they) and a **variety of expressions** to extend paragraphs.

- Look at how Juanita uses the **imperfect tense** to describe her relationship with her father in the past and her father's behaviour on holiday.
- Find examples of where Juanita talks about **other people**.
- Juanita uses the following **expressions** to extend what she says: *lo más importante es que..., lo mejor es que..., lo peor es que..., además..., por eso...* What do they mean? Choose some of them to include in your own text.

For a really impressive answer:

- Include **complex sentences** containing more than one tense. Can you find an example in the third paragraph?
- Use **a variety of negatives**. Juanita uses *tampoco* and *nadie*. Do you know what these phrases mean? Can you use them in your text?

6 ***Now write a full account of your family.***

- Adapt Juanita's text and use language from Module 4. Write at least 200 words.
- Remember, when you are describing the members of your family make sure that your adjectives agree with the nouns, for example, *Mi madre es alt**a** y delgad**a***.
- Structure your text carefully. Organise what you write in paragraphs.

General summary of your family
Introduce yourself.

Main paragraph
Describe members of your family:
- *their physical description*
- *their character*
- *your relationship with them.*

Talk about a family event in the past such as a holiday.

Conclusion
Future plans for you and your family.

7 ***Check carefully what you have written.***

- adjective agreement *(mi padre es alt**o**/mis padres son alt**os**)*
- verb endings for all the different people *(tengo, tiene, tienes, tenemos, tenéis, tienen)*
- tenses *(cuando **era** pequeña **fui** a Italia con mi padre.)*

Leer y escuchar

1 ***Choose the most suitable Spanish exchange partners for these British people. Write the name of each British person, followed by the letter of the correct Spanish person.* (4 marks)**

> Look for the **best** match between the British and Spanish writers. Don't expect to find the exact translation of the English phrases in the Spanish text. Look for words which relate to the same topic, such as 'chatting online' – *navegar por Internet*.

I chat a lot with my friends, especially online.

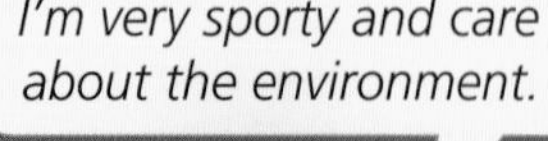

I'm very sporty and care about the environment.

I love shopping, especially for clothes!

My main interests are reading and drama.

a Soy una persona alegre y creativa. Siempre me visto bien porque me encanta la ropa elegante y la moda.

b Soy aficionado a los videojuegos y tengo uno de los móviles más avanzados del mundo. ¡Qué ilusión!

c Soy activo y optimista. Me mantengo en forma haciendo mucho ciclismo. En mi familia reciclamos casi todo.

d Soy bastante callada. Vivo con mi abuela. Paso mucho tiempo viendo la tele y tocando el piano.

e Soy simpática y habladora cuando estoy con mis amigas. También me gusta navegar por Internet.

f Soy bastante extrovertido. Voy mucho al teatro y tengo una gran colección de novelas. Quiero ser escritor.

2 ***Read Ramón's message introducing himself. For each section of the message, choose the word that best summarizes it by writing the number of each section, followed by the correct letter.* (5 marks)**

a house **b** chores
c homework **d** personality
e leisure **f** family
g routine

> Look carefully at all the English word options and don't jump to conclusions on the basis of one or two words in the Spanish text. Use all the clues in each section of the text to find the correct answer. If you're not sure of one of the answers, leave it until you've done the others. You might be able to do it by a process of elimination!

¡Hola!

1 Me llamo Ramón. Soy hijo único, pero pronto voy a tener una hermanastra. Mi madre va a casarse por segunda vez y su nuevo marido tiene una hija.

2 Mis amigos dicen que soy alegre y hablador. Mis profesores piensan que soy maduro y respetuoso. Yo creo que tengo mucho sentido del humor.

3 Ayudo mucho en casa. A veces plancho la ropa y preparo la comida, pero no me gusta mucho pasar la aspiradora o limpiar el cuarto de baño.

4 Prefiero levantarme y acostarme tarde los fines de semana, pero eso no es posible los días de colegio. También creo que ducharse es mejor que bañarse.

5 Estudio mucho en el instituto y no sé por qué tengo que estudiar más en casa. Dos o tres horas cada noche es demasiado en mi opinión.

Un saludo, **Ramón**

***In what order does Manuel always do his Saturday chores? Listen and write the letter of the correct set of pictures.* (1 mark)**

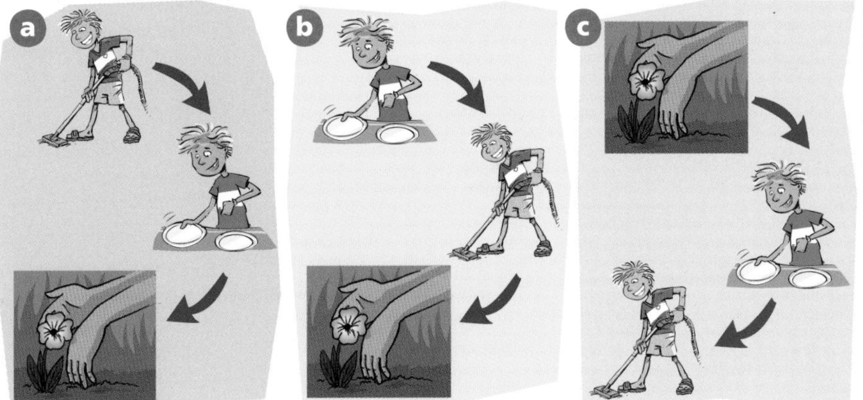

Don't jump to conclusions. Always listen right to the end of the recording. Remember, the key thing in this question is the order in which he does the tasks, so listen for words like 'first', 'next' and so on in Spanish.

***Listen to the young people's opinions on their schools. What is each person's opinion? Write each person's name followed by P (positive), N (negative) or P+N (positive and negative).* (4 marks)**

Elena

Pedro

Teresa

Carlos

You will always hear each item twice, so don't panic if you don't get it the first time. The opinions might be expressed using simple adjectives or in more complex phrases. A negative statement can sometimes be a positive opinion, e.g. 'It's good that we don't have to…'.

Listen to the conversation with Antonio, a busy film star, and answer the questions by writing the correct letters.

1 What two things did he do last week? (2 marks)
2 What two plans does he have for next week? (2 marks)

a study his film scripts
b give up smoking
c go to a film festival
d work on a TV show
e promote his new book
f work in the garden
g travel abroad
h spend time with his girlfriend

Read through the answer options before you start listening and think of what key words you would expect to hear for each. Tenses and time expressions will also be key things to listen for in a question like this. Beware of distractors, e.g. Antonio may mention things he didn't do or won't do.

Palabras

Mi familia *My family*

el abuelo	*grandfather*	Mi padre se llama…	*My father's name is…*
el bebé	*baby*	nació el… de…	*he was born on the… of…*
el hermanastro	*step brother*	enero	*January*
el hermano mayor/menor	*older/younger brother*	febrero	*February*
el hijo	*son*	marzo	*March*
el marido	*husband*	abril	*April*
el nieto	*grandson*	mayo	*May*
el padrastro	*stepfather*	junio	*June*
el padre	*father*	julio	*July*
el primo	*cousin*	agosto	*August*
el sobrino	*nephew*	septiembre	*September*
el tío	*uncle*	octubre	*October*
la madrastra	*stepmother*	noviembre	*November*
la madre	*mother*	diciembre	*December*
la mujer	*wife*	¿Cuándo es su cumpleaños?	*When is his birthday?*
Me llamo…	*My name is…*	Su cumpleaños es el… de…	*His birthday is on the… of…*
nací el… de…	*I was born on the… of…*		

¿Cómo es? *What is he/she like?*

¿De qué color son sus ojos?	*What colour are his/her eyes?*	rizado	*curly*
Tiene los ojos…	*He/She has… eyes.*	Es calvo.	*He's bald.*
¿Cómo es su pelo?	*What's his/her hair like?*	Lleva gafas.	*He/She wears glasses.*
Tiene el pelo…	*He/She has… hair.*	Tiene barba.	*He has a beard.*
blanco	*white*	Tiene bigote.	*He has a moustache.*
castaño	*brown*	Tiene pecas.	*He/She has freckles.*
gris	*grey*	¿Es…?	*Is he/she…?*
moreno	*dark*	alto/a	*tall*
negro	*black*	bajo/a	*short*
pelirrojo	*red*	delgado/a	*slim*
rubio	*blonde*	feo/a	*ugly*
corto	*short*	gordo/a	*fat*
largo	*long*	guapo/a	*attractive*
liso	*straight*	joven	*young*
ondulado	*wavy*	viejo/a	*old*

Los supervivientes *The survivors*

Soy…	*I'm…*	Me llevo mal con…	*I get on badly with…*
alegre	*pleasant*	Tenemos una relación problemática.	*We have a difficult relationship.*
ambicioso/a	*ambitious*	Antes del accidente era…	*Before the accident I was…*
creativo/a	*creative*	Me llevaba bien con…	*I used to get on well with…*
enérgico/a	*energetic*	Me llevaba mal con…	*I used to get on badly with…*
feliz	*happy*	Me casé…	*I got married…*
gracioso/a	*funny*	Me separé…	*I separated…*
honesto/a	*honest*	Me divorcié…	*I got divorced…*
optimista	*optimistic*	Teníamos una relacion de amor y odio…	*We had a love/hate relationship…*
paciente	*patient*	estar…	*to be…*
perezoso	*lazy*	casado/a	*married*
serio/a	*serious*	divorciado/a	*divorced*
tolerante	*tolerant*	soltero/a	*single*
trabajador	*hard-working*	separado/a	*separated*
Tiene (buen/mal) sentido del humor.	*He/She has a (good/bad) sense of humour.*	…años después	*…years later*
Tiene mucho sentido del humor.	*He/She has a very good sense of humour.*	Ahora…	*Now…*
Me parezco a…	*I look like…*	Luego…	*Then…*
Me llevo bien con…	*I get on well with…*		

La vida cotidiana *Daily life*

ceno pescado	*I eat fish for dinner*
desayuno fruta	*I have fruit for breakfast*
me acuesto tarde	*I go to bed late*
me baño en el mar	*I bathe in the sea*
me despierto temprano	*I wake up early*
me ducho	*I have a shower*
me lavo	*I have a wash*
me lavo los dientes	*I clean my teeth*
me levanto	*I get up*
me visto	*I get dressed*
meriendo a las cuatro	*I have tea at four o'clock*
no me afeito nunca	*I never shave*
no me peino	*I don't comb my hair*
en invierno	*in winter*
en otoño	*in autumn*
en primavera	*in spring*
en verano	*in summer*
todos los días	*every day*
desde hace un año	*for a year*
Lo que más me gusta es…	*What I like most is…*
Me encanta(n)…	*I love…*
Lo que menos me gusta es…	*What I like least is…*
Odio…	*I hate…*

Las tareas *Chores*

Arreglo mis cosas.	*I tidy up my things.*
Cocino.	*I cook.*
Hago la cama.	*I make the bed.*
Lavo los platos.	*I wash the dishes.*
Limpio mi dormitorio.	*I clean my bedroom.*
Paso la aspiradora.	*I do the vacuuming.*
Pesco.	*I fish.*
Plancho la ropa.	*I iron the clothes.*
Pongo la mesa	*I lay the table.*
Quito la mesa.	*I clear the table.*
Trabajo en el jardín.	*I work in the garden.*
nada	*nothing*
nadie	*no one*
ni… ni…	*neither… nor…*
ningún/ninguna	*no one/none at all*
nunca	*never*
tampoco	*neither/nor*
antes	*before*
ayer	*yesterday*
normalmente	*usually*
todos los días	*every day*

Otro accidente *Another accident*

(No) Me llevo bien con…	*I (don't) get on well with…*
Me llevo mal con…	*I get on badly with…*
agresivo/a	*aggressive*
alegre	*cheerful*
amable	*kind*
callado/a	*quiet*
egoísta	*selfish*
introvertido/a	*introverted*
maduro/a	*mature*
maleducado/a	*impolite*
optimista	*optimistic*
pesimista	*pessimistic*
respetuoso/a	*respectful*
simpático/a	*friendly*
sincero/a	*sincere*
tolerante	*tolerant*
valiente	*brave*
X era muy/poco…	*X was very/not very…*
No era muy…	*He/She wasn't very…*
Me vuelve loco/a.	*He/She drives me mad.*
En mi opinión…	*In my opinion…*
Pienso que…	*I think that…*
Estoy de acuerdo con…	*I agree that…*
No estoy de acuerdo con…	*I don't agree that…*
Va a ser una tragedia.	*It is going to be a tragedy.*
Va a ser una historia alegre.	*It is going to be a happy story.*
Alicia va a morir	*Alicia is going to die.*
Benedicto va a casarse con Inma	*Benedicto is going to marry Inma*
Alicia va a sobrevivir	*Alicia will survive.*
…va a enamorase de…	*he/she is going to fall in love with…*
Un equipo de rescate va a venir.	*A rescue team will come.*

Un año después *One year later*

¿Qué tipo de persona eras antes?	*What kind of person were you before?*
Antes del accidente era…	*Before the accident I was…*
¿Qué tipo de persona eres ahora?	*What kind of person are you now?*
Ahora soy mucho más…/ menos…	*Now I am much more…/less…*
¿Qué aprendiste en la isla?	*What did you learn on the island?*
Esta experiencia me enseñó…	*This experience taught me…*
Me di cuenta de que…	*I realised that…*
Además soy…	*I'm also…*
Aprendí que…	*I learnt that…*
¿Qué quieres hacer en el futuro?	*What do you want to do in the future?*
En el futuro voy a…	*In the future, I'm going to…*
Me gustaría…	*I'd like to…*
Por eso quiero…	*Therefore I want to…*

- Revising jobs and places of work
- Revising masculine and feminine nouns
- Improving your pronunciation of cognates

Repaso A trabajar

1 Lee y completa las frases con los lugares correctos. (Sobra un lugar.)

1 Soy jardinero y trabajo en un…

2 Soy profesor y trabajo en un…

3 Soy peluquero y trabajo en una…

4 Soy médica y trabajo en una…

5 Soy futbolista y trabajo en un…

6 Soy cocinera y trabajo en un…

7 Soy recepcionista y trabajo en un…

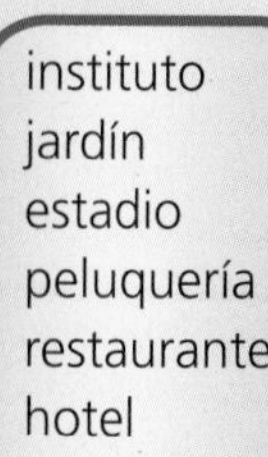

instituto
jardín
estadio
peluquería
restaurante
hotel
comisaría
clínica

2 Escucha e identifica el trabajo y el lugar. (1–11)

***Ejemplo:* 1** periodista – oficina

¿En qué trabaja usted? Soy…
Trabajo como/de…

abogad**o**/**a**, enfermer**o**/**a**, cociner**o**/**a**, camarer**o**/**a**, carpinter**o**/**a**, ingenier**o**/**a**, jardiner**o**/**a**, médic**o**/**a**, mecánic**o**/**a**, peluquer**o**/**a**,	conduct**or**(**a**) diseñad**or**(**a**) profes**or**(**a**) direct**or**(**a**)	cantante comerciante dentista futbolista periodista recepcionista soldado	**actor**/**actriz** **dependiente**/ **dependienta**

Don't use the indefinite article to explain what job you do:
Soy actriz. *I am an actress.*
Do use it in other situations:
Es una actriz muy guapa.
She is a very pretty actress.

G *Masculine and feminine nouns*

➲212

These patterns will help you remember how to change masculine nouns (e.g. job titles) into feminine nouns.

	masculine	**feminine**
Most nouns ending in **-o** become **-a**:	camarer**o**	camarer**a**
Most nouns ending in **-or** add an **-a**:	profes**or**	profes**ora**
Most nouns ending in **-ista** or **-e** do not change:	den**tista**	den**tista**
	cantant**e**	cantant**e**
These are some exceptions:	**actor**	**actriz**
	dependiente	**dependienta**

3 Traduce al español con la ayuda del diccionario.

Ejemplo: *My sister is a soldier.* – Mi hermana es soldado.

1 My sister is a soldier.
2 I am a vet.
3 My friend works as a farmer.
4 My neighbour works as a bricklayer.
5 My son is a postman.
6 Jesús is an electrician.
7 My husband is a firefighter.

Dictionary skills
When looking up words, remember that the noun will be given in the masculine singular form followed by the feminine ending **-a**: abogado, -a

4 Lee los textos. Copia y completa la tabla en inglés.

name	job	opinion of job/reason for opinion	place of work	extra information
Sergio	engineer	loves variety and...	different places	starts at 9.30am and...

Hola, me llamo Sergio y trabajo como ingeniero. Me encanta mi profesión porque me gusta la variedad y tener responsabilidades. Trabajo en lugares diferentes. Empiezo a las nueve y media y termino a las seis de la tarde.

Mi hermano se llama Dario y es actor. Le encanta su trabajo porque es muy divertido. Normalmente trabaja en la calle como estatua viviente. A veces actúa en el teatro y en la televisión. Para él la creatividad es muy importante y no le interesa nada el dinero.

Mi prima se llama Mariana y no le gusta nada su trabajo porque es bastante pesado. Es cajera y trabaja en un hipermercado cerca de Málaga. Tiene que sonreír todo el rato a los clientes. Eso no le gusta nada.

Mi nombre es Brisa y soy azafata. Trabajo para la compañía aérea española Iberia. Mi trabajo me parece muy interesante porque viajamos a Europa, África y Latinoamérica. También me gusta mucho conocer a gente de otros países y hablar idiomas diferentes.

5 Habla del trabajo de un miembro de tu familia. Contesta las preguntas.

- ¿De quién quieres hablar? (De mi hermano/tío/primo/madre/madastra/abuela, etc.)
- ¿Cómo se llama?
- ¿En qué trabaja? (Es.../trabaja como...)
- ¿Dónde trabaja?
- ¿Le gusta su trabajo? ¿Por qué?

Cognates look similar and mean the same as the English word, but they are pronounced differently!

ingeniero → is pronounced *in – hen – ie – ro*
oficina → is pronounced *oh – fee – thee – na*

Pay attention to accents too. Put the stress on the accented part of the word:

mecánico → is pronounced *meh –* ***ka*** *– nee – koh*

Listen and repeat these cognates:

secretario **actriz** **clínica** **médico**
dentista **policía** **actor**

6 Escribe un párrafo sobre el trabajo de un miembro de tu familia.

Use the questions in exercise 5 to help you plan your work.

- Describing part-time jobs
- Using **tener que** + infinitive
- Extending spoken and written answers

1 ¿Trabajas los sábados?

Escucha. Copia y completa la tabla. (1–5)

	¿Trabajo?	¿Cuándo?	¿Cuánto ganas?
1	peluquero	los fines de semana	6€ a la hora

Some words are easily confused. Use the context to be sure.

¿Cuándo…? *When…?*
¿Cuánto…? *How much…?*

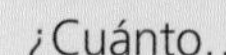

Lee las descripciones y escribe la letra correcta.

1 Los sábados tengo que cuidar a niños pequeños.
2 Todos los días tengo que levantarme muy temprano.
3 En mi trabajo tengo que servir comida y bebida a los clientes.
4 Cuando trabajo tengo que usar agua y jabón.
5 Los fines de semana tengo que vender zapatos.
6 En mi trabajo tengo que vigilar a la gente que nada en la piscina.
7 En mi trabajo tengo que cortar la hierba y plantar flores.

a

Reparto periódicos.

b

Hago de canguro.

c

Trabajo como dependienta.

d

Trabajo como camarero.

e

Lavo coches.

f

Trabajo como jardinera.

g

Trabajo como socorrista.

Read the dialogue with your partner. Then make up another dialogue using your own ideas.

- ¿En qué trabajas?
- Reparto leche, pero no me gusta mucho porque es un trabajo muy duro.
- ¿Cuándo trabajas?
- Trabajo por las mañanas de cinco a siete, por eso tengo que levantarme muy temprano, ¡qué horror!
- ¿Qué tienes que hacer?
- Tengo que repartir leche a las casas del casco viejo. También tengo que recoger las botellas vacías. Lo peor es que tengo que subir muchas escaleras.
- ¿Cuánto ganas?
- Gano seis euros con cincuenta a la hora. Gano poco, pero eso es mejor que nada.

The sections underlined show how you can extend simple sentences with connectives. Try to use phrases like **pero**, **por eso**, **también**, **lo mejor/peor es que**… as you speak.

Los sábados… Por las mañanas… Por las tardes… Todos los días… Los fines de semana…	tengo que… cuidar a niños contar historias ser amable ir bien vestido/a ser puntual vender zapatos/ropa servir comida levantarme temprano coger el autobús
Gano mucho. Gano poco.	

4 ***Read Silvana's email and choose the four statements which apply.***

1 Silvana works for eight hours a day.
2 Silvana loves working as a receptionist.
3 Silvana works part-time for her father.
4 Silvana always makes coffee for her father.
5 Silvana has to wear smart clothes.
6 Silvana does not like going in the boardroom.
7 Silvana works Saturdays.
8 Silvana has to read lots of emails.

G Tener que + *infinitive*

To say ***have to*** in Spanish use the verb **tener** followed by **que** and the **infinitive** of the main verb.

Tengo que llegar a tiempo.
I have to arrive on time.
Tuve que llegar a tiempo.
I had to arrive on time.

If you use a reflexive verb as your main verb, the pronoun stays on the end of the infinitive or goes before the verb **tener**.

Tengo que levantarme temprano.
Me tengo que levantar temprano.
I have to get up early.

¿Qué tal? Yo estoy un poco estresada. Trabajo de recepcionista a tiempo parcial en la oficina de mi padre. No me gusta nada el horario porque trabajo los sábados, de ocho de la mañana a seis de la tarde. Sin embargo, gano 8€ a la hora, que está muy bien.

Como en la mayoría de los trabajos, tengo que ir bien vestida. Me gustaría llevar vaqueros o ropa más informal los sábados porque odio llevar trajes.

Por un lado el trabajo me parece bastante interesante y variado, pero a veces es un poco difícil porque tengo que prestar mucha atención a lo que hago. Normalmente tengo que contestar al teléfono, y a veces tengo que hacer café para los clientes. ¡Qué rollo!

Aunque no me importa servir café a los clientes, me da vergüenza entrar en la sala de juntas. Mi padre es contable y sus compañeros de trabajo son muy serios. No sé, a veces son un poco antipáticos. Me dan miedo porque hablan de negocios muy complicados.

Un abrazo, **Silvana** 

los trajes = *suits*
el contable = *accountant*
la sala de juntas = *boardroom*
los negocios = *business*

5 **Lee el texto otra vez. Copia y completa la tabla.**

	horario	salario	ropa	actividades	gente
P/N/P+N					
details					

6 **Escucha. ¿Qué hacen? Escribe P (opinión positiva), N (opinión negativa), o P + N (opinión positiva y negativa). (1–4)**

***Ejemplo:* 1** sells books, P

7 ***You are working part-time in a shoe shop. Include positive and negative opinions as you write about:***

- *what you do*
- *your working hours and how much you earn*
- *what you wear and what the job entails*
- *what the clients are like*

- Describing work experience
- Using the preterite and the imperfect
- Using adverbs of time and frequency

2 Prácticas laborales

Escucha y escribe el nombre correcto. (1–6)

Eva
Hice mis prácticas laborales en una escuela.

Jorge
Fui a trabajar a una tienda de ropa.

Lilia
Hice mis prácticas laborales en una oficina.

José
Trabajé en un polideportivo.

Inmaculada
Trabajé en una empresa inglesa.

Emilio
Trabajé en un hotel.

Lee las frases. ¿Quién habla del ejercicio 1?

***Ejemplo:* 1** Lilia, Inmaculada

1 Escribí cartas y mandé correos electrónicos.
2 Hablé con los clientes en inglés.
3 Ayudé a los niños.
4 Contesté llamadas telefónicas.
5 Practiqué varios deportes.
6 Vendí ropa.
7 Di clases de natación.
8 Vigilé a los alumnos.
9 Serví comida y refrescos.

Lee los textos y las frases. Escribe E (Eugenia), S (Sebastián) o E + S (Eugenia + Sebastián) para cada frase.

1 Trabajó en una oficina.
2 El primer día no tomó nada.
3 Habló idiomas extranjeros.
4 Fue a comer algo con una compañera de trabajo.
5 Lo pasó mal el primer día.
6 Aprendió varias cosas.

1
¡Hola! Mi nombre es **Eugenia**. Hice mis prácticas laborales en una tienda de muebles. Atendía a los clientes y con algunos hablaba en inglés y francés. El primer día lo pasé mal porque no vendí nada, pero el segundo día vendí tres mesas, ¡qué guay! Conocí a Frida, una dependienta sueca. El último día fuimos juntas a una cafetería. Comí una hamburguesa y Frida tomó tortilla española. En mis prácticas lo pasé bien, pero la verdad es que no aprendí nada nuevo.

Contesta las preguntas sobre Eugenia o Sebastián.

1 ¿Dónde hizo Eugenia/Sebastián sus prácticas laborales?
2 ¿Qué hacía?
3 ¿Qué tal fue el primer día?
4 ¿Le gustó trabajar allí?
5 ¿Qué aprendió durante sus prácticas laborales?

2
Me llamo **Sebastián** y mi colegio organizó mis prácticas laborales. Fui a trabajar a una empresa internacional donde contestaba llamadas telefónicas y escribía cartas. Mi horario de trabajo era bastante duro y el primer día no comí nada porque no tuve ningún descanso, fue un día horroroso. Me gustó trabajar allí porque aprendí a mandar correos y también a trabajar en equipo.

G The preterite and the imperfect tense

➲204–206

Use the **preterite** for completed actions in the past.

	-ar verbs	**-er** verbs	**-ir** verbs	**ir** *(to go)*/**ser** *(to be)*
(yo)	trabaj**é**	com**í**	escrib**í**	fui
(tú)	trabaj**aste**	com**iste**	escrib**iste**	fuiste
(él/ella/usted)	trabaj**ó**	com**ió**	escrib**ió**	fue

El primer día **bebí** mucho café. *The first day I drank a lot of coffee.*

Use the **imperfect** to emphasise *repetition* of actions in the past, e.g. for things you did repeatedly during your work experience. Also use it to describe what specific aspects of your work experience were like, e.g. your boss.

	-ar verbs	**-er** verbs	**-ir** verbs	**ir** *(to go)*	**ser** *(to be)*
(yo)	trabaj**aba**	com**ía**	escrib**ía**	iba	era
(tú)	trabaj**abas**	com**ías**	escrib**ías**	ibas	eras
(él/ella/usted)	trabaj**aba**	com**ía**	escrib**ía**	iba	era

Todos los días **comía** un bocadillo de jamón. *Every day I used to eat a ham sandwich.*
Mi jefe **era** muy simpático. *My boss was very nice.*

5 Lee e identifica los verbos en el pretérito y en el imperfecto.

preterite	imperfect
hice	se llamaba

Mi nombre es Ana Hernández de López. En junio del año pasado hice mis prácticas en un hospital y fue increíble. Trabajé con un equipo de enfermeros estupendos. Mi jefa se llamaba María y era buenísima. Todos los días me levantaba muy temprano y cogía el metro para no llegar tarde. Me gusta ser puntual. Por las mañanas ayudaba a los enfermeros y hablaba con los pacientes. Los pacientes eran muy simpáticos. Por las tardes les servía té y hacía camas. El último día organicé una fiesta de cumpleaños para Teo, un niño enfermo de siete años.

6 *Read the text again. Which tense has been used with the following adverbs of time and frequency?*

1 en junio del año pasado
2 todos los días
3 por las mañanas
4 por las tardes
5 el último día

7 Copia y completa las preguntas con el pretérito o el imperfecto. Luego contesta sobre tus prácticas.

1 ¿Cuándo (hacer) tus prácticas laborales?
2 ¿Dónde (trabajar)?
3 ¿Con quién (trabajar)?
4 ¿Cómo (ser) tu jefe?
5 ¿Qué (hacer) todos los días?
6 ¿Qué (hacer) por las mañanas y por las tardes?
7 ¿Qué (hacer) el último día?

Use some of these adjectives to talk about the people you worked with:

agresivo/a	egoísta	nervioso/a
maleducado/a	orgulloso/a	introvertido/a
alegre	tolerante	callado/a
maduro/a	sincero/a	respetuoso/a
vago/a	hablador/a	tonto/a

- Describing future plans
- Using different verbs to talk about the future
- Forming sentences with **si...** (if...)

3 El futuro

Lee y escribe el futuro de estos famosos.

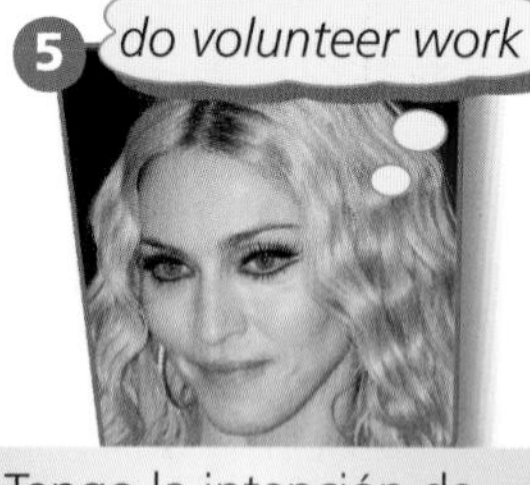

seguir estudiando
encontrar trabajo
vivir en el extranjero
trabajar como voluntario/a en…
tener una familia
tomarse un año sabático
ir a la universidad

Escucha y escribe las letras correctas. (1–5)

la gente ciega = *blind people*

Inventa cuatro preguntas sobre el futuro. Luego haz diálogos con tu compañero/a.

- ● ¿Qué vas a hacer dentro de cinco años?
- ■ Dentro de cinco años voy a…, después de… quiero…
- ● ¿Qué quieres hacer…?
- ■ Tengo la intención de…, también espero…

antes de + infinitive = before (doing) something
después de + infinitive = after (doing) something

Después de estudiar voy a viajar.
After studying I'm going to travel.

G *The future* ➲208

There are different ways to express a future event in Spanish:

1 querer + infinitive
El año que viene quiero comprar una casa.
I want to buy a house next year.

2 tener la intención de + infinitive
Tengo la intención de ir a la universidad.
I plan to go to university.

3 pensar + infinitive
Pienso comprar un coche.
I'm thinking of buying a car.

4 esperar + infinitive
Espero tomarme un año sabático.
I hope to take a year off.

5 near future tense (ir a) + infinitive
Voy a ser médico. *I am going to be a doctor.*

6 the future tense
Iré a Francia. *I will go to France.*

4 Escucha. Copia y completa la tabla en inglés. (1–5)

	If...	I will...
1	If I pass my exams	I will be an air hostess and...

G 'If' clauses ➲224

Use *if clauses* to express possibilities in the future:
Si + **present**, + **future**

Si **trabajo** mucho, **ganaré** mucho dinero.
*If **I work** a lot, **I will earn** a lot of money.*

Si apruebo mis exámenes, Si trabajo mucho, Si estudio (ciencias), Si practico más deporte, Si tengo éxito, Si (no) voy al (instituto),	**ganaré** mucho dinero. **aprenderé** un oficio. **haré** un curso de formación profesional. **iré** a la universidad. **tendré** responsabilidades. **seré** (médico/a, famoso/a…). **trabajaré** como… **escribiré** una novela. **jugaré** al fútbol en…

5 *Read Gabriela's text and answer the questions in English.*

1 How old is Gabriela?
2 What will she find hard in the future?
3 If she gets good grades, what will she do?
4 What will happen if she doesn't pass her exams?
5 What are her brother's plans for the future?
6 Where does she see herself in ten years?

¡Hola! **Me llamo** Gabriela. **Tengo** dieciséis años y **vivo** en Cali, en Colombia. No **sé** qué **va a pasar** en el futuro. **Quiero** vivir y trabajar en Cali, pero lo **veo** muy complicado. Aquí **hay** mucho desempleo y **será** difícil encontrar un buen trabajo. Si **saco** buenas notas, **iré** a la universidad para estudiar Empresariales. Sin embargo, si no **apruebo** mis exámenes, **tendré** que buscar un trabajo como dependienta o cajera en el centro comercial cerca de mi casa. Mi hermano **trabaja** como profesor y en el futuro **va a viajar** al extranjero. A mí también **me gustaría** viajar a otros países. **Estoy** segura de que **tendré** una familia y **viviré** en una casa linda, ¿pero quién **sabe**? Creo que todo **es** posible si **trabajas** mucho y si **tienes** el apoyo de tu familia.

6 Escribe sobre tu futuro.

Introducción:
¿Qué haces ahora?
Estudio, me gusta...
Desarrollo:
¿Qué piensas hacer en el futuro?
Pienso.., quiero..., espero...
Tengo la intención de...
Si...(+ present + future)
Antes de..., después de...,
¿Qué planes tienen otros miembros de tu familia?
Mi hermano/a piensa..., quiere...
Conclusión:
Todo es posible si...
Estoy seguro/a de que...

★ Try to use as many tenses as possible when writing or talking about your future plans. You can use the present tense, near future tense, future tense and the conditional (*me gustaría* + infinitive). Can you identify which colour represents which tense in exercise 5?

- Understanding job adverts and CVs
- Using the conditional with **gustar** and **poder**
- Understanding specialist vocabulary

4 Mi currículum vitae

1 Lee los anuncios. Escribe la letra correcta para cada persona.

Me llamo **Leandro** y soy una persona bastante tímida. Me gustaría trabajar de nueve a once de la mañana. El año pasado trabajé en la carnicería de un supermercado.

Me llamo **Alicia**. Nací en París, pero ahora vivo en España. Hablo francés y español. El año pasado trabajé como profesora en un instituto mixto en Madrid.

Me llamo **Juan** y busco un trabajo interesante. Soy creativo y un entusiasta de la naturaleza.

Me llamo **Fátima** y soy ama de casa. Tengo tres hijos pequeños y ¡necesito un trabajo urgentemente! Me interesa la informática y tengo un PC en casa.

a Se buscan profesores de idiomas. Interesados deben **rellenar el siguiente formulario**: http://ralimis.com/idiomas

b Se necesita recepcionista para trabajar **a tiempo parcial** en una empresa internacional. **Imprescindibles buena presencia y referencias. Incorporación inmediata**. Tfno.: 91 462 31 18

c **Se busca chico o chica joven** para una floristería. Se ofrece **horario flexible** y no es necesario tener experiencia. **Envíe una carta de presentación con currículum vitae** al Apartado de Correos 1349, Oviedo.

d **Se necesita carnicero y panadero** para trabajar durante las mañanas en el mercado. Sueldo a convenir. **Preferible con experiencia**. Interesados deben llamar al 95 248 80 39

e ¿Eres ama de casa? ¿Tienes ordenador? Importante empresa ofrece trabajo para amas de casa emprendedoras. Trabaja desde tu domicilio. **Experiencia no necesaria**.

Steps for understanding texts with specialist vocabulary

- Scan for cognates that will help you start to understand the text.
- Use the context: what are the types of phrases you would expect to see in an English job ad? Can you see any in Spanish that might mean the same thing?
- If there are words you still don't understand, use your knowledge of grammar (is it a verb, noun, adjective, etc.?) to make intelligent guesses.

2 ***Read the job ads again and write down the letter of the ad that matches these requirements (the expressions in bold will help you).***

1 I do not want to work full-time and I would like to start immediately.
2 I need to work but I have not worked previously.
3 I have good references and I am smartly presented.
4 I need to fill in a form to apply for this job.
5 I don't want a rigid work timetable and I have a covering letter ready to send.
6 I have experience working in the food industry.

3 ***Listen and write down the letter of a job from exercise 1 for each person. (1–4)***

4 Lee los currículum vitae imaginarios de Juan Pablo Montoya y Shakira. Después, lee las frases y escribe M (Montoya) o S (Shakira) o M+S (Montoya y Shakira).

Currículum Vitae

Datos personales:
Nombre: Juan Pablo
Apellidos: Montoya
Dirección: Calle los Ricos, Montecarlo, Mónaco
Móvil: 04673 4785
Correo electrónico: jpm@yahoo.es
Fecha de nacimiento: 20 de septiembre de 1975
Lugar de nacimiento: Bogotá, Colombia

Educación:
Colegio Gimnasio Campestre

Experiencia laboral:
- A los seis años corrí en triciclo.
- A los nueve años gané mi primer Campeonato Infantil Nacional de Karts.
- De 1992 a 2006 fui piloto de Fórmula 1.
- Actualmente soy piloto de NASCAR.

Idiomas: español, francés, un poco de inglés

Cualidades: entusiasta, honesto, trabajador

Pasatiempos: videojuegos, golf, windsurf

Referencias: Williams, McLaren

Currículum Vitae

Datos personales:
Nombre: Shakira Isabel
Apellidos: Mebarak Ripoll
Dirección: Calle Salsa, Miami, Florida, Estados Unidos
Móvil: 07767 259011
Correo electrónico: shakira@gmail.com
Fecha de nacimiento: 2 de febrero de 1977
Lugar de nacimiento: Barranquilla, Colombia

Educación:
Colegio Nuestra Señora de la Enseñanza

Experiencia laboral:
- Con ocho años compuse mi primera canción para mi padre: *Tus gafas oscuras*.
- Cuando tenía nueve años aparecí en varios programas de televisión y radio.
- Al cumplir los diez años gané el concurso *Buscando Artista Infantil*.
- En 2002 me hice famosa con el álbum *Servicio de lavandería*.
- Gané dos Premios Grammy y ocho Premios Grammy Latinos.

Idiomas: español e inglés

Cualidades: inteligente, positiva, viva

Pasatiempos: jardinería, naturaleza

Referencias: Sony Music

1 No vive en Europa.
2 Le interesan los deportes.
3 Le encantan las flores y las plantas.
4 Empezó su carrera cuando era muy joven.

5 Escucha y escribe M, S o M+S. (1–5)

6 Con tu compañero/a habla sobre los currículum de Montoya y de Shakira. Contesta a las preguntas.

- ¿Cómo se llama el candidato? (Se llama Juan Pablo Montoya/Shakira.)
- ¿Cuántos años tiene?
- ¿Dónde vive?
- ¿Qué hace actualmente?
- ¿Cómo es?
- ¿Qué le gusta hacer en su tiempo libre?
- Mira los anuncios en la página 94, ¿en qué podría trabajar? (Juan Pablo podría trabajar como… porque…)

G The conditional ➲210

You use this tense when you say *would* in English.
Me **gustaría** trabajar con animales.
I would like to work with animals.

When you use the conditional tense of the verb **poder** *(can, to be able to)* it is translated as *could*.
¿En qué **podría** trabajar?
What could he/she work as?
Carlos **podría** trabajar de mecánico.
Carlos could work as a mechanic.

- Understanding application letters
- Forming the perfect tense
- Conducting a job interview

5 La entrevista

1 ***Read the application letter. True, false or not mentioned? (T, F, NM)***

1. He is replying to a newspaper advertisement.
2. He is a translator.
3. He will send a CV if they are interested.
4. He is available to work part-time.
5. He knows how to use spreadsheets on the computer.
6. He has worked as the manager of a team of translators.
7. He speaks three languages.

Muy señor mío:

Me dirijo a Ud. para solicitar el puesto de traductor publicado en la página de Internet *www.ofertasdeempleoytrabajo.com*, del día 22 de febrero.

Le adjunto mi currículum vitae y como podrá ver he trabajado de traductor para varias editoriales de prestigio internacional y he traducido documentos científicos y técnicos del inglés al español, entre los que destaca el famoso libro *Ciencia para tontos*.

Soy un trabajador rápido y eficiente. Trabajo bien solo o como parte de un equipo y tengo dos años de experiencia como traductor-jefe de un equipo de ocho personas.

Soy bilingüe en inglés y español, y domino perfectamente el alemán. Además, he hecho varios cursos de informática y manejo Word, PowerPoint y Excel.

Quedo a su disposición.

Le saluda atentamente, **Guillermo Gutiérrez Barrero**

2 ***Listen and make a note of (a) what jobs these people have done, and (b) how they have used languages.*** **(1–4)**

Ejemplo: **1a** air hostess, **1b**…

3 **Escucha y empareja las frases con las preguntas que entiendas.** (1–7)

- **a** El dinero es importante. Sin embargo, este puesto ofrece mucho más que un buen sueldo.
- **b** Es manuelescobar@yahoo.es
- **c** Me parece esencial tener responsabilidades en mi trabajo.
- **d** Deseo trabajar aquí porque me apasiona este puesto y porque tengo los requisitos necesarios.
- **e** Prefiero trabajar solo, pero siempre me llevo bien con mis compañeros de trabajo.
- **f** Soy bastante optimista y mis amigos dicen que soy maduro.
- **g** He trabajado en varias empresas multinacionales y tengo siete años de experiencia.

G *The perfect tense*

➲228

The perfect tense is used to say that you *have done* something.

Forming the perfect tense:
present tense of the verb **haber** + **past participle**.
Form the past participle by taking the infinitive, removing **-ar**, **-er** and **-ir**, and adding the endings **-ado** (for **-ar** verbs) and **-ido** (for **-er** and **-ir** verbs).

(yo)	**he**	trabajado
(tú)	**has**	comido
(él/ella/usted)	**ha**	vivido
(nosotros/as)	**hemos**	etc.
(vosotros/as)	**habéis**	
(ellos/ellas/ustedes)	**han**	

Hemos trabajado mucho. *We have worked a lot.*
Ha vivido en España. *She has lived in Spain.*

Some past participles are irregular:
ser → **sido** hacer → **hecho** escribir → **escrito**
ver → **visto** poner → **puesto**

4 Escucha y lee la conversación. Copia y rellena la tabla.

nombre (guess it!)	estudios	empleo solicitado	experiencia laboral	cualidades

Pregunta: ¿Qué ha estudiado usted en el instituto?
Respuesta: He estudiado asignaturas típicas como inglés, matemáticas y ciencias, pero he tenido clases de hechizos y trucos de magia.
P: ¿Por qué quiere ser profesor de magia?
R: Quiero ser profesor porque me encanta la magia y me interesa lo sobrenatural.
P: ¿Qué experiencia laboral tiene usted?
R: He enseñado magia en un colegio privado.
P: ¿Le gusta trabajar con niños?
R: Claro que sí. Los niños son muy divertidos.
P: ¿Le interesa tener un puesto con responsabilidades?
R: Por supuesto, siempre he sido muy responsable y organizado y me gustaría demostrarlo en mi trabajo.
P: ¿Ha trabajado en equipo antes?
R: Sí, he trabajado en equipo con mis amigos, sobre todo con mi amiga Hermione.
P: ¿Qué cualidades tiene usted?
R: Soy amable, inocente y sincero.
P: ¿Cuál es su correo electrónico?
R: Es…

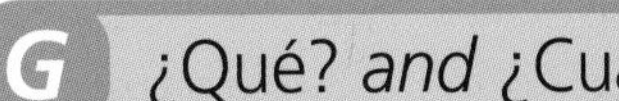

G ¿Qué? *and* ¿Cuál?

➲222

In Spanish, *what…? or which…?* are translated by the question words **¿qué…?** or **¿cuál…?**

¿Qué…? is used before a noun or a verb:
¿Qué trabajos le gustan más? *Which jobs do you like best?*
¿Qué quieres? *What do you want?*

¿Cuál…? is used when asking for more specific information, and is followed by a verb:
¿Cuál prefieres, el rojo o el verde?
Which (one) do you prefer, the red one or the green one?
¿Cuál es su dirección electrónica?
What is your email address?

5 *With a partner, write and perform a job interview.*

Quiero ser…
porque me encanta(n) / me interesa(n) / me fascina(n)…

He trabajado como…	Me interesa…
He jugado…	Lo que más me importa es…
He cantado…	trabajar en equipo
He usado…	trabajar solo/a
He mandado…	ganar un buen sueldo
He escrito…	hacer un trabajo creativo/responsable/útil
He contestado…	tener un trabajo con mucha variedad
He hablado…	hablar idiomas
He traducido…	viajar
He aprendido…	

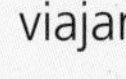

Use the questions in exercise 4 to help you. Are there any that you will need to change for your interview?

Use your imagination: you could be a celebrity (e.g. Madonna applying for a job as a singer). Remember to use the perfect tense for things you have done and work experience you have gained.

Prueba oral

Jobs

You are going to have a conversation with your teacher about part-time jobs. Your teacher will ask you the following:

- Do you have a part-time job at the moment?
- What do you do?
- Do you like your job?
- Have you done any other part-time jobs?
- What are the advantages and disadvantages of working part-time?
- What would you like to do in the future?
- Is unemployment a problem for young people?

Remember you will have to respond to an unexpected question that you have not yet prepared.
The dialogue will last between 4 and 6 minutes.

You are going to listen to Katie, an exam candidate, taking part in the above conversation with her teacher. Listen to part 1 and find the following phrases in Spanish.

1 At the moment...
2 Normally I work...
3 I work from... to...
4 It's a long day.
5 Time goes quickly.
6 I work on the cash desk.
7 In general...
8 The truth is that...
9 I don't earn much.
10 They pay me 8 euros per hour.

Listen to part 1 again. Note down in English how Katie answers the first three questions.

Listen to part 2 of Katie's conversation and note down the words that fill the gaps.

– ¿Has hecho otro trabajo a tiempo parcial en el pasado?
– Sí, he trabajado **(1)** ______ dependienta en una tienda de moda, **(2)** ______ no me gustó. **(3)** ______ he trabajado en una granja **(4)** ______ cuidaba a los animales. Tenía que levantarme todos los sábados a las cinco de la mañana y era muy duro. No quiero trabajar con animales nunca más **(5)** ______ es demasiado sucio.
– En tu opinión, ¿cuáles son las ventajas o desventajas de trabajar a tiempo parcial?
– Para mí hay muchas ventajas. **(6)** ______, los trabajos a tiempo parcial ofrecen horarios flexibles y son buenos **(7)** ______ eres estudiante **(8)** ______ si tienes hijos. Pero creo que la desventaja es el sueldo, que **(9)** ______ es suficiente **(10)** ______ trabajas a tiempo parcial. En los trabajos a tiempo completo pagan mucho más, y son mejores si quieres continuar una carrera profesional.

Look at the words you identified in exercise 3. Translate them into English.

Now listen to part 3 of Katie's conversation and answer the questions.

1 In her answer to the first question Katie uses the structure *si* + present + future. Can you spot it?
2 In the same answer she talks about the future using some structures followed by the infinitive. Which ones does she use?
3 In her answer to the second question Katie uses two adverbs. What are they and what do they mean?
4 What is the unexpected question that Katie's teacher asks and what does it mean?

Now it's your turn! Prepare your answers to the task and then have a conversation with your teacher or partner.

- Use the Grade Studio and your answers to exercises 1–5 to help you plan.
- Adapt what Katie said to talk about yourself but add your own ideas.
- Prepare your answers to the questions and try to predict what the unexpected question could be. The examiner might base this question on something you have already said, or ask something totally new!
- Record the conversation. Ask a partner to listen to it and say how well you performed.

Award each other one star, two stars or three stars for each of these categories:
- *Pronunciation*
- *Confidence and fluency*
- *Range of tenses*
- *Variety of vocabulary and expressions*
- *Using longer sentences*
- *Taking the initiative*

What do you need to do next time to improve your performance?

GradeStudio

To produce a good answer you need to be able to use a variety of structures.
- Use a **variety of tenses**, for example the present, past (preterite) and the near future or future tense correctly. Can you find examples of these in parts 1, 2 and 3?
- Give simple **opinions**. Katie uses *me gusta...* (I like), *prefiero...* (I prefer) and *odio...* (I hate) in part 1 of the conversation.
- Use simple **connectives** to extend your sentences such as *y* (and), *pero* (but), *también* (also) and *porque* (because).

To go a step further you need to use a wider variety of language.
- Use the **perfect tense** to talk about a job you **have done**. Can you find an example in exercise 3?
- Use the **imperfect tense** to talk about what you did every day in a particular job. Katie talks about her responsibilities on the farm, saying *'tenía que...'*.
- Express **points of view**. Can you find any examples of phrases that Katie uses to do this in exercise 3?
- Use **adverbs** to add detail to what you say such as *normalmente* and *desafortunadamente*.

For a really impressive answer:
- Use a **wide variety of phrases** to talk about the future. In part 3 Katie uses the future tense (I will...), *esperar* + infinitive (I hope to), *me gustaría* + infinitive (I would like to), *tener la intención* + infinitive (I intend to) and *ir a* + infinitive (I'm going to).
- Use **complex sentences** that contain more than one tense. Using *si* + present + future is one way of doing this.
- Use **relative clauses** to extend sentences. In part 2 Katie uses *donde* (where) and *cuando* (when) to link ideas in a sentence together.

Prueba escrita

1 ***Read the text and choose the correct title for each paragraph. What words/phrases support your decisions?***

a The job **b** The future **c** Who I am **d** Getting to work **e** Lunchtime

1 Me llamo Joel. Tengo quince años y estudio en el Instituto López Neyra, en Córdoba. Todos los años los alumnos de cuarto de la ESO de mi insti hacen prácticas laborales en una empresa local.

2 El mes pasado hice mis prácticas en una oficina durante quince días. Normalmente me levanto a las siete y media, y voy al instituto a pie, porque está muy cerca de mi casa. Sin embargo, cuando hacía las prácticas, me levantaba a las seis de la mañana. Cogía el tren al centro de Córdoba y después cogía el autobús. Debido a problemas en el transporte público, llegué tarde tres veces. ¡Pero por lo menos llegué a tiempo el primer día!

3 Mi jefa era la señora Brown y era muy amable. Trabajábamos en el segundo piso de un edificio grandísimo. Tenía por lo menos trece plantas y ochocientos trabajadores. Cada día mandaba correos y escribía cartas. Además, hacía llamadas telefónicas y un montón de fotocopias, e imprimía muchos documentos.

Joel

4 Normalmente teníamos una hora para comer, pero como hacía frío y ninguno de mis amigos trabajaba cerca, yo comía en la cantina. Terminábamos a las cinco y media, pero el último día salí a las tres porque no tenía nada que hacer, y mi jefe me dijo que podía salir temprano.

5 No me gustaron las prácticas. Para mí no fueron ni fáciles ni difíciles, pero resultaron muy aburridas. En el futuro no quiero trabajar en una oficina. En cambio, si tengo la oportunidad, haré algo mucho más creativo. En vacaciones me gustaría hacer más prácticas y si puedo, trabajaré en un cine o un teatro porque me fascina la cultura. ¡Que bien!

2 ***Answer the questions in English.***

1. How long was Joel's work experience?
2. What time does Joel normally get up?
3. How did Joel travel to work every day?
4. How many times did Joel arrive late to work?
5. Describe the building where Joel worked.
6. Name four things Joel did as part of his work.
7. Why did Joel eat in the canteen? Give two reasons.
8. What did Joel think about his work experience? Give two details.

3 ***Complete the sentences with the correct verbs from the text.***

1. Me ____ a las seis.
2. Después ____ el autobús.
3. Tres veces ____ tarde.
4. ____ en el segundo piso.
5. ____ por lo menos trece plantas.
6. ____ llamadas telefónicas.
7. El ultimo día ____ a las tres.
8. Las prácticas no ____ ni fáciles ni difíciles.
9. No ____ trabajar en una oficina.
10. Si ____ la oportunidad, ____ algo mucho más creativo.

4 ***Translate the sentences in exercise 3 into English.***

5 ***You might be asked to write about your work experience as a Controlled Assessment task. Use the Grade Studio to help you prepare your account.***

GradeStudio

To produce a good answer you need to use a variety of structures and express opinions.

- Joel uses the **present tense** to talk about his daily routine, the **preterite** to talk about when he was late for work and the **future tense** to talk about what job he would like to do.
- Can you find an example of where Julio uses the following **connectives** in his text: *y, además, pero, porque?*
- Find the sentence where Joel gives his opinion on his work experience. Is it positive or negative?

To go a step further you need to use a wider range of language. This might include: other tenses, such as the **imperfect**, verbs referring to a **variety of people** (I, he/she, we, they), and **different structures** for talking about the future.

- Joel uses the **imperfect tense** throughout his account to describe things he did every day: *me levantaba, cogía.* Can you find more examples of the imperfect tense in the text?
- Joel talks about **other people** in his text. Can you find examples of this?
- Joel refers to the future in a number of different ways. He uses the **conditional** *(me gustaría hacer)*, **querer + infinitive** *(quiero trabajar)* and the **future tense** *(trabajaré)*.

For a really impressive answer:

- Include a **complex sentence** with two tenses in it. Can you find an example of this in the fourth paragraph of the text?
- Use an **if** clause to talk about what you will do in the future. Can you find an example in the fifth paragraph?

6 ***Now write a full account of your work experience.***

- Adapt Joel's text and use language from Module 5. Write at least 200 words.
- If you need to look up a word in a dictionary remember that the noun or adjective will be given in the masculine singular form and you may need to change it to the feminine. Remember too that the dictionary will only give you the infinitive form of a verb. Use your memory, or verb tables, to work out the ending.
- Structure your text carefully. Organise what you write in paragraphs.

General summary of work experience

Introduce yourself.

Main paragraph

Talk about your work experience:
- *How did you get to work?*
- *Who did you work with?*
- *Describe where you worked.*
- *What did you do every day?*
- *Talk about any special incidents (the first day/the last day, etc.).*

Conclusion

How was your work experience?
What are your plans for the future?

7 ***Check carefully what you have written.***

- tenses (have you used the preterite, imperfect and future tenses correctly?)
- verb endings (correct for yourself, your boss or your colleagues?)
- accents (particularly in your verb endings!)

Palabras

A trabajar *Off to work*

un estadio	*stadium*	dependiente/ dependienta	*shop assistant*
un hotel	*hotel*	director(a)	*director*
un instituto	*school*	diseñador(a)	*designer*
un jardín	*garden*	enfermero/a	*nurse*
un restaurante	*restaurant*	futbolista	*footballer*
una clínica	*clinic*	ingeniero/a	*engineer*
una peluquería	*hairdresser's*	jardinero/a	*gardener*
Soy…	*I am a…*	mecánico/a	*mechanic*
Es…	*He/She is a…*	médico/a	*doctor*
abogado/a	*lawyer*	peluquero/a	*hairdresser*
actor/actriz	*actor/actress*	periodista	*journalist*
azafata	*air stewardess*	profesor(a)	*teacher*
camarero/a	*waiter*	recepcionista	*receptionist*
cantante	*singer*	soldado	*soldier*
carpintero/a	*carpenter*	Trabaja en…	*He/She works in…*
cocinero/a	*cook*	Le gusta…	*He/She likes…*
comerciante	*businessman/woman*	Me gusta…	*I like…*
conductor(a)	*driver*	…es importante	*…is important*
dentista	*dentist*		

¿Trabajas los sábados? *Do you work on Saturdays?*

¿Qué haces para ganar dinero?	*What do you do to earn money?*	por las mañanas	*in the mornings*
¿Cuándo trabajas?	*When do you work?*	por las tardes	*in the afternoons/evenings*
¿Qué tienes que hacer?	*What do you have to do?*	todos los días	*every day*
¿Qué opinas de tu trabajo?	*What do you think of your job?*	Tengo que…	*I have to…*
¿Cuánto ganas?	*How much do you earn?*	coger el autobús	*catch the bus*
Gano …€ a la hora.	*I earn …€ an hour.*	contar historias	*tell stories*
Gano mucho.	*I earn a lot.*	cuidar a niños	*look after children*
Gano poco.	*I earn little.*	ir bien vestido/a	*dress well*
Hago de canguro.	*I'm a babysitter*	levantarme temprano	*get up early*
Lavo coches.	*I wash cars.*	ser amable	*be nice*
Reparto periódicos.	*I deliver newspapers.*	ser puntual	*be on time*
Trabajo como camarero/a.	*I work as a waiter/waitress.*	servir comida	*serve food*
Trabajo como dependiente/a.	*I work as a shop assistant.*	vender zapatos/ropa	*sell shoes/clothes*
Trabajo como jardinero/a.	*I work as a gardener.*	Es un trabajo…	*It's a… job.*
Trabajo como socorrista.	*I work as a lifeguard.*	difícil	*difficult*
los fines de semana	*at weekends*	duro	*hard*
los sábados	*on Saturdays*	interesante	*interesting*

Prácticas laborales *Work experience*

¿Dónde trabajaste?	*Where did you work?*	Hablaba con los clientes.	*I used to talk to clients.*
Trabajé en…	*I worked in…*	Leía correos electrónicos.	*I used to read emails.*
Hice mis prácticas laborales en…	*I did my work experience in…*	Practicaba varios deportes.	*I used to practise sports.*
Fui a trabajar a…	*I went to work at…*	Salía a comprar bocadillos y café.	*I used to go out to buy sandwiches and coffee.*
un polideportivo	*a sports centre*	Vigilaba a los alumnos/as.	*I used to supervise the students.*
una empresa inglesa	*an English company*	¿Qué hiciste el último día?	*What did you do on the last day?*
una escuela	*a school*	Ayudé a los niños.	*I helped the children.*
una oficina	*an office*	Contesté llamadas telefónicas.	*I answered the phone.*
una tienda de ropa	*a clothes shop*	Escribí cartas y mandé correos electrónicos.	*I wrote letters and sent emails.*
¿Cuándo hiciste tus prácticas laborales?	*When did you do your work experience?*	Hablé con los clientes.	*I talked to the customers.*
¿Con quién trabajaste?	*Who did you work with?*	Hablé varios idiomas extranjeros.	*I spoke several foreign languages.*
¿Cómo era tu jefe?	*What was your boss like?*	Leí correos electrónicos.	*I read emails.*
¿Qué hacías todos los días?	*What did you used to do every day?*	Practiqué varios deportes.	*I practised various sports.*
¿Qué hacías por la mañana y por la tarde?	*What did you used to do in the morning and in the afternoon?*	Salí a comprar bocadillos y café.	*I went out to buy sandwiches and coffee.*
Ayudaba a los niños.	*I used to help the children.*	Vigilé a los alumnos.	*I supervised the pupils.*
Contestaba llamadas telefónicas.	*I used to answer the phone.*	Lo pasé bomba/mal.	*I had a great/bad time.*
Escribía cartas y mandaba correos electrónicos.	*I used to write letters and send emails.*		

El futuro *The future*

Quiero…	*I want to…*
Voy a…	*I'm going to…*
Pienso…	*I'm thinking of…*
Tengo la intención de…	*I plan to…*
Me gustaría…	*I'd like to…*
Espero…	*I hope to…*
encontrar trabajo	*get a job*
ir a la universidad	*go to university*
seguir estudiando	*continue studying*
tener una familia	*have a family*
tomarse un año sabático	*take a year off*
trabajar como voluntario/a en…	*work as a volunteer in…*
vivir en el extranjero	*live abroad*
Si apruebo mis exámenes…	*If I pass my exams…*
Si estudio…	*If I study…*
Si practico más deporte…	*If I practise more sport…*
Si tengo éxito…	*If I'm successful…*
Si trabajo mucho…	*If I work hard…*
aprenderé un oficio.	*I will do an apprenticeship.*
escribiré una novela.	*I will write a novel.*
ganaré dinero.	*I will earn money.*
haré un curso de formación profesional	*I will do a professional training course.*
iré a la universidad.	*I will go to university.*
jugaré al fútbol en…	*I'll play football in…*
seré famoso/a.	*I will be famous.*
seré…	*I will be a…*
tendré responsabilidades.	*I will have responsibilities.*
¿Qué vas a hacer dentro de cinco años?	*What are you going to do in five years?*
Dentro de cinco años voy a…	*In five years, I'm going to…*

Mi currículum vitae *My CV*

A los… años	*At the age of…*
Cuando tenía… años…	*When I was… years old…*
busqué/encontré…	*I searched for/I found…*
comencé/empecé a…	*I started…*
compuse…	*I composed…*
dejé de…	*I stopped…*
escribí…	*I wrote…*
estudié…	*I studied…*
gané/perdí…	*I won/I lost…*
me hice…	*I became…*
trabajé en/para/como…	*I worked in/for/as…*
viajé…	*I travelled…*
el anuncio	*(job) advert*
Se busca(n)…/Se necesita(n)…	*…required*
a tiempo parcial/completo	*part/full-time*
buena presencia y referencias	*good appearance and references*
deben llamar a…	*you should call…*
dominio del inglés	*able to speak English*
envíe una carta de presentación	*send a covering letter*
experiencia no necesaria	*experience not necessary*
horario flexible	*flexible hours*
incorporación inmediata	*starting immediately*
interesados…	*if you're interested…*
preferible con experiencia	*preferably with experience*
rellenar el siguiente formulario	*fill in the following form*
nombre	*first name*
apellidos	*surname*
dirección	*address*
teléfono	*telephone number*
móvil	*mobile number*
correo electrónico	*email address*
fecha de nacimiento	*date of birth*
lugar de nacimiento	*place of birth*
educación	*education*
experiencia laboral	*work experience*
idiomas	*languages*
otros datos	*other information*

La entrevista *The interview*

Muy Señor mío	*Dear Sir*
Me dirijo a Ud. para…	*I am writing to you to…*
Le adjunto…	*I attach…*
quedo a su disposición	*I await your reply*
le saluda atentamente	*yours sincerely*
¿Qué ha estudiado usted en el instituto?	*What have you studied at school?*
¿Por qué quiere ser…?	*Why do you want to be a…?*
¿Qué experiencia laboral tiene usted?	*What work experience do you have?*
¿Le gusta trabajar con…?	*Do you like to work with…?*
¿Le interesa tener un puesto con responsabilidades?	*Are you interested in a job with responsibilities?*
¿Ha trabajado en equipo antes?	*Have you worked in a team before?*
¿Qué cualidades tiene usted?	*What qualities do you have?*
¿Cuál es su correo electrónico?	*What's your email address?*
quiero ser… porque es importante…	*I want to be… because it's important to…*
me encanta(n)	*I love…*
me interesa(n)	*I am interested in…*
me fascina(n)	*I am fascinated by…*
ganar un buen sueldo	*earn a good salary*
hablar idiomas	*speak languages*
hacer un trabajo creativo/responsable/útil	*do a creative/responsible/useful job*
tener un trabajo con mucha variedad	*have a job with a lot of variety*
trabajar en equipo	*work in a team*
trabajar solo/a	*work alone*
viajar	*travel*
He aprendido…	*I have learnt…*
He cantado…	*I have sung…*
He contestado al teléfono.	*I have answered the phone.*
He escrito cartas.	*I have written letters.*
He hablado idiomas extranjeros.	*I have spoken foreign languages.*
He jugado al fútbol.	*I have played football.*
He mandado correos.	*I have sent emails.*
He trabajado como…	*I have worked as*
He traducido…	*I have translated…*
He usado Internet/Word/PowerPoint/Excel.	*I have used the internet/Word/PowerPoint/Excel.*
Lo que más/menos me importa es…	*What matters most/least to me is…*
me interesa…	*I am interested in…*
el puesto	*the job*
el sueldo	*the salary*
tener responsabilidades	*having responsibilities*

- Revising TV programmes and films
- Using definite/indefinite articles and **algún**
- Expressing a range of opinions

Repaso 1 *La tele y el cine*

1 Escucha y escribe la letra correcta. (1–8)

Ejemplo: **1** b

a 
las películas del Oeste

b 
los programas de deportes

c 
las películas de terror

d 
el telediario/las noticias

e 
las películas de artes marciales

f 
los documentales

g 
los concursos

h 
las series de policías

i 
los dibujos animados

j 
las películas de amor/románticas

k 
las telenovelas

l 
las películas de ciencia-ficción

¿Qué ponen en la tele hoy/esta tarde/mañana?
¿Quieres venir a mi casa a ver…?
¿Quieres ir al cine a ver…?
¿Te apetece ir al cine?
(No) me apetece ir al cine.
¿Para qué sesión?
¿A qué hora empieza el programa/la película?
Dos entradas para…, por favor.

2 Escucha otra vez. ¿A qué hora ponen el programa/la película? (1–8)

a la una
a la**s** dos/tres/cuatro/etc.
a la/las… y media
y/menos (cinco/diez/cuarto/veinte/etc.)

3 Lee la conversación y luego las frases falsas. Después corrige las frases falsas.

Ejemplo: **1** Charo está **bien**.

1 Charo está fatal.
2 A Charo no le apetece ir al cine esta noche.
3 Ponen una película de amor.
4 A Charo le gustan mucho las películas de acción porque son educativas.
5 La película empieza a las diez y ocho.
6 Termina a las diez y cuarto.

Juan: Hola, Charo. ¿Qué tal?
Charo: Pues… Bien, gracias.
Juan: ¿Quieres ir al cine esta noche?
Charo: De acuerdo. ¿Qué ponen?
Juan: Ponen *El increíble Hulk*. ¿La conoces? Es una película de acción.
Charo: Claro que sí, tío. Me gustan mucho las películas de acción porque son emocionantes y divertidas.
Juan: Empieza a las ocho y diez.
Charo: Vale. ¿A qué hora termina?
Juan: Creo que termina a las diez y media.

4 Escucha. Copia y completa la tabla. (1–5)

	película/programa	opinión ♥ / ✗	¿Por qué?
1	películas de guerra	♥	emocionantes, informativas e…

el/un programa…	la/una película…	los/algunos programas…	las/algunas películas…
mal**o**	mal**a**	mal**os**	mal**as**
tont**o**	tont**a**	tont**os**	tont**as**
curios**o**	curios**a**	curios**os**	curios**as**
entretenid**o**	entretenid**a**	entretenid**os**	entretenid**as**
educativ**o**	educativ**a**	educativ**os**	educativ**as**
lent**o**	lent**a**	lent**os**	lent**as**
larg**o**	larg**a**	larg**os**	larg**as**
emocionante	emocionante	emocionantes	emocionantes
inolvidable	inolvidable	inolvidables	inolvidables

5 Rellena los espacios en blanco y escribe dos preguntas más. Luego haz una conversación.

- ● ¿Te gustan las películas de ___?
- ■ Sí, algunas son ___, pero otras son ___.
- ● ¿Te interesan los ___?
- ■ Generalmente ___. Hay algunos que son ___.
- ● ¿Prefieres ver la tele ___ ir al ___?
- ■ Prefiero ___.
- ● ¿___?
- ■ ¿___?

Remember to use the definite article after opinion verbs and when talking generally about something:

Odio **las** películas de aventuras. *I hate adventure films.*
Los documentales son informativos. *Documentaries are informative.*

Use the indefinite article (**unos/unas**) when you want to refer to some rather than all the films:
Ponen **unas** películas muy buenas este fin de semana.
They are showing some very good films this weekend.

Some can also be translated as **algún(algunos)/alguna(s)**:
Algunos concursos son buenos. *Some game shows are good.*
Tengo **algunos** DVD de Tarantino. *I have some Tarantino DVDs.*

6 Escucha. Copia y completa la tabla. (1–4)

	película	número de entradas	sesión	precio de entradas en total	comida/ bebida
1	Juno	2	las 8:00	12€	palomitas

Pues…, ¿me da… entradas para…?, por favor.
¿Para qué sesión? (Para la sesión de…)
¿Cuánto cuesta una entrada?
¿Quiere palomitas de maíz, caramelos o refrescos?
Sí, quiero…, por favor.
¿Cuánto es? (Son… con…)

Narnia
La Brújula Dorada
Kung Fu Panda
El Caballero Oscuro
27 Vestidos
Juno
Superman

- Talking about hobbies and pocket money
- Using conjugated verbs and infinitives
- Introducing variety into your spoken Spanish

Repaso 2 *La paga*

escuchar **1** **Escucha y escribe las letras correctas. (1–5)**

Ejemplo: **1** e,…

patinar/hacer patinaje
nadar/hacer natación
hacer atletismo
jugar al fútbol
hacer equitación/montar a caballo
jugar al tenis de mesa/ping-pong
jugar al voleibol
jugar al golf
jugar al baloncesto
esquiar/hacer esquí

escuchar **2** ***Listen again. Note down any expressions with infinitives that you hear.***

Ejemplo: prefiero hacer, me gusta jugar,…

G *Infinitives v. conjugated verbs*

Verbs can be used in the infinitive or they can be conjugated (i.e. have their endings changed according to who is doing the action, and the tense required).

Infinitives

Expressions with **infinitives** are very important as they will add variety to what you say and help you sound impressive. Here are some useful expressions which are followed by an infinitive. What do they all mean?

Me gusta	**Suelo**	
Me encanta	**Odio**	**+** **jugar** al fútbol
Prefiero	**Antes de**	
Quiero	**Después de**	

Conjugated verbs

You can also use conjugated verbs in the present tense to talk about your hobbies:
Juego al rugby. *I play rugby.*
Hacemos ciclismo. *We go cycling.*

Try to use both expressions with the infinitive and conjugated verbs in your work.

hablar **3** **Con tu compañero/a, pregunta y contesta.**

- ¿Qué deportes te gustan?
- ¿Qué deportes haces en el colegio?
- ¿Sueles hacer deporte al aire libre?
- ¿Prefieres jugar al fútbol o al tenis de mesa?
- ¿Con qué frecuencia nadas?

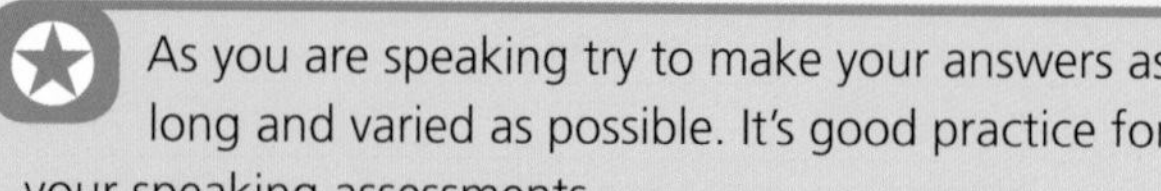

As you are speaking try to make your answers as long and varied as possible. It's good practice for your speaking assessments.

- Answer in whole sentences.
- Look carefully at the verbs in the questions. Are they conjugated verbs or structures with an infinitive? Try to include the same in your answer.
- You could add in adverbs of frequency as well: **todos los días** *(every day)* **dos veces al mes** *(twice a month)*, **una vez a la semana** *(once a week)*, **los miércoles** *(on Wednesdays)*, **nunca** *(never)*.
- Make up another question or two to ask your partner.

4 **Lee el texto de Tina. Decide si las frases son verdaderas, falsas o no se mencionan en el texto. Escribe V, F o NM.**

Hola, me llamo Tina y en mi tiempo libre me encanta hacer muchas cosas distintas. En casa me gusta jugar con mi ordenador. Suelo chatear por Internet con mi novio y también descargo música. A veces mando correos electrónicos a mi hermana que vive en Estados Unidos. Me interesa la lectura y leo mucho, sobre todo libros de misterio. Además, toco el bajo en un grupo y escribo letras de canciones, aunque nunca canto.

Mis padres me dan veinte euros al mes y casi siempre me los gasto en revistas de música. Normalmente las compro cada quince días. Mis padres dicen que malgasto mi dinero, pero no es verdad. A veces ahorro para comprar algo más caro como ropa, o como el bajo que compré el año pasado.

el bajo = *the bass*

1 Tina hace poco en su tiempo libre.
2 En su tiempo libre, a Tina le gusta ir al cine.
3 Tina chatea por Internet y descarga música.
4 A Tina le gusta leer.
5 Tina toca un instrumento.
6 Tina nunca recibe dinero de sus padres.
7 No compra nada.
8 Solamente ahorra su dinero.

5 ***Listen to these people talking about their pocket money. Copy and fill in the table.*** **(1–5)**

	How much?	How often?	Spend, save or both?	Extra details
1	30€	monthly		

G Direct object pronouns ➲214

When you are talking about something, but don't want to repeat a noun twice, you can use a pronoun instead (in English these are words like *it* and *them*).

Compro **revistas**. **Las** compro cada quince días.
I buy ***magazines****. I buy* ***them*** *every fortnight.*
Ahorro **dinero**. **Lo** ahorro para comprar ropa.
I save ***money****. I save* ***it*** *to buy clothes.*

The pronoun you use depends on the noun it replaces:

	singular	plural
masc.	el dinero → **lo**	los libros → **los**
fem.	la revista → **la**	las revistas → **las**

Remember to put the pronoun *in front of* the verb that goes with it.

Mis padres me dan… Mi padre/madre me da… Recibo… al día a la semana al mes cada (quince) días	Compro revistas/caramelos/ropa… Me lo gasto en maquillaje/libros/saldo para el móvil… Lo/La/Los/Las compro todas las semanas. Ahorro dinero para comprar algo más caro.
	Sé que malgasto el dinero, pero no me importa. No malgasto el dinero. Antes tenía menos paga, pero ahora… Es muy importante ahorrar para el futuro. Es importante divertirse.

6 ***Write a text like Tina's. Describe the following:***

- *Your hobbies: what you do and when. (Use a variety of verbs, structures with the infinitive and adverbs of frequency.)*
- *Your pocket money: how much you used to get, how much you get now and what you do with it.*

- Describing sports and sporting events
- Referring to the past and the present
- Listening for the relevant information

1 El campeonato

1 Escucha. Copia y completa la tabla. (1–4)

	sports they do regularly	sports done recently	used to do
1	jogging		

a practicar béisbol

b hacer patinaje

c jugar al billar

d ir de pesca

e hacer footing

f hacer gimnasia

g hacer vela

h jugar a la pelota vasca

i hacer alpinismo

Always read the question carefully. If the question asks what someone did in the past, look for past tense verbs and past time expressions:

- **Preterite verbs** (*practiqué*, *hice*, *jugué*, *fui*, etc.) will refer to completed actions.
- **Imperfect verbs** (*practicaba*, *hacía*, *jugaba*, *iba*, etc.) will refer to things people used to do.

If a question asks what someone normally does, look for present tense verbs and present tense time expressions. These are the verbs you have known for the longest: *practico*, *hago*, *juego*, *voy*.

escribir **2** Escribe los verbos correctos.

1 Diego Maradona (**marcar**) tres goles. *(scored)*
2 Raúl (**jugar**) en el Real Madrid. *(used to play)*
3 Fernando Torres y José Antonio Reyes (**jugar**) en la Copa de Europa 2008. *(played)*
4 Yo (**participar**) en el campeonato. *(participated)*
5 El equipo inglés (**ganar**) el partido. *(won)*

ZONA CULTURA

La Pelota Vasca

This is a sport which originated in the Basque country and is now also played in some other northern regions of Spain and a few Latin American countries. It is similar to handball and is played in a *frontón* (a court with walls) with two teams of one or two players. Players use their hand, a racket or a basket to hit the ball.

3 ***Read the text and work out what the words in red mean. Then write some notes about Matías:***

- *his sporting activities at school*
- *his favourite player*
- *other sports he has tried*

¡Hola! Me llamo Matías. Me encanta el deporte y lo practico muy a menudo. Antes jugaba mucho al fútbol, pero ahora el tenis es mi deporte favorito. Juego bien y soy miembro del **equipo titular** del cole. **Entrenamos** dos veces a la semana y tenemos por lo menos tres partidos cada sábado.

Para mí, Rafael Nadal es el mejor jugador porque puede correr rápido, **golpea** bien **la pelota** y marca puntos sin problemas. Antes yo era **hincha** de Carlos Moyá, pero ahora ¡mi jugador preferido es Nadal! El miércoles pasado mis amigos y yo jugamos al hockey sobre **hielo** por primera vez. Me pareció muy difícil. Aunque sé jugar al hockey sobre **hierba**, no podía **mantenerme en pie** sobre el hielo durante el partido. ¡Patiné fatal y no marqué ningún gol!

4 Habla de los deportes.

- Tu opinión del deporte:
  Me encanta, me interesa, me gusta… porque…
- Los deportes que practicas en el colegio:
  En el cole suelo…
  Juego en el equipo de…
  Entrenamos en el polideportivo/la piscina… una vez a la semana…
- Los deportes que practicas en tu tiempo libre:
  En mi tiempo libre practico/hago/juego al/a la…
- Los deportes que hacías en el pasado. *(Use the imperfect to say what you used to do!)*:
  Antes/cuando era más pequeño/a practicaba/hacía/jugaba…
- ¿Antes eras hincha de algún deportista? ¿Y ahora?
  En el pasado era hincha de… Ahora soy hincha de…
- Lo que hiciste la semana pasada/el mes pasado.
  (Use the preterite to say what you did last week):
  Ayer/anteayer… jugué un partido de… Participé en un campeonato de… Jugué con…
  Jugué contra otro equipo/colegio/otra persona. Marqué (dos) goles… Gané…

5 *Read about Fernando Torres. Look at the phrases in red and work out the English. Then decide if the statements are true, false or not mentioned. Write T, F or NM.*

Fernando Torres "El Niño" – Una biografía

Fernando Torres es un futbolista español que juega en la posición de **delantero**. Es también uno de los mejores jugadores del mundo.

Fernando Torres nació en Madrid y es **el menor** de tres hermanos. Era un apasionado del fútbol desde que era muy pequeño. Comenzó su carrera profesional en 2001 en el famoso club de fútbol español Atlético de Madrid. Aquí marcó **una media de** quince goles **por temporada**. En 2007 el club inglés Liverpool FC **lo fichó** por treinta y seis millones de euros. "El niño" también juega para la Selección Nacional Española. En 2006 participó en la Copa Mundial de Fútbol, y marcó el mayor número de goles del equipo español de la historia. También participó en la Copa de Europa 2008, y marcó el gol que dio la victoria al equipo español.

Su extraordinaria **capacidad goleadora** junto a su **juventud**, le han convertido en un ídolo para millones de personas, sean o no **aficionadas** a este deporte. Torres es un verdadero campeón. ¡**Es un crack**!

1 He started playing when he was 18.
2 He does not have any brothers or sisters.
3 He was bought by Liverpool for sixty-three thousand euros.
4 He scored the most goals for Spain in the 2006 World Cup.
5 He has a great goal scoring capacity.

- Talking about extreme sports
- Using a range of adjectives and opinion phrases
- Decoding texts

2 Los deportes de riesgo

Decoding texts

Even if you don't understand every word in a reading text, use what you do understand as a source of clues to help you find the right answer.

- Can you tell from clues in the text what kind of sport is being referred to? (water sport, winter sport, etc.)

escuchar **1** **Escucha y lee. Empareja el texto con la foto correcta. (1–5)**

1 Estamos en Miami. Hace calor y el mar está precioso. Hoy por fin, es el día del Campeonato Mundial de este deporte tan emocionante, que está de moda entre muchos jóvenes que hacen esquí acuático.

2 Bienvenidos a los Juegos Olímpicos de Invierno de Vancouver de 2010. Esta mañana se puede disfrutar viendo un deporte espectacular. Hoy las condiciones en las pistas son ideales para esta competición.

3 Bienvenidos a la Feria de San Isidro… Señoras y señores, ¡qué tarde de toros nos espera! ¡Bravos y nobles! Les presento a los toreros y a los toros…

4 Aquí hay una escuela de buceo maravillosa donde se puede disfrutar de la naturaleza submarina. En el agua se puede ver una gran variedad de peces, delfines y corales.

5 En esta película se puede ver un ejemplo de un deporte de riesgo sorprendente y fascinante. Es un deporte urbano que ahora se practica en las calles de muchas ciudades del mundo.

a 
el wakeboard

b ***el parkour***

c 
el snowboard

d 
la corrida

e 
el submarinismo

leer **2** **¿Estás listo/a para hacer deportes de riesgo? Haz el test para comprobarlo.**

Test: Deportes de riesgo

1 Si estás solo/a en casa, te gusta…
- **a** sentarte en el sofá y ver la tele.
- **b** navegar por Internet.
- **c** ponerte tus zapatillas de deporte e ir a hacer footing.

2 En el colegio tus asignaturas preferidas son…
- **a** la geografía o la historia.
- **b** la educación física o el dibujo.
- **c** el inglés o las matemáticas.

3 En tu opinión, eres una persona…
- **a** tranquila.
- **b** trabajadora y activa.
- **c** egoísta pero divertida.

4 Prefieres hacer deportes como…
- **a** el golf o el tenis.
- **b** el esquí o el rugby.
- **c** el fútbol o el baloncesto.

Resultados
Puntos:
1 a-1, b-2, c-3
2 a-1, b-2, c-3
3 a-1, b-3, c-2
4 a-1, b-2, c-3

Entre 0–5:	Te gusta la tranquilidad y no te interesan los deportes de riesgo. Lo tuyo es leer libros, ver DVD e ir de compras.
Entre 6–10:	Los deportes de riesgo no son para ti. Haz un deporte de equipo menos peligroso como el fútbol, el tenis o el hockey. Si no quieres ser miembro de un equipo, puedes hacer natación o equitación.
Entre 11–15:	¡Tú vales para esto! Sin duda los deportes de riesgo te van a gustar. Puedes practicar el wakeboard, el snowboard o lo que quieras.

escuchar 3 ***Listen and write speaker 1, speaker 2 or speaker 3 for each question below. There are two questions too many.*** **(1–3)**

a Who can't afford to do high risk sport?
b Who is scared of doing high risk sport?
c Who does high risk sports on holiday?
d Who watches a lot of high risk sport on TV?
e Who can't stand extreme sport?
f Who would like to do high risk sport at some point?
g Who favours wakeboard and parkour in particular?
h Who feels that there are better ways to enjoy life than doing extreme sport?

> Each speaker talks at some length and you might not understand everything the first time you hear it. First listen to each person to try to get a feel for the gist of what they say. Do they seem to have positive or negative views of extreme sport? Do they mention other types of sport as well?

hablar 4 **Habla de los deportes de riesgo con tu compañero/a. Lee las preguntas y haz tus propias preguntas.**

- ¿Te gusta hacer deporte?
- ¿Qué opinas de los deportes de riesgo?
- ¿Qué opinas del/de la…? *(choose a high risk sport to complete the question).*
- ¿Haces algún deporte de riesgo a menudo?
- ¿Si tienes bastante dinero en el futuro, harás algún deporte de riesgo?
- ¿?
- ¿?

Me encanta(n)…	porque es/son…	En mi opinión/A mi modo de ver, este tipo de deporte es demasiado…
Me gusta(n)…	difícil(es)	
Me fascina(n)…	impresionante(s)	
Me interesa(n)…	emocionante(s)	Lo(s) veo en la tele/en Internet.
Me interesa(n) más…	sorprendente(s)	Lo(s) hago… veces al año.
Me da(n) miedo…	seguro(s)	Hice… en mis vacaciones el verano pasado.
Odio…	peligroso(s)	
Prefiero…	arriesgado(s)	Me gustaría hacer… porque es…
No soporto…	caro(s)	
	barato(s)	Si tengo dinero en el futuro, haré…
	fácil(es)	Te puedes divertir de otra manera.

escribir 5 **Escribe un artículo sobre un deporte de riesgo. Contesta las preguntas:**

- *What is your opinion of extreme sports? Why?*
- *Is there an extreme sport that you are most interested in?*
- *Where do you see it? (TV, Internet)*
- *Do you do any extreme sports? Did you do any in the past?*
- *Would you like to do any in the future? Why/Why not?*
- *Can you give any further information about an extreme sport?*

- Making arrangements to go out
- Using the present continuous
- Taking part in an extended conversation

3 ¿Quedamos?

1 Escucha y lee. Copia y completa la tabla.

What are they doing now?	Message left
Mustafa is…	

Abuela: ¿Dígame?
María: Hola. ¿Está Mustafá?
Abuela: ¿De parte de quién?
María: Soy María del Carmen.
Abuela: Un momento. Mustafá…, Mustafá… Lo siento, no está. Está jugando al fútbol en el parque con su hermano. ¿Quieres dejarle algún recado?
María: ¿Puede decirle que voy a ir al polideportivo esta tarde?
Abuela: ¿Al polideportivo? De acuerdo.
María: Gracias. ¡Hasta luego!
Abuela: ¡Hasta luego!

2 ***Now listen to some further dialogues and continue to fill in the table from exercise 1.*** **(1–3)**

G *The present continuous*

➲226

The present continuous is used when you are doing something at a certain moment (I am playing cards). It is formed by taking the present tense of the verb **estar** and the **present participle** of the verb.

	estar *(to be)*	**present participle**
(yo)	estoy	descans**ando**
(tú)	estás	hac**iendo**
(él/ella/usted)	está	escrib**iendo**
(nosotros/as)	estamos	etc.
(vosotros/as)	estáis	
(ellos/ellas/ustedes)	están	

To form the present participle you take the infinitive, remove the **-ar**, **-er** or **-ir** and add the endings: **-ando**, **-iendo**, **-iendo**

Estoy viendo la televisión. *I am watching television.*
No **estoy haciendo** nada. *I am not doing anything.*

Irregular present participles include: leer → **leyendo**, dormir → **durmiendo**

3 ***Write a short paragraph about what you are doing at the moment.***

Últimamente estoy… porque…
También estoy… y…
No estoy…
Tampoco estoy…

4 ***Read the dialogue and write the red verbs in the correct form. Careful: they are all stem-changing verbs.***

Ana: Hola, Leonardo. ¿Qué haces?
Leo: Nada, estoy descansando un poco.
Ana: ¿(1) **Querer** ir al cine esta tarde?
Leo: Lo siento, pero esta tarde no (2) **poder**.
Ana: ¡Vaya! ¿Por qué?
Leo: Porque tengo que salir con mis padres.
Ana: Pues… ¿Te apetece ir al polideportivo mañana a jugar al voleibol?
Leo: Sí, sí, me apetece un montón. Juego mucho con mi hermano y siempre gano. Después (3) **poder** tomar algo en la cafetería. ¿A que hora quedamos?
Ana: ¿A las cuatro y media? El partido de voleibol (4) **empezar** a las cinco.
Leo: (5) **Preferir** quedar un poco más tarde, ¿a las cinco menos cuarto?
Ana: Vale. ¿Dónde quedamos?
Leo: En la estación de metro.

G Stem-changing verbs (radical changing verbs) ➲200

Stem-changing verbs are verbs which have changes to the vowels in their stem. In the present tense, these changes affect: *I*, *you*, *he/she* and *they*. For example:

poder *(can, to be able to)*

p**ue**do	*(I can)*	podemos	*(we can)*
p**ue**des	*(you can)*	podéis	*(you, plural can)*
p**ue**de	*(he/she can)*	p**ue**den	*(they can)*

There are four types of changes:

1 o → ue p**o**der *(to be able to)*, d**o**rmir *(to sleep)*, v**o**lver *(to return)*
2 e → ie qu**e**rer *(to want)*, pref**e**rir *(to prefer)*, emp**e**zar *(to start)*
3 e → i p**e**dir *(to ask for)*, rep**e**tir *(to repeat)*
4 u → ue j**u**gar *(to play)*

The most common stem-changing verbs are from the first two groups.

5 Escucha y contesta las preguntas para cada diálogo. (1–3)

a What are they doing?
b What is suggested as an activity?
c Can they do it? (If not, give the excuse.)
d What else is suggested?
e When do they arrange to meet?
f Where do they arrange to meet?

No puedo ir porque…	Tengo que…
estoy ocupado/a.	hacer los deberes.
estoy leyendo.	hacer de canguro.
estoy viendo…	salir con mis padres.
no me apetece.	limpiar mi dormitorio.
no tengo dinero.	quedarme en casa.
voy a salir con…	trabajar.
ya he quedado con…	visitar a…

6 Haz el diálogo con tu compañero/a. Usa el diálogo del ejercicio 4 como modelo. Luego inventa tu propio diálogo.

- ● Washing the dog because very dirty.
- ■ Football match – Saturday afternoon?
- ● Can't: have to visit aunt.
- ■ Football in park, Sunday?
- ● Yes! Afterwards, can go to the cinema.
- ■ Meet at 3.15?
- ● 3.30 better. Have to do homework beforehand.
- ■ Meet in the park?
- ● No – meet at the bus station.

The bullets are just a sketch of what you might say. Use the dialogue in exercise 4 as a model and try to include as much language as possible.

Exclamations	*Phrases for gaining time*
¡Qué guay!	Pues… *Well…*
¡Claro (que sí)!	Bueno… *Well…*
¡Qué bien!	A ver… *Let's see…*
¡Qué pena!	Vale… *Okay…*
¡Vaya!	

- Writing reviews
- Using the personal a to talk about other people
- Using absolute superlatives

4 Una crítica

1 ***Look at this image from the film* Pan's Labyrinth. *Which adjectives would you use to describe the scene? Write a few sentences in Spanish.***

Ejemplo: *Esta escena de la película me parece sorprendente…*

me parece…
es…
- deprimente
- misteriosa
- bonita/hermosa
- original
- emocionante
- fascinante
- rara/extraña
- fea
- mágica
- terrorífica
- sorprendente
- impresionante
- triste
- feliz/alegre

2 **Escucha y lee el texto sobre la película *El Laberinto del fauno*. Busca las frases en el texto (en negrita).**

1 the characters
2 the sound effects
3 it tells the story of
4 the special effects
5 create a mysterious atmosphere
6 I would recommend it because
7 the film deals with
8 certain scenes
9 acts in the role of
10 a fairytale
11 I have just seen
12 developed into

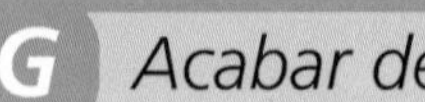

G *Acabar de*

228

When you want to say that you have just done something, use **acabar de** + **infinitive**
The verb **acabar** works like a normal **-ar** verb.
Sentences with **acabar de** don't translate word for word into English.

Acabo de **leer** un libro muy interesante.
I have just read a very interesting book.
¿Acabas de **mandar** un correo?
Have you just sent an email?

Acabo de ver una película increíble que se llama *El laberinto del fauno,* ambientada en 1944, cinco años después del final de la Guerra Civil Española. **Cuenta la historia de** Ofelia, una niña de trece años que tiene que irse a vivir a un pequeño pueblo en el norte de España con su madre y su nuevo padrastro, el villano de la historia. El padrastro se llama Vidal y es un capitán de la guardia fascista muy cruel.

Una noche, Ofelia descubre las ruinas de un laberinto donde vive un fauno, una criatura fantástica que le hace una increíble revelación: Ofelia es la princesa de un mundo mágico. **La película trata de** la historia de Ofelia entre dos mundos: la realidad de la dictadura franquista y este mundo mágico.

Lo que más me gusta de la película son **los personajes** fantásticos del mundo mágico. Ivana Baquero **interpreta el papel de** Ofelia y es una actriz excelente. **Los efectos sonoros** y **los efectos especiales** consiguen **crear un ambiente de misterio**. La fotografía es espectacular; **algunas escenas** son durísimas y otras son bellísimas. El final de la película es a la vez triste y feliz.

En realidad, la película es **un cuento de hadas** narrado por Guillermo Del Toro, el famoso director de *Blade 2* y *Hellboy.* Al principio creí que era una película de aventuras tipo *Narnia,* pero después **se convirtió en** una historia muy seria. **La recomendaría porque** no sólo es una película de terror y suspense, sino que también es una historia con sentimiento.

3 **Lee el texto y escoge las cuatro frases correctas.**

1 The thirteen year old girl discovers a magical world.
2 There are four types of monster in the film.
3 The film is not about war.
4 The villain is the cruel step-father.
5 There are no special effects in the film.
6 The film takes place in Spain.
7 The reviewer did not like the film.

G Absolute superlatives ➲218

In English absolute superlatives are made by adding the words *very*, *really*, *extremely*, etc., to an adjective. To express the same in Spanish add **-ísimo** to the end of an adjective. If the adjective ends in a vowel, remove it before adding this ending.

Difícil *(difficult)* → dificil**ísimo** *(incredibly difficult)*
Hermoso *(beautiful)* → hermos**ísimo** *(so beautiful)*

The ending **-ísimo** changes in the same way as adjectives ending with **-o**.
El actor es guap**ísimo**. *The actor is extremely handsome.*
Las actrices son guap**ísimas**. *The actresses are extremely beautiful.*

4 **Habla de artistas, autores, actores o músicos.**

- ¿Qué autor/artista/actor/actriz/músico admiras más? ¿Por qué?
- Adoro a JK Rowling porque sus libros son interesantísimos. Me fascinan los libros de JK Rowling porque son divertidísimos.

Admiro a… Adoro a… Odio a…	porque sus pinturas son porque sus películas son porque sus libros son porque su música es	interesantísimo/a(s). divertidísimo/a(s). rarísimo/a(s). feísimo/a(s). bellísimo/a(s). buenísimo/a(s). anticuadísimo/a(s). aburridísimo/a(s).
Me gustan Me encantan Me interesan Me fascinan	las pinturas de… porque son las películas de… porque son los libros de… porque son la música de… porque es	

The personal a

Remember to use the personal **a** when you are talking about your feelings/opinions of *other people* with verbs like: **adorar** *(to love)*, **admirar** *(to admire)*, **odiar** *(to hate)*.

Admiro **a** Penélope cruz porque es una actriz buenísima.
I admire Penélope cruz because she is an excellent actress.
Adoro **a** Joan Miró, el artista español. *I love Joan Miró, the Spanish artist.*
Odio **a** Picasso. *I hate Picasso.*

5 **Escucha. Copia y completa la tabla en inglés. (1–6)**

	What is discussed? (film, book, etc.)	Opinion ♥ / ♥✗	Information
1	film	♥	sound effects are mysterious and atmospheric

El guión es una adaptación de una historia original de…
la banda sonora
los efectos especiales

6 **Escribe sobre una película que te interese.**

- *Whose films do you want to write about? their work?* Adoro a… Me fascinan las películas de… porque son… Voy a escribir sobre…
- *What does it deal with? Who are the main characters/actors?* Trata de…, los personajes principales son…, …actúa en el papel de…
- *What story does it tell? How does it end?* Cuenta la historia de…, tiene un final…
- *Highlight certain aspects of the film.* Lo que más me gusta de la película es/son… el guión, la banda sonora, los efectos especiales, la historia, los personajes, la fotografía…

- Talking about new technology
- Revising comparatives
- Using language of debate

5 La tecnología

1 ***Read the texts and think of an appropriate word for each gap. Then listen to check if the speaker used the same words.***

1 En mi (a) ______ siempre paso muchas horas navegando por (b) ______. Tengo mi propia (c) ______ web donde escribo sobre mi vida y mis pasatiempos. También uso mucho *Facebook* para saber lo que hacen mis amigos.

2 Hoy en día mucha (a) ______ tiene un ordenador portátil, en vez de un ordenador de sobremesa. (b) ______ que los ordenadores portátiles (c) ______ más útiles. Con un ordenador portátil puedo ver DVD cuando viajo en tren o en coche.

3 Siempre compro cosas como (a) ______, libros, o artículos de segunda mano en páginas (b) ______ como *eBay*. En mi (c) ______, las compras por Internet son bastante seguras.

4 Me (a) ______ usar mi ordenador y mando (b) ______ electrónicos a todos mis amigos. Todo el mundo lo hace hoy en día, ¡incluso mi abuela! El problema es que (c) ______ recibo mucho correo basura de gente que quiere venderme tonterías.

2 **Lee las opiniones del ejercicio 1 y busca las frases en español.**

1 I spend a lot of hours
2 I use
3 nowadays
4 a laptop
5 second hand
6 quite safe
7 even my grandma!
8 spam
9 to sell me stupid things

Remember that, when you are giving your opinion, using comparatives will help to add variety, and variety can make you sound impressive if you are also accurate.

más + adjective + **que**…	*more… than…*
menos + adjective + **que**…	*less… than…*
mejor que…	*better than…*
peor que…	*worse than…*
tan + adjective + **como**…	*as… as…*

Remember to make your adjectives agree with the nouns you are describing:

Tu ordenador portátil es **más caro que** mi PC.
Your laptop is more expensive than my computer.

You can also compare two activities using verbs in the **infinitive**:
Hacer compras por Internet es **más** cómodo **que ir** al centro comercial. *Shopping on the Internet is more convenient than going to the shopping centre.*

3 **Escucha. Copia y completa la tabla en inglés. (1–4)**

	comparing	opinion?
1	*online shopping and shopping centres*	*online shopping faster and…*

los correos electrónicos		es/son…	
las cartas tradicionales		más/menos… que…	
los chats		baratos/as	caros/as
comprar por Internet		peligrosos/as	seguros/as
comprar en el centro comercial		rápidos/as	lentos/as
los CD	iTunes	divertidos/as	cómodos/as
las fotografías tradicionales	*Facebook*	necesarios/as	importantes

4 Haz un diálogo con tu compañero/a.

- ¿Qué opinas de los correos electrónicos / los ordenadores portátiles / las compras por Internet / los móviles / *Facebook* / los libros electrónicos?
- Para mí los correos electrónicos son… Son más/menos… que…

En mi opinión…
Para mí…
Pienso que/creo que…
Por un lado… por otro lado…
Me parece que…
A mi modo de ver…

5 Lee los textos y escribe M (María), J (Juan) or M+J (María y Juan).

Who…

1 uses the Internet to do homework?
2 has friends in other countries through the Internet?
3 thinks that the Internet has its disadvantages?
4 mentions activities with friends away from the computer?
5 has parents who think there are dangers?
6 says they use the Internet with care?
7 feels the Internet is necessary these days?

María

Uso mucho el ordenador en mi tiempo libre. Por las tardes, después de hacer mis deberes, descargo música y chateo con mis amigas. Tengo amigas por todo el mundo gracias a esta tecnología. Mis padres piensan que los chats son peligrosos porque puede haber criminales, por ejemplo, adultos con malas intenciones que se hacen pasar por gente de nuestra edad. Sin embargo, yo siempre uso los chats con cuidado, y nunca doy ni mi número de teléfono, ni información personal a las personas con quien hablo. ¡Nunca!
Otra cosa que suelo hacer por Internet es comprar de todo. Vivo lejos de nuestro centro comercial y no hay autobuses hasta allí. Creo que comprar por Internet garantiza precios más baratos y es mucho más cómodo. No puedo vivir sin Internet.

Juan

Hola, ¿que tal? ¿Internet? A mi modo de ver Internet es esencial hoy en día porque la gente lo usa en el trabajo, en los institutos, en su tiempo libre y tiene muchas ventajas. En mi caso, lo uso para hacer mis deberes todos los días, ya que cuando tengo que escribir algo, navego por Internet para buscar información. Es más fácil, más rápido y más entretenido que ir a la biblioteca.
En mi tiempo libre, por las tardes y los fines de semana, lo uso para jugar a videojuegos con amigos que están en otros países. Una desventaja de Internet es que muchas veces juegas solo y no ves a los amigos que viven en el mismo barrio. Por supuesto también tengo amigos que viven cerca de mi casa. Jugamos al fútbol o charlamos. No paso todo mi tiempo con el ordenador.

hacerse pasar por = *pretending to be*

6 Escribe sobre las ventajas y desventajas de Internet.
Plan a text that covers the following points:

- *How often you use the Internet and what for:* Uso Internet todos los días. Lo uso para jugar…, chatear…, mandar…, ver…, descargar… Suelo…
- *Your opinion of the things you do (use phrases of opinions and comparatives):* A mi modo de ver… Es más… que…
- *Mention any advantages:* Tiene muchas ventajas, por ejemplo se puede descargar…, mandar…
- *Mention a disadvantage that you, your parents or your friends see in the Internet:* Una desventaja es que…

Prueba oral

Leisure

You are going to be interviewed by your teacher. You will play the role of a young actor or actress and your teacher will play the role of the interviewer. Your teacher could ask you the following:

- Tell me a bit about yourself – name, age, profession, etc.
- What sort of films do you prefer? Why?
- Which actor or actress do you admire most? Why?
- Do you prefer to go to the cinema or watch a DVD at home?
- Do you think the Internet will destroy traditional cinemas?
- Have you made a film recently?

Remember you will have to respond to an unexpected question. The dialogue will last for between 4 and 6 minutes.

You are going to hear Cheryl, an exam candidate, taking part in the above interview with her teacher. Listen to part 1. Which of the first three questions above will Cheryl use each of the following phrases to answer? Then listen to part 1 again to check whether you were right.

1 es una pregunta difícil…
2 me encantan sus películas…
3 me encanta todo tipo de películas…
4 tiene mucho talento al interpretar a sus personajes
5 vivo sola pero…
6 hace papeles en inglés y en español
7 los personajes como Bugs Bunny
8 es una actriz buenísima

hace un papel = *to act a part*
los personajes = *characters*

Listen to part 1 again. Copy and complete the table below about the actress, Mónica.

age	nationality	city lives in	favourite type of film (2 details)	reasons for favourite actor and actress (4 details)

Listen to part 2 of Cheryl's interview and note down the words that fill the gaps.

– Pues, a mí me gusta Russell Crowe. ¿Prefieres ir al cine o ver un DVD en casa?
– Normalmente veo DVD porque (1) ___ estar en casa. Pero (2) ___ ponen una película increíble la veo en el cine. (3) ___, prefiero ver las películas de acción en el cine (4) ___ los efectos especiales son mejores en la gran pantalla. El sábado pasado llovía, y (5) ___ alquilé el DVD de Gladiador. Lo vi en casa, (6) ___ sin duda, esas pelis son mejores en el cine.
– ¿Crees que Internet va a destruir los cines tradicionales?
– No. (7) ___ es mucho mejor ver algunas películas en el cine. (8) ___, siempre habrá cines tradicionales porque la gente prefiere ver las películas en la gran pantalla. (9) ___, (10) ___ descargar una película es necesario tener un ordenador bueno. ¡No todos tenemos buenos ordenadores!

la gran pantalla = *the big screen*

Look at the words you identified in exercise 3. How would you describe them? Can you think of any others?

- connectives to add information
- phrases to express a point of view

Read the text from exercise 3 again. Can you find the two direct object pronouns that Cheryl used?

Now listen to part 3 of Cheryl's interview and answer the questions.

las escenas = *scenes*
grabar = *to film*

1. Which tense is the first question and the beginning of the answer in? Can you explain why this tense is used?
2. Can you spot an example of the present continuous tense in her first answer?
3. What is the unexpected question that Cheryl's teacher asks and what does it mean?

Now it's your turn! Prepare your answers to the task and then do the interview with your partner or your teacher.

- Use the Grade Studio and your answers to exercises 1–6 to help you plan.
- Adapt what Cheryl said as the actress Mónica but add your own ideas.
- Prepare your answers to the questions and try to predict what the unexpected question could be. The examiner might base this question on something you have already said, or ask something totally new!
- Record the conversation. Ask a partner to listen to it and say how well you performed.

Award each other one star, two stars or three stars for each of these categories:
- *Pronunciation*
- *Confidence and fluency*
- *Range of tenses*
- *Variety of vocabulary and expressions*
- *Using longer sentences*
- *Taking the initiative*

What do you need to do next time to improve your performance?

GradeStudio

To produce a good answer you need to be able to use a variety of structures.
- Use a **variety of tenses**. Try to include past (preterite), present and future tenses. Can you find examples of these in Cheryl's answers?
- Give simple **opinions**. Cheryl uses phrases like *'me encanta(n)'* and *'prefiero…'*. Can you think of any others?
- Use **adjectives** to describe things. Cheryl uses *'divertido'* to describe cartoons. Can you think of others that would apply to films or TV programmes?

To go a step further, you need to use a wider variety of language.
- Use the **preterite** to talk about completed actions in the past and the **perfect tense** to talk about general experiences (as in exercise 6).
- Use a **wider range of connectives** like the ones you identified in exercise 3: *por eso* (because of this), *además* (what's more) and *por ejemplo* (for example).
- Express your **point of view**. Cheryl uses *'creo que…'* and *'a mi modo de ver…'* but which other ones could you use?

For a really impressive answer:
- **Express your point of view** and **justify it**. Can you find sentences in exercise 3 where Cheryl does this?
- Use complex tenses like the **present continuous tense** to talk about what you are doing at the moment (as in exercise 6).
- Rather than repeat a noun twice, try to use **direct object pronouns**: *'Me gustan las películas de terror.'* → *'Las veo una vez al mes.'*
- Use an **absolute superlative**. Cheryl uses *'buenísima'* to describe Penélope Cruz.

Prueba escrita

Read the text and choose the correct title for each paragraph. What words/phrases support your decisions?

a The author **b** The novel **c** A passion for reading **d** Future reading

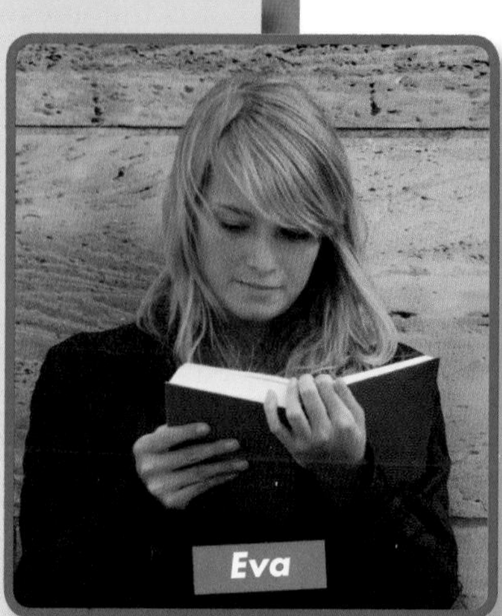

1 Me encanta leer. Mi pasión por la lectura empezó cuando tenía ocho años. Leo muchísimo, ¡normalmente leo un libro a la semana! Lo que más me gusta leer son novelas que tratan de fantasía o de ciencia ficción, pero la verdad es que me gusta leer cualquier cosa.

2 Ahora estoy leyendo una novela impresionante de una autora española que se llama Laura Gallego. Se titula *La hija de la noche* y es un libro de misterio. Cuenta la historia de un pueblo francés del siglo catorce donde pasan cosas extrañas. Para empezar, en este pueblo hay vampiros. La protagonista es Isabelle, una joven que vive desde hace poco tiempo en el pueblo y que nunca sale de casa. Me gusta mucho Isabelle porque es un personaje bastante complejo. A mí me encantan las historias de vampiros y por eso siempre me interesa leer algo sobre este tema. Sin embargo, no me gustan las historias de miedo, solo las de misterio.

3 Laura Gallego nació el 11 de octubre de 1977 en Valencia. A los once años escribió su primer libro, una historia fantástica, con su amiga Miriam. Hasta ahora ha escrito más de dieciséis novelas. Además, le gusta viajar, dormir, hacer deporte, y le encantan los animales.

4 En el futuro me gustaría leer más novelas sobre otros países, porque quiero aprender de otras culturas. También quiero leer más libros en español, creo que leeré alguna obra de Isabel Allende y de Gabriel García Márquez. Es más difícil leer en español que en inglés, pero me gusta.

Answer the questions in English.

1 When did Eva's love of reading start?
2 What nationality is the author of the book that Eva is reading?
3 In which country is the story set?
4 What is the name of the main character in *La hija de la noche*?
5 Where was the author of *La hija de la noche* born?
6 How old was the author when she wrote her first book?
7 Why does Eva want to read books about other countries?

Find the equivalent of these expressions in Spanish in the text.

1 My passion for reading started when…
2 What I like reading most…
3 …novels which are about…
4 I am reading…
5 …whose name is…
6 It tells the story of…
7 The main character is…
8 …because she is quite a complex character.
9 I would like to read more novels about…

You might be asked to write a review of a book or a film as a Controlled Assessment task. Use the Grade Studio to help you prepare your account.

GradeStudio

To produce a good answer you need to use a variety of structures and use simple connectives to extend your sentences.

- Find four examples in the first paragraph where Eva uses the **present tense** to talk about her love of reading.
- Find two examples in the third paragraph where Eva uses the **preterite** to talk about the life of the author of her book.
- Find an example in the fourth paragraph where Eva uses the **future tense** to talk about what she wants to read in the future.
- Find five examples of simple **connectives** that Eva uses in her text.

To go a step further you need to use a wider range of language. This might include: other tenses such as the **present perfect**, verbs referring to a **variety of people** (I, he/she, we, they) and **detailed opinions**.

- Look at how Eva uses the **perfect** tense to say how many books Laura Gallego has written.
- Look at how Eva uses the **present continuous** to say what she is reading at the moment.
- Find examples of where Eva talks about **other people**.
- Eva uses more **varied expressions** to give detailed **opinions**: *'Lo que más me gusta...'*

For a really impressive answer:

- Include **complex sentences** with two tenses in them. Eva says: *'Mi pasión por la lectura empezó cuando tenía ocho años.'* Can you find three more examples of a complex sentence in the text?
- Use **adverbs**. Eva uses *'normalmente'* and *'siempre'*. Can you use some adverbs in your own text?
- Include more **unusual words** like *'donde'* and *'cuando'* to extend your sentences. Can you find examples of these in the text? What do they mean?

Now write a review of a book, film or painting.

- Adapt Eva's text and use language from Module 6. Write at least 200 words.
- If you need to write something which is not in the book then keep it simple. When you look up words in a dictionary make sure that you choose the right one by looking carefully at any examples given.
- Structure your text carefully. Organise what you write in paragraphs.

General summary of your review

Introduce yourself and talk about your hobbies. What sort of books do you like?

Main paragraph

Introduce the subject of your review:
- *What is it called and who is it by?*
- *Who are the characters and what is the story about?*
- *Why did you like it?*
- *Who is the author? Where does the author come from?*

Conclusion

What sort of books would you like to read in the future?

Check carefully what you have written.

- spelling and accents (accents on preterite, imperfect and future verbs?)
- verb endings (correct when talking about other people: *nació, escribió*?)
- adjective agreement (correct when describing a book, author or character?)

1 ***Read the two adverts from job agencies in Spain. Which agency could each person apply to for a job? Write the letter of each statement followed by M (Agencia Miraflores), P (Agencia Pedrosa) or M+P (Agencia Miraflores and Agencia Pedrosa).*** **(6 marks)**

Agencia Miraflores

Trabajo de verano

¡Oportunidades para jóvenes!

Si tienes más de 21 años ofrecemos puestos de 16 a 24 horas a la semana

Buscamos a:

* camareros
* dependientes
* cajeros
* recepcionistas
* jardineros
* secretarias

¿Hablas bien tres idiomas europeos?

¿Sabes usar programas informáticos?

¡Necesitas un poco de experiencia!

Agencia Pedrosa

Trabajo a tiempo parcial

¡Salarios buenos y horarios flexibles!

Si tienes 17 años como mínimo y buscas trabajo interesante podemos ofrecerte puestos de 5 a 12 horas por semana

¿Sabes trabajar de canguro, servir bebidas y comida, lavar coches, repartir periódicos o trabajar con el ordenador?

¿No tienes experiencia de trabajo?

¡No importa - tenemos trabajo para ti!

a I'm 17 and don't have much experience.
b I would like to work in a café or restaurant.
c I would like to do some babysitting.
d I want to use my Spanish, French and English.
e I want to work in a shop and I can use a till.
f I have good ICT and computer skills.

In this type of task some answers will be in only one of the texts and some will be in both texts, so read both texts carefully. Take your time and don't rush to give the first answer that you find. The information in the question may be expressed differently in the texts, e.g. 'work in a café or restaurant' – *servir bebidas y comida*.

2 ***Read Sofía's letter about a trip to the cinema and decide whether the statements below are T (true), F (false) or NM (not mentioned).*** **(4 marks)**

a Sofía has been to the cinema with her boyfriend.
b She had a drink during the film.
c It wasn't her favourite kind of film.
d She plans to download the soundtrack tomorrow.

la banda sonora = *soundtrack*

¡Hola Ana!

Estoy escribiendo esta carta para decirte que he pasado una noche estupenda en Sevilla. ¡He visto una película fantástica! La protagonista es mi actriz favorita, Penélope Cruz, que es una superestrella. Comí palomitas de maíz durante la sesión y después fui a una cafetería a tomar una Coca-Cola porque tenía mucha sed. En general prefiero las comedias, pero esta película romántica es inolvidable. Ya he descargado la banda sonora y mañana voy a comprar el DVD.

Un abrazo, **Sofía**

3 ***Teresa shows you an email (on page 123) she has received from her friend Alberto in reply to an invitation. Read the email and write the correct letter for each answer.***

1 How do you think Teresa will feel about Alberto's reply to her invitation? (1 mark)
a amused **b** disappointed **c** delighted

2 What kind of attitude do you think Alberto has to money? (1 mark)
a work hard, save hard **b** earn a lot, spend a lot **c** work little, spend a lot

3 What kind of person do you think Alberto is? (1 mark)
a caring **b** selfish **c** reliable

¡Hola, Teresa! Gracias por tu invitación para salir esta semana. Ya sé que hace mucho tiempo que no nos vemos, pero la verdad es que voy a la biblioteca el lunes, a la piscina el martes, a mi clase de música el miércoles, a casa de mi abuela el jueves y al teatro el viernes. Así que estoy muy ocupado en este momento.

Tengo un problema. Mi padre no me da suficiente paga y necesito mucho dinero. No tengo ganas de buscar trabajo - es aburrido y soy un poco perezoso. Tengo la intención de viajar y tomarme un año sabático antes de ir a la universidad, pero no me queda nada en el banco. ¿Por qué papá no me da más dinero?

No sé si voy a tener mucho tiempo o dinero en el futuro, pero escríbeme pronto. Me gusta recibir tus noticias. Un abrazo, **Alberto**

***Listen to the debate about extreme sports. What does each person think? Write each person's name followed by a, b or c.* (4 marks)**

a in favour
b against
c no strong feelings either way

Jaime
Luisa
Pepe
Rosa

Listen for positive and negative adjectives, which tell you what someone's attitude is. Also listen for expressions like *a favor de* (in favour of), *en contra de* (against) and *me da/dan igual* (I don't mind). Remember that negatives can also completely change the meaning of a sentence.

***Listen to two people giving opinions on their jobs. What* positive *aspects of their jobs do they mention? For each person, write the correct letter for each of the headings.* (2 marks for each person)**

Teresa

Example: **Past job:** c
Present job:
Future job:

a holidays
b uniform
c independence
d responsibility
e colleagues

Tomás

Past job:
Example: **Present job:** b
Future job:

a boss
b customers
c salary
d hours
e travel

In 'time frame' questions like this listen carefully for the tenses the speakers use (especially the verb endings) and time phrases. Beware of 'distractors'. Some things will be mentioned, but not necessarily as positive aspects of the job. So, listening for positive and negative adjectives will help you.

Listen to Miguel talking about his new exercise programme and answer the questions.

1 What were two advantages to Miguel of doing the programme? (2 marks)
2 What were two disadvantages of doing it? (2 marks)
3 Afterwards, how did he feel the programme had been? (1 mark)
a pointless **b** easy **c** challenging
4 What would he do differently on another occasion? (1 mark)
a improve his attitude and motivation
b find a 'buddy' to train with
c not listen to his parents

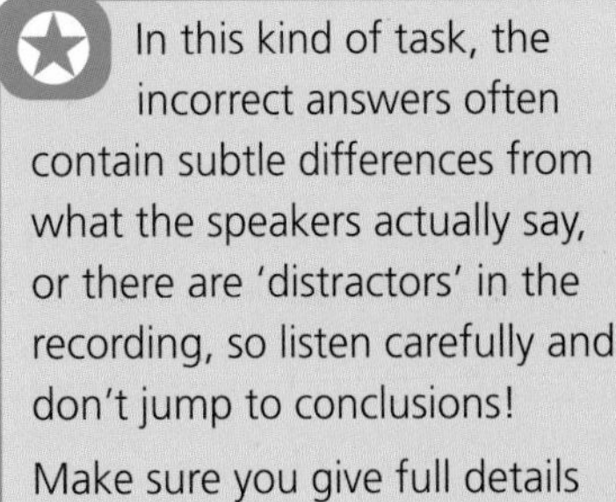
In this kind of task, the incorrect answers often contain subtle differences from what the speakers actually say, or there are 'distractors' in the recording, so listen carefully and don't jump to conclusions!

Make sure you give full details in your answer, or you may lose marks.

Palabras

La tele y el cine *Television and cinema*

el telediario/las noticias	*news*
las películas de amor/las películas románticas	*love films*
las películas de artes marciales	*martial arts films*
las películas de ciencia-ficción	*sci-fi films*
las películas de terror	*horror films*
las películas del Oeste	*Westerns*
las series de policías	*detective series*
las telenovelas	*soap operas*
los concursos	*game shows*
los dibujos animados	*cartoons*
los documentales	*documentaries*
los programas de deportes	*sports programmes*
¿Qué ponen en la tele hoy/esta tarde/mañana?	*What's on TV today/this afternoon/this morning?*
¿Quieres venir a mi casa a ver…?	*Do you want to come to my house to watch…?*
¿Quieres ir al cine a ver…?	*Do you want to go to the cinema to see…?*
¿Quieres ver… en el cine?	*Do you want to see… at the cinema?*
¿Te apetece ir al cine?	*Do you fancy going to the cinema?*
(No) me apetece ir al cine.	*I (don't) fancy going to the cinema.*
¿Para qué sesión?	*For which showing?*
¿A qué hora empieza la película?	*What time does the film start?*
Dos entradas para…, por favor.	*Two tickets for…, please.*
curioso/a	*curious*
educativo/a	*educational*
emocionante	*moving*
entretenido/a	*entertaining*
inolvidable	*unforgettable*
largo/a	*long*
lento/a	*slow*
malo/a	*bad*
tonto/a	*stupid*
Quiero… entradas para… de las tres y cuarto, por favor.	*I'd like… tickets for… at 3.15, please.*
Pues…, ¿me da… entradas para…?, por favor.	*Well…, could you give me… tickets for…, please?*
¿Para qué sesión?	*For which showing?*
Para la sesión de…	*For the… showing.*
¿Cuánto cuesta una entrada?	*How much is a ticket?*
¿Quiere palomitas de maíz, caramelos o refrescos?	*Do you want popcorn, sweets or drinks?*
Sí, quiero, por favor.	*Yes, can I have… please?*
¿Cuánto es?	*How much is it?*
Son… con…	*They are… with…*

La paga *Pocket money*

los lunes/martes	*on Mondays/Tuesdays*
nunca	*never*
siempre	*always*
todos los días	*every day*
una vez a la semana/una vez al mes	*once a week/month*
Después de…	*After…*
Antes de…	*Before…*
patinar/hacer patinaje	*skate*
nadar/hacer natación	*swim*
hacer atletismo	*do athletics*
jugar al fútbol	*play football*
hacer equitación/montar a caballo	*go horse-riding*
jugar al tenis de mesa/ping-pong	*play table tennis*
jugar al voleibol	*play volleyball*
jugar al golf	*play golf*
jugar al baloncesto	*play basketball*
esquiar/hacer esquí	*ski*
mis padres me dan…	*my parents give me…*
mi padre/mi madre me da…	*my dad/my mum gives me…*
recibo…	*I get…*
a la semana	*per week*
al día	*per day*
al mes	*per month*
cada quince días	*every fortnight*
compro…	*I buy…*
caramelos	*sweets*
libros	*books*
maquillaje	*make-up*
revistas	*magazines*
ropa	*clothes*
saldo para el móvil	*top-ups for my mobile*
Lo gasto en…	*I spend it on…*
Lo/La/Los/Las compro todas las semanas.	*I buy it/them every week.*
Ahorro dinero para comprar algo más caro.	*I save money to buy something more expensive.*
Sé que malgasto el dinero, pero no me importa.	*I know that I waste my money but I don't mind.*
No malgasto el dinero.	*I don't waste my money.*
Antes tenía menos dinero, pero ahora…	*Before I used to get less money but now…*
Es muy importante ahorrar para el futuro.	*It's very important to save for the future.*
Es importante divertirse.	*It's important to have fun.*

El campeonato *The championship*

hacer alpinismo	*go climbing*
hacer footing	*go jogging*
hacer gimnasia	*do gymnastics*
hacer patinaje	*skate*
hacer vela	*sail*
ir de pesca	*go fishing*
jugar a la pelota vasca	*play Basque pelota*
jugar al billar	*play snooker*
practicar béisbol	*play baseball*
En el cole suelo…	*At school I usually…*
Juego en un equipo de…	*I play for a… team.*
Entrenamos en el polideportivo/la piscina… una vez a la semana	*We train at the sports centre/pool… once a week.*
En mi tiempo libre hago/juego al…	*In my free time, I do/play…*
Soy hincha de…	*I'm a fan of…*
anteayer	*the day before yesterday*
ayer	*yesterday*

Los deportes de riesgo *Extreme sports*

el parkour	*parkour (free running)*
el snowboard	*snowboarding*
el submarinismo	*diving*
el wakeboard	*wakeboarding*
la corrida	*bullfighting*
Me encanta(n)…	*I love…*
Me gusta(n)…	*I like…*
Me fascina(n)…	*I'm fascinated by…*
Me interesa(n)…	*I'm interested in…*
Me interesa(n) más…	*I'm more interested in…*
Me da(n) miedo…	*I'm scared of…*
Odio…	*I hate…*
Prefiero…	*I prefer…*
No soporto…	*I can't stand…*
porque es/son…	*because it's/they are…*
arriesgado/a	*risky*
barato/a	*cheap*
caro/a	*expensive*
difícil	*difficult*
emocionante	*exciting*
fácil	*easy*
impresionante	*impressive*
peligroso/a	*dangerous*
seguro/a	*safe*
sorprendente	*surprising*
En mi opinión/A mi modo de ver…	*In my opinion/The way I see it…*
este tipo de deporte es demasiado…	*this type of sport is too…*
Lo(s) veo en la tele/en Internet.	*I watch it/them on the TV/Internet.*
Lo(s) hago… veces al año.	*I do it/them… times a year.*
Hice… durante mis vacaciones el verano pasado.	*I did… during my holidays last summer.*
Me gustaría hacer…	*I'd like to do…*
Si tengo dinero en el futuro, haré…	*If I have money in the future, I will…*
Te puedes divertir de otra manera	*You can enjoy yourself in other ways.*

¿Quedamos? *Shall we meet?*

Estoy…	*I am…*
viendo la televisión	*watching TV*
leyendo un libro	*reading a book*
comiendo…	*eating…*
no estoy haciendo nada	*I'm not doing anything*
¿A qué hora quedamos?	*What time shall we meet?*
¿Dónde quedamos?	*Where shall we meet?*
¡Claro que sí!	*Of course!*
¡Qué bien!	*Great!*
¡Qué guay!	*How cool!*
¡Qué lástima!	*What a pity!*
¡Qué pena!	*What a shame!*
Lo siento. No puedo ir porque…	*I'm sorry I can't come because…*
Estoy ocupado/a.	*I am busy.*
No me apetece.	*I don't feel like it.*
No tengo dinero.	*I don't have any money.*
Voy a salir con…	*I am going to go out with…*
Ya he quedado con…	*I have already agreed to meet…*
Tengo que…	*I have to…*
hacer de canguro	*babysit*
hacer los deberes	*do my homework*
limpiar	*clean*
quedarme en casa	*stay at home*
salir con mis padres	*go out with my parents*
trabajar	*work*
visitar a…	*visit…*

Una crítica *A review*

Me parece…	*It seems… to me.*
Admiro a…	*I admire…*
Adoro a…	*I adore…*
Odio a…	*I hate…*
porque sus películas son…	*because his/her films are…*
porque su música es…	*because his/her music is…*
las pinturas de… porque son…	*…'s paintings because they are…*
las películas de… porque son…	*…'s films because they are…*
los libros de… porque son…	*…'s books because they are…*
la música de… porque es…	*…'s music because it is…*
aburridísimo/a(s)	*really boring*
anticuadísimo/a(s)	*really old-fashioned*
bellísimo/a(s)	*really beautiful*
buenísimo/a(s)	*really good*
divertidísimo/a(s)	*really fun*
feísimo/a(s)	*really ugly*
interesantísimo/a(s)	*really interesting*
rarísimo/a(s)	*really strange*
el artista	*artist*
el autor	*author*
el músico	*musician*
el actor/la actriz	*actor/actress*
la banda sonora	*soundtrack*
la fotografía	*photography*
los efectos especiales	*special effects*
los personajes	*characters*
Cuenta la historia de…	*It tells the story of…*
Trata de…	*It's about…*

La tecnología *Technology*

las cartas tradicionales	*traditional letters*
comprar por Internet	*internet shopping*
las fotografías tradicionales	*traditional photographs*
los CD	*CDs*
los chats	*chatrooms*
los correos electrónicos	*e-mail*
más/menos… que	*more/less… than*
barato/a	*cheap*
peligroso/a	*dangerous*
rápido/a	*fast*
divertido/a	*funny, amusing*
necesario/a	*necessary*
seguro/a	*safe*
lento/a	*slow*
cómodo/a	*comfortable*
Me parece que…	*It seems to me that…*
Para mí…	*For me…*
Pienso que/Creo que…	*I think that…*
Por un lado… por otro lado…	*On one hand… on the other hand…*
Hoy en día	*Nowadays*
el correo basura	*spam*
el móvil	*mobile*
el ordenador de sobremesa	*desktop computer*
el ordenador portátil	*laptop*
la página web	*web page*

- Talking about your home
- Using prepositions
- Using relative clauses

Repaso *Hogar, dulce hogar*

1 Con tu compañero/a, describe estas casas.

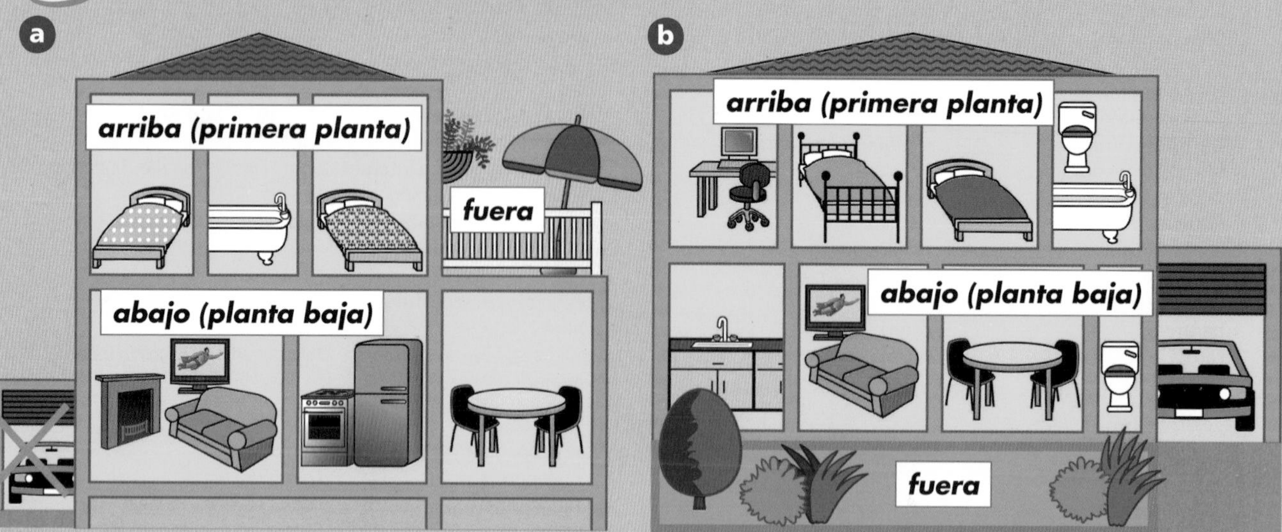

Vivo en… un piso / una casa / un apartamento / un chalé.
Tiene muchas/pocas habitaciones.

abajo	hay	un aseo	un cuarto de baño	un salón
arriba	tenemos	una cocina	un dormitorio	un jardín
fuera		un comedor	un estudio/despacho	
		una terraza	un garaje	

2 Escucha y escribe el nombre de la habitación en español. (1–6)

Questions often begin with a question word.
¿**Dónde** está mi toalla? ***Where*** *is my towel?*
This word can also be used (without an accent) in the middle of a sentence in a relative clause.
Esta es la habitación **donde** veo la televisión.
This is the room ***where*** *I watch TV.*
Can you spot examples of this in exercise 2?

3 Escucha y repite. Luego empareja los dibujos con las palabras correctas.

la alfombra	el espejo	el lavaplatos	la silla
el armario	la estantería	la moqueta	el sofá
la butaca/el sillón	el horno	la nevera/el frigorífico	la televisión
la cama	la lámpara	el ordenador	la ventana
el equipo de música	la lavadora	la puerta	

Write descriptions of a room, mentioning the furniture, but not the name of the room. See if your classmates can guess which room it is.

Example: Esta es la habitación donde hay una lámpara, una silla,…

With your partner, play a guessing game. Try to use all the prepositions in the grammar box below correctly.

- ● Está al lado de la mesa, a la izquierda.
- ■ ¿Es al armario?
- ● Sí, es correcto.
  No. Prueba otra vez.

G *Prepositions*

Prepositions show the relationship of one thing to another.

delante de	*in front of*
detrás de	*behind*
encima de	*on*
debajo de	*under*
al lado de	*next to*
a la derecha de	*on the right of*
a la izquierda de	*on the left of*
entre	*between*

de + el → del
de + la → de la

La lavadora está **al lado del** lavaplatos.
The washing machine is next to the dishwasher.

Escucha y empareja las respuestas con las preguntas. (1–8)

Ejemplo: **1** f

- **a** ¿Vives en una casa o en un piso?
- **b** ¿Qué hay abajo?
- **c** ¿Qué hay arriba?
- **d** ¿Qué hay fuera?
- **e** ¿Puedes describir el salón en tu casa?
- **f** ¿Qué haces normalmente en el salón?
- **g** ¿Qué tienes en tu dormitorio?
- **h** ¿Te gusta tu dormitorio?

En la primera planta hay…
En la planta baja hay…
En las paredes hay…
En el suelo hay…
Es la habitación donde me lavo el pelo…
Tengo que compartir mi habitación con…
Tengo que dormir en el mismo cuarto que…
Necesito tener mi propia habitación porque…

Use the questions in exercise 6 to write a description of your house. Try to extend your sentences as much as possible, using relative clauses with donde _and a variety of prepositions._

- Talking about different types of houses
- Using a variety of phrases to express opinions
- Justifying opinions

1 ¿Cómo es tu casa?

Escucha y escribe la letra de la foto correcta y los adjetivos. (1–5)

Ejemplo: **1** e – pequeña,…

a

b

c

d

e

Vivo en…		Está…
un chalé	adosado/a	en un pueblo
una casa	aislado/a	en la ciudad
un piso	antiguo/a	en las afueras
un apartamento	bonito/a	en el campo
una granja	cómodo/a	en la costa
un bloque de pisos	feo/a	en la playa
un edificio	moderno/a	en la montaña
un rascacielos	nuevo/a	
	pequeño/a	
	viejo/a	
	grande	

Listen again to the people talking about where they live. Write P (positive), N (negative) or P + N (positive and negative). Note any extra details you understand. **(1–5)**

Example: **1** P – a bit small but very comfortable house,…

Lo bueno es que…	hay…	(un) aparcamiento	(un) ascensor
Lo malo es que…	no hay…	(un) ático	(un) garaje
Lo que más me gusta es que…	tenemos…	(un) jardín (con césped)	(un) patio
Lo que menos me gusta es que…	no tenemos…	(un) sótano	(una) terraza
		habitaciones grandes	(una) piscina
		mucho/poco espacio	calefacción

Describe tu casa.

Ejemplo: Vivo en… Está en… y es… Me gusta porque… pero lo malo es que…

4 Mira la casa de Shakira y la casa de Rosa. Lee los textos. ¿Qué significan las palabras en rojo? ¿De qué casa hablan?

La casa de Shakira

La casa de Rosa

1 *No soporto la gente que vive con tanto lujo…, con toda la pobreza que hay en el mundo.* ***Manuela***

2 *Me encanta esta casa porque es modesta y muy cómoda si quieres vivir en el centro de una ciudad. Es un lugar ideal si tienes mascotas.* ***José***

3 *¡Qué casa tan bonita! La verdad es que me encanta porque es elegante y clásica. Además, tiene unas vistas a la piscina y al mar maravillosas. Lo único malo es que es muy cara.* ***Claudia***

4 *Yo pienso que esta casa es perfecta para Shakira porque es una buena persona que se preocupa por los demás, y se merece este lujo.* ***David***

5 *Prefiero la casa pequeña. Creo que el dinero no da la felicidad.* ***Isa***

6 *Me dan rabia las casas de la gente rica. Es importante tener una casa pequeña si te preocupa el medio ambiente.* ***Inés***

soportar = *to tolerate*

5 Lee los textos otra vez. Copia y completa la tabla en inglés.

	opinion	justification
1	can't tolerate people living in…	lots of poverty in the world

6 ***With your partner, discuss the following questions.***

- ¿Qué piensas de la casa de Rosa? ¿Por qué?
- ¿Qué opinas de la casa de Shakira? ¿Por qué?
- ¿En cuál de las dos casas te gustaría vivir? ¿Por qué?
- ¿Estás de acuerdo con (Manuela/José/etc.)? ¿Por qué?
- ¿Qué opinas de vivir en una granja en el campo? ¿Por qué?
- ¿Qué opinas de vivir en las afueras? ¿Por qué?
- ¿Qué piensas de vivir en la montaña? ¿Por qué?

In order to produce an impressive answer in your speaking and writing, use a variety of opinion phrases:

Pienso que…
Opino que…
Me da(n) rabia…
No soporto…
(No) Estoy de acuerdo con…
Me encanta vivir en…
Odio vivir en…

And make sure you justify your opinions!
…porque…

7 Escribe un texto y contesta a las preguntas.

¿Dónde vives?
¿En qué tipo de casa vives?
¿Dónde está?
¿Cómo es?

¿Cuántas habitaciones hay?
¿Qué hay fuera de tu casa?
¿Qué opinas de tu casa? ¿Por qué?

- Talking about your neighbourhood
- Using the imperfect and present tenses
- Understanding **tan** and **tanto/a** (so, so much, so many)

2 Mi barrio

1 Lee los textos y empareja las letras con los números.

a Mi pueblo es muy bonito. Es un lugar con mucha historia y hay muchos monumentos de interés. Es muy conocido y en verano vienen muchos turistas.

b Vivo en una importante ciudad industrial. Lo bueno es que hay muchas cosas que hacer, pero no es muy tranquila. Siempre hay mucho ruido, y también hay mucha contaminación debido a las fábricas y al enorme tráfico de la ciudad.

c Vivo en un barrio donde hay mucha pobreza. Es un barrio histórico, pero aquí no vienen turistas porque está muy sucio y no hay nada que hacer.

1 Sin embargo, el ayuntamiento dice que van a poner una zona peatonal en el centro. Es una idea muy buena. El centro estará limpio y no habrá ruidos.

2 Lo único que hay es una pista de tenis muy vieja, pero dicen que pronto van a construir un polideportivo con acceso gratis para los del barrio.

3 Hay muchas tiendas de regalos y postales para los visitantes, pero necesitamos algo para los jóvenes, como un polideportivo. Antes había una biblioteca en el pueblo, pero desafortunadamente la cerraron.

2 Busca estas frases en los textos.

a The good thing is that there are lots of things to do.
b Lots of tourists come in summer.
c We need something for the teenagers.
d There is nothing to do.
e The only thing that there is…
f The centre will be clean.

3 Escucha y escribe las preguntas en español. (1–6)

4 *With your partner talk about the two places below. Use your imagination and the questions from exercise 3.*

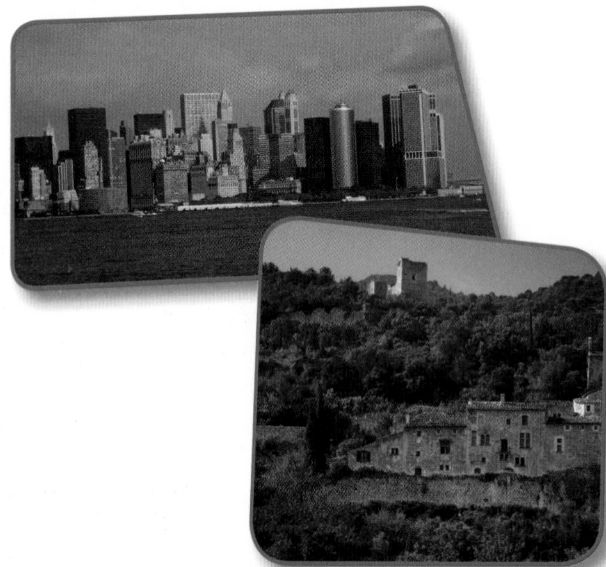

Vivo en un pueblo/una ciudad…
histórico/a, moderno/a, pequeño/a
turístico/a, grande, importante, industrial

Mi barrio/pueblo/ciudad es…
bonito/a, conocido/a, feo/a, ruidoso/a, tranquilo/a

Hay…
un centro comercial
un polideportivo
una biblioteca
un cine
una pista de tenis
muchas cosas que hacer
mucho que hacer
muchos lugares de interés
mucha contaminación
parques
salas de juegos
restaurantes
discotecas
bares

No hay…
polideportivo
mucha contaminación
centro comercial
mucho que hacer

(No) Está sucio/a, limpio/a, aislado/a.

5 Escucha y lee. Apunta los datos siguientes en inglés.

- Julio's life in the past…
- Julio's life now…

UN ADOLESCENTE SEVILLANO EN 1939

Reportero: ¿En qué tipo de casa vivías?

Julio: Vivía en una casa pequeña y modesta. ¡No había edificios tan grandes como hoy en día! Ahora vivo en un piso moderno y grande.

Reportero: Cuando eras joven, ¿cuáles eran los pasatiempos preferidos de los adolescentes?

Julio: A ver…, hacíamos cosas más simples que los pasatiempos de hoy en día. Jugábamos en la calle a la pelota o a la goma. Solo había un cine y no había discotecas, ni tampoco polideportivos. La vida era más lenta. Hoy en día los jóvenes tienen más oportunidades que nosotros: viajar, practicar deportes de riesgo, etc…

Reportero: ¿Cuál era tu juego o tu juguete preferido cuando eras adolescente?

Julio: Después de la Guerra Civil no había mucho dinero para juguetes. ¡Éramos tan pobres! Yo iba en la bicicleta de mi padre, y ese era mi juguete favorito. Ahora, mi juguete favorito es mi motocicleta, je, je.

Reportero: ¿Cómo era Sevilla hace setenta años?

Julio: Era muy diferente. Las calles estaban más sucias que ahora y había más basura, pero el río no estaba tan contaminado. No había tanto tráfico, ni tantos coches como ahora porque solo los ricos tenían coches. Ahora hay mucho tráfico porque todo el mundo tiene coche.

Julio Rubio, 75 años

G *So…, so much…, so many…*

tan + adjective **tan** barato/a	*so + adjective* *so cheap*
tanto/a + noun **tanto** tráfico	*so much + noun* *so much traffic*
tantos/as + noun **tantos** coches	*so many + noun* *so many cars*

As you have seen, *the imperfect tense* is used for descriptions in the past. It can translate as *used to*.
In the interview with Julio there are many examples of this. Look out for verbs like these. What do they mean?
había; vivía, vivías; hacía, hacíamos; iba, íbamos; jugábamos, jugaban; era, eras, éramos, eran; teníamos, tenían; comíamos
Julio also uses the present tense to talk about what things are like now. Can you find four examples of this?

6 Lee el texto otraz vez. Contesta a estas preguntas en inglés.

1. Where did Julio use to live?
2. What did young people like to do?
3. What does he say about young people now?
4. What is his favourite 'toy' nowadays?
5. What did the city used to be like?

7 Describe dónde vives ahora y dónde vivías en el pasado.

Ahora	En el pasado
Vivo en…	Vivía en…
Es…	Mi abuelo dice que antes era…
Está…	Estaba…
(No) Hay…	(No) Había…
Lo bueno/malo es que…	Lo bueno/malo era que…
Juego/voy/tengo…	Jugaba/iba/tenía…

In order to produce an impressive answer you need to use a variety of tenses and complex structures in your writing:

- examples of **tan** and **tanto**: no había **tantos** turistas
- examples of comparatives: era **más/menos**… **que** hoy en día
- examples of sentences using the imperfect and present tenses: cuando **era** joven **había**…, pero **ahora** hay…

- Talking about how you would change your city
- Using the conditional
- Developing a checklist to improve accuracy

3 Mi ciudad hoy y mañana

1 Empareja los dibujos con las frases.

a 
b 
c 
d 
e 
f 
g 
h 
i 
j 
k 

En mi ciudad…
1 hay muchos turistas.
2 hay mucho tráfico.
3 hay mucha basura.
4 hay muchos habitantes.
5 hay muchas tiendas.
6 hay una zona peatonal.
7 hay muchos museos y muchas galerías de arte.
8 no hay muchos árboles.
9 no hay muchos espacios verdes.
10 no hay red de transporte público.
11 no hay muchas áreas de ocio.

2 Escucha. Copia y completa la tabla. (1–4)

	positive	negative	improvements to be made
1	lots of trees and…	not much to do	build a bowling alley and…

G The conditional

➲210

You already know the conditional from phrases like **me gustaría** (I would like), **podría** (I/he/she could) and **debería** (I/he/she should).

Most verbs in the conditional translate as *would*: I would go, I would do, etc. To form the conditional, add imperfect endings of -er/-ir verbs to the infinitive:

	beber *(to drink)*		
(yo)	beber**ía**	(nosotros/as)	beber**íamos**
(tú)	beber**ías**	(vosotros/as)	beber**íais**
(él/ella/usted)	beber**ía**	(ellos/ellas/ustedes)	beber**ían**

A few verbs use an irregular future stem instead of the infinitive:

poner	*to put*	→	**pondr**ía	*I would put*
poder	*can*	→	**podr**ía	*I would be able*
tener	*to have*	→	**tendr**ía	*I would have*
salir	*to go out*	→	**saldr**ía	*I would go out*
hacer	*to do/make*	→	**har**ía	*I would do/make*
haber	*there is/are*	→	**habr**ía	*there would be*

deberían construir = *they should build*

The conditional looks very similar to the imperfect because the word endings look the same. However, the conditional is easy to spot as it will always have '**r**' just before the end of the word. Listen and decide whether you are hearing a conditional verb or not.

3 Escucha y lee. Luego contesta a las preguntas en inglés. (1–2)

1 What is Ramón worried about?
2 What does he do each day?
3 What is the town where he lives like?
4 What would Ramón do to improve the town?
5 What is Ruth's town like?
6 What would she like to do later in life?
7 What would she build?
8 What does she say about cars?

Me llamo **Ramón**. Me preocupa mucho el medio ambiente, y por eso soy miembro de un grupo ecologista. Creo que tenemos que cambiar nuestra manera de vivir. Me gusta mucho la lectura y todos los días escribo un blog sobre el medio ambiente.
Vivo en una ciudad donde hay mucha contaminación. Hay mucho tráfico, y lo malo es que también hay mucha basura. No hay ni árboles, ni espacios verdes, ¡es una pena!
Deberíamos mejorar nuestro entorno. Deberíamos construir áreas de ocio con árboles para los jóvenes. Me gustaría mejorar la red de transporte público, así habría menos coches y menos contaminación. Un sistema de alquiler de bicicletas sería una idea muy buena. También construiría casas sostenibles, es importante para nuestro futuro.

Me llamo **Ruth**.
Vivo en una ciudad tranquila e histórica en el sur de España. No hay muchas tiendas, y no hay muchas diversiones para los jóvenes.
Antes había una biblioteca, pero la cerraron. Lo malo es que nos aburrimos. En el futuro me gustaría mucho trabajar para mejorar los servicios que nuestra ciudad ofrece a los jóvenes. Haría muchas cosas, por ejemplo, pondría más áreas de ocio como parques y museos. Construiría un polideportivo, un estadio y ¡hasta una bolera! Renovaría el centro de la ciudad, pondría muchos árboles, y lo convertiría en zona peatonal, sin coches, porque contaminan y hacen ruido.

4 Busca el equivalente de estas frases en el texto.

a we should improve
b I would like to improve
c it would be
d I would build
e I would do
f I would put
g I would renovate
h I would convert

5 Con tu compañero/a, habla de tu ciudad/pueblo.

- ● Describe tu ciudad/pueblo, ¿cómo es hoy en día?
- ■ Es…, hay…, no hay…
- ● ¿Qué harías para proteger el medio ambiente?
- ■ Pondría árboles, espacios verdes, un sistema de alquiler de bicicletas y una buena red de transporte. Construiría casas sostenibles.
- ● ¿Qué harías para los jóvenes deportistas en tu ciudad?
- ■ Construiría áreas de ocio, una bolera, un centro cultural juvenil, un cine, un polideportivo…
- ● ¿Cómo sería la red de transporte en tu ciudad ideal?
- ■ Sería/tendría…

Sistema de alquiler de bicicletas en Sevilla.

6 Escribe tus respuestas a las preguntas del ejercicio 5.

As you write, it's useful to identify **three** things that you might get wrong and check your work for those. For this task, these could be the following:

- missing accents in conditional verbs
- incorrect conditional stems (check that you are using the correct infinitive form or an irregular stem if needed)
- incorrect endings on mucho/much**a**/much**os**/much**as**

- Shopping for clothing
- Using direct object pronouns
- Using **este**, **ese** and **aquel**

4 El centro comercial

1 Escucha y lee los textos. ¿Qué significan las frases en azul? (1–5)

¡Una ganga! = *What a bargain!*
¡Menos mal! = *What a relief!*

Simón

No hay muchas tiendas en nuestra ciudad, y por eso compro todo por Internet. **¡Hago mis compras sin moverme de casa!** No tengo que hacer cola para pagar porque lo pago en un segundo.

María

Me gusta comprar por Internet porque hay mucha variedad, y **porque los precios son económicos**. En este momento estoy buscando unas zapatillas de deporte de edición limitada, y seguro que las encuentro en Internet.

Belén

A mí me gusta reutilizar las cosas y la semana pasada compré un bolso de marca de segunda mano. Lo compré en *eBay* y solo pagué 2€. ¡Una ganga!

Raúl

Ir de compras con tus amigos puede ser muy divertido. Anteayer fui de compras con dos amigos a un centro comercial nuevo. Tengo que ver los artículos de ropa antes de comprarlos.

José

Me gusta la ropa alternativa de estilo *hippie funky*. La **suelo comprar en tiendas de diseño porque las cadenas no me gustan.** En Madrid, donde vivo, hay muchas tiendas de diseño, ¡menos mal!

2 Lee los textos otra vez y contesta.

1. Where do they mention that they enjoy buying clothes? Why?
2. Can you spot 5 direct object pronouns?

3 Escucha. Copia y completa la tabla en inglés. (1–3)

	where they shop?	reason
1	*shopping centres*	*cheaper, shops close later*

4 Con tu compañero/a, pregunta y contesta.

- ● ¿Adónde vas de compras normalmente?
- ■ Normalmente voy… Compro…
- ● ¿Qué opinas de comprar cosas por Internet?
- ■ Me gusta/Odio comprar por Internet porque…
- ● ¿Dónde te gusta comprar? ¿En grandes almacenes, en cadenas, en tiendas pequeñas o en tiendas de diseño?
- ■ Me gusta comprar en…
- ● ¿Adónde fuiste de compras la última vez y qué compraste?
- ■ Fui de compras a… con… Compré…
- ● ¿Vas a comprar algo la semana que viene?
- ■ La semana que viene voy a…

Direct object pronouns ➲214

Remember: pronouns need to match the noun they replace.

Compro **un libro**.	→	**Lo** compro.
Compro **los guantes**.	→	**Los** compro.
Compro **una gorra**.	→	**La** compro.
Compro **las gafas**.	→	**Las** compro.

When using direct object pronouns with the present and preterite tenses, the pronoun goes before the verb. Can you find two examples of this in the texts above?

When using direct object pronouns with the near future tense and verbs like *querer* + infinitive, the pronoun can go in two different places:

- before *ir* and *querer*
  → **lo** voy a comprar, **lo** quiero comprar
- joined onto the infinitive at the end of the phrase → voy a comprar**lo**, quiero comprar**lo**

- Look at which tense is used in each question and answer using the correct tense.
- Use ideas from the texts above.
- Try to use a pronoun instead of repeating a noun twice.

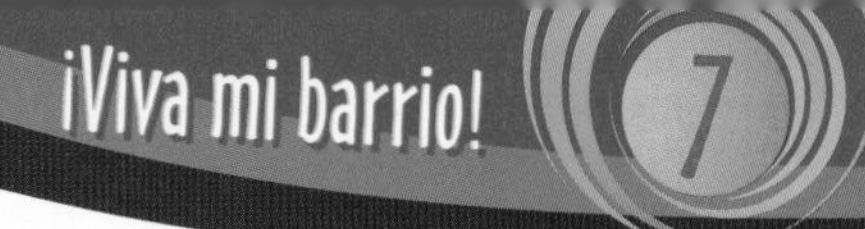

5 Listen and read the dialogue between Penélope and Mónica. Make a note of the following:

1 The items they look at.
2 Which items do they need in a bigger or smaller size?
3 Which items do they buy?

Mónica: (1) Estoy buscando un abrigo, Penélope.
Penélope: Y yo estoy buscando un bañador. Quería uno nuevo para las vacaciones.
M: (2) Mira estas sandalias rojas. ¿Te gustan, Penélope?
P: No, no me gustan nada. ¡Qué mal gusto tienes, de verdad!
M: (3) Me gusta mucho aquella sudadera naranja. Y esta blusa amarilla de algodón…
P: ¡Uf! ¡Qué feas! Un momento… (4) ¿Ves ese abrigo morado? ¿Lo ves?
M: Sí, sí. Ya lo veo, Penélope.
P: Perdone, perdone, (5) este abrigo morado… lo quería más pequeño, por favor.
Dependienta: ¿Qué talla quería?
P: La 40.
Dependienta: Aquí lo tiene.
P: (6) ¿Me lo puedo probar?
Dependienta: Por supuesto. (7) ¿Qué tal con esos guantes morados de lana?…
P: ¡Qué elegantes! Los voy a comprar – ¡el abrigo y los guantes!
M: ¿Y yo qué compro?

6 Read the dialogue again. What do the underlined phrases mean? Make sure you translate the demonstrative adjectives correctly.

G Demonstrative adjectives

These are words like *this*, *that*, *these* and *those*, and are used to identify things. They need to match the noun that they go with:

este abrigo ***this** coat* **esta** blusa ***this** blouse*

	singular		plural	
	masc.	**fem.**	**masc.**	**fem.**
this	**este** abrigo	**esta** blusa	**estos** abrigos	**estas** blusas
that	**ese** abrigo	**esa** blusa	**esos** abrigos	**esas** blusas
those… over there	**aquel** abrigo	**aquella** blusa	**aquellos** abrigos	**aquellas** blusas

7 Escucha. Copia y completa la tabla en inglés. (1–4)

	items looked at	items finally bought
1	woollen trousers brown silk tie	woollen trousers

una bolsa un bolso un cinturón una corbata una gorra un sombrero	de cuero de seda de algodón de lana
unos guantes unos calcetines unas gafas de sol	de lunares

- Giving presents and making complaints
- Using indirect object pronouns
- Extending sentences by giving reasons

5 Regalos y quejas

1 ***Look at the departments in this store. With a partner, brainstorm things you might buy in each department, using a dictionary if necessary.***

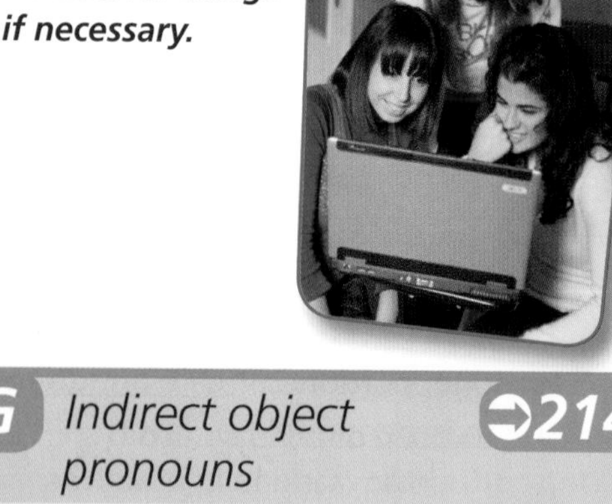

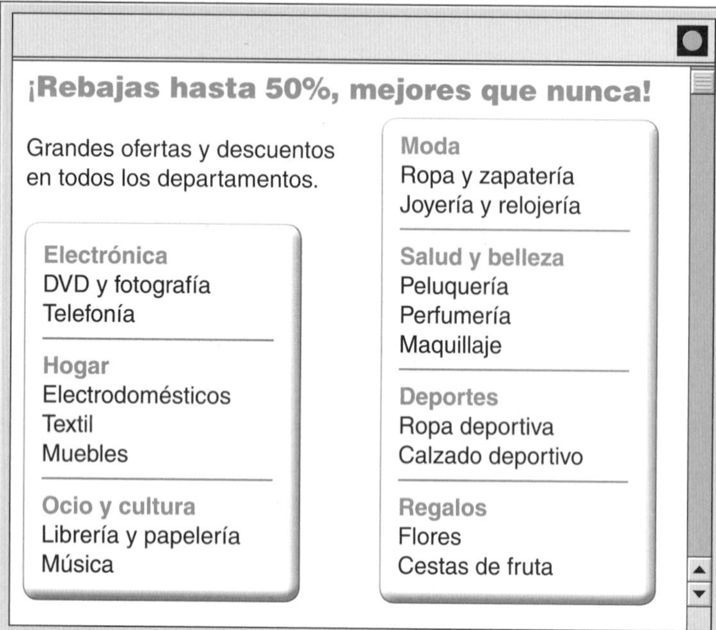

¡Rebajas hasta 50%, mejores que nunca!

Grandes ofertas y descuentos en todos los departamentos.

Electrónica
DVD y fotografía
Telefonía

Hogar
Electrodomésticos
Textil
Muebles

Ocio y cultura
Librería y papelería
Música

Moda
Ropa y zapatería
Joyería y relojería

Salud y belleza
Peluquería
Perfumería
Maquillaje

Deportes
Ropa deportiva
Calzado deportivo

Regalos
Flores
Cestas de fruta

G *Indirect object pronouns*

➲214

me	*to me*
te	*to you*
le	*to him/to her/to you (formal sing.)*
nos	*to us*
os	*to you*
les	*to them/to you (formal pl.)*

In the present or preterite tenses the pronoun comes before the verb:
Le di una pulsera.
I gave a bracelet ***to him/her***.

When you are using the near future tense the pronoun can go at the beginning of the sentence or on the end of the infinitive:
Les voy a dar un libro./Voy a dar**les** un libro.
I am going to give a book ***to them***.

2 **Escucha y contesta a las preguntas en inglés.** (1–5)

- **a** Who are they buying a present for?
- **b** What is the occasion?
- **c** What are they buying and why?
- **d** Which department of the store do they need to visit?

3 **Lee el texto y contesta a las preguntas en inglés.**

1. Which four presents are suggested?
2. What makes each present good for Father's Day, according to the text?

Para el día de la madre/del padre Para Navidad Para mi/tu/su cumpleaños	me te le os les	voy a	regalar comprar	un anillo, un collar un reloj de plata/oro un libro, un DVD una pulsera unas zapatillas de deporte

Porque me/te/le/les encanta(n).

El domingo es el día del padre. ¿Qué le vas a regalar a tu papá?
Un buen regalo para un padre viajero es una maleta con ruedas, o un maletín para el ordenador. Para los amantes del vino, una caja de 12 botellas sería una buena elección.
Las pulseras no son exclusivas de las mujeres. Esta pulsera de cuero y metal es discreta, y muy apropiada para la primavera. Aquí lo encontrarás todo, desde zapatillas a relojes, gafas de sol...

4 Lee el texto otra vez. ¿Verdadero (V), falso (F) o no se menciona en el texto (NM)?

1 Un buen regalo para alguien que no viaja es una maleta.
2 Una noche de hotel para la familia es muy romántica.
3 El vino puede ser un regalo muy bueno.
4 Las pulseras son solo para las mujeres.
5 Es importante pensar en el estilo del padre.

5 Con tu compañero/a, haz estos diálogos.

- ● ¿Qué le regalaste a tu madre para el día de la madre el año pasado?
- ■ Le regalé… porque…
- ● ¿Qué les regalaste a tus abuelos para Navidad?
- ■ Les regalé… porque…
- ● ¿Qué le vas a regalar a tu madre para su cumpleaños este año?
- ■ Le voy a comprar… porque …
- ● ¿Qué le vas a regalar a tu padre para el día del padre?
- ■ Le voy a regalar… porque…
- ● ¿Qué les vas a regalar a tus padres/tus hermanos/tus abuelos para Navidad?
- ■ Les voy a regalar… porque…

> ★ Extend what you say with reasons, giving as much detail as you can!
> Porque…
> Le/Les interesa mucho todo tipo de música, especialmente la música de…
> Es fan de…
> Le/Les gustan los libros de…
> Le/Les fascinan las películas de…
> Le/Les encanta la joyería.

6 Escucha y escribe la letra correcta. (1–5)

***Ejemplo:* 1** d

a

b

c

d

e

Quería cambiar este/esta…	Está estropeado/a. Es demasiado grande, pequeño/a. Tiene un agujero. Está roto/a. No funciona.
¿Tiene el recibo? Le voy a dar otro/a… Lo siento, es imposible cambiar o hacer un reembolso sin el recibo.	No tengo el recibo. Quería un reembolso. Quiero hablar con el director. Me parece inaceptable.

7 Escucha otra vez. Copia y completa la tabla en inglés.

	What did they buy?	What is the problem?	What would they like to do?	Were they successful?
1	*suitcase*	*damaged*		

Prueba oral

Home and local area
You are going to have a conversation with your teacher about your home and local area. Your teacher could ask you the following:

- What is your town like?
- What did your town use to be like?
- What is your opinion of your town?
- What will your town be like in the future?
- What would your ideal town be like?

Remember that you will have to respond to an unexpected question that you have not yet prepared. The dialogue will last between 4 and 6 minutes.

You are going to listen to Ted, an exam candidate, taking part in the above conversation with his teacher. Listen to part 1 and complete the following sentences in English.

1. Bristol is quite…
2. There are modern areas with a lot of…
3. The good thing is that…
4. My grandfather says that in the past the city was…
5. There were fewer… and fewer…
6. Because of this, children…
7. There were shops in the centre but there was no…

Listen to part 1 again. Note down the Spanish phrases which helped you to answer these questions.

Listen to part 2 of Ted's conversation and note down the missing words and phrases.

– ¿Qué opinas de tu ciudad?
– A ver, (1) ______ me encanta porque es una ciudad grande y hay muchas cosas que hacer, pero por otro lado hay (2) ______. En verano mucha gente viene a visitar Bristol y (3) ______. Lo que más me gusta son los parques y áreas de ocio, pero (4) ______ hay mucha contaminación a causa del tráfico. Muchas personas usan el coche (5) ______ ir en autobús. ¡Qué pena!
– ¿Cómo será tu ciudad en el futuro?
– En el futuro construirán rascacielos en Bristol sin duda. Muchas personas necesitan casas y no hay casas para todos. (6) ______ no es una idea (7) ______ si el diseño de los rascacielos está bien. También (8) ______ habrá menos tráfico en el centro de la ciudad porque habrá más zonas peatonales. Creo que será mejor así.

Translate your answers to exercise 3 into English.

Now listen to part 3 of Ted's conversation and answer the questions.

1. How does Ted say 'it would have a very good transport network'?
2. Ted uses four more conditionals in his answer to the first question. What are they?
3. In his answer to the first question, Ted uses a sentence with more than one tense in it. Can you spot it?
4. What is the unexpected question that Ted's teacher asks and what does it mean?
5. Ted says '*no te lo pierdas*' when he recommends to see the Cabot Tower. What does this mean?

Now it's your turn! Prepare your answers to the task and then have a conversation with your teacher or partner.

- Use the Grade Studio and your answers to exercises 1–5 to help you plan.
- Adapt what Ted said to talk about yourself but add your own ideas.
- Prepare your answers to the questions and try to predict what the unexpected question could be. The examiner might base this question on something you have already said, or ask something totally new!
- Record the conversation. Ask a partner to listen to it and say how well you performed.

Award each other one star, two stars or three stars for each of these categories:

- *Pronunciation*
- *Confidence and fluency*
- *Range of tenses*
- *Variety of vocabulary and expressions*
- *Using longer sentences*
- *Taking the initiative*

What do you need to do next time to improve your performance?

GradeStudio

To produce a good answer you need to be able to use a variety of structures.

- Use the **present tense** to talk about your city as it is now, for example '*mi ciudad es...*', '*en mi ciudad hay...*'
- Use the **future tense** to talk about what your city will be like in the future: '*mi ciudad será...*', '*habrá...*'
- Use simple **opinions** and descriptions with **adjectives**. Ted uses phrases like '*Bristol me gusta mucho*' (I like Bristol a lot) and '*hay barrios históricos*' (there are historic areas).
- Use simple **connectives** to extend your sentences such as *y* (and), *pero* (but), *también* (also) and *porque* (because).

To go a step further you need to use a wider variety of language.

- Vary your language by referring to **people other than yourself**. Ted refers to kids in his city in the past: '*Los niños jugaban en la calle.*'
- State your **point of view** with more varied language. Which phrases does Ted use to do this in exercise 3?

For a really impressive answer:

- Use **complex sentences** containing more than one tense. Did you find the complex sentence in exercise 5?
- Add variety to your descriptions by using ***tan*** **+ adjective** (so) or ***tanto(s)/tanta(s)*** (so many).
- Give **points of view** and make sure you **justify them**. Can you find examples of where Ted does this in exercise 3?

Prueba escrita

Read the text and answer the questions in English.

1 How does Lía describe her neighbourhood? Give two details.
2 Why does Lía not complain about sharing her room? Give two details.
3 How did the children use to play when Lía's grandmother was a child?
4 Why does Lía like listening to her grandmother's stories?
5 Why doesn't Lía like the traffic?
6 How would Lía improve Seville? Give two details.

Vivo en un bloque de pisos en Sevilla, en el barrio de Triana, que es un barrio histórico muy famoso. El edificio es muy antiguo, tiene mucho carácter y me gusta bastante. Lo que no me gusta tanto, es que tengo que compartir mi dormitorio con mi hermana menor porque mi abuela ahora vive con nosotros. Sin embargo, no me quejo porque el dormitorio es muy espacioso y me llevo bien con mi hermana. Por lo general, paso mucho tiempo en el patio que compartimos con los vecinos del edificio. Es muy agradable charlar allí a la sombra. ¡Qué placer!

A menudo mi abuela nos cuenta su vida en Sevilla cuando era joven. No había tantos coches como ahora y todo era más tranquilo. Dice que todos los niños jugaban en la calle con una pelota. En casa no tenían nevera, ni lavadora, ni lavaplatos. Mi abuela y sus hermanos tenían que hacer muchas tareas en casa. Además, había mucha pobreza. ¡Qué horror! También dice que en aquellos días no había tanta contaminación como ahora, y todo estaba más limpio. Me encanta escuchar sus historias porque son muy interesantes y porque tenía una vida muy diferente a la mía.

Hoy en día Sevilla es muy diferente. Tiene muchos habitantes y es muy turística. Hay mucho tráfico y me da rabia porque los coches contaminan y hacen mucho ruido. Mejoraría la red de transporte y pondría un sistema de alquiler de monopatines. Lo bueno es que tenemos unos espacios verdes muy bonitos en la ciudad y bastantes monumentos maravillosos. Claro que hay maneras de mejorar mi ciudad, pero siempre será la mejor del mundo ¡por lo menos desde mi punto de vista!

Find the equivalent of these expressions in Spanish in the text. Copy them out under the following headings: present, imperfect or conditional.

1 ...is a famous, very historic neighbourhood.
2 What I don't like that much...
3 However, I don't complain...
4 ...my grandmother tells us about her life in Seville when she was young.
5 ...they didn't use to have a fridge, nor a washing machine...
6 ...in those days there wasn't as much pollution as nowadays...
7 These days Seville is very different.
8 I would improve the transport system...

3 *leer* ***Look at the text again. Make a list of words and phrases used to do these things:***

- give opinions
- extend sentences/paragraphs with extra information

4 *escribir* ***You might be asked to write about your local area as a Controlled Assessment task. Use the Grade Studio to help you prepare your account.***

GradeStudio

To produce a good answer you need to use a variety of structures, describe things using adjectives and express opinions.

- Lía uses the **present tense** to talk about what her house **is** like and the **future tense** to say that, for her, Seville **will** always be the best city in the world.
- Find examples of how Lía uses **adjectives** in her text to describe her neighbourhood, the block of flats and the good things in Seville.
- Find the sentence where Lía gives her **opinion** about her city.

To go a step further you need to use a wider range of language. This might include tenses, such as the **imperfect**, longer sentences with **opinion phrases** and **exclamations**.

- Lía uses the **imperfect tense** to talk about what Seville **used to be** like when her grandmother was a child. Find five examples of how Isabel uses the imperfect tense.
- Lía uses a number of phrases to express her **opinion** such as *'lo que no me gusta'*, *'lo bueno es que'*, *'claro que'*, *'desde mi punto de vista'*. Choose some expressions (not all of them) that you would like to include in your own text.
- Put some real **exclamations** into your text to make the description more expressive. Where has Lía done this?

For a really impressive answer:

- Include a **complex sentence** with more than one tense in it. Can you find a sentence in the second paragraph where Lía has combined the present and the imperfect?
- Lía uses the **conditional** to talk about how she would change Seville. Find two examples of how Lía uses the conditional tense.
- Use **qualifiers** like *'tan'*, *'tanto'* and **phrases of opinion** like *'me da rabia'*. Do you know what these phrases mean? Can you use them in your text?

5 *escribir* ***Now write a full account of your local area.***

- Adapt Lía's text and use language from Module 7. Write at least 200 words.
- Remember to make your adjectives agree with the nouns that they describe. If you look the adjective up in a dictionary it will be given in the masculine singular form.
- Structure your text carefully. Organise what you write in paragraphs.

General summary of area

Where do you live? Who do you live with?
What is your house like?
What is the area like?

Main paragraph

Give details of what the area used to be like:
- *What were children's lives like?*
- *How were people's lives different to how they are today?*
- *How was the local area different to how it is today?*

Conclusion

What is your local area like now?
What would you do to change your area?
Give your overall opinion of your local area.

6 *escribir* ***Check carefully what you have written.***

- spelling and accents (adjectives agree with the noun that they are describing?)
- verb endings (correct endings on imperfect and conditional verbs?)
- tenses (use the imperfect tense to talk about what things used to be like)

Palabras

Hogar, dulce hogar *Home, sweet home*

Vivo en…	*I live in…*
un apartamento	*an apartment*
un chalé	*a chalet*
un piso	*a flat*
una casa	*a house*
arriba	*upstairs*
abajo	*downstairs*
fuera	*outside*
hay…	*there is…*
tenemos…	*we have…*
un aseo	*a toilet*
un comedor	*a dining room*
un cuarto de baño	*a bathroom*
un cuarto	*a room*
un dormitorio	*a bedroom*
un estudio/despacho	*a study*
un garaje	*a garage*
un jardín	*a garden*
un salón	*a lounge*
una cocina	*a kitchen*
una habitación	*a room*
una terraza	*a terrace*
el armario	*wardrobe*
el equipo de música	*stereo*
el espejo	*mirror*
el horno	*oven*
el lavaplatos	*dishwasher*
el ordenador	*computer*
el sofá	*sofa*
la alfombra	*carpet*
la butaca/el sillón	*armchair*
la cama	*bed*
la estantería	*bookcase*
la lámpara	*lamp*
la lavadora	*washing machine*
la moqueta	*carpet*
la nevera/el frigorífico	*fridge*
la puerta	*door*
la silla	*chair*
la televisión	*TV*
la ventana	*window*
a la derecha de	*on the right of*
a la izquierda de	*on the left of*
al lado de	*next to*
debajo de	*under*
delante de	*in front of*
detrás de	*behind*
encima de	*on*
entre	*between*
En la planta baja hay…	*On the ground floor, there is/are…*
En la primera planta hay…	*On the first floor, there is/are…*
En las paredes hay…	*On the walls, there is/are…*
En el suelo hay…	*On the floor, there is/are…*
Es la habitación donde me lavo el pelo, …	*It's the room where I wash my hair, …*
Tengo que compartir mi habitación con…	*I have to share my room with…*
Tengo que dormir en el mismo cuarto que…	*I have to sleep in the same room as…*
Necesito tener mi propia habitación porque…	*I need to have my own room because…*

¿Cómo es tu casa? *What's your house like?*

Vivo en…	*I live in…*
un bloque de pisos	*a block of flats*
un edificio	*building*
un rascacielos	*a skyscraper*
una granja	*a farm*
adosado/a	*semi-detached*
aislado/a	*detached*
antiguo/a	*old*
bonito/a	*nice*
cómodo/a	*comfortable*
feo/a	*ugly*
grande	*large*
moderno/a	*modern*
nuevo/a	*new*
pequeño/a	*small*
viejo/a	*old*
Está…	*It is…*
en la ciudad	*in the city*
en un pueblo	*in a town*
en las afueras	*in the outskirts*
en el campo	*in the countryside*
en la costa	*on the coast*
en la playa	*by the beach*
en la montaña	*in the mountains*
Lo bueno es que…	*The good thing is that…*
Lo malo es que…	*The bad thing is that…*
Lo que más me gusta es que…	*What I like most is that…*
Lo que menos me gusta es que…	*What I like least is that…*
Hay/No hay…	*There is/isn't (are/aren't)…*
Tenemos/No tenemos…	*We have/don't have…*
calefacción	*heating*
habitaciones grandes	*large rooms*
mucho/poco espacio	*a lot/not much space*
un aparcamiento	*a parking space*
un ascensor	*a lift*
un ático	*an attic*
un garaje	*a garage*
un jardín (con césped)	*a garden (with lawn)*
un patio	*a patio*
un sótano	*a cellar*
una terraza	*a terrace*
una piscina	*a swimming pool*

Mi barrio *My neighbourhood*

Vivo en un pueblo/una ciudad…	*I live in a… town/a… city*	parques	*parks*
grande	*large*	restaurantes	*restaurants*
histórico/a	*historic*	salas de juegos	*amusement arcades*
importante	*important*	un centro comercial	*a shopping centre*
industrial	*industrial*	un cine	*a cinema*
moderno/a	*modern*	un polideportivo	*a sports centre*
pequeño/a	*small*	una biblioteca	*a library*
turístico/a	*tourist*	una pista de tenis	*a tennis court*
Mi barrio/pueblo/ciudad es…	*My neighbourhood/town/city is…*	muchas cosas que hacer	*a lot of things to do*
bonito/a	*nice*	mucho que hacer	*a lot to do*
conocido/a	*well-known*	muchos lugares de interés	*a lot of places of interest*
feo/a	*ugly*	mucha contaminación	*a lot of pollution*
ruidoso/a	*noisy*	No hay…	*There isn't/aren't…*
tranquilo/a	*quiet*	(No) Está…	*It is(n't)…*
Hay…	*There is/are…*	Mi abuelo/a dice que antes era…	*My grandfather/grandmother says that before it used to be…*
bares	*bars*		
discotecas	*discos*		

Mi ciudad *My city*

En mi ciudad…	*In my city…*	no hay muchos árboles	*there aren't many trees*
hay mucha basura	*there is a lot of rubbish*	no hay muchos espacios verdes	*there aren't many green spaces*
hay muchas tiendas	*there are a lot of shops*	no hay red de transporte público	*there is no public transport network*
hay mucho tráfico	*there is a lot of traffic*	Deberíamos construir… para los jóvenes.	*We should build… for young people.*
hay muchos habitantes	*there are a lot of inhabitants*	una bolera	*a bowling alley*
hay muchos museos y muchas galerías de arte	*there are a lot of museums and art galleries*	un centro cultural para jóvenes	*a cultural centre for young people*
hay muchos turistas	*there are a lot of tourists*	un cine	*a cinema*
hay una zona peatonal	*there is a pedestrian zone*	un polideportivo	*a sports centre*
no hay muchas áreas de ocio	*there aren't many leisure areas*		

El centro comercial *The shopping centre*

Estoy buscando…	*I'm looking for…*	unas gafas de sol	*sunglasses*
un abrigo	*a coat*	unos calcetines	*socks*
una bolsa	*a handbag*	unos guantes	*gloves*
un bolso	*a bag*	de algodón	*made of cotton*
un cinturón	*a belt*	de cuero	*made of leather*
un sombrero	*a hat*	de lana	*made of wool*
una corbata	*a tie*	de seda	*made of silk*
una gorra	*a cap*	de lunares	*spotted*

Regalos y quejas *Presents and complaints*

para el día de la madre/del padre	*for Mother's/Father's Day*	Está estropeado/a.	*It's broken.*
para Navidad	*for Christmas*	Es demasiado grande/pequeño/a.	*It's too big/small.*
para mi/tu/su cumpleaños	*for my/your/his/her birthday*	Tiene un agujero.	*It has a hole.*
me voy a regalar…	*I'm going to give myself…*	Está roto/a.	*It's broken.*
te/os voy a comprar…	*I'm going to buy you…*	No funciona.	*It doesn't work.*
le/les voy a regalar…	*I'm going to give him/her/them…*	¿Tiene el recibo?	*Have you got a receipt?*
un anillo	*a ring*	Le voy a dar otro/a…	*I am going to give you another…*
un collar	*a necklace*	No tengo el recibo.	*I don't have the receipt.*
un DVD	*a DVD*	Quería un reembolso.	*I'd like a refund.*
un libro	*a book*	Quiero hablar con el director.	*I want to speak to the manager.*
un reloj de plata/oro	*a silver/gold watch*	Me parece inaceptable.	*It's unacceptable.*
una pulsera	*a bracelet*	Lo siento, es imposible cambiar o hacer un reembolso sin el recibo.	*I'm sorry, it's not possible to exchange or give your money back without a receipt.*
unas zapatillas de deporte	*trainers*		
unos pendientes	*earrings*		
Quería cambiar este/esta…	*I'd like to change this…*		

- Talking about the body and illnesses
- Using reflexive verbs in the perfect tense
- Finding strategies to remember vocab

Repaso 1 *Pasándolo mal*

Escucha y escribe la letra o las letras correctas. (1–8)

Ejemplo: **1** h, j

Me duele(n)…
Te duele(n)…
Le duele(n)…

Tengo dolor de…
Tienes dolor de…
Tiene dolor de…

***Listen and write down what hurts and for how long.* (1–6)**

Ejemplo: **1** eyes, 2 weeks

No me encuentro bien. Me siento mal.	Tienes mala cara.
¿Cuánto (tiempo) hace que te duele? ¿Desde cuándo? ¿Desde hace cuánto tiempo?	Desde hace… un día/mes una semana/hora dos horas/días/semanas/meses
	Desde… el martes pasado ayer/anteayer esta mañana/tarde

el cuerpo = *body*

G Doler 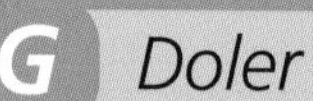

➲202

Doler *(to hurt)* changes its stem from **o** to **ue**. It works in the same way as **gustar**.

Me duele **el** pie.	*My foot hurts.*
Te duele **la** cabeza.	*Your head hurts.*

Remember to use **duelen** for plural nouns (feet, eyes, etc.) or more than one part of the body.

Le duelen **los** brazos. *His/Her arm hurts.*

Remember to use the definite article to talk about body parts in Spanish.

Haz diálogos con tu compañero/a.

- ● No me encuentro bien.
- ■ ¿Qué te pasa?
- ● Me duele(n)… Tengo dolor de…
- ■ ¿Cuánto tiempo hace que te duele?/¿Desde cuándo?
- ● Desde hace… Desde…
- ■ ¡Vaya!, ¡qué mal! / Tranquilo/a, ¡eso no es nada! / ¡Pobrecito/a!

★ To learn and remember words that are completely different from the English, it is helpful if you can think of a story behind the word to jog your memory. For example:

La garganta – sounds like "gargle" and you use your <u>throat</u> to do this.

Can you think of any of your own?

Escucha. Copia y completa la tabla. (1–5)

	Problems	How did they get the injury?	Suggested treatment
1	*arm hurts,...*	*playing basketball*	*rest,...*

estar pachucho/a = *to feel under the weather*

Me he roto la pierna.

¡Ay! Me he cortado el pie.

Me he torcido el tobillo.

Me he quemado la espalda.

Tengo una insolación.

Tengo tos.

Tengo fiebre. Tengo frío/calor.

Tengo gripe.

Estoy enfermo.

Estoy cansada. Tengo sueño.

Tengo un resfriado.

Tienes que…
Debes…
Hay que…
- beber mucha agua.
- descansar.
- ponerte esta crema.
- tomar este jarabe.
- tomar una aspirina.
- ponerte una tirita.
- ir al hospital inmediatamente.

Habla con tu compañero/a. Estás enfermo/a.

- ● ¿Qué te pasa?
- ■ Estoy pachucho/a. Me duele(n)… Tengo… Estoy… Me he…
- ● ¡Vaya! ¿Desde cuándo?
- ■ Desde…/Desde hace…
- ● ¿Qué te pasó?/¿Qué hiciste?
- ■ Tuve un accidente jugando…, nadando…, esquiando…, haciendo…
- ● Ay, ¡qué mal!/Tienes que… y debes…
- ■ Vale, muchas gracias.

G *The perfect tense*

➲228

Use the perfect tense to say you have broken, twisted, burned or cut a part of your body. The verbs are reflexive, because these are things you have done to yourself. Remember to include the reflexive pronoun (me, te, se, etc.) right at the beginning, before the rest of the verb:

cortarse	*to cut*
Me he cortado.	*I have cut myself.*
torcerse	*to twist/sprain*
Se ha torcido el brazo.	*He has twisted his arm.*

- Buying food
- More vocab strategies
- Number practice

Repaso 2 ¿Cuánto es?

Escucha y lee. Escribe la letra correcta. (1–15)

Ejemplo: los melocotones – e

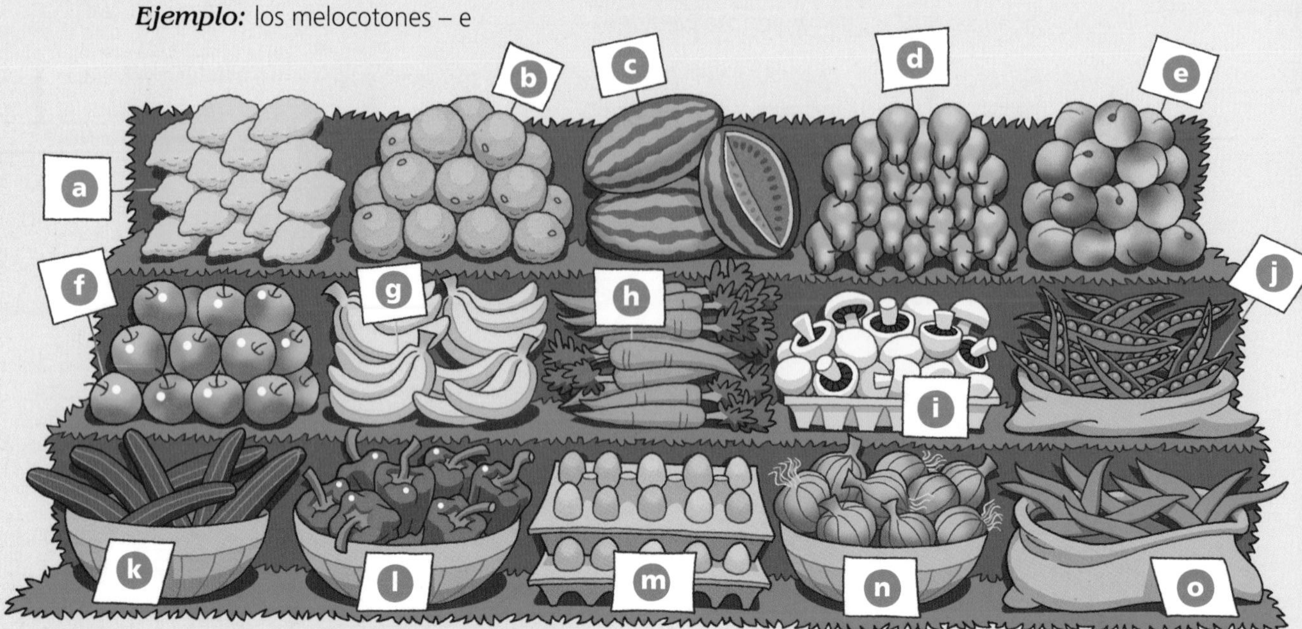

los melocotones	los melones	las zanahorias
los huevos	los champiñones	las naranjas
los guisantes	los pepinos	las peras
los limones	los pimientos rojos	las judías verdes
los plátanos	las cebollas	las manzanas

Lee la lista de la compra. Copia y completa la tabla.

frutas	verduras y legumbres	bebidas	otros alimentos

quinientos gramos de queso
medio kilo de tomates
un kilo de lentejas
dos kilos de melones
una barra de pan
una pastilla de mantequilla
un paquete de azúcar
un paquete de arroz
una botella de aceite (de oliva)
una lata de atún
un cartón de leche/zumo de naranja
una caja de galletas/pasteles

Sorting big groups of vocabulary into categories will help you learn them by breaking them down into smaller chunks. When you have written out the items in exercise 2, take a minute to look at each list before covering it up and writing the items down again. After you've done this with each list, close your book and see how many of the items you can write correctly from memory.

3 Lee los precios y escribe los números correctos.

Ejemplo: **1** – 9,50€

1 Nueve euros con cincuenta =
2 Ocho euros con veinticinco céntimos =
3 Diez euros con setenta y cinco =
4 Once euros con sesenta =
5 Catorce euros con cuarenta =
6 Quince euros con ochenta y cinco céntimos =

It is very important to learn numbers carefully, as they crop up in almost every topic area. Prices sometimes include the word **con**, which separates euros and cents. Cents tend to be in multiples of five, but not exclusively.

4 Escucha. ¿Qué compran? Copia y completa la tabla. (1–8)

	comida y bebida	cantidad	precio
1	*vinagre*	*2 botellas*	*8 euros*

¿En qué puedo servirle?	100 cien	gramos de…
Deme…, por favor.	200 doscientos	
Lo siento, no queda(n)…	300 trescientos	
Aquí tiene. ¿Algo más?	400 cuatrocientos	
No, nada más.	500 quinientos	
¿Cuánto es?/¿Cuánto cuesta(n)?	Medio kilo / Un kilo / Dos kilos de…	
Son… euros con… en total.	Media/Una docena de huevos.	

5 Lee la conversación. Escribe la letra correcta.

- ● Buenas tardes. ¿En qué puedo servirle?
- ■ Hola, buenas tardes. Deme tres barras de pan, por favor.
- ● Lo siento, pero solo quedan dos barras.
- ■ De acuerdo, está bien.
- ● ¿Algo más?
- ■ Sí, necesito una pastilla de mantequilla y tres latas de tomates.
- ● No quedan latas de tomates. Aquí tiene la mantequilla.
- ■ Vale.
- ● ¿Es eso todo?
- ■ No. Deme también dos cartones de leche, por favor. ¿Cuánto es?
- ● A ver… Las barras cuestan tres euros con sesenta y cinco, más la mantequilla y la leche, son seis euros con setenta y cinco.
- ■ Muy bien. Aquí tiene. ¡Gracias!
- ● Muchas gracias, ¡adiós!

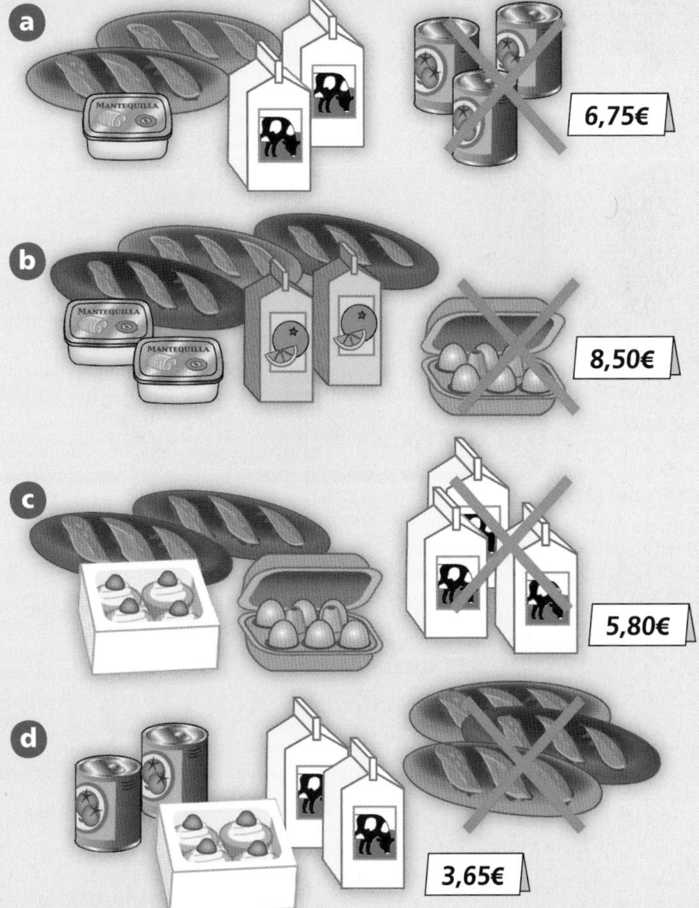

6 Haz diálogos con tu compañero/a. Usa las imágenes del ejercicio 5.

- Talking about how to stay in good shape
- Using the present and imperfect
- Using a variety of verbs to talk about mealtimes

1 Estar en forma

1 **Escucha a los famosos. Escribe la letra correcta. (1–4)**

Sara Baras

Gael García Bernal

Salma Hayek

Rafael Nadal

a

b

c

d

e

Para estar en forma… Para no engordar…		
siempre a menudo normalmente frecuentemente de vez en cuando raramente rara vez no nunca	como bebo desayuno ceno suelo comer suelo beber intento comer intento beber	zumo, leche, café, té, verduras, legumbres, fruta, ensalada, lechuga, pescado, gambas, merluza, pollo, filetes, carne de cerdo/cordero/ternera, huevos, yogur, queso, comida basura/rápida, perritos calientes, hamburguesas, pasteles, dulces, churros.
Contiene(n) No contiene(n)	mucho/a, poco/a, demasiado/a	fibra, sal, grasa, azúcar.
	muchos/as, pocos/as, demasiados/as	vitaminas, proteínas.

2 **Lee las preguntas y rellena los espacios en blanco.**

intentas desayunas bebidas raramente
qué cenas beber mediodía basura

1 ¿___ te gusta comer?
2 ¿Qué comes al ___ normalmente?
3 ¿Qué ___ cada mañana?
4 ¿Qué ___ por la noche?
5 ¿Qué sueles ___ todos los días?
6 ¿Qué comes ___?
7 ¿Qué ___ evitar?

Remember that the verbs for *to eat* are different in Spanish depending on the time of day! **Comer** can also be used to talk about eating generally.

Desayunar	**Desayuno** cereales.	*I eat cereal for breakfast.*
Comer	**Como** pescado.	*I eat fish (for lunch).*
Merendar	**Meriendo** fruta.	*I eat fruit for tea.*
Cenar	**Ceno** ensalada.	*I eat salad for dinner.*

3 Habla de tu estilo de vida. Contesta a las preguntas.

- ¿Qué comes normalmente?
- Por lo general suelo comer…
  Desayuno… Como… Meriendo… Ceno…
  Intento comer… porque contiene(n)…
- ¿Qué bebes cada día?
- Bebo mucho/a… Bebo muy poco/a… porque…
- ¿Qué comida intentas evitar?
- Intento evitar… porque…

4 Escucha y contesta a las preguntas para cada persona en inglés. (1–5)

a Does the person have a healthy lifestyle now? Explain your answer.

b Did the person have a healthy lifestyle in the past? Explain your answer.

Ahora – (yo) como, bebo, duermo, juego, voy, hago
Antes – (yo) comía, bebía, dormía, jugaba, iba, hacía

Remember that the imperfect tense is used to describe things you used to do, while the present tense is used for describing current habits. Listen for **-ía** or **-aba** at the end of verbs to recognise the imperfect. Key time markers like **ahora** (now), **antes** (previously) and **cuando era joven** (when I was young) will also help you to understand what you are hearing.

5 ¿Qué haces para estar en forma? Escribe un párrafo.

- *Your food and drink likes and dislikes:* Me encanta comer/beber… Odio… Prefiero… porque…
- *What you eat and drink every day:* Cada día como… bebo… Suelo comer/beber…
- *What you try to avoid:* Intento evitar…
- *What you used to eat and drink:* Hace tres años comía… bebía…
- *What you do to stay fit:* Dos veces a la semana hago… voy… juego… Soy miembro de…

6 Lee el texto y contesta a las preguntas en inglés.

1. Name the factors that prevent children from burning sufficient calories (five are mentioned).
2. Name at least three benefits which doing regular physical exercise can bring.
3. Name at least two types of activity that can be done every day.
4. Name at least two activities that should not be done for more than two hours a day.

¡No a la obesidad!

Los chicos se mueven poco, pasan mucho tiempo frente a la tele y al ordenador, y van en coche o autobús a todos lados. Tampoco practican deporte y tienen poca educación física en el colegio. Esta rutina cada vez más sedentaria no ayuda a combatir la sobredosis calórica que ingieren.
La práctica regular de actividad física aporta numerosos beneficios: el descanso y el sueño, la prevención de enfermedades crónicas y mejora la concentración.

Es fundamental acompañar una dieta equilibrada y variada con una actividad física regular:

- **Moverse cada día:** caminar, tareas del hogar, juegos activos o pasear al perro.
- **3–5 veces a la semana:** actividades y deportes vigorosos como fútbol, como mínimo 20 minutos en cada sesión.
- **2–3 veces a la semana:** actividades para potenciar la flexibilidad y la fuerza como baile, flexiones, artes marciales…
- **Menos de 2 horas:** ver la televisión, jugar con videojuegos y con el ordenador.

- Reading problem pages and giving advice
- Using the conditional and future tense
- Giving extended answers while speaking

2 ¿Llevas una vida sana?

Lee y decide si las frases son verdaderas (V), falsas (F) o no se mencionan en el texto (NM).

1 José no está delgado.
2 Le gusta comer perritos calientes los fines de semana.
3 A José no le gusta nada la fruta.
4 A José no le funcionan las dietas.
5 A José le encantan las actividades deportivas.
6 Prefiere ver la televisión.

Querida Tía Tita:

Estoy muy preocupado porque estoy gordo. Me gustaría perder peso porque las chicas del cole no quieren salir conmigo. Ellas están delgadísimas. La verdad es que como bien, no como comida basura y evito la comida rápida, pero no puedo perder peso. ¡No sé por qué!

Hace dos años pesaba diez kilos menos y comía mucho chocolate. Antes comía dulces todo el tiempo, y ahora solo como bombones o churros el fin de semana. He hecho varias dietas, pero no me han dado ningún resultado. No hago ejercicio porque odio los deportes. Prefiero jugar al ajedrez o navegar por Internet. ¿Qué debería hacer para no engordar?

José, Cádiz

Querido José:

Es evidente que te gustaría adelgazar y por eso estás tan estresado. ¡No te preocupes! A la mayoría de las chicas les encantaría parecerse a las modelos de las revistas de moda, pero muchas modelos son anoréxicas. La delgadez extrema es muy peligrosa y mata a mucha gente: no comer nada no es saludable. No deberías escucharles. Yo en tu lugar, haría más ejercicio. No deberías pasar tanto tiempo en casa. Si no te gusta hacer deporte, podrías utilizar la escalera en vez del ascensor, o ir a pie en lugar de ir en autobús. Así perderías peso.

Tía Tita

perder peso/adelgazar = *to lose weight*
matar = *to kill*
Yo en tu lugar = *in your situation*

Lee otra vez la carta de Tía Tita del ejercicio 1. Busca 6 verbos en el condicional.

Ejemplo: te gustaría

Escucha las tres conversaciones y contesta a las preguntas en inglés. (1–3)

a What is wrong?
b What advice are they given?
c What will they do in the future?

Use the **conditional** to give advice in Spanish where you say *would* or *should* in English:

Yo en tu lugar, **comería** mucha fruta.
*In your position, **I would eat** a lot of fruit.*
Deberías cambiar tu dieta.
***You should** change your diet.*

Use the **future** to talk about things you *will* do:
De ahora en adelante **comeré** más fruta.
*Fom now on **I will eat** more fruit.*

The conditional and the future share the same irregular stems:

			conditional	*future*
hacer	*to do/make*	→	**har**ía	**har**é
tener	*to have*	→	**tendr**ía	**tendr**é
salir	*to go out*	→	**saldr**ía	**saldr**é

hablar 4 ***Give advice to your partner. Try to extend your answers as much as possible each time.***

- Me siento mal porque estoy engordando mucho.
- Oye, pues deberías ponerte en forma. Para adelgazar, deberías comer más fruta. Además, yo en tu lugar, haría más deporte después del cole.
- Vale, tienes razón. De ahora en adelante comeré…

1 *Me siento mal porque estoy engordando mucho.*

2 *Quiero llevar una vida más sana.*

3 *Soy adicto/a al ordenador. Me paso el día jugando a los videojuegos y no tengo amigos.*

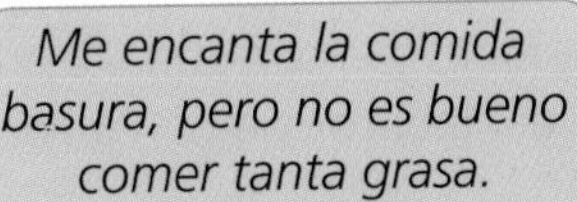

4 *Me encanta la comida basura, pero no es bueno comer tanta grasa.*

5 *No sé por qué, pero estoy cansado/a todo el tiempo.*

6 *Odio hacer deporte, pero me gustaría estar en forma.*

Giving advice		Accepting advice
(No) Deberías…	Yo en tu lugar,…	Vale, tienes razón.
ponerte en forma.	(no) cambiaría mi estilo de vida.	En el futuro…
preocuparte.	compraría caramelos sin azúcar.	cambiaré…
Para perder peso/adelgazar, deberías…	comería más/menos…	compraré…
Para estar en forma, deberías…	bebería más/menos…	comeré…
Para llevar una vida más sana, deberías…	intentaría comer/hacer…	beberé…
Para no estar cansado/a, deberías…	haría más deporte.	haré…
Para sentirte mejor, deberías…	empezaría a hacer/practicar/jugar…	empezaré…
		intentaré…

escribir 5 Escribe una carta para una de las personas en el ejercicio 4.

Querido/a…:
¡No te preocupes! Aquí tienes algunos consejos que te pueden ayudar.
Yo en tu lugar,…
Para…

(No) deberías…
Ya sé que es difícil, pero todo es posible si tienes una actitud positiva.
¡Suerte!
Tío/a (tu nombre)

- Talking about issues facing young people
- Understanding phrases with the subjunctive
- Using the present tense and the conditional

3 Los jóvenes

Lee y empareja las personas con los textos.

Ejemplo: **1** Natalia

pertencer a = *to belong to*
las pandillas = *gangs*

1 Hoy en día hay muchos problemas que afectan a los jóvenes. Para mí el problema más preocupante es el alcoholismo. Muchos de mis amigos salen de copas todo el tiempo y beben demasiado. Eso no es bueno para la salud.

2 La sociedad española debe reconocer el hecho de que muchos jóvenes llevan cuchillos u otras armas habitualmente. No sólo son los jóvenes que pertenecen a pandillas juveniles, sino también adolescentes que quieren protegerse de la violencia callejera.

3 Muchos de mis amigos fuman porros para relajarse. No es una droga dura y creo que es igual que el alcohol. En España es legal fumar marihuana o cultivarla en casa, pero tendrás problemas con la policía si la compras o la vendes.

4 El tabaquismo es un problema que afecta a muchos jóvenes españoles. El humo es muy perjudicial para los pulmones y el corazón. Ahora las cajetillas llevan advertencias muy duras sobre los riesgos del tabaco como "Fumar puede matar", pero dejar de fumar es difícil

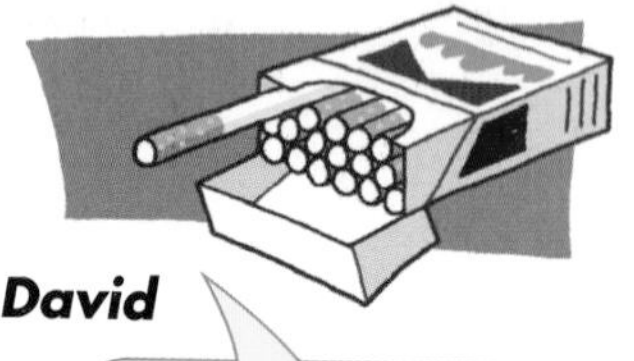

David

*Creo que **fumar** es peligroso.*

Ignacio

*Me da igual **tomar drogas blandas**. No es una cosa muy seria.*

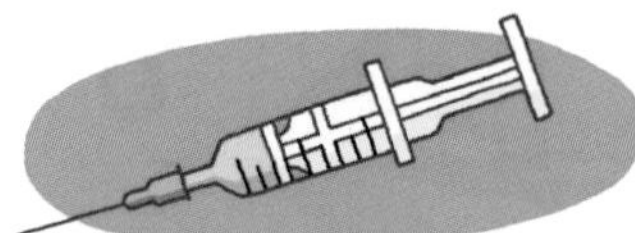

Marisa

*Reconozco que **tomar drogas duras** es muy peligroso.*

Natalia

*Sé que **beber alcohol** es perjudicial para la salud.*

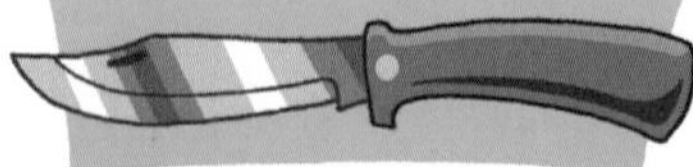

Pablo

*A mi modo de ver, **llevar navajas** es una tontería.*

Escucha. Copia y completa la tabla en inglés. (1–4)

	things they do	extra details	things they don't do/wouldn't do
1	smoke	smokes from time to time but...	take drugs

Habla con tu compañero/a.

- ¿Qué opinas de fumar/tomar drogas blandas…?
- En mi opinión fumar es una perdida de tiempo y tendría miedo de los riesgos.
- ¿Tienes algún vicio?
- Sí/No. A veces bebo/fumo/tomo/llevo…
- ¿Por qué no fumarías/tomarías/beberías/llevarías…?
- No fumaría/tomaría/bebería/llevaría… porque…

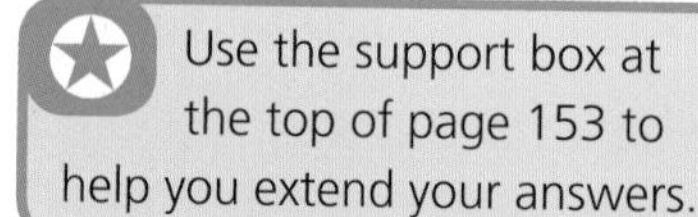

Use the support box at the top of page 153 to help you extend your answers.

En mi opinión… Creo que… A mi modo de ver… Por un lado…, por otro lado… Me da igual… Tendría miedo de…	fumar cigarrillos tomar drogas blandas tomar drogas duras beber alcohol llevar navajas vivir en un barrio violento la dependencia hacerme drogadicto/alcohólico los riesgos morir	 es una pérdida de tiempo/dinero. es una tontería. es peligroso. ☺ no me parece una cosa seria. es inofensivo. es divertido y mis amigos lo hacen. se puede dejar fácilmente.

leer 4 Lee el texto y contesta a las preguntas en inglés.

Hola, Nicolás. ¿Cómo estás? Yo estoy muy preocupada por mi amiga Camila. Creo que toma heroína. Todo empezó hace cuatro meses, en una fiesta. Camila bebió mucha cerveza, estaba un poco borracha, y probó una pastilla de éxtasis con su novio, Mauri. Este chico tiene veinte años y es drogadicto, pero es muy guapo y Camila está enamorada de él. No vale la pena hablar mal de Mauri porque Camila no me escucha.

Al principio Camila tomaba dos o tres pastillas de éxtasis a la semana y luego empezó a tomar cocaína, a pesar de los consejos de sus amigos. Ahora está tomando heroína. Camila dice que no es drogadicta, y que tomar drogas es igual que emborracharse, pero yo creo que Camila necesita un programa de rehabilitación porque está fuera de control.

No creo que Camila pueda dejar de tomar drogas sin ayuda profesional, por eso la semana que viene voy a hablar con nuestra tutora del cole. Sin embargo, sé que al hablar con una profesora corro el riesgo de perder mi amistad con Camila. Ojalá Camila deje de tomar drogas. ¿Y tú, qué harías? Un beso, ***Alexa***

1 Who is Alexa concerned about and why?
2 How did the problem start? Give three details.
3 Who is Mauri and why does he have a strong influence over Camila?
4 Which drugs has Camila tried so far?
5 What do her friends feel about the situation? Explain your answer.
6 Does Camila feel that she is a drug addict? Why/Why not?
7 What does Alexa feel that Camila needs and why?
8 What is Alexa going to do next week?
9 What might happen as a result?

escribir 5 Escribe un correo electrónico de Nicolás a Alexa.

G *Ojalá*

➲230

This is a word which means *let's hope* or *if only*.

- You can use it on its own in conversations to mean *let's hope so*.
  – En el futuro los jóvenes no van a llevar navajas.
  – **¡Ojalá**!
- You can use **ojalá** as part of a phrase, but you must use the **subjunctive** with it.

Ojalá no **fumes** más.
Let's hope you don't smoke any more.
Ojalá **puedas** dejar de fumar.
Let's hope you can give up smoking.

For more information on how to form the subjunctive and for other uses of the subjunctive see p. 230

Prueba oral

Interview with a homeless person

You are going to be interviewed by your teacher. You will play the role of a homeless person and your teacher will play the role of the interviewer. Your teacher could ask you the following:

- Tell me about yourself – name, age, brothers and sisters, etc.
- Why are you living on the streets?
- Describe a typical day for you.
- What do you normally eat and drink?
- What is the most serious problem for homeless people?
- What would you like to do in 5 years time?

Remember you will have to respond to an unexpected question that you have not yet prepared.
The dialogue will last between 4 and 6 minutes.

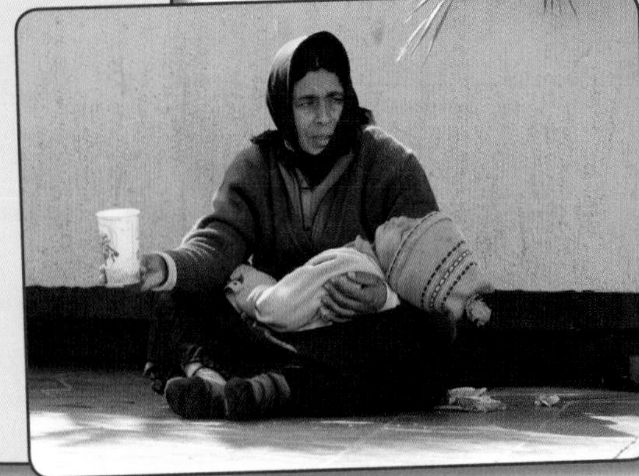

You will hear Jamie, an exam candidate, being interviewed by his teacher. Part 1 of the conversation covers the first three questions. Are Jamie's statements below in answer to the first, second or third question? Listen to part 1 to check whether you were right.

1. Me levanto temprano porque es incómodo dormir en la calle.
2. Nací el 20 de mayo.
3. Charlo con ellos todo el día y busco comida.
4. Yo no podía encontrar un trabajo.
5. Tengo dos hermanos menores.
6. Mis padres se divorciaron.
7. Vivo aquí, en las calles de Málaga.
8. Empecé a vivir en la calle.
9. Mi madre no tenía dinero.
10. A veces la gente me da dinero.

Listen to part 1 again and summarise:

- Why he is living on the streets
- What a typical day is like for him

Listen to part 2 of Jamie's conversation and note down the words that fill the gaps.

– Describe un día típico para ti… ¿Qué comes y bebes normalmente?
– ¡No llevo una vida muy sana! (1) ____ comer pizza de una pizzería cerca de la calle (2) ____ duermo. Hay una camarera muy simpática (3) ____ siempre me da una porción de pizza. De vez en cuando hay gente buena que me compra un café (4) ____ hace frío. (5) ____ también bebo mucho alcohol. Lo bebo sobre todo en invierno cuando hace frío.

– ¿Cuál es el problema más serio para los jóvenes sin techo?
– (6) ____, el problema más serio es el alcoholismo. (7) ____ hay muchas drogas en la calle. Drogas blandas y drogas duras. (8) ____ alcohol y de la droga, los jóvenes sin techo tienen muchos problemas de salud. El año pasado un amigo mío murió (9) ____ tomar una sobredosis de heroína. La experiencia ha sido muy dura para mí. (10) ____ evitar las drogas, pero es muy difícil porque la vida parece mejor después de tomar drogas.

Look at the words you identified in exercise 3. What do they mean? Which of the following are they used for?

- adding information within a sentence
- helping to structure a paragraph
- adding variety to the language

Now listen to part 3 of Jamie's interview and answer the questions.

1 Jamie says '*Ojalá pueda dejar de vivir en la calle*'. What does '*dejar de*' mean? What verb form does he use in this sentence and why?
2 Jamie says 'This is what I want most'. Can you write the words he uses in Spanish to express this?
3 What is the unexpected question that Jamie's teacher asks and what does it mean?
4 Which tenses does he use in answer to the unexpected question? Which time expressions does he use with each tense?

Now it's your turn! Prepare your answers to the task and then do the interview with your partner or teacher.

- Use the Grade Studio and your answers to exercises 1–5 to help you plan.
- Adapt what Jamie said but add your own ideas.
- Prepare your answers to the questions and try to predict what the unexpected question could be. The examiner might base this question on something you have already said, or ask something totally new!
- Record the conversation. Ask a partner to listen to it and say how well you performed.

Award each other one star, two stars or three stars for each of these categories:

- *Pronunciation*
- *Confidence and fluency*
- *Range of tenses*
- *Variety of vocabulary and expressions*
- *Using longer sentences*
- *Taking the initiative*

What do you need to do next time to improve your performance?

GradeStudio

To produce a good answer you need to be able to use a variety of structures.

- Use a **range of tenses**. Jamie uses the preterite tense and present tenses in answer to the first two questions. Look through the questions and plan how you could answer them.
- Use **connectives** to extend your sentences such as *porque, pero, y* and *también*.
- Use **adjectives** to describe people and situations. Jamie uses these in the first three questions: *tranquila, incómodo, difícil*. Can you remember what he used them to describe?

To go a step further you need to use a wider variety of language.

- Jamie uses the **imperfect tense** to describe how his life used to be. Can you incorporate the imperfect tense into your own interview?
- Use **adverbs of frequency** and **time expressions** to add more detail to what you say. Which does Jamie use in exercise 3?
- Refer to **other people** a well as yourself so that you use a range of verb forms. Which other people does Jamie refer to in the course of his interview?

For a really impressive answer:

- Use **complex sentences** that contain more than one tense. In part 3 Jamie uses the present tense and the imperfect tense, '*Cuando no vivía en la calle hacía mucho deporte, pero ahora no es posible.*'
- Use phrases like *ójala* with the **subjunctive**, '*Ójala pueda dejar de tomar drogas.*'
- Use **relative pronouns** to link ideas in a sentence, such as *donde* (where), *cuando* (when) and *que* (which/who) to add information to sentences. Can you find examples of these in exercise 3?

Prueba escrita

Read the text and answer the questions in English.

1 Whose advice for a healthy lifestyle does James quote?
2 What foods does James like to eat?
3 What steps does he take to keep healthy? Give three details.
4 What two things would he never do?
5 How much did James weigh three years ago?
6 Why was James overweight previously? Give three details.
7 What made him lose weight?
8 Why does James want to eat well when he is at university? Give two reasons.

Me llamo James y tengo quince años. Creo que llevo una vida bastante sana. Cuando era pequeño mi abuela me decía 'Desayuna como un rey, come como un príncipe y cena como un mendigo.' Es un buen consejo para llevar una vida sana y reconozco que el desayuno es muy importante. Me gusta desayunar cereales y a veces tostadas. También me gusta comer carne con verduras o pescado con ensalada, y me encanta la fruta. Para mantenerme en forma, siempre intento evitar la comida basura, pero de vez en cuando como alguna hamburguesa. También bebo mucha agua porque es muy buena para la salud. Además, me gusta practicar deporte ya que el ejercicio aeróbico ayuda a eliminar grasa del cuerpo. En general llevo una vida sana y creo que evito tomar cosas perjudiciales, por ejemplo, nunca tomaría drogas ni tampoco fumaría.

La verdad es que mi vida ha cambiado radicalmente. Hace tres años comía demasiado y pesaba más de ochenta kilos. El problema era que comía muy mal, siempre iba a restaurantes de comida rápida y nunca hacía deporte. No tenía energía para nada. Un día mi amigo Pepe me invitó a ir a la playa, pero no fui porque no quería ponerme en bañador delante de mis amigos. ¡Qué vergüenza! Ese día decidí cambiar mi vida y ahora es muy diferente. Tengo mucho más energía y estoy más contento.

Dentro de unos años iré a la universidad y me gustaría mantenerme en forma. Sé que mucha gente no come bien lejos de casa, pero intentaré comer lo mejor posible para no engordar, y para evitar sentirme tan deprimido como antes. ¡Ojalá pueda comer bien con el poco dinero que tenga!

Find the equivalent of these expressions in Spanish in the text.

1 It is good advice…
2 I try to avoid junk food…
3 …aerobic exercise helps to eliminate fat.
4 I would never take drugs…
5 The truth is that my life has changed radically.
6 The problem was that…
7 That day I decided to change my life…
8 …now it's very different.
9 Within a few years I will go to university…
10 I hope I can eat well…

3 ***Tick the sentences from exercise 2 that are not in the present tense. Identify the tense used for these.***

4 ***You might be asked to write about healthy lifestyles as a Controlled Assessment task. Use the Grade Studio to help you prepare your account.***

GradeStudio

To produce a good answer you need to use a variety of structures.

- Look at how James uses the **present tense** in the first paragraph to talk about his lifestyle now.
- Look at how he uses the **preterite** in the second paragraph to talk about the time that he decided to change his lifestyle. Can you find three verbs in the preterite?
- James talks about his lifestyle hopes for the future using the **future tense**. Can you find two verbs in the future tense?
- Find five examples of **simple connectives** that James uses in the first paragraph to extend his sentences.

To go a step further you need to use a wider range of language.

- Find six examples of how James uses the **imperfect tense** to talk about what his lifestyle used to be like.
- Find an example of how James uses the **perfect tense** to talk about how his life has changed and the **conditional** to talk about what he would or wouldn't do.
- James uses a number of **phrases** to **extend his sentences** and structure his text. What do these mean: *'creo que…', 'reconozco que…', 'la verdad es que…', 'sé que…'*?

For a really impressive answer:

- Include a **complex sentence** with two tenses in it. Can you find an example of this in the second paragraph of the text?
- Use ***para*** **+ infinitive** to extend your sentences. Can you find three examples where James uses this?
- Use ***ojalá*** **+ subjunctive**. Can you see where James uses this in the third paragraph?

5 ***Now write a full account of your lifestyle.***

- Adapt James's text and use language from Module 8. Write at least 200 words.
- If you need to write something which is not in the book then keep it simple. When you look up a word in a dictionary make sure that you choose the right one. Look carefully at any examples given. Cross-check by looking the Spanish word up in the Spanish-English part of the dictionary.
- Structure your text carefully. Organise what you write in paragraphs.

General summary of the topic

Introduce yourself
Do you think that you have a healthy lifestyle?

Main paragraph

Talk about your lifestyle
- *What do you eat?*
- *What exercise do you do?*
- *What are your opinions on smoking, alcohol, drugs, etc.?*

How did your lifestyle use to be?
Why did you change it?

Conclusion

What sort of lifestyle will you have in the future?

6 ***Check carefully what you have written.***

- spelling (a lot of food items are cognates, but they may be spelt differently *hamburguesa, cereales*)
- accents on verbs (correct in the imperfect, conditional, future and preterite?)
- verbs (imperfect and the future with the correct endings and an irregular stem if necessary?)

Leer y escuchar

1 ***Read the article about moving house. Where did the removal men actually put these items of furniture? Write the letter of the correct room for each item of furniture.*** **(4 marks)**

Historias de mudanzas

¡Cuando nos mudamos de casa, los empleados de las compañías de mudanzas no siempre ponen los muebles en las habitaciones apropiadas! He aquí varias historias curiosas…

Al llegar a nuestra nueva casa no vimos la nevera. Buscamos por toda la casa y por fin la encontramos en el garaje. ¡Qué raro!
Juanita, Madrid

Yo creo que lo normal es poner el sofá en el salón, pero nosotros descubrimos nuestro sofá en la cocina. ¡Me enfadé mucho!
Pilar, Valencia

Mis instrucciones fueron muy claras: hay que poner la lámpara en el dormitorio grande. ¿Dónde la pusieron? En el cuarto de baño. ¿Cómo es posible?
Marga, Bilbao

¡Qué horror! Cuando llegamos al nuevo apartamento nuestra cama estaba en el comedor. ¡No me lo podía creer!
Julio, Salamanca

1 fridge
2 sofa
3 lamp
4 bed

a bathroom
b bedroom
c kitchen
d dining room
e living room
f garage

2 ***Read the article about where people live. Do these young people like the areas of the town they live in? For each person, write Yes or No and give a reason for your answer.*** **(4 marks)**

a Javier **b** Alicia **c** Carlos **d** Marta

Yo vivo en el norte de la ciudad. Creo que es divertido porque hay un polideportivo estupendo, pero mi hermano dice que es aburrido porque no hay mucha gente. ***Javier***

Según mucha gente el barrio del este es muy industrial y sucio. A mí me parece fantástico porque aquí están todas las tiendas modernas y quays. ¡Mola mogollón!
Carlos

Mi casa está en el sur de la ciudad. Detesto vivir aquí porque los edificios son viejos. Los monumentos históricos, sin embargo, gustan mucho a los turistas. ***Alicia***

Vivir en el centro de la ciudad es horrible. A mi hermana le gusta la vida nocturna aquí, pero yo no estoy de acuerdo con ella. En mi opinión las calles son muy ruidosas. ***Marta***

3 ***Read the advice column on page 159 and answer the questions.***

1 What advice does Conchita ask for? (1 mark)
2 What does Tía Tita suggest Conchita's real problem might be? Write the correct letter. (1 mark)
a greed **b** showing off **c** unhappiness

In a challenging task like this, you will need to use reading strategies to work out the meaning of unfamiliar language. Look for near-cognates and words you recognise from other contexts, like *perdido* and *menos*.

You might also be expected to draw your own conclusions about someone's feelings from clues in the text.

La Tía Tita, tu consejera sentimental

Querida Tía Tita,

Necesito ayuda. ¿Cómo puedo dejar de gastar todo mi dinero en ropa?

Conchita, Barcelona

Cuando vas a las tiendas y piensas 'me gusta este vestido' o 'me encanta esa camiseta' o 'adoro aquellos pantalones' es porque estás tratando de llenar un vacío. Piensa menos en lo material y céntrate en tus sentimientos. Quizás para ti sentirte feliz sea más importante que comprar ropa. ¿Hay alguna cosa que has perdido o alguna persona a quien echas de menos en tu vida?

Un saludo, Tía Tita

1 ***Listen to Carmen describing her home town and answer the questions.***

1 How does she describe her home town? Write the correct letter. (1 mark)
a modern but ugly **b** industrial but dirty **c** historical but touristy

2 What was the worst aspect of her home town in the past? Write the correct letter. (1 mark)
a quality of the shops **b** traffic pollution **c** leisure facilities

3 What are they planning to do to improve the town? (1 mark)
a clean up the town centre **b** improve public transport **c** build more houses

> In this type of task, listen carefully for small words, such as negatives, as these can completely change the meaning of what someone says. Listen for the detail, in order to separate a correct answer from a 'distractor'.

2 ***Listen to a family comparing a former house and a new flat. What does each person think of their new flat? Write B (better than), W (worse than) or S (similar to) their former house? (4 marks)***

1 Julio
2 Mamá
3 Papá
4 Elena

> In this task, you need to distinguish between people talking about the past and the present. So listen carefully for tenses and time expressions. It's also essential to know the words *igual* (equal, same) and *el/la/los/las mismo(s)/misma(s)* (the same).

3 ***Listen to Miguel talking about healthy food and answer the questions.***

1 What exactly is Miguel's comment about yoghurt? (1 mark)

2 Does Miguel feel that supermarkets are being honest about healthy food? Yes or No? Give a reason for your answer. (1 mark)

3 What does Miguel plan to do in the future? Mention 2 things. (2 marks)

4 In conclusion, how would you describe Miguel's attitude to healthy food? (1 mark)
a responsible **b** indifferent **c** critical

> You don't need to answer in full sentences, but you do need to give full details, especially when you see the word 'exactly'.
> At this level, there will often be a question that asks you to draw a conclusion, based on all the evidence in the text (see question 4)

Palabras

Pasándolo mal *Feeling ill*

el brazo	*arm*
el codo	*elbow*
el estómago	*stomach*
el pie	*foot*
la boca	*mouth*
la cabeza	*head*
la espalda	*back*
la garganta	*throat*
la mano	*hand*
la nariz	*nose*
la pierna	*leg*
la rodilla	*knee*
las muelas/los dientes	*teeth*
los oídos/las orejas	*ears*
los ojos	*eyes*
Le duele(n)…	*His/her… hurts*
Me duele(n)…	*My… hurts*
Te duele(n)…	*Your… hurts*
Tengo dolor de…	*I have …ache*
Tiene dolor de…	*He/She has …ache*
Tienes dolor de…	*You have …ache*
No me encuentro bien./Me siento mal.	*I don't feel well.*
Tienes mala cara.	*You don't look well.*
¿Cuánto (tiempo) hace que te duele?	*How long has it been hurting you?*
¿Desde cuándo?	*Since when?*
¿Desde hace cuánto tiempo?	*For how long?*
Desde hace…	*For…*
Desde…	*Since…*
Estoy cansado(a)./Tengo sueño.	*I'm tired.*
Estoy enfermo.	*I'm ill.*
Me he cortado el pie.	*I've cut my foot.*
Me he quemado la espalda.	*I've burnt my back.*
Me he roto la pierna.	*I've broken my leg.*
Me he torcido el tobillo.	*I've twisted my ankle.*
Tengo fiebre.	*I've got a temperature.*
Tengo frío/calor.	*I'm cold/hot.*
Tengo gripe.	*I've got flu.*
Tengo tos.	*I've got a cough.*
Tengo un resfriado.	*I've got a cold.*
Tengo una insolación.	*I've got sunburn.*
Tienes que…	*You have to…*
Debes…	*You should…*
beber mucha agua	*drink a lot of water*
descansar	*rest*
ir al hospital inmediatamente	*go to hospital immediately*
ponerte esta crema	*put this cream on*
ponerte una tirita	*put a plaster on*
tomar este jarabe	*take this syrup*
tomar una aspirina	*take an aspirin*

¿Cuánto es? *How much is it?*

las cebollas	*onions*
las judías verdes	*green beans*
las manzanas	*apples*
las naranjas	*oranges*
las peras	*pears*
las zanahorias	*carrots*
los champiñones	*mushrooms*
los guisantes	*peas*
los huevos	*eggs*
los limones	*lemons*
los melocotones	*peaches*
los melones	*melons*
los pepinos	*cucumbers*
los pimientos rojos	*red peppers*
los plátanos	*bananas*
¿En qué puedo servirle?	*How can I help you?*
Deme…, por favor.	*Give me…, please.*
Lo siento, no queda(n)…	*I'm sorry, I've got no… left.*
Aquí tiene. ¿Algo más?	*Here you are. Anything else?*
No, nada más.	*No, nothing else.*
¿Cuánto es?	*How much is it?*
¿Cuánto cuesta(n)?	*How much does it/do they cost?*
Son… euros con…	*They are… euros and…*
…gramos de…	*…grams of…*
medio kilo/un kilo/dos kilos de…	*half a kilo/one kilo/two kilos of…*
media/una docena de huevos halfa	*half a/a dozen eggs*
un cartón de leche	*a carton of milk*
un paquete de azúcar/arroz	*a packet of sugar/rice*
una barra de pan	*a stick of bread*
una botella de aceite	*a bottle of oil*
una caja de galletas	*a box of biscuits*
una lata de atún	*a tin of tuna*
una pastilla de mantequilla	*a packet of butter*

Estar en forma *Being in shape*

Para estar en forma…	*To be in shape…*
Para no engordar…	*To not put on weight…*
siempre	*always*
a menudo	*often*
frecuentemente	*frequently*
de vez en cuando	*sometimes*
raramente	*rarely*
raras veces	*occasionally*
nunca	*never*
(no) como/bebo	*I (don't) eat/drink*
desayuno	*I eat breakfast*
ceno	*I eat dinner*
suelo beber	*I usually drink*
suelo comer	*I usually eat*
intento beber	*I try to drink*
intento comer	*I try to eat*
intento evitar	*I try to avoid*
el café	*coffee*
el cordero	*lamb*
el pescado	*fish*
el pollo	*chicken*
el queso	*cheese*
el té	*tea*
el yogur	*yogurt*
el zumo	*juice*
la carne de cerdo	*pork*
la comida basura/rápida	*junk/fast food*
la ensalada	*salad*
la fruta	*fruit*
la leche	*milk*
la lechuga	*lettuce*
la merluza	*hake*
la ternera	*veal*
las gambas	*prawns*
las hamburguesas	*hamburgers*
las tartas con nata	*cream cakes*
las verduras	*vegetables*
los churros	*donuts*
los dulces	*sweets*
los filetes	*steak*
los huevos	*eggs*
las legumbres	*vegetables*
los pasteles	*cakes*
los perritos calientes	*hot dogs*
Contiene(n) …	*It contains (They contain) …*
No contiene(n) …	*It doesn't (They don't) contain…*
demasiado/a	*too much*
mucho/a	*a lot*
poco/a	*a little*
el azúcar	*sugar*
la sal	*salt*
la fibra	*fibre*
la grasa	*fat*
las proteínas	*proteins*
las vitaminas	*vitamins*

¿Llevas una vida sana? *Do you lead a healthy life?*

(No) Deberías…	*You should(n't)…*
ponerte en forma	*get in shape*
preocuparte	*worry*
Para perder peso/adelgazar, deberías…	*To lose weight/slim down, you should…*
Para estar en forma, deberías…	*To be in shape, you should…*
Para llevar una vida más sana, deberías…	*To lead a healthier life, you should…*
Para no estar cansado/a, deberías …	*To not be tired, you should…*
Para sentirte mejor, deberías…	*To feel better, you should…*
Yo, en tu lugar,…	*In your place, I…*
(no) cambiaría mi estilo de vida	*I would(n't) change my lifestyle*
bebería más/menos…	*I would drink more/less…*
comería más/menos…	*I would eat more/less…*
compraría caramelos sin azúcar	*I would buy sugar-free sweets*
empezaría a hacer/practicar/jugar…	*I would start to do/practise/play…*
haría más deporte	*I would do more sport*
intentaría comer/hacer…	*I would try to eat/do…*
Vale. Tienes razón.	*OK. You're right.*
En el futuro…	*In the future…*
beberé	*I will drink*
cambiaré	*I will change*
comeré	*I will eat*
compraré	*I will buy*
empezaré	*I will begin*
haré	*I will do*
intentaré	*I will try*

Los jóvenes *Young people*

En mi opinión…	*In my opinion…*
Creo que…	*I think that…*
A mi modo de ver…	*As I see it…*
Por un lado…, por otro lado…	*On one hand…, on the other hand…*
Me da igual…	*I'm not bothered…*
Tendría miedo de…	*I would be afraid of…*
beber alcohol	*drinking alcohol*
fumar cigarrillos	*smoking cigarettes*
llevar navajas	*carrying knives*
tomar drogas blandas	*taking soft drugs*
tomar drogas duras	*taking hard drugs*
vivir en un barrio violento	*to live in a rough neighbourhood*
la dependencia	*addiction*
hacerse drogadicto/alcohólico	*to become a drug addict/an alcoholic*
los riesgos	*the risks*
morir	*to die*
es peligroso	*is dangerous*
es una pérdida de tiempo/dinero	*is a waste of time/money*
es una tontería	*is stupid*
es divertido	*it's fun*
mis amigos lo hacen	*my friends do it*
no me parece una cosa seria	*it doesn't seem a serious thing to me*
se puede dejar fácilmente	*you can give up easily*
es inofensivo	*is harmless*

- Talking about the environment
- Using the conditional of **deber**
- Using a variety of expressions to give your point of view

Repaso *Cambios medioambientales*

1 Completa las frases. Después empareja la frase con una foto.

la sequía = *drought*

1 En nuestra ciudad…
2 Mucha gente va…
3 Hay demasiado…
4 El aire y el agua están …
5 No hay espacios…
6 Hay muchas…
7 No llueve lo suficiente y por eso…

I …la sequía es un problema en nuestra región.
II …hay mucha basura.
III …verdes, solo hay edificios.
IV …fábricas.
V …en coche o en moto.
VI …muy contaminados.
VII …tráfico y atascos.

a

b

c

d

e

f

g

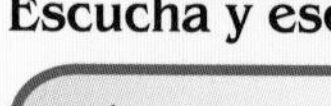

2 Escucha y escribe las letras correctas. (1–5)

Deberíamos…
a comprar productos ecológicos.
b consumir menos energía.
c plantar más árboles.
d proteger la naturaleza.
e reciclar el papel y el vidrio.
f reducir la contaminación.
g mantener el aire limpio/el agua limpia.
h usar más el transporte público.
i mejorar la red de transporte público.
j usar el agua de forma responsable.

No deberíamos…
k malgastar el agua.
l tirar basura al suelo.

G *(Se) Debería + infinitive* 210

Use the conditional of **deber** *(must)* followed by an **infinitive** to say what people *should* do:

deber**ía**	*I should*	+ **plantar** / **proteger** / **consumir**
deber**ías**	*you should*	
deber**ía**	*he/she should*	
deber**íamos**	*we should*	
deber**íais**	*you should*	
deber**ían**	*they should*	

Deberíamos plantar más árboles.
We should plant more trees.

To say that *one should* do something without specifying who should do it, use **se debería + infinitive:**
Se debería plantar más árboles.
One should plant more trees.

3 Escucha a estas personas. Copia y completa la tabla en inglés. (1–3)

	area lived in	problems	solutions
1	industrial area in Gijón	a lot of pollution,…	should improve transport network,…

Gastar can mean *spend* for money, or *use* for energy. The opposite is **malgastar** (to waste, i.e. use badly).

Con tu compañero/a, pregunta y contesta, cambiando los datos subrayados.

- ¿Dónde vives?
- Vivo en un barrio industrial cerca de Londres.
- ¿Qué problemas medioambientales hay en tu región?
- Hay varios problemas. El mayor problema es que hay mucha contaminación; por ejemplo, hay muchas fábricas y mucho tráfico. Otro problema es que no hay espacios verdes.
- ¿Qué deberíamos hacer para proteger el medio ambiente?
- Creo que primero deberíamos usar más el transporte público. También deberíamos comprar productos ecológicos.

Use a model to help you answer the questions, but add in your own information.

Vary what you say as much as possible using phrases you have seen before to give your point of view:

Opino que...
A mi modo de ver...
Para mí...
Por un lado..., por otro lado...

Lee el texto y busca estas frases en español.

a you can help too
b reduce your consumption
c before you throw something away
d recyle
e separate rubbish
f always respect the environment

Tú también puedes ayudar al planeta practicando '**la ley de las 3 R**':
Reducir: reduce tu consumo. Compra y gasta solo lo que necesites.
Reutilizar: antes de tirar algo, piensa si lo has gastado del todo y si ya no sirve para nada más.
Reciclar: El papel, el plástico y el vidrio se pueden reutilizar o reciclar. Separa la basura.
Y sobre todo hay que respetar: RESPETA el medio ambiente ¡siempre!

Everything in its place. Where would you leave each object?

- ¿En qué lugar dejarías una botella de plástico vacía?
- La dejaría en el contenedor amarillo o la reutilizaría otra vez para beber agua.

una botella de plástico vacía	un libro
una manzana	un tetrabrick de leche vacío
una bolsa de plástico	una botella de cristal vacía
un periódico	un bote de champú gastado

dejar = *to leave*

el contenedor azul – papel y cartón	**el contenedor verde – vidrio**	**el contenedor amarillo – envases de plástico, tetrabrick**	**el contenedor de compostaje**	**el frigorífico**	**la basura**
			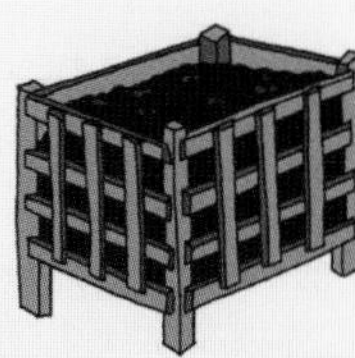		

Escribe un artículo sobre el medio ambiente. Hay que mencionar:

Problemas medioambientales en tu región	Para proteger el medio ambiente...
• El mayor problema es que...	• Creo que primero deberíamos...
• Otro problema es que...	• También deberíamos...
	• Podríamos...

- Talking about global issues
- Using the present subjunctive
- Listening for high numbers

1 El mundo hoy en día

1 Escucha y lee. Empareja los textos con las fotos.

Jorge: *Hay problemas medioambientales en todo el planeta. Me preocupan **el calentamiento global** y **el agujero de la capa de ozono**.*

María: *Actualmente los problemas más preocupantes son **la crisis económica** y **el precio de la gasolina**.*

Paco: *En España existen problemas como **los sin techo**, gente que no tiene hogar y que vive en la calle. También **el paro** es preocupante. Hay muchos parados, es decir, gente sin trabajo.*

Alicia: *Me preocupan **la discriminación** y **el racismo**. ¿Por qué no podemos vivir juntos?*

Eduardo: *Es increíble que haya tanta **pobreza** y **hambre** en el mundo.*

Juanita: *Me da miedo **el terrorismo** porque es una amenaza global.*

Miguel: *Para mí **la justicia** y **la igualdad** son importantes, así como **el respeto**, **la solidaridad** y **los derechos humanos**... 'Todos los seres humanos nacen libres e iguales en derechos y dignidad...'*

Katia: *Me preocupa **la delincuencia** hoy en día. ¿Qué vamos a hacer?*

1 

2 

3 

4 

5 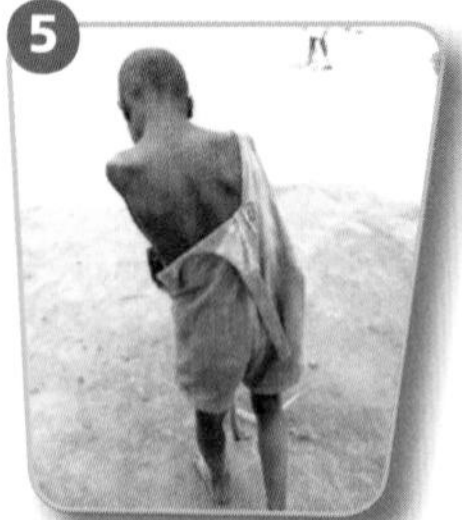

6 

7 

8 

2 Lee los textos otra vez y escribe las palabras en rojo en inglés.

3 Con tu compañero/a, pregunta y contesta.

- ¿Cuál es para ti el problema más serio hoy en día?
- Opino que...
- No estoy de acuerdo contigo. Para mí...

> When you want to say that you are concerned or worried about something, you can use:
> Me preocupa(n)... *I am worried by...*
> ...es/son preocupante(s). *...is/are worrying.*

Opino que... Para mí... A mi modo de ver... A mi parecer... Creo que... Estoy de acuerdo contigo. No estoy de acuerdo contigo.	el calentamiento global el agujero de la capa de ozono la crisis económica el precio de la gasolina	es el problema más serio. es un problema muy serio. no es un problema tan serio.
	los sin techo y el paro la discriminación y el racismo la pobreza y el hambre el terrorismo y la delincuencia	son los problemas más serios. son unos problemas muy serios. no son unos problemas tan serios.

4 Lee el texto. Escribe un resumen en inglés de los pensamientos de Paco.

Pienso que es importante que luchemos contra la discriminación y el racismo.
Es increíble que haya tanta pobreza en el mundo.
No es justo que el terrorismo exista y que muera tanta gente inocente.
Es importante que trabajemos para acabar con el hambre en el mundo.
Es esencial que luchemos contra el calentamiento global y que salvemos la Tierra.
Es necesario que no dañemos la naturaleza y que no contaminemos los ríos y el aire.

5 Here are the infinitive verbs in the text. Find the subjunctive forms in Paco's manifesto.

1 existir – *to exist*
2 contaminar – *to pollute*
3 luchar – *to fight*
4 trabajar – *to work*
5 salvar – *to save*
6 morir – *to die*
7 dañar – *to damage*
8 haber – *there is/there are*

G *The present subjunctive* ➲230

The subjunctive is used to express feelings. You have already seen it with **ojalá** *(let's hope that…)*. In Spanish it is also used in sentences with this structure:

Es + adjective + que… | Es **importante** que… / Es **esencial** que… / Es **necesario** que… / Es **increíble** que… / Es **terrible** que…

To form the present subjunctive take the **yo** form from the present tense, but add different endings:

	usar *(to use)*	**proteg**er *(to protect)*	**consum**ir *(to consume)*
(yo)	us**e**	protej**a**	consum**a**
(tú)	us**es**	protej**as**	consum**as**
(él/ella/usted)	us**e**	protej**a**	consum**a**
(nosotros/as)	us**emos**	protej**amos**	consum**amos**
(vosotros/as)	us**éis**	protej**áis**	consum**áis**
(ellos/as/ustedes)	us**en**	protej**an**	consum**an**

Some verbs are irregular, but the endings follow the patterns above.
Here is the *I form*:

dar *(to give)*	d**é**	ir *(to go)*	*vaya*
ser (to be)	*se***a**	*haber* (there is/*are*)	hay**a**

6 Escucha y escribe la cifra correcta. (1–8)

1 El ____ de la población mundial disfruta del 70% de la riqueza del planeta.
2 ____ millones de personas no tienen acceso a comida suficiente para alimentarse.
3 ____ millones de personas sobreviven con menos de un euro diario.
4 ____ millones de personas no tienen acceso al agua potable.
5 ____ millones de personas están infectadas con el VIH/SIDA, y la gran mayoría no recibe ningún tratamiento.
6 ____ millones de niños y niñas mueren cada año antes de cumplir los cinco años de edad por causas evitables.
7 El ____ de las personas pobres del planeta son mujeres.
8 ____ habitante de un país rico emite ____ veces más dióxido de carbono a la atmósfera que ____ de África subsahariana.

When listening for numbers and percentages, don't panic!
Listen, then write. Listen the second time to check your answer.
80% = el ochenta por ciento
1000 = mil
2000 = dos mil
6792 = seis mil setecientos noventa y dos
1 000 000 = un millón
2 000 000 = dos millones
1 000 000 000 = mil millones

- Considering problems facing the planet
- Negative commands
- Using cognates and context to understand a text

2 ¡Cuida tu planeta!

Read and match each phrase in English with the correct Spanish. Then listen. Which phrase is mentioned each time? Write the correct letter. **(1–6)**

- **a** Don't use so much energy.
- **b** Separate rubbish.
- **c** Re-use plastic bags.
- **d** Don't waste paper.
- **e** Don't use fossil fuels.
- **f** Don't pollute water.
- **g** Don't use detergents with phosphates.
- **h** Don't pollute the environment.

1. Reutilice las bolsas de plástico.
2. No contamine el medio ambiente.
3. Separe la basura.
4. No ensucie el agua.
5. No malgaste el papel.
6. No use detergentes con fosfatos.
7. No utilice combustibles fósiles.
8. No consuma tanta energía.

ensuciar = *to make dirty*

escuchar 2 **Escucha otra vez. Escribe la letra correcta.**

- **a** Water is vital for the survival of all living organisms.
- **b** Phosphates damage aquatic ecosystems.
- **c** We are consuming more and more, and we have to stop.
- **d** We have to leave a healthy planet to our children.
- **e** Never forget that for you to use paper, a tree has died.
- **f** Help our planet to be a pleasant place to live.

hablar 3 ***With a partner, read the phrases below out loud and match each one to an order from exercise 1.***

- ● Es necesario que protejamos los árboles.
- ■ No malgaste el papel.

1. **Es necesario que protejamos los árboles.**
2. **Es esencial que apaguemos las luces.**
3. ***Es importante que conservemos el planeta.***
4. **Es necesario que protejamos la vida marina.**
5. ***Es importante que reciclemos la basura.***
6. **Es esencial que encontremos alternativas a los combustibles fósiles.**

G *The present subjunctive* ➲230

The present subjunctive is also used:

For formal positive commands where a person you would call *usted* is being addressed.
cuid**ar** = *to look after*
¡Cuid**e** el medio ambiente! (usted)
Look after the environment.

In *all* negative commands:
consum**ir** = *to consume*
No consum**as** demasiada energía. (tú)
Don't consume too much energy.
No consum**a** demasiada energía.(usted)
Don't consume too much energy.

4 Escucha y empareja estos títulos con los artículos.

1 La contaminación del aire
2 Cuidemos nuestros bosques y árboles
3 El calentamiento global del planeta

a Una de las mayores amenazas de nuestro planeta es el calentamiento global, provocado por el efecto invernadero (el aumento de CO_2 en la atmósfera).
La quema de combustibles fósiles (petróleo, carbón y gas) emite grandes cantidades de CO_2. Para reducir las emisiones, la única solución es quemar menos cantidad de estos combustibles, y utilizar otros no contaminantes.
El objetivo de Greenpeace es luchar por un cambio en las políticas energéticas en favor del ahorro, la utilización eficiente de la energía y el desarrollo de las energías limpias y renovables.

b Uno de los problemas medioambientales más graves que tenemos es la contaminación del aire. El uso abusivo del transporte particular contribuye mucho a la contaminación del aire y a la lluvia ácida.
Para tener un aire más limpio, es necesario que ayudemos a mejorar nuestro entorno, para legar a nuestros hijos un ambiente sano.
¡Deje el coche en casa!

c Las selvas y los bosques de nuestro planeta tienen árboles centenarios. El Amazonas es uno de los ecosistemas más diversos del mundo. Aquí puedes encontrar la mitad de las especies de toda la Tierra. Muchas de esas especies están en peligro de extinción a causa de la deforestación. Además, en el Amazonas se produce una buena parte del oxígeno que respiramos. Sin embargo, cada año cortamos grandes extensiones de árboles…

Reading is about using what you know to help you understand new words. You can use cognates and context to help you understand the meaning of a text. There are many Spanish words, which look and sometimes sound similar to English words.

For example, you know that *efecto = effect*.

You are puzzled by the word invernadero, but within the context of climate change, you can work out that it means 'greenhouse'.

5 *Make a list of ten cognates in the three texts. Write the English.*

6 *Now use cognates and context to find the following phrases in Spanish in the texts.*

1 threats
2 the increase
3 to burn
4 development
5 clean and renewable energies
6 environmental
7 we cut
8 our environment
9 rainforests and woods
10 half
11 in danger
12 extinction

7 Lee los textos otra vez. Completa las frases en inglés.

1 Global warming… the planet.
2 Burning fossil fuels produces…
3 Greenpeace believes we should develop…
4 One of the most serious problems we face is…
5 The abuse of… contributes to this problem.
6 The jungles and forests on our planet have…
7 The Amazon is one of…
8 The Amazon produces…

8 Diseña un póster.

- *Use slogans from exercise 3 and the texts above.*
- *Use negative commands from exercise 1 above.*

Ejemplo: Muchas especies están en peligro porque cortamos demasiados árboles.
Es muy importante que protejamos los árboles. No malgaste el papel.

- Looking at local solutions to global problems
- Using the imperfect and present tenses
- Gaining thinking time when speaking

3 Piensa globalmente

Haz este cuestionario. Escribe frases enteras.

Ejemplo: **1** Para ahorrar agua, es mejor ducharse.

en vez de + infinitivo = *instead of + ing*

TEST

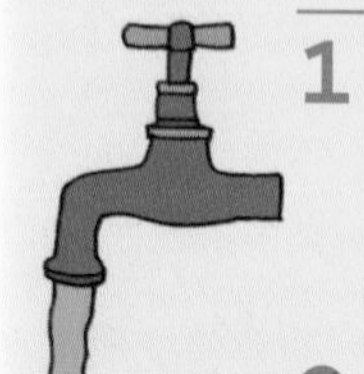

1 Para ahorrar agua, es mejor…
- **a** ducharse.
- **b** bañarse/darse un baño.

2 Para reducir la contaminación del aire, es mejor…
- **a** andar o ir en bici, en vez de usar el coche.
- **b** usar más el coche.

3 Para consumir menos energía, es mejor…
- **a** encender las luces y enchufar los electrodomésticos.
- **b** apagar las luces y desenchufar los electrodomésticos.

4 Para respetar nuestro entorno, es mejor…
- **a** comprar productos locales.
- **b** comprar productos de países lejanos.

5 Para evitar contaminar el medio ambiente, es mejor…
- **a** llevar una bolsa a la compra.
- **b** pedir una bolsa de plástico.

6 Para luchar contra el calentamiento global, es mejor…
- **a** ver la televisión.
- **b** hacerse miembro de un grupo ecologista.

Look at the quiz for 2 minutes, then shut your books and see how much your partner can remember in Spanish about how to help the environment.

- ● ¿Qué deberíamos hacer para proteger el medio ambiente?
- ■ A ver… para ahorrar agua, es mejor ducharse.
- ● ¿Qué más?
- ■ Pues… un momento…, para consumir menos energía, es mejor…

Use the following expressions to play for time when you are speaking:

A ver… **Un momento…**
Pues… no lo sé. **Espera…**

***Listen to these suggestions for recycling and reusing items. Answer the questions in English.* (1–5)**

1 What could you use the other side of the paper for? (Mention 3 things)
2 What are the advantages of reusable coffee filters?
3 What do they suggest you do with toys when you have grown out of them? (Mention 2 details)
4 What are you reminded of with regard to other children?
5 Which material can be useful if recycled? What do they recommend you do with it?

4 Escucha y lee. Contesta a las preguntas en inglés.

a How did Fabio use to behave?
b How has he changed his lifestyle?

El medio ambiente nos preocupa a todos. **Tengo** suerte porque **gano** mucho dinero, pero **quiero** legar a mis hijos un mundo sano, así que por eso he cambiado mi comportamiento.
Antes **tenía** un *Hummer* e **iba** a todas partes en coche, incluso para visitar a mis vecinos. Ahora **conduzco** un coche híbrido y además **cojo** la bici a menudo; o si no, **ando**.
Antes no **pensaba** en proteger el medio ambiente. **Llevaba** ropa de marca muy cara y a menudo **compraba** cosas que no necesitaba. Ahora **reutilizo** todo: papel, bolsas de la compra... También **compro** todo de segunda mano y **doy** mi ropa vieja a la tienda de segunda mano Oxfam.
Antes no **separaba** la basura. Sin embargo, ahora **reciclo** el vidrio, el papel y el plástico, y **pongo** todo en el contenedor correcto.
Antes nunca **cuidaba** del jardín, pero ahora **cultivo** de todo: fruta, legumbres y flores. También **pongo** mis residuos orgánicos en el contenedor de compostaje. **Reduzco** mi consumo al máximo.

Fabio antes

Fabio ahora

5 Describe cómo ha cambiado su vida esta estrella.

Antes siempre... /a menudo... /nunca...

Ahora siempre... /a menudo... /nunca...

G Present tense, irregular verbs ➲202

Some of these verbs belong to a group of verbs that are slightly irregular in the *I form* of the present tense:

conducir	*to drive*	→	condu**zco**	*I drive*
reducir	*to reduce*	→	redu**zco**	*I reduce*
poner	*to put*	→	pon**go**	*I put*

As you write, try to make your sentences as extended and complex as possible. This will help you sound more impressive in your speaking and writing.

- Combine present and imperfect tenses in one sentence.
- Join lots of ideas together with connectives.

Antes siempre **iba** en una limusina muy grande y **consumía** mucha gasolina, **pero** ahora **voy** en bicicleta a menudo y **consumo** muy poca energía.

✓	✗
comprar productos ecológicos	malgastar dinero en cosas inútiles
apagar las luces	comprar productos de países lejanos
consumir poca energía/agua/gasolina	encender las luces
comprar ropa de segunda mano en Oxfam	comprar ropa nueva cada semana
ir en bicicleta	ir en una limusina muy grande
separar la basura y reciclar	pedir siempre bolsas de plástico
utilizar el contenedor de compostaje	consumir mucha agua/energía/gasolina
dar dinero a organizaciones benéficas	bañarse cuatro veces al día

- Talking about global citizenship
- Using **si** + present + future
- Writing an extended text

4 Voluntarios

Escucha y escribe la letra correcta. (1–6)

Silvana

Mustafá

Gabriel

Sabrina

Si pago un poco más por los productos de comercio justo,

Juan Pablo

Isabel

a mejoraré la sociedad, ayudaré a los demás y haré algo útil.
b transformaremos el mundo y acabaremos con la pobreza.
c tendrá la posibilidad de sobrevivir.
d cuidaremos el medio ambiente.
e más personas tendrán una vida digna.
f los trabajadores tendrán mejores salarios.

Busca siete verbos en el futuro en el ejercicio 1 y escríbelos en inglés.

Con tu compañero/a, haz estos diálogos.

- ¿Cómo te llamas?
- ¿De dónde eres?
- ¿Por qué quieres trabajar como voluntario/a? (Si…)

1
Name: Pablo
Nationality: Spanish
Goals as a volunteer:
Help others
More people will have a dignified life
Finish poverty and transform the world

2
Name: Esther
Nationality: German
Goals as a volunteer:
Do something useful and educate people
Better pay for workers and improve society

G Sentences with Si… (If…) ➲208

Si + present tense, + **future tense**
Use this construction to talk about things that are likely to happen:

Si educamos a la gente, **transformaremos** el mundo.
If we educate people, we will change the world.

Si trabajo como voluntario, **mejoraré** la sociedad.
If I work as a volunteer, I will improve society.

For the part of the sentence that uses the future tense, there are some irregular future stems that you will need to remember:

hacer → **har**é   poner → **pondr**é
tener → **tendr**é   salir → **saldr**é

Si is a very useful connective for creating complex sentences with more than one tense. It will help you to aim for the highest marks in your speaking and writing assessments.

4 Lee los textos y contesta a las preguntas en inglés para cada persona.

Me llamo **Germán** y soy voluntario de Cruz Roja en España desde hace un año y medio. Colaboro en un programa de ayuda a personas mayores.
Creo que antes era un poco egoísta. En mi tiempo libre escuchaba música, mandaba correos electrónicos o navegaba por Internet, hasta que un día vi un anuncio: 'Tus minutos muertos pueden ganar vidas.' Llamé y aquí estoy.
Si te haces voluntario, conocerás a gente nueva y tendrás experiencias muy positivas. Doy mi tiempo, pero recibo amistad, que es una cosa preciosa.
El año pasado fui a un evento de Cruz Roja y lo pasé realmente bien. Fue muy divertido. Además, conocí a mi novia que también es voluntaria de esta organización humanitaria…

Me llamo **Silvia** y hace ocho meses me hice voluntaria de un grupo ecologista. A los diecisiete años fui de vacaciones a África con una amiga, y eso cambió mi vida. Vi la sequía y la pobreza de este continente, y me hice voluntaria en cuanto volví a casa. Creo que he cambiado porque antes no tenía tiempo para colaborar con organizaciones humanitarias. Sin embargo, ahora sé que si trabajamos juntos, cambiaremos el mundo. Creo que es muy importante que todo el mundo tenga una vida digna.
Ser voluntario es una experiencia muy buena y gracias a la cual conoces a mucha gente. Si te haces voluntario, ayudarás a los demás y sobre todo, te ayudarás a ti mismo.

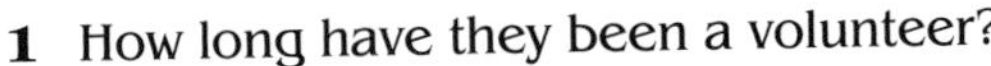

1 How long have they been a volunteer?
2 What type of organisation do they volunteer with?
3 What were they like before they became a volunteer?
4 Why did they sign up?
5 What do they say about being a volunteer? (give three details)

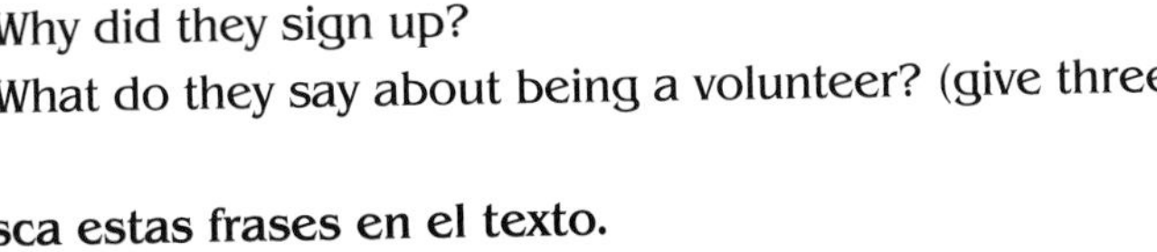

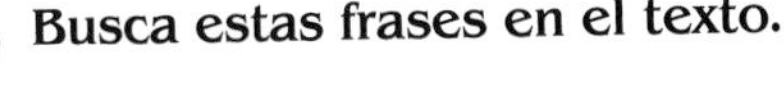

5 Busca estas frases en el texto.

1 Before, I think I was a bit selfish.
2 If you become a volunteer, you will get to know new people.
3 You'll have very positive experiences.
4 I became a volunteer as soon as I came back home.
5 If we work together, we will change the world.
6 If you volunteer, you will help others.

6 Escucha a Isabel y contesta a las preguntas en inglés.

1 How long has she been a volunteer?
2 What sort of work does she do? (give two details)
3 What are the people like that she works with? (give three details)
4 Why did she sign up?
5 Who in particular would she recommend volunteering to?

7 Eres Luis. Escribe un párrafo sobre tus aspiraciones.

As you write your text try to include these:

- Sentences with '**si** + present + future'
- Sentences with the subjunctive like 'Es importante que…'

Nombre: Luis
País: Argentina
Idiomas: inglés y español
Pasatiempos: cocinar, escribir en mi blog, jugar al fútbol
Voluntario: desde hace 6 meses
Trabajo: en un hospital en Ecuador
Motivación: ayudar a la gente enferma, conocer otra cultura, hacer algo útil

- Talking about homelessness
- The pluperfect tense
- Using different time frames

5 Sin techo, sin derecho

1 ***Read the text on homeless people and make notes on what the numbers in bold represent.***

Tres millones de personas viven en la calle en Europa. En España **30 000** no tienen hogar, pero tienen una historia y un nombre...

Los hombres son el **82,7** por ciento de las personas sin hogar, mientras que las mujeres llegan al **17,3** por ciento. Por otra parte, el **29,9** por ciento de las personas que viven en España sin hogar tienen entre 18 y 30 años y el **40** por ciento entre 31 y 44, mientras que **casi la mitad** de todas ellas son extranjeras.

2 **Escucha y lee. Contesta a las preguntas en inglés.**

1 When was Arantxa homeless?
2 How was it for her?
3 Did she manage to get out of it?

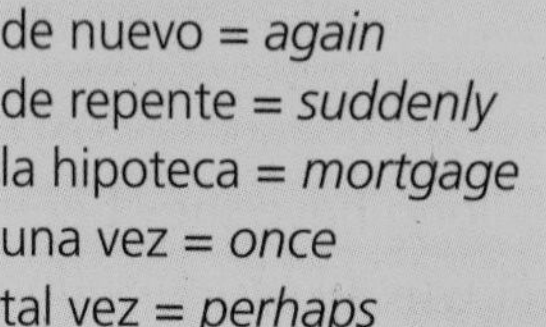

de nuevo = *again*
de repente = *suddenly*
la hipoteca = *mortgage*
una vez = *once*
tal vez = *perhaps*

Reportero: ¿Cómo te llamas?
Arantxa: Me llamo Arantxa.
R: ¿Cuántos años tienes, Arantxa?
A: Tengo veinticuatro años.
R: Y Arantxa, te quedaste sin techo hace unos años, ¿verdad?
A: Sí, hace cuatro años.
R: ¿Qué te pasó exactamente?
A: Pues, primero perdí a mi papá y luego a mi mamá, así que no tenía dinero, ni familia y no sabía qué hacer. En esa época estaba estudiando en la universidad y no podía pagar la hipoteca, así que empecé a dormir en la calle. Hasta entonces mi madre siempre me había dado dinero y había cuidado de mí, pero después de su muerte me quedé sin nada. Anteriormente había vivido una vida sin problemas, y de repente me encontré sola y sin dinero.
R: Debió de ser una experiencia terrible para ti, Arantxa.
A: Lo pasé muy mal. En la calle hay problemas muy graves como el consumo de alcohol y de drogas, la violencia... Nunca había visto tanta indignidad en mi vida. La exclusión social es un gran problema en nuestra sociedad.
R: ¿Cómo saliste de esta situación?
A: Decidí reincorporarme a la sociedad de nuevo, pero no sabía cómo hacerlo. La reinserción es muy difícil. Un día conocí a un voluntario que trabajaba para una organización humanitaria y me ayudó mucho. Ahora trabajo para esta organización, 'Café y bollos para los sin hogar', y vivo en un piso en el centro.
R: ¿Qué planes de futuro tienes?
A: A ver, en el futuro me gustaría viajar. Me encantaría conocer otros países y tener nuevas experiencias. Me preocupa mucho el medio ambiente, sobre todo el calentamiento global. Tal vez trabajaré en este campo, pero si puedo ayudar a los demás, seré feliz...

Contesta a las preguntas en inglés.

1 How did Arantxa end up on the street? (two details)
2 What had her life been like previously?
3 What problems did Arantxa see amongst the homeless? (four details)
4 Who helped her get off the street?
5 What does she do now?
6 Does she have plans for the future? (two details)
7 What is Arantxa concerned about?
8 What will Arantxa be happy to be doing?

Escribe los verbos en amarillo del texto en inglés.

Escucha y apunta los datos siguientes en inglés. (1–4)

a Why did they became homeless?
b How did they get out of homelessness?
c What are they doing now?

Había comprado una casa.	Encontré trabajo.	Trabajo en…
Había empezado a estudiar.	Hablé con una organización caritativa.	Tengo novia y otra casa.
Había perdido mi trabajo.	Me decidí a cambiar todo.	Trabajo con los sin techo.
Había dado a luz a un niño.	Me quedé con un amigo y empecé a buscar trabajo.	Tengo una familia.

Imagina una entrevista con un sin techo. Utiliza estas preguntas.

1 ¿Cómo te llamas?
2 ¿Cuántos años tienes ?
3 Te quedaste sin techo hace unos años, ¿verdad?
4 ¿Qué habías hecho antes de estar sin techo?
5 ¿Qué te pasó exactamente?
6 ¿Cómo saliste de esta situación?
7 ¿Qué planes de futuro tienes?

Act out your conversation for the class.

G *The pluperfect tense*

The pluperfect is used to talk about what someone *had* done, referring to an action in the past which precedes another action. The pluperfect is formed in a similar way to the perfect tense, but instead of using **he cambiado**, **has cambiado**, etc., use **the imperfect of haber** + **past participle**:

(yo)	**había**	
(tú)	**habías**	cambi**ado**
(él/ella/usted)	**había**	+ com**ido**
(nosotros/as)	**habíamos**	viv**ido**
(vosotros/as)	**habíais**	
(ellos/ellas/ustedes)	**habían**	

Hasta entonces **había jugado** al voleibol todos los días.
Until that time, I had played volleyball everyday.

Anteriormente **había trabajado** en una tienda.
Previously I had worked in a shop.

Remember, to form the past participle:
- take the infinitive or the verb
- remove **-ar**, **-er** or **-ir**
- add **-ado** for **-ar** verbs / **-ido** for **-er** and **-ir** verbs

Environment

You are going to have a conversation with your teacher about current problems facing the planet. Your teacher could ask you the following:

- What environmental problems are there in your region?
- What should we do to protect the environment?
- What shouldn't we do?
- How have you changed your life to protect the environment?
- Would you like to work as a volunteer?

Remember that you will have to respond to an unexpected question that you have not yet prepared.
The dialogue will last between 4 and 6 minutes.

You are going to listen to Helen, an exam candidate, taking part in the above conversation with her teacher. Listen to part 1 of the conversation and put these phrases in the order in which you hear them.

1 Otro problema es que…
2 Creo que primero…
3 …sin pensar.
4 El mayor problema…
5 …por ejemplo,…
6 …hay varios problemas.
7 Mucha gente usa su vehículo…

Listen to part 1 again. Note down in English how Helen answers the first two questions.

Listen to part 2 of Helen's conversation and note down the words that fill the gaps.

– ¿Qué no hay que hacer?
– A ver… tengo una lista larga: no utilice combustibles fósiles, no ensucie el agua, no use detergentes con fosfatos porque son peligrosos. (1) ____ deberíamos proteger la vida marina. (2) ____ ahorrar energía no deberíamos dejar la luz encendida (3) ____ salimos de una habitación. (4) ____ deberíamos malgastar el papel, (5) ____ en el colegio. Hay que pensar en los árboles.

– ¿Cómo has cambiado tu vida para proteger el medio ambiente?
– Antes no pensaba en proteger el medio ambiente, (6) ____ en el pasado, (7) ____ separaba la basura. Tampoco llevaba una bolsa a la compra. No había oido hablar del calentamiento global. (8) ____ ahora soy más respetuosa con mi entorno. Cuando voy de compras con mi madre, le digo que (9) ____ compremos productos ecológicos. (10) ____, en casa siempre desenchufo los electrodomésticos para consumir menos energía.

Look at the words you identified in exercise 3. How would you describe them?

- phrases to express a point of view
- connectives
- negatives

5 ***Now listen to part 3 of Helen's conversation and answer the questions.***

1 Helen uses the structure *si* + present + future in her answer to the first question? Can you spot two examples?
2 What is the unexpected question that Helen's teacher asks and what does it mean?
3 In her answer to the second question Helen says '*Es esencial que luchemos contra el calentamiento global*'. What form of the verb *luchar* does she use?

6 ***Now it's your turn! Prepare your answers to the task and then have a conversation with your teacher or partner.***

- Use the Grade Studio and your answers to exercises 1–5 to help you plan.
- Adapt what Helen said to talk about yourself but add your own ideas.
- Prepare your answers to the questions and try to predict what the unexpected question could be. The examiner might base this question on something you have already said, or ask something totally new!
- Record the conversation. Ask a partner to listen to it and say how well you performed.

Award each other one star, two stars or three stars for each of these categories:

- *Pronunciation*
- *Confidence and fluency*
- *Range of tenses*
- *Variety of vocabulary and expressions*
- *Using longer sentences*
- *Taking the initiative*

What do you need to do next time to improve your performance?

GradeStudio

To produce a good answer you need to be able to use a variety of structures.

- **Vary your language** by referring to **the past** and **the present**. Helen talks about environmental problems in the present tense but she mentions that her mum recently bought a bike (using the preterite to refer to the past).
- Use simple **connectives** to extend your sentences such as *y* (and), *también* (also), *pero* (but), *porque* (because).
- Use **adjectives** to add detail to what you say. Helen uses these in her first two answers: *terribles, pequeñas, importantes*.

To go a step further you need to use a wider variety of language.

- Helen uses the **imperfect** to say what her behaviour **used to be** like.
- Helen uses the **conditional** to say what we should do: *Deberíamos utilizar más el transporte público.*
- Try to talk about **other people** so that you use a greater variety of verbs. Can you find examples of where Helen does this?
- Express your **point of view**. Look again at exercise 3 to find expressions that Helen uses to do this.

For a really impressive answer:

- Include an example of the **subjunctive**. Helen uses the subjunctive in the following ways: *Es esencial que luchemos..., Es importante que compremos..., Ojalá lo podamos hacer.*
- Use the **pluperfect tense**. Can you find an example of this in part 2 of the conversation?
- Use **complex sentences** with two tenses in them. Helen does this when she uses sentences with *si* + present + future.

Prueba escrita

Read the text and answer the questions in English.

1 What is the main problem, and its cause, in Amy's city?
2 What made Amy decide to change her life? Give two details.
3 What world problems is Amy most worried about? Give two details.
4 How does Amy describe Greenpeace?
5 What does Amy suggest we should do to help save the planet? Give three details.
6 Where would Amy like to live?
7 How has Amy's character changed? Give two details.

Amy

Me llamo Amy y vivo en Manchester. Mi ciudad es muy grande y para mí el mayor problema es la contaminación, a causa del tráfico existente. Lo veo de primera mano porque mi hermano menor tiene asma y sufre debido al humo, por eso me di cuenta de que hay que modificar nuestro modo de vivir y decidí cambiar mi vida.

Hay muchos problemas en el mundo, pero lo que más me preocupa es el medio ambiente y el calentamiento global. Opino que hay que llevar una vida más sostenible, y por eso me hice miembro de Greenpeace, una organización que lucha por la defensa del medio ambiente. Me enseñó cosas que podía hacer para cambiar mi vida. Por ejemplo, antes me bañaba con frecuencia, ahora casi siempre me ducho porque así utilizo menos agua. Antes mi familia tenía un coche muy grande, pero ahora tenemos un coche híbrido y yo tengo una bicicleta. También, mientras que antes tirábamos todo a la basura, ahora reciclamos el vidrio, el papel y el plástico.

A mi modo de ver, es muy importante que cuidemos el planeta. Deberíamos apagar la luz y desenchufar los electrodomésticos cuando salimos de un cuarto. Deberíamos comprar menos y reutilizar las cosas. Además, siempre deberíamos llevar una bolsa a la compra, en vez de pedir una de plástico. Son cosas pequeñas, pero muy importantes.

Si un día me hago voluntaria de Greenpeace, viajaré y conoceré otras culturas. Me encantaría vivir en las casas sostenibles de Puerto Rico. ¡Qué guay! Anteriormente nunca había pensado mucho en proteger el medio ambiente, pero he cambiado bastante. Ahora creo que soy una persona mucho más generosa y alegre. Si cuidamos la salud del planeta, el mundo será un lugar mejor.

Find the equivalent of these expressions in Spanish in the text.

1 The biggest problem is… because of…
2 I see it first hand…
3 I realised that…
4 I decided to change my life.
5 …what worries me most is…
6 …one must lead a more sustainable life…
7 …in my view it is very important that…
8 …I will travel and I will get to know different cultures.
9 Formerly, I had never thought much about…
10 …the world will be a better place.

Look at the text again. Make a list of verbs in these tenses:

- present perfect
- imperfect
- future
- conditional
- pluperfect

You might be asked to write about your world view as a Controlled Assessment task. Use the Grade Studio to help you prepare your account.

GradeStudio

To produce a good answer you need to use a variety of structures.

- Amy uses the **present tense** to talk about the most important problem that affects her.
- Find two examples in the first paragraph where Amy uses the **preterite** to talk about how she changed her life.
- Find two examples in the fourth paragraph where Amy uses the **future tense** to talk about what she will do in the future.
- Amy uses **simple connectives** such as *y* (and), *también* (also), *pero* (but) and *porque* (because) to extend her sentences. Can you find examples in her text?

To go a step further you need to use a wider range of language.

- Find examples of where Amy uses the **imperfect tense**, the **perfect tense** and the **conditional tense**.
- Amy uses **adverbs** to describe her actions. Can you find two examples in the fourth paragraph?
- Amy uses a **variety of phrases** to help to structure her text and extend sentences: *antes..., ahora..., por eso..., a mi modo de ver..., opino que...* Do you know what all of these mean?

For a really impressive answer:

- Use more **complex tenses**, like the **pluperfect**. Can you find an example of this in the fourth paragraph of the text?
- Use the **subjunctive**. In the third paragraph Amy says: *'es muy importante que cuidemos el planeta.'* Do you understand what this means? Can you use a subjunctive in your own text?
- Include a **complex sentence** with two tenses in it, for example, a *si* clause to talk about what will happen if you do something. Can you find two examples of this in the text?

Now write a full account of your world view.

- Adapt Amy's text and use language from Module 9. Write at least 200 words.
- If you need to write something which is not in the book then keep it simple. When you look up words in a dictionary make sure that you choose the right one. Look carefully at any examples given. Cross-check by looking the Spanish word up in the Spanish-English part of the dictionary.
- Structure your text carefully. Organise what you write in paragraphs.

General summary of your world view

Where do you live?
What problems affect you?

Main paragraph

What issues worry you?
What changes have you made in your life?
What do you think we should do to improve things?

Conclusion

What would you like to do in the future?
How were you different in the past and how have you changed?

Check carefully what you have written.

- spelling and accents (cognates spelt correctly with correct accents *contaminación, tráfico, planeta?*)
- verb endings (correct verb endings in the subjunctive?)
- tenses (correct use of the auxiliary verb with the pluperfect tense *haber: había, habías, habíamos?*)

Read the newspaper article about environmental problems. Which group of people does each paragraph of the article refer to? Write the correct letter for each paragraph. (5 marks)

a smokers
b lorry drivers
c commuters
d gardeners
e fishermen
f householders
g pedestrians

Look for clues such as words or phrases related to each group of people in the grid, e.g. another word for *las personas que andan por las calles*?

¿Quién es responsable de los problemas del medioambiente?

1 Uno de los problemas medioambientales de la ciudad es la basura. Es responsabilidad de la gente que anda por la calle y tira basura al suelo.

2 Hoy en día hay muchos periódicos gratis. La gente que viaja al trabajo en tren y autobús y lee uno de esos periódicos gratuitos casi nunca los recicla.

3 Nos gusta respirar aire sin humo de tabaco en bares, restaurantes y edificios públicos. Desgraciadamente hay muchas colillas en el suelo cerca de las puertas de entrada o salida.

4 Sabemos que reciclar es bueno, pero a veces no hacemos lo suficiente para ayudar en casa. Si todo el mundo separa su basura, podremos sin duda reciclar más plástico y metal.

5 La cantidad de comida que tiramos todos los días es una barbaridad, pero muchos productos vegetales son reciclables. Todos los que cultivan flores y legumbres conocen el valor de reciclar productos vegetales.

Read the letter to a newspaper about world problems and answer the questions.

Muy señor mío:
Me preocupan mucho los problemas del Tercer Mundo y cuando veo las tristes caras de los niños sin hogar y sin comida, empiezo a preguntarme por qué los países desarrollados les dejan morir. Esta situación me enfurece y quisiera protestar en voz alta.
Se dice que el futuro está en manos de los jóvenes y entiendo muy bien que ellos piensen en la posibilidad de una crisis económica y de paro. Me parece, sin embargo, que los jóvenes no tienen miedo a eso, y tampoco ignoran los problemas porque creo que ven las cosas exactamente como son.
En general el mundo está más preparado para aceptar los derechos humanos de los individuos puesto que el nivel de educación es mejor que antes. En mi opinión el trabajo más importante para el mundo del futuro, es aprender a llevarse mejor los unos con los otros.
Le saluda atentamente, *Enrique Fernández*

1 How does Enrique feel about Third World problems? Write the correct letter. (1 mark)
a sad **b** unconcerned **c** angry

2 According to Enrique, what is young people's attitude to the future? (1 mark)
a optimistic **b** realistic **c** simplistic

3 What does Enrique see as the biggest challenge for the world? (1 mark)
a reducing unemployment
b understanding one another better
c granting everyone their human rights

Listen to Vicente talking about when he was homeless. Write the correct letters.

1 When did Vicente become homeless? (1 mark)
   a after his 16th birthday
   b before sitting his exams
   c during the school holidays
2 How long was it before he got a place in a hostel? (1 mark)
   a 8–10 months
   b 12–14 months
   c 16–18 months
3 On what date did he eventually move into a flat? (1 mark)
   a Tuesday 3 June
   b Thursday 13 June
   c Thursday 30 July

Make sure you know numbers, dates, months and times really well. It's also important to know words like *antes* and *después* so you can work out the order in which things happened.

Listen to four people talking about the problems of being homeless. Identify the problem each person mentions. Write the correct letter for each person. (4 marks)

1 Inés
2 Nacho
3 Pilar
4 Felipe

a money
b clothes
c addiction
d hunger
e discrimination
f loneliness

In a task like this you are listening for gist, so you don't need to understand every word. Try to pick out key words or cognates which relate to the answer options.

Listen to a former homeless girl, Pepa, talking about the decisions that changed her life. What decisions did she take and what were the consequences for her? For each number, write down the missing decision or consequence, in English. (4 marks)

Decision	Consequence
find a hostel	1
2	understand her options
sell magazines	3
4	get qualifications

Look carefully at the examples (in the grey boxes in the grid) to see the kind of answers you are expected to give. Bear in mind that Pepa may sometimes mention the consequence before the decision

Palabras

Cambios medioambientales *Environmental changes*

Deberíamos…	*We should…*
comprar productos ecológicos	*buy green products*
consumir menos energía	*use less energy*
mantener el aire limpio/el agua limpia	*keep the air/water clean*
mejorar la red de transporte público	*improve the public transport network*
plantar más árboles	*plant more trees*
proteger la naturaleza	*protect nature*
reciclar papel y vidrio	*recycle paper and glass*
reducir la contaminación	*reduce pollution*
usar el agua de forma responsable	*use water responsibly*
usar más el transporte público	*use public transport more*
No deberíamos…	*We shouldn't…*
malgastar el agua	*waste water*
tirar la basura al suelo	*throw rubbish on the ground*

El mundo hoy en día *The world today*

Opino que…	*I think that…*
Para mí…	*For me…*
A mi modo de ver…	*As I see it…*
A mi parecer…	*It seems to me…*
Creo que…	*I think that…*
Estoy de acuerdo contigo.	*I agree with you.*
No estoy de acuerdo contigo.	*I don't agree with you.*
el agujero de la capa de ozono	*the hole in the ozone layer*
el calentamiento global	*global warming*
el hambre	*hunger*
el paro	*unemployment*
el precio de la gasolina	*the price of oil*
el racismo	*racism*
el respeto	*respect*
el terrorismo	*terrorism*
la crisis económica	*economic crisis*
la delincuencia	*delinquency*
la discriminación	*discrimination*
la igualdad	*equality*
la justicia	*justice*
la pobreza	*poverty*
la solidaridad	*solidarity*
los derechos humanos	*human rights*
los sin techo	*the homeless*
es el problema más serio	*is the most serious problem*
es un problema muy serio	*is a very serious problem*
no es un problema tan serio	*is not such a serious problem*
Es esencial que…	*It's essential that…*
Es importante que…	*It's important that…*
Es increíble que…	*It's incredible that…*
Es necesario que…	*It's necessary that…*
Es terrible que…	*It's terrible that…*

¡Cuida tu planeta! *Look after your planet!*

No utilice combustibles fósiles.	*Don't use fossil fuel.*
No ensucie el agua.	*Don't pollute water.*
No consuma tanta energía.	*Don't use so much energy.*
No contamine el medio ambiente.	*Don't pollute the environment.*
No use detergentes con fosfatos.	*Don't use detergents with phosphates.*
No malgaste el papel.	*Don't waste paper.*
Reutilice las bolsas de plástico.	*Re-use plastic bags.*
Separe la basura.	*Separate rubbish.*

Piensa globalmente *Think globally*

Para ahorrar agua, es mejor…	*In order to save water, it's better to…*
Para reducir la contaminación del aire, es mejor…	*In order to reduce air pollution, it's better to…*
Para consumir menos energía, es mejor…	*In order to use less energy, it's better to…*
Para respetar nuestro entorno, es mejor…	*In order to respect our surroundings, it's better to…*
Para evitar contaminar el medio ambiente, es mejor…	*In order to avoid polluting the environment, it's better to…*
Para luchar contra el calentamiento global, es mejor…	*In order to fight against global warming, it's better to…*
apagar las luces	*turn off the lights*
comprar productos ecológicos	*buy green products*
comprar ropa de segunda mano en Oxfam	*buy second-hand clothes from Oxfam*
consumir poca energía/agua/gasolina	*use less energy/water/oil*
dar dinero a organizaciones benéficas	*give money to charitable organisations*
ir en bicicleta	*travel by bicycle*
separar la basura y reciclar	*separate rubbish and recycle*
utilizar el contenedor de compostaje	*use a compost bin*
bañarse cuatro veces al día	*have a bath four times a day*
comprar productos de países lejanos	*buy products from faraway countries*
comprar ropa nueva cada semana	*buy new clothes every week*
consumir mucha agua/energía/gasolina	*use a lot of water/energy/oil*
encender las luces	*turn on the lights*
ir en una limusina muy grande	*travel in a very large limousine*
malgastar dinero en cosas inútiles	*waste money on useless things*
pedir siempre bolsas de plástico	*always ask for plastic bags*

Voluntarios *Volunteers*

Si apadrino a un niño del tercer mundo, …	*If I foster a child from the third world, …*
Si educamos a la gente, …	*If we educate people, …*
Si me hago miembro de Oxfam, …	*If I become a member of Oxfam, …*
Si me hago voluntaria, …	*If I become a volunteer, …*
Si pago un poco más por los productos de comercio justo, …	*If I pay a bit more for fairtrade products,…*
Si reciclamos y reutilizamos, …	*If we recycle and reuse, …*
acabaremos con la pobreza	*we will end poverty*
ayudaré a los demás y haré algo útil	*I will help others and I will do something useful*
cuidaremos el medio ambiente	*we will look after the environment*
los trabajadores tendrán mejores salarios	*workers will have better salaries*
más personas tendrán una vida digna	*more people will have a dignified life*
mejoraré la sociedad	*I will improve society*
tendrá la posibilidad de sobrevivir.	*he/she will have the possibility of surviving*
transformaremos el mundo.	*we will change the world*
¿Cómo te llamas?	*What's your name?*
¿De dónde eres?	*Where are you from?*
¿Por qué quieres trabajar como voluntario?	*Why do you want to work as a volunteer?*

Sin techo, sin derecho *No roof, no rights*

había comprado una casa	*I had bought a house*
había dado a luz a un niño	*I had given birth to a child*
había empezado a estudiar	*I had begun to study*
había perdido mi trabajo	*I had lost my job*
me decidí a cambiar todo	*I decided to change everything*
encontré trabajo	*I found work*
hablé con una organización caritativa	*I spoke with a charitable organisation*
me quedé con un amigo y empecé a buscar trabajo	*I stayed with a friend and I started to look for work*
tengo novio/a y otra casa	*I have a boy/girlfriend and another house*
tengo una familia	*I have a family*
trabajo con los sin techo	*I work with the homeless*
trabajo en…	*I work in…*

Te toca a ti A

Match the profiles to the holidays. There is one holiday too many.

1 Me llamo Manuel. Tengo dieciocho años. Soy un poco tímido. No salgo mucho. Me encanta leer. Leo mucho. Todos los días escribo un blog en el que hablo sobre mis ideas y mis sentimientos. Mi vida es tranquila. Creo que hay demasiado ruido en el mundo.

2 Me llamo Isabel. Tengo diecisiete años. Me preocupa el medio ambiente. Reciclo todo y me gusta la idea de un turismo sostenible. No quiero que mis vacaciones afecten al medio ambiente.

3 Me llamo Trevor y tengo veinte años. Me encanta el buceo. El año pasado buceé en Costa Rica y este año me gustaría bucear en España, que está más cerca.

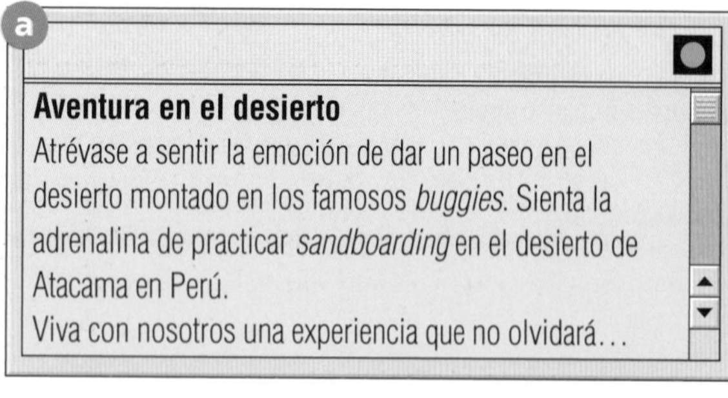

a

Aventura en el desierto
Atrévase a sentir la emoción de dar un paseo en el desierto montado en los famosos *buggies*. Sienta la adrenalina de practicar *sandboarding* en el desierto de Atacama en Perú.
Viva con nosotros una experiencia que no olvidará…

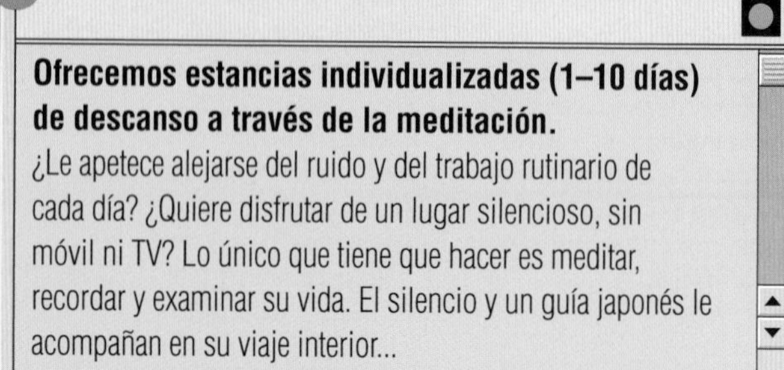

b

Ofrecemos estancias individualizadas (1–10 días) de descanso a través de la meditación.
¿Le apetece alejarse del ruido y del trabajo rutinario de cada día? ¿Quiere disfrutar de un lugar silencioso, sin móvil ni TV? Lo único que tiene que hacer es meditar, recordar y examinar su vida. El silencio y un guía japonés le acompañan en su viaje interior...

c

Vacaciones ecológicas y turismo responsable
Escocia es un lugar fantástico con muchas opciones de ocio a pie, en bicicleta o a caballo. Las emisiones de carbono durante unas vacaciones en Escocia son insignificantes. Además, puede pescar su propia cena…

d

Centro de submarinismo – Lanzarote
Si deseas combinar tus vacaciones de surfing con el buceo en las bonitas playas de Lanzarote, tenemos varios paquetes con alojamiento incluido dentro del parque natural de Caleta de Famara…

Write down the letters of the five sentences that are true about the text.

Mis vacaciones fueron inolvidables. El hotel estaba en la montaña, pero no era nada lujoso. Era muy sencillo. Hice alpinismo y senderismo todos los días. Un día hice caída libre y tuve miedo, pero ¡fue maravilloso!

Una noche fui a una clase de flamenco y me gustó bastante, pero prefiero los deportes de alto riesgo. Por las tardes, nadé en la piscina del hotel, pero no era climatizada. El jueves, monté en bici y visité un castillo. Era del siglo XVI – impresionante.

Nuria

a Nuria stayed in the mountains.
b The hotel was luxurious.
c She went climbing and hiking every day.
d She was scared when she went sky diving.
e She didn't enjoy her salsa class.
f The swimming pool wasn't heated.
g On the Friday she went on a bike ride and visited a castle.
h The castle dated from the sixteenth century.

1 Match up the texts to the correct hotel. There is one text too many.

1

Me alojé en un hotel que era magnífico. Tenía tres plantas y 91 habitaciones. Tenía bar y un restaurante. También tenía varias tiendas y una peluquería.
Lo mejor del hotel era que podías aparcar en el sótano. A veces puede ser difícil aparcar en Cancún. Fue una experiencia fantástica.

2

Pasé unas vacaciones muy románticas en este hotel, que estaba en la zona residencial de la ciudad y que tenía cinco estrellas. Tenía bar y restaurante. También tenía una piscina al aire libre y una cancha de tenis. Fuimos alguna vez al centro de fitness.

3

Me quedé en un hotel muy moderno y lujoso que estaba en el centro de la ciudad. Tenía bar y restaurante. Me encantó la comida. También había piscina climatizada. Las habitaciones eran enormes y muy cómodas.

4

Mis vacaciones en México fueron estupendas. Me quedé en un hotel de tres estrellas que era muy acogedor. El hotel estaba en la costa. Tenía piscina, sauna y gimnasio. También había bar. Estaba muy bien. Lo mejor del hotel era que tenía una discoteca genial.

2 Write out this dialogue in the correct order. Start with the green sentence.

- **a** Sí, necesito la habitación ahora, quiero cambiar de habitación inmediatamente.
- **b** Muy bien. Gracias.
- **c** **¿Qué le pasa, señora?**
- **d** Lo siento mucho. Voy a llamar al técnico y al servicio de limpieza. ¿Quiere algo más?
- **e** A ver… No, lo siento. No tengo habitaciones libres. El hotel está completo.
- **f** Por supuesto. Voy a llamar al director y pedir un descuento.
- **g** Quiero hacer una reclamación. Mi habitación está sucia y la luz no funciona.
- **h** Pues… por lo menos quiero un descuento…

3 Write ten sentences about the weather and holiday activities in the past.

Ejemplo: Ayer hizo sol y fui a la piscina.

Te toca a ti A

Write out the words in the word snakes with the correct punctuation, then match the sentences to the pictures.

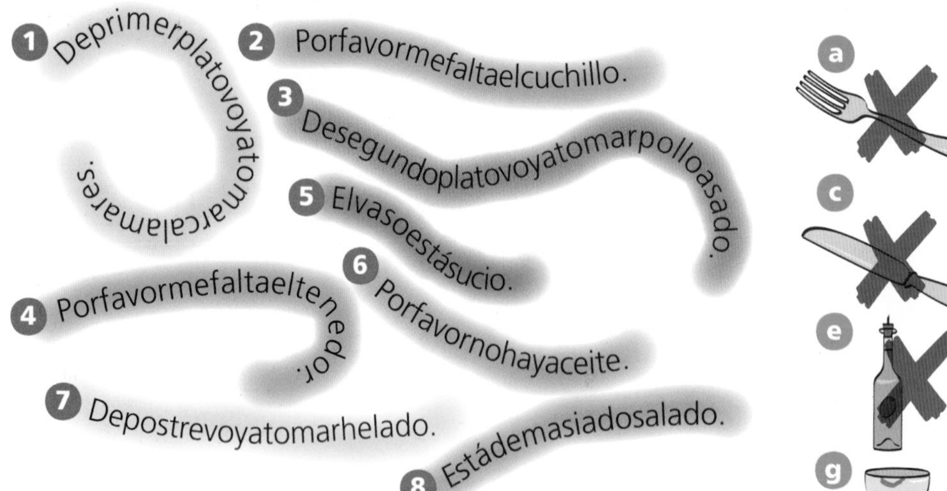

1 Deprimerplatovoyatomarcalamares.
2 Porfavormefaltaelcuchillo.
3 Desegundoplatovoyatomarpolloasado.
4 Porfavormefaltaeltenedor.
5 Elvasoestásucio.
6 Porfavornohayaceite.
7 Depostrevoyatomarhelado.
8 Estádemasiadosalado.

Elige el resumen correcto.

a Juan liked the food, but thought the drinks were expensive.

b Juan loved the restaurant, but thought it was too small.

c Juan thought the food and drinks were expensive.

En pleno centro de Sevilla hay uno de los bares de tapeo más típicos de la ciudad. De precio está muy bien, es muy barato. Cuando pides una bebida, te ponen una tapa. Las mejores eran las de calamares fritos. Ponen música española moderna. Lo malo es que era un bar pequeño.

Comida: 8
Calidad del servicio: 8
Ambiente: 10
Calidad / Precio: 7

Lo que más me gustó:
Los calamares fritos y el ambiente

Lo que menos me gustó:
Era un bar pequeño.

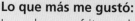

Write the questions out correctly, then translate them into English.

1 ?Sevilla en se ¿ver Qué puede
2 museo? Cuándo el ¿abre
3 el ver hay Qué que museo? en¿
4 ¿al se museo? Cómo va
5 ¿tiempo Cuánto el? dura viaje

Answer the questions in exercise 3 using the advert below.

Venga al Museo de Bellas Artes de Sevilla, en Sevilla
Impresionante colección de arte español, de la época medieval a la moderna.
Abierto: Martes a domingo: de 10.00 a 13.00 de la mañana y de 14.00 a 20.00 de la tarde.
Para llegar, coja las líneas C1, C2 hasta el paseo de Cartuja. Está a 10 minutos del centro.

1 Match up the two halves of the sentence, then translate them into English.

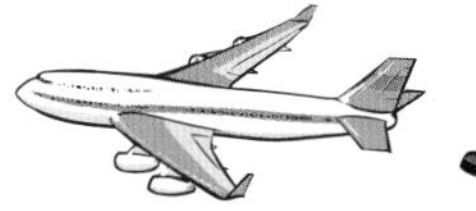

1 No me gusta nada viajar en,...
2 Me gusta mucho mi independencia...
3 Cojo siempre el autobús porque es barato...
4 Normalmente cojo los transportes públicos...
5 Prefiero ir a pie porque creo...
6 No me gusta esperar y prefiero...

a y puedo leer o escuchar música.
b que de esta forma no contamino.
c por eso prefiero ir en coche.
d llegar rápidamente, por eso cojo un taxi.
e autocar porque la gente me molesta.
f porque no son caros y por respeto al medio ambiente.

2 Read the text and answer these questions in English.

1 What does it mean if you:
  a move your fan with your left hand?
  b move your fan with your right hand?
  c throw your fan down?

2 What should you do with your fan if you want:
  a someone to wait for you?
  b someone to come and talk to you?
  c to tell someone they are cruel?

El lenguaje de los abanicos

Los principales gestos del lenguaje de los abanicos son:

1 Moverlo con la mano izquierda. *Nos observan.*	5 Abrirlo despacio. *Espérame.*
2 Moverlo con la mano derecha. *Quiero a otro.*	6 Abrirlo con la mano izquierda. *Ven y habla conmigo.*
3 Arrojarlo con la mano. *Te odio.*	7 Golpearlo cerrado sobre la mano izquierda. *Escríbeme.*
4 Abrirlo y cerrarlo. *Eres cruel.*	8 Dejarlo deslizar sobre los ojos. *Vete, por favor*

3 Read what Antonia says and correct the mistakes in the sentences.

El año pasado fui a Sevilla con una amiga y nos encantó. Fuimos en tren e hicimos muchas cosas: fuimos de excursión en autobús, compré recuerdos en las tiendas, fui al parque de María Luisa, donde di una vuelta en bicicleta, y vi una obra maravillosa de Lorca en el teatro Lope de Vega. Lo que menos me gustó fue la corrida en la plaza de toros, fue cruel. El año que viene voy a ir de vacaciones otra vez con mi amiga. Vamos a ir a Córdoba. Vamos a ir a la mezquita y yo voy a sacar fotos para mi blog.

1 No les gustó Sevilla.
2 Fue con su madre.
3 Fueron en avión.
4 Montó a caballo.
5 Lo que menos le gustó fue la visita al teatro Lope de Vega.
6 Le gustó la corrida en la plaza de Toros.
7 El año que viene va a ir de vacaciones con su familia.
8 No va a hacer turismo.

Te toca a ti A

Copy and complete the sentences with the correct missing words. Then write the sentences in English.

1 Me ____ las matemáticas porque no son difíciles.
2 Mi profesor de ciencias es bastante ____.
3 Siempre llevo mis ____ a mis clases.
4 Las clases ____ a las ocho y media todos los días.
5 No voy al club de ____ porque no me interesa.

severo	encantan
odio	cuadernos
ajedrez	profesora
empiezan	

Copy and complete the sentences with the correct times. Then write the sentences in English.

1 Tengo matemáticas a las ____.

4 María tiene dibujo ____.

2 Tienen inglés a las ____.

5 Pepe tiene educación física ____.

3 Tenemos alemán a ____.

6 Tenemos geografía ____.

Write these sentences in Spanish.

Ejemplo: *Normally I go to school by bus.*
Normalmente voy al colegio en autobús.

1 Normally I go to school by bike.
2 I never go to school by car.
3 I always go to school by tube.
4 I sometimes go to school by train.
5 I walk to school every day.
6 During winter I go to school by bus.

You are writing an email to a new Spanish penfriend. Include the following information:

- *your name and age*
- *how you go to school*
- *the school subjects you study*
- *what you take to class (books, dictionary, etc.)*
- *describe your best day at school including times you have your subjects*
- *give your opinion on your favourite/worst school subjects and teachers*

Voy al instituto en...
Estudio español...
Siempre llevo mis libros a clase y a veces...
El mejor día es el lunes porque tengo español a las..., después tengo...
Me encanta(n)/odio... porque es/son... entretenido/a(s)/complicado/a(s).
El profesor de... es...

5 Read José's text and then find the Spanish for the sentences that follow.

Estoy en cuarto de la ESO y tengo diez asignaturas. Mi instituto es grandísimo y siempre hay que cumplir muchas normas, por eso no me gusta nada. Por ejemplo, está prohibido llevar joyas y piercings. En clase está prohibido escuchar tu MP3, no se permite mandar mensajes de texto y tampoco se permite comer chicle. ¡Qué rollo! No se puede hacer nada. Tampoco me gustan los profesores porque son antipáticos, nunca sonríen y sus clases son aburridas. Lo bueno es que no llevamos uniforme, así que siempre llevo unos vaqueros y una camiseta. Si hace calor, llevo unos pantalones cortos y una gorra. El mayor problema de mi instituto es el acoso escolar. La semana pasada unos alumnos mayores atacaron a mi mejor amigo y tuvo que darles todo el dinero que tenía. ¡Fue terrible! Antes en mi colegio había muy buen ambiente, pero todo ha cambiado últimamente. Creo que es culpa de toda la violencia que hay en nuestra sociedad. Estoy contento porque el año que viene no vuelvo al instituto. Voy a trabajar en una zapatería.

- **a** I am in Year 11.
- **b** My school is really big.
- **c** There are always lots of rules to follow.
- **d** You can't send texts.
- **e** You can't do anything.
- **f** They never smile.
- **g** If it is hot…
- **h** The biggest problem in my school.
- **i** Some older students attacked my best friend…
- **j** He had to give them all the money he had.
- **k** Our society…
- **l** I am going to work in a shoe shop.

Remember to use a dictionary or glossary pages when working through a text on your own. Note down any new words in a vocabulary book or in your exercise book, so that you can look over them as part of your revision later on.

6 Read the text again and answer the following questions in English.

1. How many subjects does José study?
2. Why does he not like his school? (2 reasons)
3. What does he like about his school?
4. Name two school rules he mentions.
5. Describe what he wears to school when it is not hot.
6. What happened to his best friend recently?
7. What is José happy about?

7 Write about the worst school ever. Be as negative as you can. Include information on:

- *the teachers*
- *the rules*
- *the uniform*
- *the clubs*
- *the issues (describe something bad that has happened recently)*

Use as many of the these negative adjectives as you can:

antipático	severo
complicado	difícil
aburrido	terrible
violento	malo
feo	pesado
tonto	perezoso

Te toca a ti A

1 Answer these questions for the people below in full sentences.

- ¿Cuántos años tiene…?
- ¿De qué color son sus ojos?
- ¿Cómo es su pelo?
- ¿Cómo es de carácter?

Normalmente es…
Por lo general es…
A veces puede ser…

Luis – 16 years old

Normally: sincere, respectful, tolerant, cheerful

Sometimes can be: quiet, pessimistic

Angélica –14 years old

Normally: aggressive, selfish, quiet, violent

Sometimes can be: mature, optimistic

2 Pretend you are Alicia. Describe your day.

Ejemplo: **a** Por la mañana muy temprano me despierto…

a Por la mañana muy temprano

b Luego

c Después

d Por la tarde

e Un poco más tarde

f Por la noche

3 Unjumble these questions and then answer them for yourself.

1 usted? se ¿Cómo llama
2 es ¿Cuál nacionalidad? su
3 ¿Tiene relación una alguien de con de familia? su amor y odio
4 se de quién su lleva familia? bien ¿Con
5 quién ¿A parece? se
6 le ¿Qué hacer? gusta

Follow the lines to find the words and write them out. Then match the English to the Spanish.

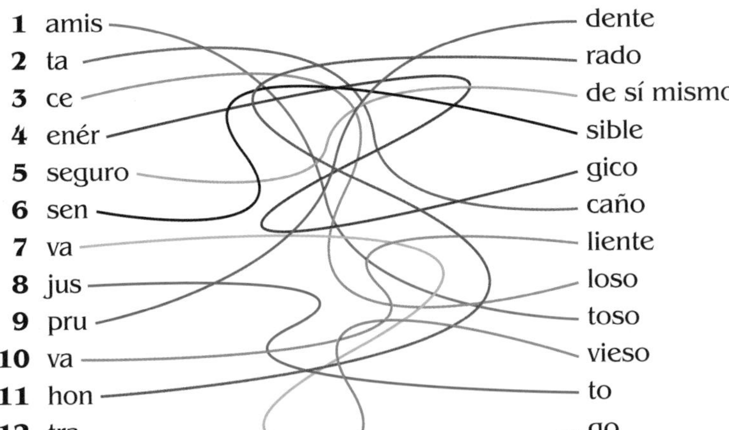

1 amis	dente	a brave
2 ta	rado	b energetic
3 ce	de sí mismo	c sure of oneself
4 enér	sible	d fair
5 seguro	gico	e sensitive
6 sen	caño	f mean
7 va	liente	g jealous
8 jus	loso	h lazy
9 pru	toso	i wise, prudent
10 va	vieso	j friendly
11 hon	to	k honourable, respectable
12 tra	go	l naughty

Beware of false friends:
sensible = *sensitive, not sensible*
vago/a = *lazy, not vague*

Read these texts and then decide which two adjectives from exercise 1 could describe each person.

1 Tengo mucho sentido del humor y creo que soy amable. Mis amigos son muy importantes para mí. Me gusta mucho salir con ellos. Charlamos y nos divertimos. Salgo tres o cuatro veces a la semana. Me encanta hacer deporte y luego ir a la cafetería. *Aitor*

2 Normalmente soy creativo y no soy muy ambicioso. No me gusta nada trabajar.
Prefiero navegar por Internet, mandar mensajes con mi móvil o jugar con mi ordenador.
A veces cojo el teléfono de mi hermana y mando mensajes a sus amigas. Le da rabia cuando lo hago, pero a mí me parece que es muy divertido. Magec

3 No me gusta nada hacer regalos a la gente. No quiero gastar mi dinero así. Estoy ahorrando para mis vacaciones. Trabajo solo para mí, no tengo ganas de gastar mi dinero en otras personas vagas que no quieren trabajar. Yo sé que tengo razón. *Laura*

Read the text and answer the questions in English.

1 When was Alonso's accident?
2 How did he feel after the accident? Mention two details.
3 What was his character like before the accident?
4 How has he changed?
5 What question does he ask at the end of the text?

Hace dos años tuve un grave accidente de coche en una autopista. Afortunadamente llevaba puesto el cinturón de seguridad. Estuve en el hospital varias semanas sin hacer nada. Ese accidente cambió mi vida. Después del accidente tenía miedo a conducir y tampoco podía dormir. Ahora duermo bien, pero no quiero conducir. Antes del accidente era enérgico, extrovertido y estaba seguro de mí mismo. Ahora soy mucho más tímido. Creo que tengo muchos miedos y además estoy preocupado todo el tiempo. Creo que sufro un trauma. No soy muy feliz. ¿Alguien podría darme algún consejo? ***Alonso***

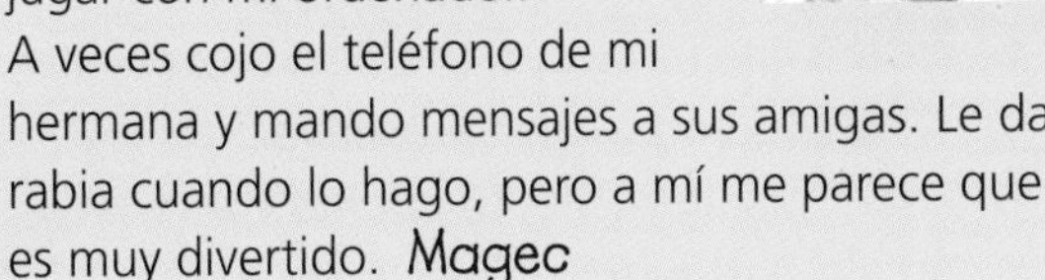

1 ***Read the sentences and fill in the correct job. Then translate each sentence into English.***

1 A veces trabaja en una ambulancia. Es m_____.
2 Te lava, te corta y te seca el pelo. Es p_____.
3 Cuida de tu boca y tus dientes. Es d_____.
4 Corre con un balón en un estadio. Es f_____.
5 Escribe artículos para periódicos y revistas. Es p_____.
6 Contesta al teléfono y ayuda a los clientes. Es r_____.

2 ***Read the emails and complete the sentences with the correct name.***

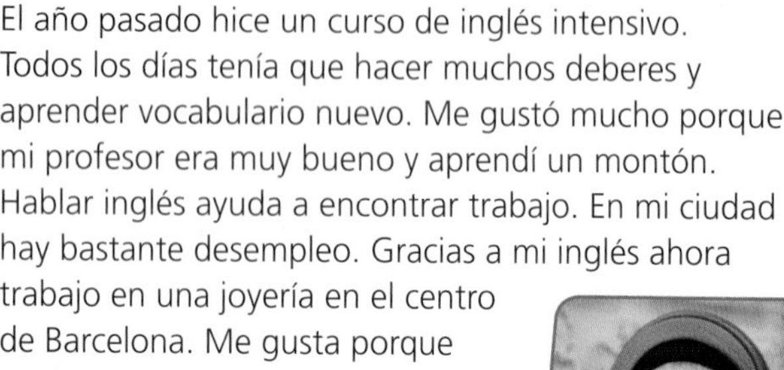

El año pasado hice un curso de inglés intensivo. Todos los días tenía que hacer muchos deberes y aprender vocabulario nuevo. Me gustó mucho porque mi profesor era muy bueno y aprendí un montón. Hablar inglés ayuda a encontrar trabajo. En mi ciudad hay bastante desempleo. Gracias a mi inglés ahora trabajo en una joyería en el centro de Barcelona. Me gusta porque me hacen descuentos y así puedo comprar accesorios más baratos. Lo malo es que me pagan poco y que tengo que trabajar los sábados.
Un beso,
Lina

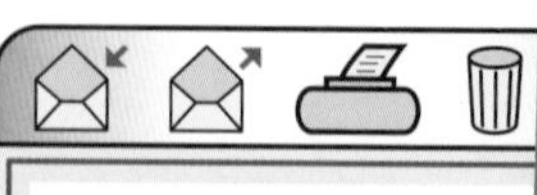

Hola, ¿qué tal?
Trabajo en una peluquería. Todos los días tengo que lavar, cortar y secar el pelo a los clientes y también tengo que barrer el suelo. Me gusta mi trabajo y gano mucho dinero, pero mi jefe es un pesado y quiero cambiar de trabajo. El año pasado trabajé de dependienta en una zapatería donde vendía zapatos y hablaba con los clientes. No me gustaba mucho el trabajo y ganaba poco dinero, pero mi jefa era muy maja. Necesito dinero, así que de momento voy a seguir aquí, ¡qué rollo!
Un abrazo,
María

Ejemplo: **1** Lina currently works in a shop.

1 _____ currently works in a shop.
2 _____ studied last year.
3 _____ got a job because she speaks English.
4 _____ wants to change jobs.
5 _____ is not paid well.
6 _____ has to sweep the floors every day.
7 _____ has to work Saturdays.
8 _____ used to talk to clients every day.
9 _____ had a great boss last year.
10 _____ lives in an area with unemployment.

3 ***Copy the table and fill in the missing verbs.***

infinitivo	**pretérito (él/ella)**	**imperfecto (él/ella)**
trabajar	trabajó	trabajaba
comenzar		comenzaba
	terminó	
		escribía
beber		
	habló	
		vendía

leer **1** ***Read the word snake and write out the sentence correctly.***

Misprácticaslaboralesfueronbastantedivertidasporquetrabajéconniñosytodoslosdíashacíavelaporlasmañanasyjugabaaltenisporlastardes.

2 ***Read the text. Copy and complete it with the correct words.***

noches | gustaría | telefónicas | parcial | pagan | gustó | cansado | limpio | trabajé | dieciocho | enfermeros

Me llamo Eugenia y tengo (1) ______ años. Todavía vivo en casa de mis padres en Oviedo. Trabajo a tiempo (2) ______ en un hospital. Tengo que ayudar a los (3) ______. Organizo el historial de cada paciente, contesto llamadas (4) ______ y también (5) ______ los suelos. Me gusta mi trabajo, pero me (6) ______ mal y a veces tengo que trabajar de (7) ______. El trabajo nocturno es muy difícil porque es muy (8) ______. El año pasado (9) ______ en una clínica privada y no me (10) ______ porque trabajaba siempre de noche. En el futuro me (11) ______ estudiar enfermería.

3 ***Translate Eugenia's text from exercise 2 into English. Use a dictionary if necessary.***

4 ***Read the information on this Mexican website and find the Spanish for:***

A your skills
B young people like you
C help you and support you
D the important process of choosing a career
E the following questions
F on this exciting journey

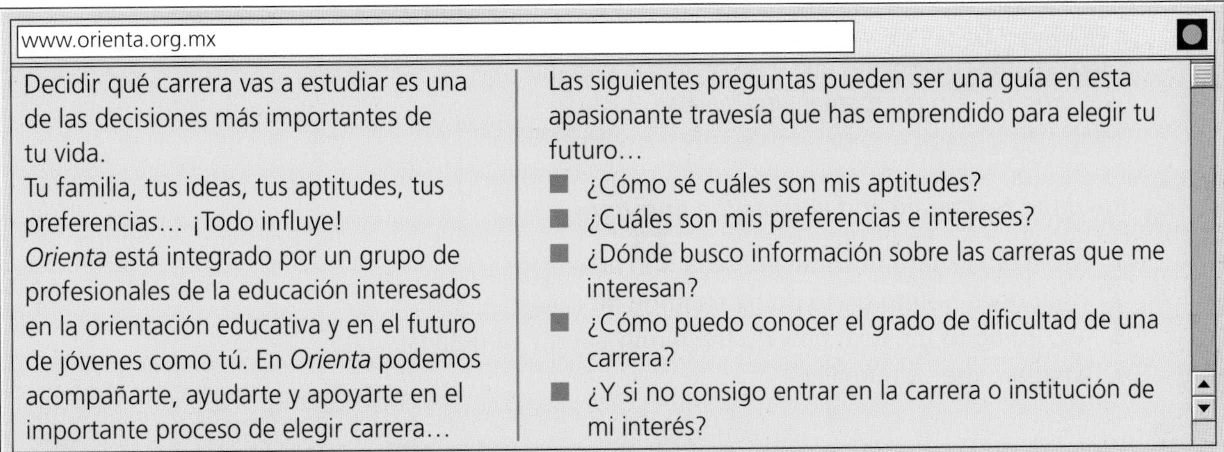

www.orienta.org.mx

Decidir qué carrera vas a estudiar es una de las decisiones más importantes de tu vida.
Tu familia, tus ideas, tus aptitudes, tus preferencias… ¡Todo influye!
Orienta está integrado por un grupo de profesionales de la educación interesados en la orientación educativa y en el futuro de jóvenes como tú. En *Orienta* podemos acompañarte, ayudarte y apoyarte en el importante proceso de elegir carrera…

Las siguientes preguntas pueden ser una guía en esta apasionante travesía que has emprendido para elegir tu futuro…

- ¿Cómo sé cuáles son mis aptitudes?
- ¿Cuáles son mis preferencias e intereses?
- ¿Dónde busco información sobre las carreras que me interesan?
- ¿Cómo puedo conocer el grado de dificultad de una carrera?
- ¿Y si no consigo entrar en la carrera o institución de mi interés?

5 ***Read the website again and find the Spanish for these questions.***

1. What are my likes and preferences?
2. And what if I don't get chosen for the career or college of my choice?
3. Where do I find information about the careers that interest me?
4. How can I know how hard each career is?
5. How do I know what my skills are?

6 ***Summarise in English what the website* Orienta *does.***

Te toca a ti A

Read the text on the artist* Botero *and find the Spanish for these phrases.

a The characters he paints are really fat.
b He is illustrating a normal scene.
c They are sitting next to an apple tree.
d They represent an altered reality.

Adoro al artista colombiano Fernando Botero. Lo esencial de sus pinturas es la forma grande o exagerada de sus dimensiones. Los personajes que pinta están gordísimos y de esta manera, intenta hacer una crítica a la sociedad de su tiempo.

Botero nació el 19 de abril de mil novecientos treinta y dos en Medellín, Colombia. Tiene dos hermanos que se llaman Juan David y Rodrigo. El pintor se interesó por el arte cuando era tan solo un niño.

Mi pintura favorita de Botero se llama *Familia*. En este cuadro Botero está ilustrando una escena cotidiana. Se trata de un grupo familiar que está reunido en un jardín o un parque en el que aparecen el padre, la madre, los hijos y el perro. Me parece que el padre es el personaje principal de la pintura. Toda la familia parece seria y un poco triste. Están sentados al lado de un manzano y están cayendo manzanas por todas partes. Los colores que usa Botero son bastante oscuros, por eso representan una realidad alterada.

Read the text again and answer the questions.

1 When did Botero become interested in art?
2 What does Botero try to do by painting fat figures?
3 According to the text, how do the family seem? (2 details)
4 What are the colours like?

Write about your opinion on going to the cinema and watching television. Include:

- *your favourite types of film and why you like them:*
  Me fascinan las películas de… porque son…
- *your favourite types of TV programmes and why you like them:*
  Me interesan los programas de… porque son más/menos… que…
- *what your friends like:*
  A mi amigo John le gustan las películas…, pero para mí son…
- *which activity you prefer and why:*
  Prefiero ir al cine/ver la tele porque…

1 Find the odd one out for each list of sports.

1 fútbol	tenis	equitación	baloncesto
2 natación	vela	windsurf	alpinismo
3 pesca	parkour	esquí acuático	paracaidismo
4 wakeboard	footing	snowboard	esquí
5 golf	béisbol	billar	gimnasia

2 Read the sentences and write the verb in the correct tense and person for each.

1 Cuando estaba de vacaciones, todos los días *(jugar)* al fútbol con mis hermanos en la playa.
2 Ayer yo *(hacer)* vela por primera vez.
3 La semana pasada mis amigos y yo *(jugar)* al voleibol.
4 El año que viene yo *(hacer)* esquí con mi amiga Cristina.
5 Mi padre siempre *(hacer)* deporte los sábados por la mañana.
6 Anoche fui al polideportivo y *(jugar)* a la pelota vasca.
7 Hoy por la tarde, a las tres, María *(jugar)* al tenis y luego va a comer una hamburguesa.
8 Antes los chicos de mi clase *(hacer)* patinaje después del cole.

3 Read the text and complete the phrases with the correct information.

1 Jaime's favourite sport is…
2 He does this sport with…
3 He describes his favourite sport as… because…
4 His family's boat size is…
5 His father has…
6 His boat is equipped with… (one detail)
7 In the future he would like to…
8 He would like to visit…
9 He learnt a lot when he…
10 He now has a Recreational Skipper Vessel licence and he had to go offshore up to… miles.

Me llamo Jaime y mi deporte preferido es la vela. La practico todos los fines de semana con mi familia. La vela es un deporte bastante emocionante porque nunca se sabe qué tiempo va a hacer, y si va a hacer viento o no. A mí me gusta salir en nuestro velero (es un barco de vela de cinco metros) con mis hermanos, mi madre y mi padre. Mi padre tiene mucha experiencia con veleros, y ha participado en los circuitos de regatas profesionales como *Zegna, Godó, Freixenet, Príncipe de Asturias, Copa Breitling, Copa del Rey,* etc.

Nuestro velero se llama *Felicidad*. La navegación es a vela, aunque el velero también dispone de motor. El barco está equipado con todo el material necesario para la navegación, así como material de seguridad (chalecos salvavidas) y menaje de cocina. Además, cuenta con una radio-CD para poner la música que nos gusta. Normalmente el almuerzo se hace a bordo. Comemos bocadillos de jamón o queso, o algo fácil de preparar. Normalmente al atardecer volvemos a tierra.

En el futuro me gustaría trabajar como marinero, y navegar todos los días. Me encantaría visitar otros países de Europa y quizás del Caribe. El verano pasado hice un curso de vela y pasé tres días navegando en un barco de vela de siete metros, donde aprendí muchas cosas nuevas. Hice estas prácticas de vela para obtener el título de *Patrón de Embarcación de Recreo*. Tuve que navegar entre islas y hasta una distancia de doce millas paralelas a la costa. ¡Fue increíble!

4 Now write a summary of Jaime's text in Spanish, giving the main points:

- *his opinion:* El deporte preferido de Jaime es… A Jaime le gusta…
- *his family and sailing:* La familia de Jaime tiene… La familia sale… hace…
- *his recent experience:* Jaime hizo…
- *his future plans:* (En el futuro) Jaime quiere… A Jaime le encantaría…

Answer these questions in English.

a Which rooms are in the main wing?
b What separates this area from the main bedroom and the guest bedroom?
c Which rooms are in the smaller wing?
d What shape is the floor plan?

La casa de aluminio

La Casa Aluminio está dividida en dos alas.

El ala principal tiene un amplio espacio habitable, donde se encuentran la sala de estar, la cocina y el comedor. Una pared separa este espacio de la habitación de matrimonio y de la de los invitados.

El ala secundaria tiene dos habitaciones, un estudio y un espacio común para usos múltiples. Los dos espacios públicos dan al patio exterior, que completa la forma rectangular de la planta.

el ala = *the wing*
la planta = *the floor*

Write out this conversation in the correct order.

a ¿Qué?¿No se puede cambiar sin el recibo? Me parece inaceptable.
b Pues no, no lo tengo.
c Pues... no se puede cambiar sin el recibo.
d Quería cambiar este collar de oro. Lo compré para mi madre, pero no le gusta.
e Sí, quisiera hablar con el director ahora mismo.
f Lo siento, ¿quiere hablar con el director?
g Muy bien, ¿tiene el recibo?

Translate this survey into English.

¿Qué opinión tienes de comprar por Internet?

a No lo he probado.
b No lo he probado, pero quiero hacerlo pronto.
c Solo compro por Internet si es más barato.
d Prefiero comprar en tiendas. Prefiero ver y tocar los artículos.
e Creo que no es seguro y no me da mucha confianza.

leer 1 Read the text. Choose the correct information.

Nuestra actriz más internacional, Penélope Cruz, y su hermana Mónica han diseñado una colección especial de prendas para la marca *Mango* que consta de 25 piezas, e incluirá también algunos accesorios.
La moda de los famosos que crean sus propias colecciones para las firmas de ropa está más de moda que nunca.

la prenda = *the garment*
constar de = *to consist of*

1 Penélope and Mónica Cruz have designed…
  - **a** a special collection for *Mango*.
  - **b** all of *Mango's* clothes.
  - **c** three collections for *Mango*.

2 The collection consists of…
  - **a** bags.
  - **b** accessories.
  - **c** garments and accessories.

3 Celebrity endorsements are…
  - **a** less common nowadays.
  - **b** more and more popular.
  - **c** less and less successful.

leer 2 Read and write the name of the appropriate person.

Who…

1. would build sustainable housing?
2. would make sure the public transport was good?
3. would build a sports centre?
4. thinks a city should be multicultural?
5. would create lots of places for recreation?
6. thinks there should be green spaces?
7. would introduce a system for renting bikes?
8. would build a bowling alley and maybe a cinema?

¿Cómo debería ser la ciudad ideal?

Martín: *Deberían construir una bolera, y quizás un cine para los jóvenes.*

Antonio: *Se debería construir un centro cultural, y también un polideportivo para los jóvenes.*

Diego: *Tendría una red de transporte muy buena.*

Rosalía: *En mi ciudad ideal me gustaría tener muchos espacios verdes.*

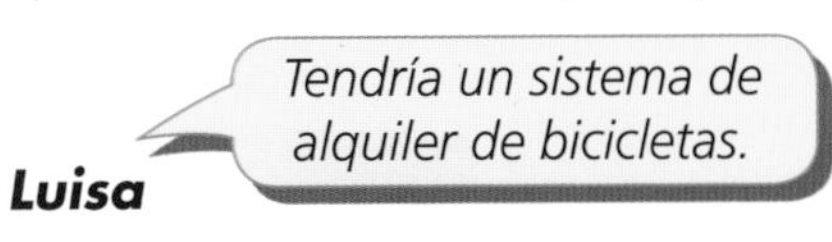
Tendría un sistema de alquiler de bicicletas.

Luisa

Ángel: *Yo construiría casas sostenibles.*

Soledad: *La ciudad debería ser multicultural, con gente de todo el mundo.*

Bea: *Construiría muchas áreas de ocio: parques, museos y estadios.*

escribir 3 Write a description of these cities.

a

skyscrapers
big
lots to do
but…
dirty
polluted
no parks
no green spaces

b

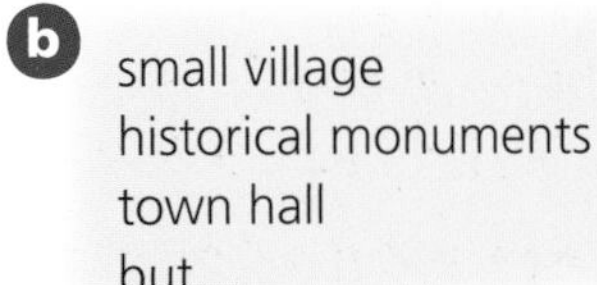

small village
historical monuments
town hall
but…
no sports centre
no shopping centre
nothing to do

Te toca a ti A

1 *Read the phrases and solve the puzzles by writing in the correct word.*

1 una lata de ______ (dainsras)
2 una botella de ______ (verezca)
3 medio kilo de ______ (estomat)
4 un paquete de ______ (cúraza)
5 una caja de ______ (asgellat)
6 un bote de ______ (féac)
7 una bolsa de ______ (taapsta stifra)
8 un cartón de ______ (helec)
9 una barra de ______ (nap)
10 una docena de ______ (shevuo)

2 *Read the phrases and put the statements in order. Start with the healthiest diet and finish with the unhealthiest diet.*

Tomo mucho pescado como merluza o trucha a menudo, y no como carne roja. No me gusta la fruta y tampoco como verdura.

Me gusta comer mucho, pero solo carne roja o pasta. La verdura y la fruta no me gustan nada. Me encanta tomar café y fumar después de comer.

Creo que llevo una dieta equilibrada, pero creo que bebo demasiados refrescos y tomo postres. Me encanta el chocolate.

Para no engordar, no como nunca comida rápida y evito comer sal o grasas. Como de todo, excepto chocolate. Como carne, pescado, verdura y fruta, pero con moderación.

3 *Translate the sentences in exercise 2 into English.*

Ejemplo: **1** I often eat fish like hake or trout and I try to avoid red meat.

4 *Read the postcard and decide if the statements are True (T), False (F) or Not mentioned (NM).*

1 Sandra travelled there by aeroplane.
2 Sandra is having bad weather on holiday.
3 Sandra had an accident in the morning.
4 She went on a boating trip with her aunt and uncle.
5 She has not broken anything.
6 She cut her foot.
7 She can sunbathe on the beach now.

¡Hola Marta! ¿Qué tal? Estoy de vacaciones aquí en Pals, en la Costa Brava. Hace sol y el tiempo es perfecto, pero no puedo hacer deporte porque tengo la pierna mal. Hoy por la mañana he ido de excursión en barco con mis abuelos, pero al llegar al puerto me he caído al agua en medio de unas rocas. Me he cortado la pierna y me he torcido el codo. ¡Me duele mucho! He tenido que ir al hospital para hacerme una radiografía, pero afortunadamente no me he roto nada. Tengo que tomar unas aspirinas para el dolor. Por lo menos puedo ir a la playa para relajarme y tomar el sol, que ya sabes que me encanta.
Un abrazo,
Sandra

Take the healthy lifestyle survey. Summarise in English the advice you are given for your results.

1 Desayunas…
- a todos los días. Te gustan los cereales o la fruta con yogur.
- b casi todos los días, pero hay veces que no tienes hambre.
- c solo los fines de semana. No tienes tiempo para desayunar entre semana.

2 En un restaurante, cuando tienes sed bebes…
- a agua mineral sin gas o con gas. Es muy sano.
- b un refresco. Te gustan las burbujas.
- c zumo de fruta. Prefieres algo con sabor.

3 Cuando tienes hambre en casa comes…
- a un poco de queso o una loncha de jamón.
- b una manzana o un plátano.
- c unos caramelos o unas galletas con pepitas de chocolate.

4 Comes verduras…
- a todos los días. Hay que comer cinco frutas o verduras diferentes al día.
- b tres veces a la semana. No me gustan mucho, pero con kétchup están buenas.
- c una vez cada seis meses. Las verduras son para los conejos.

5 Comes pescado…
- a una vez a la semana con patatas fritas.
- b tres veces a la semana. Te gusta el marisco.
- c si te obliga tu madre/padre. El pescado huele mal.

6 Antes de dormir te gusta…
- a beber un vaso de leche, a veces con azúcar.
- b comerte un paquete grande de bombones.
- c tomar un té de menta. Te ayuda a descansar.

7 Duermes…
- a pocas horas. Dormir es para la gente que no tiene vida social.
- b muchas horas. Eres muy perezoso.
- c ocho horas, lo recomendable. No quieres perder el día.

8 Practicas deporte…
- a a menudo con tus amigos. Jugar es divertirse.
- b una vez al año. Lo tuyo son los videojuegos en el sofá.
- c rara vez durante la semana. Tienes que estudiar.

9 Para perder peso…
- a comes menos. Los platos pequeños son perfectos.
- b bebes más refrescos, así no puedes comer demasiado.
- c no haces nada. Es demasiado trabajo.

10 Lo más importante es…
- a divertirse.
- b comer bien y hacer ejercicio.
- c no tener hambre.

una pérdida de tiempo = *a waste of time*
una loncha de = *a slice of*
pepitas de chocolate = *chocolate chips*
huele mál = *it smells bad*
un pequeño lujo = *a little treat*

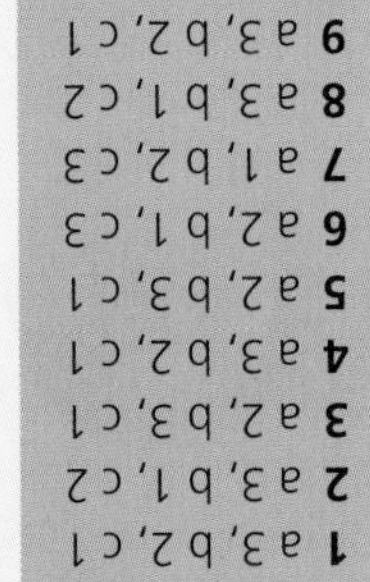

Los resultados:
1 a 3, b 2, c 1
2 a 3, b 1, c 2
3 a 2, b 3, c 1
4 a 3, b 2, c 1
5 a 2, b 3, c 1
6 a 2, b 1, c 3
7 a 1, b 2, c 3
8 a 3, b 1, c 2
9 a 3, b 2, c 1
10 a 1, b 3, c 2

25–30 puntos
¡Felicidades! Estás en forma y llevas una vida muy sana. Deberías continuar así, sin embargo, a veces tienes que permitirte un pequeño lujo (como unos caramelos o un poco de chocolate) porque la vida es demasiada corta.

18–24 puntos
Piensas que llevas una vida bastante sana, pero en realidad no tanto como piensas y no estás en forma. No comes ni suficiente fruta, ni cuidas de tu cuerpo como deberías. Tienes que beber más agua y comer más comida sana.

10–17 puntos
Deberías cuidar mejor de tu cuerpo. No estás en forma, ni quieres estarlo. Es una lástima porque la salud es lo más importante. Nunca es demasiado tarde para empezar a cuidarse. Deberías seguir estos consejos: haz más ejercicio, come más fruta y verdura y bebe más agua. ¡Dile sí a la vida!

Write about your eating habits and lifestyle. Use your answers from the survey to make interesting phrases. Remember to change the verb endings from tú to yo and add in connectives where possible.

Ejemplo: **Desayuno** rara vez durante la semana **porque** no **tengo** tiempo.

Te toca a ti A

1 ***Match each object with the time you think it would take to decompose.***

¿Sabes cuántos años tienen que pasar para la degradación natural de las cosas que tiramos al suelo?

1 pañuelo de papel
2 periódico
3 colilla de cigarro
4 chicle
5 cáscara de fruta
6 encendedor de plástico
7 vaso de vidrio

a de 3 meses a 2 años
b de 1 a 5 años
c 4.000 años
d de 3 a 12 meses
e 3 meses
f 100 años
g 5 años

2 ***Complete these sentences in English.***

1 Finca Bellavista is located…
2 The houses are up in the…
3 They use… energy.
4 There is a… garden.
5 It is possible to…

Casas sostenibles en los árboles de la Finca Bellavista, Puerto Rico.

La Finca Bellavista se encuentra en las montañas de la costa sur del Pacífico. En la Finca se pueden encontrar estas casas en lo alto de los árboles, unas casas con principios de sostenibilidad, ya que utilizan energía hidroeléctrica y solar, y además tienen tratamiento y distribución centralizada de agua, centro de reciclaje y jardín comunitario.

Incluso estando inmerso en la naturaleza, es posible conectarse a Internet a través de un enlace libre de antena. Yo me conectaría sin duda, ¡no puedo vivir sin Internet!

3 ***Write a paragraph saying what we need to do to protect the planet.***

¿Qué tenemos que hacer para proteger el planeta?

No utilice combustibles fósiles.
No ensucie el agua.
No consuma demasiada energía.
No contamine el medio ambiente.
No use detergentes con fosfatos.
No malgaste el papel.

Es importante que protejamos los ríos.
Es esencial que apaguemos las luces.
Es importante que conservemos el planeta.
Es esencial que encontremos alternativas a los combustibles fósiles.
Es necesario que protejamos la vida marina.

1 Read the text and find the Spanish for:

1 world citizen	**3** equality	**5** peace	**7** liberty
2 homeland	**4** flag	**6** war	**8** inheritance

¿Eres tú ciudadano del mundo?

Las características del ciudadano del mundo:

- **Tiene** una nacionalidad, pero una sola patria… la Tierra.
- **Puede** hablar muchos idiomas, pero un solo lenguaje… la Igualdad.
- **Admira** su bandera, pero **defiende** un solo símbolo… la Paz.
- **Combate** en muchas batallas, pero **lucha** en una única guerra… la Libertad.
- **Vive** en un pedazo del universo y su familia se apellida Continente, compuesto por 5 Hermanos: América, Europa, Asia, África y Oceanía.
- **Respeta** y **protege** lo que le dejó en herencia la Señora Madre de la familia Continente… la Naturaleza.

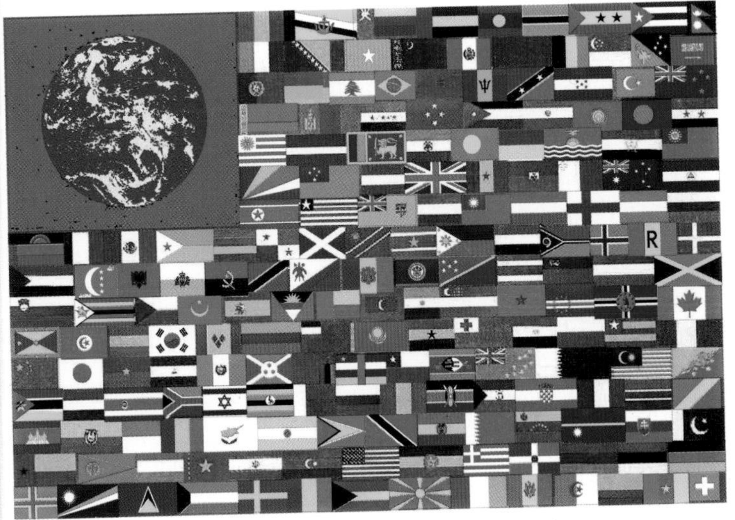

2 Read the text again and translate the verbs in orange into English.

3 Match up the objectives to the topics.

Ejemplo: **1** d

Los objetivos del milenio:

1. Acabar con la pobreza y el hambre.
2. Conseguir que todos los niños y niñas vayan al colegio.
3. Que los hombres y las mujeres sean iguales.
4. Intentar que no mueran los niños por causas evitables.
5. Mejorar la salud de todas las madres del mundo.
6. Prevenir el SIDA.
7. Trabajar todos para mejorar el mundo.

a la igualdad de género
b la educación primaria universal
c la mortalidad infantil
d garantizar la sostenibilidad
e combatir las enfermedades
f crear una asociación mundial
g la salud materna

4 Look at the phrases 1-7 in exercise 3 above. Write a manifesto using verbs in the subjunctive.

Ejemplo: Es importante que acabemos con la pobreza y el hambre.
Es esencial que….
Es necesario que…

Gramática / Hay que saber bien

The present tense – regular verbs

What is it and when do I use it?

The present tense is used to talk about the present. You use it to talk about:

- What usually happens: Siempre **escucho** música pop. *(I always **listen** to pop music.)*
- What things are like: La playa **es** preciosa. *(The beach **is** beautiful.)*
- What is happening now: **Vivo** en Bournemouth. *(I **live** in Bournemouth.)*

Why is it important?

Verbs are the building blocks of language. Using the correct tense helps people understand what you say.

Things to watch out for

The verb ending is the important part. This tells you 'who' is speaking.

How does it work?

Regular verbs

- To form the present tense you replace the infinitive ending (*-ar*, *-er* or *-ir*) with the present tense endings like this:

	escuchar *(to listen)*	**com**er *(to eat)*	**viv**ir *(to live)*
(yo)	escuch**o**	com**o**	viv**o**
(tú)	escuch**as**	com**es**	viv**es**
(él/ella/usted)	escuch**a**	com**e**	viv**e**
(nosotros/as)	escuch**amos**	com**emos**	viv**imos**
(vosotros/as)	escuch**áis**	com**éis**	viv**ís**
(ellos/ellas/ustedes)	escuch**an**	com**en**	viv**en**

Stem-changing verbs

- Stem-changing verbs are formed in the same way as regular present tense verbs. However, their stem changes in these forms: I, you (sing.), he/she/it, they. The vowel change always occurs on the last vowel before the infinitive ending. They are usually regular in their endings. There are three common groups.

	o → ue	**e → ie**	**e → i**
	p**o**der *(to be able)*	quer**e**r *(to want)*	p**e**dir *(to ask)*
(yo)	p**ue**do	qu**ie**ro	p**i**do
(tú)	p**ue**des	qu**ie**res	p**i**des
(él/ella/usted)	p**ue**de	qu**ie**re	p**i**de
(nosotros/as)	podemos	queremos	pedimos
(vosotros/as)	podéis	queréis	pedís
(ellos/ellas/ustedes)	p**ue**den	qu**ie**ren	p**i**den

- Other examples of stem-changing verbs are:

u / o → ue

j**u**gar	→	j**ue**go	*(I play)*
c**o**star	→	c**ue**sta	*(it costs)*
ac**o**starse	→	me ac**ue**sto	*(I go to bed)*
d**o**rmir	→	d**ue**rmo	*(I sleep)*

enc**o**ntrar	→	enc**ue**ntro	*(I meet/find)*
ll**o**ver	→	ll**ue**ve	*(it rains)*
v**o**lver	→	v**ue**lvo	*(I come back)*

The verb *jugar* (to play) is the only example of a verb that has the stem change from **u → ue**.

e → ie

desp**e**rtarse	→	me desp**ie**rto	*(I wake up)*
emp**e**zar	→	emp**ie**zo	*(I start)*
ent**e**nder	→	ent**ie**ndo	*(I understand)*
n**e**var	→	n**ie**va	*(it snows)*
p**e**nsar	→	p**ie**nso	*(I think)*
p**e**rder	→	p**ie**rdo	*(I lose)*
pref**e**rir	→	pref**ie**ro	*(I prefer)*
recom**e**ndar	→	recom**ie**ndo	*(I recommend)*

e → i

rep**e**tir	→	rep**i**to	*(I repeat)*
s**e**rvir	→	s**i**rvo	*(I serve)*
v**e**stirse	→	me v**i**sto	*(I get dressed)*

Preparados

1 Fill in the gaps with the correct form of the verb.

1 Me llamo Silvana y **vivo** en Barcelona. *(vivir)*
2 Todos los días ____ con mis amigos y ____ por Internet. *(chatear/navegar)*
3 De vez en cuando ____ con el ordenador o con la Wii. *(jugar)*
4 ____ música por las tardes. *(descargar)*
5 No ____ vivir sin música. *(poder)*
6 ____ inglés, pero no me gusta mucho. *(estudiar)*
7 ____ estudiar informática. *(preferir)*
8 ____ en mi blog todos los días. *(escribir)*
9 De vez en cuando ____ algo por Internet. *(comprar)*
10 No ____ mucho. *(leer)*

Listos

2 Underline the correct verb to complete each sentence.

1 Mis clases ***empiezas*** / <u>***empiezan***</u> / ***empiezo*** a las ocho.
2 Todos los días ***lleva / llevan / llevo*** mi mochila.
3 Ellos ***necesitamos / necesita / necesitan*** unos bolígrafos, una regla y sus cosas.
4 Mi amigo Carlos ***pueden / puede / puedo*** ir andando.
5 Yo ***prefiero / prefieres / preferimos*** ir en bici.
6 A veces, en el recreo, nosotros ***jugamos / juega / jugáis*** al tenis.
7 Mi amiga Silvia ***prefiero / prefieres / prefiere*** las asignaturas prácticas.
8 No le gusta el inglés porque ***odia / odias / odio*** memorizar palabras.
9 Yo ***odian / odio / odias*** cantar en el coro.
10 ¿Y tú qué ***prefieres / preferís / prefieren***?

¡Ya!

3 How do you say...? Write out the answers.

1 At lunchtime I drink something. *A la hora de comer bebo algo.*
2 In class, I listen and write.
3 In the summer, we play basketball outside.
4 My friends prefer to go to the language club.
5 Elena can speak Spanish.
6 Now she wants to learn German.
7 Jim and Samir speak English.
8 My father recommends French.
9 He loses always.
10 Do you speak Spanish?

Gramática Hay que saber bien

The present tense – reflexives and irregular

What are reflexive verbs and when do I use them?
Reflexive verbs are verbs that include a reflexive pronoun. They describe actions that we do to ourselves.

What are irregular verbs and when do I use them?
Irregular verbs do not follow the normal patterns of regular *-ar*, *-er* and *-ir* verbs. Many of the most common and most useful verbs in Spanish are irregular.

Why are irregular and reflexive verbs important?
You can't speak a language without knowing a wide range of verbs, and some of the most important verbs like **to be**, **to have**, **to do** and **to go** are irregular.

Things to watch out for

- With reflexive verbs always check you have used the correct reflexive pronoun.
- You must learn irregular verbs by heart. Sometimes, just the ***yo*** form is irregular.

How does it work?

Reflexive verbs

Reflexive verbs describe an action which you do to yourself. They are formed in the same way as regular present tense verbs but they include a reflexive pronoun.

- In the **infinitive**, the pronoun is shown at the end of the verb *(ducharse)*.
- In the **present tense**, the pronoun precedes the verb and depends on the person *(**me** ducho)*.

	ducharse *(to shower)*	**despertarse** *(to wake up)*
(yo)	**me** ducho	**me** despierto
(tú)	**te** duchas	**te** despiertas
(él/ella/usted)	**se** ducha	**se** despierta
(nosotros/as)	**nos** duchamos	**nos** despertamos
(vosotros/as)	**os** ducháis	**os** despertáis
(ellos/ellas/ustedes)	**se** duchan	**se** despiertan

Irregular verbs

These verbs are irregular in the ***yo*** form (the first person singular), but regular in the other forms.

conducir	*(to drive)*	→	conduzco
conocer	*(to know/meet)*	→	conozco
dar	*(to give)*	→	doy
hacer	*(to make/do)*	→	hago
poner	*(to put)*	→	pongo

saber	*(to know)*	→	sé
salir	*(to go out)*	→	salgo
tener	(to have)	→	tengo
traer	*(to bring)*	→	traigo

- Other verbs have more irregularity.

	ser *(to be)*	**estar** *(to be)*	**ir** *(to go)*
(yo)	soy	estoy	voy
(tú)	eres	estás	vas
(él/ella/usted)	es	está	va
(nosotros/as)	somos	estamos	vamos
(vosotros/as)	sois	estáis	vais
(ellos/ellas/ustedes)	son	están	van

- Look at the verb tables on pages 232–233 for more irregular present tense verbs.

Preparados

1 Complete these sentences with the correct form of the verb.

1. Me despierto a las siete. *(despertarse, yo)*
2. ______ a las siete y diez. *(levantarse, yo)*
3. Mis padres ______ a las seis. *(levantarse)*
4. ¿A qué hora ______? *(levantarse, tú)*
5. Luego ______. *(ducharse, yo)*
6. Después ______. *(vestirse, yo)*
7. No ______. *(peinarse, yo)*
8. ______ a las once. *(acostarse, yo)*
9. Mi hermano y yo ______ *(acostarse, nosotros)* más tarde el fin de semana.
10. ¿A qué hora ______? *(acostarse, tú)*

Listos

2 Complete the table with the 'you' form and the 'he/she' form. Watch out for the reflexive pronouns and possessives.

Yo	1 Me levanto todos los días y 2 me digo que mi vida va a cambiar. 3 Pienso que 4 soy una persona simpática. Ya 5 conozco a mucha gente y 6 tengo muchos amigos. En el futuro 7 quiero encontrar a alguien con quien reírme. ¿Dónde está esa persona? No lo 8 sé. Cuando 9 me despierto y cuando 10 me acuesto está cerca.
Tú	1 Te levantas todos los días y 2 ______ que tu vida va a cambiar. 3 ______ que 4 ______ una persona simpática. Ya 5 ______ a mucha gente y 6 ______ muchos amigos. En el futuro 7 ______ encontrar a alguien con quien reírte. ¿Dónde está esa persona? No lo 8 ______. Cuando 9 ______ y cuando 10 ______ está cerca.
Él/Ella	1 Se levanta todos los días y 2 ______ que su vida va a cambiar. 3 ______ que 4 ______ una persona simpática. Ya 5 ______ a mucha gente y 6 ______ muchos amigos. En el futuro 7 ______ encontrar a alguien con quien reírse. ¿Dónde está esa persona? No lo 8 ______. Cuando 9 ______ y cuando 10 ______ está cerca.

¡Ya!

3 Complete these sentences with the correct form of the verb.

1. Salgo a las ocho. *(salir)*
2. Por la noche yo ______ mis deberes. *(hacer)*
3. Mis padres ______ mucho. *(salir)*
4. Yo ______ el autobús, pero tú ______ el tren. *(coger)*
5. Cada mes le ______ un regalo a mi novio. *(hacer)*
6. ¿Cómo se llama? No lo ______. *(saber)*
7. Mis amigos y yo ______ natación los sábados. *(hacer)*
8. Yo siempre ______ muy bien. *(drive)*
9. Mis padres ______ una casa muy bonita. *(tener)*
10. Yo ______ a mucha gente. *(conocer)*

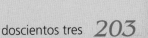

Gramática / Hay que saber bien

The preterite

What is it and when do I use it?

The preterite is known as the 'simple past'. It is used to talk about completed actions in the past.

Fui a la playa. (*I **went** to the beach.*) **Comió** un bocadillo. (*He **ate** a sandwich.*)

Why is it important?

You often want to say what you or someone else did. Without the preterite you could not tell a story in Spanish.

Things to watch out for

- Some forms of regular verbs in the preterite take an accent. Be careful that you use accents correctly as using them incorrectly can change the meaning of a word.
  escuch**o** (*I listen*) escuch**ó** (*he listened*)
- Irregular verbs don't take accents in the preterite.
- The verbs *ir* and *ser* are the same in the preterite.

How does it work?

Regular preterite verbs

- The preterite tense is formed by taking the infinitive of a verb, removing the infinitive endings (*-ar*, *-er* or *-ir*), and then adding the following preterite endings. Note that *-er* and *-ir* verbs take the same endings in the preterite.

	visitar (*to visit*)	**comer** (*to eat*)	**salir** (*to go out*)
(yo)	visit**é**	com**í**	sal**í**
(tú)	visit**aste**	com**iste**	sal**iste**
(él/ella/usted)	visit**ó**	com**ió**	sal**ió**
(nosotros/as)	visit**amos**	com**imos**	sal**imos**
(vosotros/as)	visit**asteis**	com**isteis**	sal**isteis**
(ellos/ellas/ustedes)	visit**aron**	com**ieron**	sal**ieron**

- When you are using stem-changing verbs make sure you have the correct infinitive:
  encuentro (*I find*) → encontr**ar** (*infinitive: to find*) → encontré (*I found*)

Irregular preterite verbs

- The most common irregular verbs are:

	ser/ir (*to be/to go*)	**ver** (*to see*)	**hacer** (*to do/make*)	**tener** (*to have*)
(yo)	fui	vi	hice	tuve
(tú)	fuiste	viste	hiciste	tuviste
(él/ella/usted)	fue	vio	hizo	tuvo
(nosotros/as)	fuimos	vimos	hicimos	tuvimos
(vosotros/as)	fuisteis	visteis	hicisteis	tuvisteis
(ellos/ellas/ustedes)	fueron	vieron	hicieron	tuvieron

- Other irregular preterite verbs include:
  dar (*to give*) estar (*to be*) andar (*to walk*) poder (*to be able to*) poner (*to put*)
  querer (*to want*) saber (*to know*) traer (*to bring*) venir (*to come*) decir (*to say*)
  (Go to the verb tables on page 232 to see some of them.)
- Some preterite verbs have **irregular spellings** in just the first person singular (yo). For example:
  sacar → sa**qu**é (*I got*) cruzar → cru**c**é (*I crossed*) jugar → ju**gu**é (*I played*)
  tocar → to**qu**é (*I played*) empezar → empe**c**é (*I started*) llegar → lle**gu**é (*I arrived*)
- Some have **irregular spellings** in the third person singular (él/ella/usted) and plural (ellos/ellas/ustedes):
  caer → ca**y**ó/ca**y**eron (*he/she fell, they fell*) leer → le**y**ó/le**y**eron (*he/she read, they read*)

Preparados

1 Copy the sentence and write the correct form of the verb in brackets. Then translate each sentence into English.

1 La semana pasada yo (***leer***) un libro muy bueno. *leí – Last week I read a very good book.*
2 Ayer yo (***comprar***) palomitas y me gasté todos mis ahorros.
3 La semana pasada mi amiga (***comer***) paella.
4 Mis amigos y yo (***tener***) una fiesta para celebrar mi cumpleaños.
5 ¿Cuándo (***ir***) a la piscina? Ayer no te vi.
6 Mis vacaciones (***ser***) increíbles.
7 Ayer mis amigos y yo no (***hacer***) nada.
8 Anteayer fui en metro al centro y (***ver***) una obra de teatro.
9 Mi hermano (***estudiar***) ocho asignaturas en el colegio.
10 Mi madre (***hacer***) vela hace dos días.

Listos

2 Look at the list of phrases and decide if the verbs are in the present or the preterite. Then translate each verb into English.

1 ***Tomo*** el desayuno a las diez. *present – I have*
2 ***Fuimos*** al museo antes de comer.
3 ***Hace*** mucho sol aquí.
4 Mi amigo ***decidió*** comprar unos recuerdos.
5 ***Practiqué*** natación en el polideportivo cerca de mi casa.
6 Nunca ***hago*** mis deberes.
7 ***Observé*** a la gente en el restaurante.
8 En el colegio ***comemos*** a las doce y media.
9 Anoche mis amigos ***fueron*** al cine.
10 Silvia ***jugó*** al fútbol el sábado.

¡Ya!

3 Write the following story in the past. Change all the present tense verbs into the preterite.

Fui a la bolera…

¡Un buen día!

(1) ***Voy*** a la bolera y (2) ***juego*** a los bolos con mis amigos. (3) ***Bebemos*** refrescos, pero no (4) ***comemos*** nada. Mis padres me (5) ***dan*** cuatro euros para gastar el fin de semana y con eso (6) ***es*** suficiente para salir por la tarde. En casa (7) ***limpio*** el suelo, mis hermanas (8) ***lavan*** los platos y mis abuelos (9) ***cocinan***. (10) ***Es*** un rollo. Por la tarde (11) ***salgo*** y (12) ***voy*** al cine con mi novio. Después (13) ***vamos*** al centro comercial a comprar un regalo para un amigo. Finalmente, (14) ***llego*** a casa, pero no (15) ***hago*** mis deberes. (16) ***Leo*** un poco y (17) ***mando*** mensajes de texto a mi novio. (18) ***Me acuesto*** a las diez y (19) ***me duermo*** pronto.

Gramática | Hay que saber bien

The imperfect tense

What is it and when do I use it?

The imperfect tense is another way of talking about the past. It is used in Spanish to describe:

- repeated actions in the past:

  Comíamos a las dos todos los días. *(We **ate** at two every day.)*
- background details (what someone or something was like or was doing):

  El hotel **era** muy grande. *(The hotel **was** very big.)*
- what people used to do and what things used to be like:

  Antes **vivía** con mis abuelos, pero ahora vivo sola. *(I **used to live** with my grandparents, but I live on my own now.)*

Why is it important?

To tell a story in the past successfully you need to be able to use the imperfect for descriptions and repeated actions.

Things to watch out for

You use the **preterite** for single events in the past and the **imperfect tense** for repeated or continuous actions in the past.

How does it work?

- The **imperfect tense** is formed by taking the infinitive of a verb, removing the infinitive endings (*-ar, -er, -ir*) and then adding the following endings. Note that *-er* and *-ir* verbs take the same endings in the imperfect.

	hablar *(to speak)*	**hac**er *(to do/make)*	**viv**ir *(to live)*
(yo)	habl**aba**	hac**ía**	viv**ía**
(tú)	habl**abas**	hac**ías**	viv**ías**
(él/ella/usted)	habl**aba**	hac**ía**	viv**ía**
(nosotros/as)	habl**ábamos**	hac**íamos**	viv**íamos**
(vosotros/as)	habl**abais**	hac**íais**	viv**íais**
(ellos/ellas/ustedes)	habl**aban**	hac**ían**	viv**ían**

- There are three verbs that are irregular in the imperfect tense.

	ir *(to go)*	**ser** *(to be)*	**ver** *(to see)*
(yo)	**iba**	**era**	**veía**
(tú)	**ibas**	**eras**	**veías**
(él/ella/usted)	**iba**	**era**	**veía**
(nosotros/as)	**íbamos**	**éramos**	**veíamos**
(vosotros/as)	**ibais**	**erais**	**veíais**
(ellos/ellas/ustedes)	**iban**	**eran**	**veían**

- The imperfect tense of ***haber*** and ***hay*** (there is) is ***había*** (there was/were). *Había* is very useful for describing what things used to be like.

  Había mucha gente en la tienda. *(**There were** a lot of people in the shop.)*

Preparados

1 Translate the sentences into English. Write the correct letters next to each sentence to explain why the imperfect is required – RA (repeated action in the past), BD (background detail in the past) or UT ('used to' phrase).

1. Durante las vacaciones me levantaba a las nueve cada día.
   During the holidays I got up at nine o'clock every day. (RA)
2. Por la mañana me despertaba a las seis.
3. Mi piso en Madrid era muy pequeño.
4. Había mucha gente en la clase.
5. Antes me gustaba comer comida rápida.
6. Rafael era una persona simpática, pero ahora es antipático.
7. En el camping, María cocinaba para su madre.
8. En el verano íbamos a la playa todos los días.
9. En el hotel había una piscina climatizada.
10. En mi instituto había mucho acoso escolar, pero ahora no.

Listos

2 Read Eva's description of what she did last weekend. Identify and write down all the verbs that she uses in the imperfect tense and their English meanings.

¡El fin de semana pasado fue horrible! Me levanté tarde y no encontraba las llaves. Siempre pongo mis llaves al lado del móvil en el comedor, pero no estaban allí. Tuve que buscarlas por todos lados. Finalmente, a las nueve y media, y con más de una hora de retraso, encontré las llaves en mi dormitorio, salí de casa y fui al trabajo. Antes cogía el metro para ir al trabajo, pero ahora el metro cuesta demasiado y siempre voy en autobús. El año pasado trabajaba en una tienda de discos, pero lo odiaba. Ahora estoy más contenta porque trabajo en una tienda de ropa. Sólo ganaba cinco euros a la hora en la tienda de discos, pero ahora gano mucho más. La tienda de discos era bastante pequeña y solo tenía música de los años sesenta y setenta. ¡Qué aburrimiento! **Luisa**

3 Now describe the events in English in the table.

Actions in the past (preterite)	Background details or repeated action (imperfect)]
Eva got up late.	*She couldn't find her keys.*

¡Ya!

4 Complete the sentences with either the preterite or imperfect tense.

1. Fui de vacaciones a España y el hotel donde nos quedamos *era* *(ser)* bastante lujoso.
2. Ayer mis amigos ______ *(despertarse)* tarde porque el despertador no funcionaba.
3. Antes Juan ______ *(beber)* mucho café, pero ahora no porque quiere llevar una vida más sana.
4. Mis padres y yo ______ *(vivir)* en una casa adosada en el campo, pero ahora vivimos en las afueras.
5. Mi abuela ______ *(ir)* al mercado todos los sábados.
6. Antes ______ *(haber)* mucha gente en la playa porque estaba limpia, pero ahora no hay nadie.
7. Mi abuelo era muy alto y ______ *(tener)* el pelo negro como yo.
8. Hicimos los deberes el domingo y después ______ *(ir)* al cine.
9. Mi hermano ______ *(ordenar)* su dormitorio una vez a la semana, pero ahora no tiene tiempo y lo hace una vez al mes.
10. Recargué mi móvil y luego ______ *(ir)* a casa de mis amigos.

The future tense

The near future tense

What is it and when do I use it?

The near future is used to describe 'what is going to happen' (for example, tonight, tomorrow, next week, etc.). It is the most common tense in Spanish for describing future plans.

Voy a ir a jugar a los bolos. *(I **am going to go** bowling.)*

Why is it important?

You often want to say what you or someone else is going to do.

Things to watch out for

Don't forget to use the preposition **a** when using the near future.

How does it work?

To form the future, you need to use ***ir*** (in the present tense) + ***a*** + **infinitive verb**

(yo)	voy	a	comer
(tú)	vas		jugar
(él/ella/usted)	va		tener
(nosotros/as)	vamos		salir
(vosotros/as)	vais		comprar
(ellos/ellas/ustedes)	van		hacer

The future tense

What is it and when do I use it?

The future tense is used to describe what 'will happen' in the future.

El polideportivo **será** muy grande. *(The sports centre **will be** very big.)*

Why is it important?

You often want to say what you or someone else will do.

Things to watch out for

Don't forget to use the correct accents on future tense verbs.

How does it work?

To form the future tense of most verbs, you take the infinitive of the verb and add the following endings.

(yo)	hablar**é**
(tú)	hablar**ás**
(él/ella/usted)	hablar**á**
(nosotros/as)	hablar**emos**
(vosotros/as)	hablar**éis**
(ellos/ellas/ustedes)	hablar**án**

These endings are the same for *-ar*, *-er* and *-ir* verbs.

- These verbs have irregular stems in the future but the endings are the same as for regular verbs.

decir	*(to say)*	→	**dir**é	saber	*(to know)*	→	**sabr**é
hacer	*(to do/make)*	→	**har**é	salir	*(to leave/go out)*	→	**saldr**é
poder	*(to be able to)*	→	**podr**é	tener	*(to have)*	→	**tendr**é
poner	*(to put)*	→	**pondr**é	venir	*(to come)*	→	**vendr**é
querer	*(to want)*	→	**querr**é	haber	*(there is/are)*	→	**habrá**

Preparados

1 Rewrite the sentence to include the missing part of the immediate future tense.

1 I am going to buy a flat. – Voy comprar un piso. *Voy a comprar un piso.*
2 My friends are going to go to the cinema. – Mis amigos van a al cine.
3 Today my father is going to cook. – Hoy mi padre a cocinar.
4 We are going to visit museums. – Vamos a visitar algunos museos.
5 Maite is going to prepare for her exams. – Maite va preparar sus exámenes.
6 Fernando is going to download music. – Fernando a descargar música.
7 People are going to smoke less. – La gente va fumar menos.
8 We are going to eat more fruit. – Vamos a más fruta.
9 I am going to go to France. – Voy ir a Francia.
10 They are going to go on the bus. – a ir en autobús.
11 I am going to buy a necklace. – Voy a un collar.
12 Today you are going to play football. – Hoy vosotros a jugar al fútbol.

Listos

2 Change all of the verbs from the immediate future into the future tense. Watch out for the irregular ones!

Ejemplo: *va a ser* → *será*

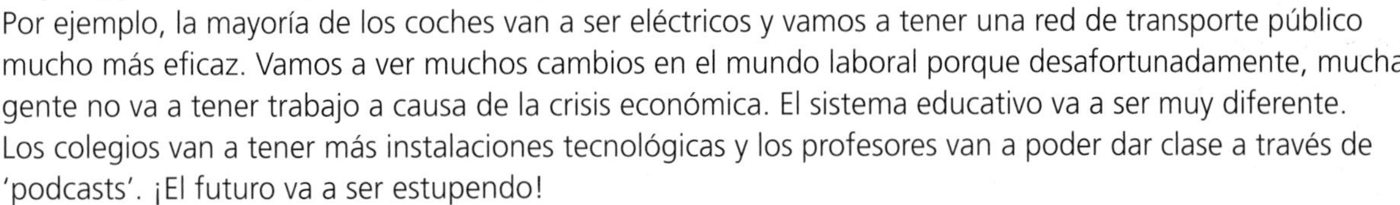

En el futuro, el mundo va a ser muy diferente porque la tecnología va a mejorar, y va a ser una parte aún más importante de nuestra vida cotidiana. Por ejemplo, la mayoría de los coches van a ser eléctricos y vamos a tener una red de transporte público mucho más eficaz. Vamos a ver muchos cambios en el mundo laboral porque desafortunadamente, mucha gente no va a tener trabajo a causa de la crisis económica. El sistema educativo va a ser muy diferente. Los colegios van a tener más instalaciones tecnológicas y los profesores van a poder dar clase a través de 'podcasts'. ¡El futuro va a ser estupendo!

3 Translate the text into English.

¡Ya!

4 Read the interview and complete the sentences or questions with the correct future tense of an appropriate verb.

haber ser ser tener jugar hacer tocar existir estudiar practicar hacer

A: ¿Cuántos alumnos (1) *estudiarán* español el año que viene?
B: Pues, no lo sé, pero el colegio (2) ____ más de quinientos alumnos en total.
A: ¿(3) ____ un club de fotografía?
B: Sí. El club de fotografía (4) ____ los lunes a la hora de comer.
A: ¿Y tú, (5) ____ algún deporte?
B: Si tengo tiempo, (6) ____ al béisbol los viernes, o (7) ____ natación los martes. Todo depende, porque también (8) ____ la trompeta en la orquesta.
A: En tu opinión, ¿cuáles (9) ____ los principales problemas para los jóvenes de tu colegio?
B: Pues, es una lástima, pero creo que siempre (10) ____ el acoso escolar.
A: Si el acoso escolar nunca desaparece, ¿tú qué (11) ____ para proteger a los alumnos?

The conditional

What is it and when do I use it?
The conditional is used to describe what you **would** do in the future.
Me encantaría trabajar con ordenadores. *(I **would love** to work with computers.)*

Why is it important?
You need the conditional to talk successfully about your future plans and ideas.

Things to watch out for
Don't confuse conditional verbs with imperfect verbs. The conditional is formed by using the future stem and adding the imperfect endings.

How does it work?
The conditional is formed in the same way as the future tense. You take the infinitive of the verb and add the following endings (these are the same for *-ar*, *-er* and *-ir* verbs):

	comer *(to eat)*
(yo)	comer**ía**
(tú)	comer**ías**
(él/ella/usted)	comer**ía**
(nosotros/as)	comer**íamos**
(vosotros/as)	comer**íais**
(ellos/ellas/ustedes)	comer**ían**

- The verbs which have irregular stems in the future also have irregular stems in the conditional. For example:

  hacer *(to do/make)* → **har**ía, **har**ías… *(would do)*
  poder *(to be able to)* → **podr**ía, **podr**ías… *(would be able to)*
  tener *(to have)* → **tendr**ía, **tendr**ías… *(would have)*

  Other verbs which have irregular stems in the future and therefore the conditional are listed on pages 232–233.

- The conditional of haber is ***habría*** *(there would be).*

- The conditional can be used to express future ideas by using the verb ***gustar*** followed by **an infinitive**.
  En el futuro, **me gustaría hablar** más idiomas.
  *(In the future, I **would like to speak** more languages.)*

- The conditional of ***poder*** + **an infinitive** is used to express the notion of something that you could do.
  Podríamos ir al cine.
  *(We **could go** to the cinema.)*

- The conditional of ***deber*** + **an infinitive** is used to express the notion of something that you ought to do.
  Deberíamos reciclar los productos plásticos.
  *(We **should recycle** plastic items.)*

Preparados

1 Here are some sentences about an ideal world. Make sure the correct conditional is used in each one.

1 ¿Cómo ***(ser)*** un mundo ideal para ti? *sería*
2 En un mundo ideal, mi hermano ***(trabajar)*** y ***(tener)*** un buen sueldo.
3 Mis padres ***(comprar)*** un barco muy rápido y ***(hacer)*** esquí acuático los fines de semana.
4 ¡Mi profesor de español no ***(hablar)*** nada en español, ¡sólo en inglés!
5 Mi novia me ***(regalar)*** un anillo de oro y me ***(decir)***: 'Te quiero'.
6 Mi abuelo ***(vivir)*** mucho más tiempo y ***(cumplir)*** cien años.
7 Mis amigos y yo ***(salir)*** cada fin de semana e ***(ir)*** al centro comercial o al cine.
8 Mi hermana ***(querer)*** irse de casa.
9 Mi hermano ***(dejar)*** de ser obrero y ***(ser)*** un actor famoso.
10 Finalmente, yo ***(ganar)*** mucho dinero y ***(poder)*** ayudar a la gente pobre de África.

Listos

2 What would you do if you had the time? Translate these examples into Spanish.

1 My brother would play football a lot more. *Mi hermano jugaría al fútbol mucho más.*
2 My friends would go swimming every day.
3 I would send text messages to all my family.
4 Manuel would go to the cinema every Sunday.
5 Rosa would watch television every evening.
6 My mother would go to an art gallery every weekend.
7 Would you go to the beach to sunbathe?
8 You would all ride your bicycles.
9 I would visit a museum every month.
10 My friends would have more parties.

¡Ya!

3 What would you like to do in the future? Write three sentences.

a Dentro de dos años me gustaría…
b Dentro de cinco años me…
c Dentro de diez años…

4 Give advice to your friends. What would you do in their position? Use as many of the verbs in the box as you can.

beber comer comprar deber hacer jugar poder salir tener

1 Fumas demasiado. *Yo fumaría menos y haría más ejercicio.*
2 Bebes demasiado alcohol.
3 Estudias poco.
4 No haces deporte.
5 Duermes muy poco.
6 Nunca escuchas música.
7 Comes demasiada comida basura.
8 Tomas drogas.
9 No hablas con tus padres.
10 No tienes novia.

Gramática / Hay que saber bien

Nouns and articles

Nouns

What are they and when do I use them?
Nouns are words that name things, people and ideas. You use them all the time.

Why are they important?
Nouns form the basis of a language, so you cannot speak Spanish without them!

Things to watch out for
Gender does **not** refer to whether a boy or a girl would have or use that item! For example, *el vestido* (dress) is a masculine word. However, people have the gender according to whether they are female or male.

la madre *(the mother)* el padre *(the father)*

How do they work?
In Spanish each noun has a gender: masculine or feminine.
Generally nouns ending in **-o** are masculine *(**el** libr**o**)* and those ending in **-a** are feminine *(**la** cas**a**)*.
However, there are exceptions which you need to learn, for example: *el día, el problema, la mano, la foto.*

- There are some other endings that are generally either masculine or feminine.
  - **Masculine:** nouns ending in ***-or*** *(actor, pintor)*, ***-ón*** *(peatón, salchichón)* and ***-és*** *(escocés, estrés).*
  - **Feminine:** nouns ending in ***-ción*** *(tradición, educación)*, ***-dad*** and ***-tad*** *(ciudad, libertad).*
- To form the plural of nouns you normally add:

-s to words ending in a vowel

bolígraf**o** *(pen)* → bolígraf**os** *(pens)*
cas**a** *(house)* → cas**as** *(houses)*

-es for words ending in a consonant

actor *(actor)* → actor**es** *(actors)*

- Nouns which end in -z in the singular, end in **-ces** in the plural.

ve**z** *(time)* → ve**ces** *(times)*

Articles

What are they and when do I use them?
Articles are used with nouns. There are definite articles ***el / la*** (the) and indefinite articles ***un / una*** (a, an) and ***unos / unas*** (some).

Why are they important?
Articles are important as they give information about the nouns.

How do they work?

- In Spanish the **definite article** changes according to whether the noun is masculine or feminine, singular or plural.

el piso *(the flat)* → **los** piso**s** *(the flats)*
la casa *(the house)* → **las** casa**s** *(the houses)*

- The definite article is sometimes used in Spanish where we don't use it in English. You need to use it to:
  - Talk about languages (except when the language comes straight after a verb):

El inglés es fácil. *(English is easy.)*
Hablo español bien. *(I can speak Spanish well.)*
Ella habla francés. *(She can speak French.)*

- Refer to school subjects (except when the subject comes straight after a verb):
  La geografía es genial. *(Geography is great.)* Estudio religión. *(I study religion.)*
- Express an opinion, for example, *me gusta* or *me encanta*:
  Me encanta el inglés. *(I love English.)* La asignatura es interesante. *(The subject is interesting.)*
- Refer to days of the week and mean 'on…':
  Voy al cine el sábado. *(I am going to the cinema on Saturday.)*

- The **indefinite article** also changes according to whether the noun is masculine or feminine, singular or plural.
  un piso *(a flat)* → **unos** pisos *(some flats)*
  una casa *(a house)* → **unas** casas *(some houses)*
- The indefinite article is sometimes not used in Spanish where we do use it in English. You do not need to use it when:
  - You talk about jobs:
    Soy médico. *(I am a doctor.)* Es profesor. *(He is a teacher.)*
  - It comes after the verb ***tener*** in negative sentences:
    No tengo coche. *(I don't have a car.)* No tengo clase ahora. *(I don't have a class now.)*
  - It comes after ***sin*** or ***con***:
    Salí con gorra. *(I went out with a hat on.)* Escribo con boli. *(I write with a pen.)*
    Sin duda. *(Without a doubt.)*

Preparados

1 Write the plural form of the following nouns.

1 pintor
2 ambición
3 ordenador
4 inglés
5 ciudad
6 pez
7 mesa
8 coche
9 avión
10 mujer

Listos

2 Complete these sentences with the correct article.

1 Me gusta ____ francés.
2 Le gustan ____ matemáticas.
3 Prefiero ____ películas de terror.
4 ¿Tienes ____ bolígrafo?
5 Tiene ____ casa en el campo.
6 ____ hombres son muy viejos.
7 Me encanta ____ verano.
8 Siempre voy a la piscina ____ sábados.
9 Habla muy bien ____ japonés.
10 ____ historia es muy interesante.

¡Ya!

1 Fill in the gaps with the correct article. Be careful, you may not need to use one.

1 Mi madre no habla francés.
2 Estudio ____ matemáticas, ____ español y ____ geografía.
3 ____ asignatura que más me gusta es ____ informática.
4 ____ inglés es muy difícil.
5 Mi padre es ____ profesor.
6 Mi hermana va a ____ discoteca ____ viernes.
7 ¿No tienes ____ tiempo?
8 En el futuro quiero ser ____ cantante.
9 Tenemos que hacer el examen sin ____ calculadora.
10 Hablas muy bien ____ español.

Pronouns

Pronouns

What are they and when do I use them?
Pronouns are used in place of a noun, to avoid repeating it.

Why are they important?
Using pronouns correctly is a very good way to add variety to your language.

Things to watch out for
Remember to make sure that the pronoun agrees with the noun it replaces.

How do they work?

- **Subject pronouns** are often only used for emphasis in Spanish, because the verb ending usually indicates who is doing the action.

  yo tú él ella usted nosotros/as vosotros/as ellos ellas ustedes

- **Object pronouns** can be direct or indirect.

Direct	**Indirect**
me	me *(me)*
te	te *(you)*
lo/la	le *(him/her/it/you, sing., formal)*
nos	nos *(us)*
os	os *(you)*
los/las	les *(them/you, plural, formal)*

  – Direct: **Lo** compré. *(I bought **it**.)*
  Los veo allí. *(I see **them** over there.)*

  – Indirect: **Le** compré un regalo. *(I bought **him/her** a present. = I bought a present **for him/her**.)*
  Te voy a escribir. *(I am going to write **to you**.)*

- Object pronouns normally go:
  – Before the verb:
  Lo tengo. *(I have it.)*
  Lo he hecho. *(I have done/made it.)*
  – After the negative word:
  No **lo** tengo. *(I don't have it.)*
  Nadie **lo** hace. *(No-one does it.)*
  – Attached to the end or before the near future tense and the present continuous.
  Voy a hacer**lo**. / **Lo** voy a hacer. *(I am going to do it.)*
  Estoy haciéndo**lo**. / **Lo** estoy haciendo. *(I am doing it.)*
  – Attached to the end of the imperative.
  Haz**lo**. *(Do it.)*

Preparados

1 Rewrite these sentences using direct object pronouns.

1. Quiero el abrigo más grande. *Lo quiero más grande.*
2. Quiero las botas más grandes.
3. Quiero el vestido más corto.
4. Quiero el impermeable más largo.
5. Quiero la sudadera más grande.
6. Quiero las zapatillas deportivas más pequeñas.
7. No quiero estas botas.
8. ¿Has comprado los zapatos?
9. Estoy leyendo un libro.
10. Quiero comprar el coche.

Listos

2 Rewrite and improve these sentences using direct and indirect object pronouns.

1. Da el libro a Juan.
2. Escucho a Marta.
3. Enseñaste el libro a Carmen.
4. Regaló unos pendientes a su madre.
5. Daré la casa a vosotros.
6. Escribo a mi abuelo cada mes.
7. Estoy haciendo mis deberes.
8. Nadie tiene el perro.
9. Mandaron un mensaje a mí.
10. Compré un regalo para sus padres.

¡Ya!

3 Translate these sentences into Spanish.

1. I gave her some books.
2. I write to her every day.
3. I am going to write to you (plural).
4. My grandmother is going to give us money.
5. I told them everything.
6. They sent me messages.
7. I will show it to you later.
8. I sent you an email.
9. Are you listening to me?
10. Give it to me!

Gramática — Hay que saber bien

Adjectives

What are they and when do I use them?
Adjectives are describing words. You use them to describe a noun, a person or thing and to give extra information.

Why are they important?
To describe things you are talking or writing about. They make your work more interesting and personal.

Things to watch out for

- In Spanish adjectives have to 'agree' with the person or thing they describe. They may have different endings in the masculine, feminine, singular and plural.
- Most Spanish adjectives come after the noun.

How do they work?
These are the common patterns of adjective endings.

Adjectives ending in:	Masculine singular	Feminine singular	Masculine plural	Feminine plural
-o/-a	baj**o**	baj**a**	baj**os**	baj**as**
-e	impresionant**e**	impresionant**e**	impresionant**es**	impresionant**es**
-or/-ora	habla**dor**	habla**dora**	hablador**es**	hablador**as**
in consonant	azul	azul	azul**es**	azul**es**

- Some adjectives of nationality which do not end in ***-o*** follow different patterns.

Ending in ***-s***	inglés	ingles**a**	ingles**es**	ingles**as**
Ending in ***-l***	español	español**a**	español**es**	español**as**

- Some adjectives don't change and always take the masculine singular form. They are mostly:
  – Colours made up of two words: azul claro, rojo oscuro…
- The majority of adjectives will come after the noun that they are describing.
  Una casa pequeña. *(A small house.)*
  Un edificio impresionante. *(An impressive building.)*
- However, there are a few adjectives that always come before the noun.
  mucho, poco…
  primero, segundo, tercero…
  próximo, último, alguno, ninguno
  No tengo **mucho** tiempo. *(I don't have lots of time.)*
  La **próxima** clase empieza a las diez. *(Next class starts at ten.)*
- Some adjectives are shortened when they come before a masculine singular noun.
  bueno *(good)* → buen Hace **buen** tiempo.
  malo *(bad)* → mal Hace **mal** tiempo.
  primero *(first)* → primer Vivo en el **primer** piso.
  tercero *(third)* → tercer Es el **tercer** hijo.
  alguno (some, any) → algún ¿Tienes **algún** bolígrafo?
  ninguno *(none)* → ningún No, no tengo **ningún** bolígrafo.
- **Grande** is shortened when it comes before both a masculine and a feminine noun.
  Es un/a **gran** actor/actriz. *(He/She's a great actor/actress.)*

Preparados

1 Choose the correct adjective.

1 Vivo en una ciudad *pequeñas / pequeña*.
Vivo en una ciudad pequeña.
2 Mis padres están ***divorciados / divorciadas***.
3 Tengo que llevar una falda ***amarillas / amarilla***.
4 Mi profesor de inglés es más ***antipáticos / antipático*** que mi profe de francés.
5 Las montañas cerca de mi casa son ***preciosas / preciosa***.
6 Mi mejor amiga es ***galés / galesa***.
7 Trabajo en una ***gran / grande*** empresa.
8 Me encanta la Coca-Cola, pero es menos ***sana / sanas*** que el agua.
9 Los problemas de los jóvenes son bastante ***serias / serios***.
10 Estas chicas son ***españoles / españolas***.

Listos

2 Look at the picture and describe Madrid. Put an appropriate adjective that agrees with the noun, in each space.

antiguos blancos famoso hermosos histórica
interesantes largas pequeña rojos ruidosa

Madrid es una ciudad bastante (1) histórica. Tiene muchos edificios (2) ______ y muchas calles (3) ______. Madrid es más (4) ______ que Londres, pero es tan (5) ______ como cualquier capital famosa. En Madrid hay muchos museos (6) ______, pero no hay playa porque está en el centro del país. En Madrid los taxis son (7) ______ y algunos de los autobuses son (8) ______, como en Londres. Muchos edificios tienen balcones (9) ______ y en esta foto se puede ver un gran edificio (10) ______ al fondo.

¡Ya!

3 Rewrite these sentences using the adjective provided. Make sure that the ending and the position of the adjective is correct. If there is more than one possibility for its position, write them both.

1 Mi novio se llamaba Juan. *(primero)* Mi primer novio se llamaba Juan.
2 Me gusta leer libros. *(divertido)*
3 Mi primo vive en el piso. *(tercero)*
4 Las chicas son guapas. *(español)*
5 Compré unas medias. *(azul oscuro)*
6 Para mí es un problema. *(serio)*
7 Rafael siempre lleva gafas. *(pequeño)*
8 Me gusta mi trabajo porque tengo un jefe. *(bueno)*
9 Fuimos a una hermosa ciudad. *(inglés)*
10 Ana no tiene mascota. *(ningún)*
11 Vivimos en una casa. *(grande)*

Gramática / Hay que saber bien

Comparative and superlative adjectives

What are they and when do I use them?
They are the forms of adjectives (bigger, more expensive, as cute as, less chatty than, the funniest) which you use when you are comparing things.

- Use **comparative adjectives** to compare two things and say one is bigger, better, worse etc. than the other.
- Use **superlative adjectives** to compare more than two things and say one is the best, worst, biggest etc.

Why are they important?
Comparing is one step further than just describing.

How do they work?

- The **comparative** is formed by using the correct form of the adjective with the following constructions:
  - **Más** + [adjective] + **que** *(more + [adjective] + than)* Juan es más alto que Julio.
  - **Menos** + [adjective] + **que** *(less + [adjective] + than)* Marta es menos lista que Ana.
  - **Tan** + [adjective] + **como** *(as + [adjective] + as)* José es tan alto como Luis.
- The **superlative** is formed by using the correct form of the adjective with the following construction:
  el/la/los/las + **más/menos** + [adjective]
  Mi hermana es la más alt**a**. *(My sister is the tallest.)*
- There are the **irregular** ones.

Adjective	Comparative	Superlative		
bueno *(good)*	mejor *(better)*	el/la mejor	los/las mejores	*(the best)*
malo *(bad)*	peor *(worse)*	el/la peor	los/las peores	*(the worst)*

- To add extra emphasis to an adjective you can add ***-ísimo***, after removing the final vowel where necessary. These are called absolute superlatives.
  malo *(bad)* → mal**ísimo** *(extremely bad)* La película es malísima.
  fácil *(easy)* → facil**ísimo** *(incredibly easy)* El inglés es facilísimo.

Preparados

1 Make a comparison using the information provided (+ *más* / – *menos*).

1 Ana + yo (tall) *Ana es más alta que yo.*
2 José – Antonio (attractive)
3 Paulina + Federico (intelligent)
4 my brother – my sister (active)
5 my mother + my father (thin)
6 my female friend – my male friend (boring)

Listos

2 Write the correct superlative statement.

1 Este restaurante es *(best)* de la ciudad.
2 Mi casa es *(most modern)*.
3 Tu coche es *(fastest)*.
4 Nuestro perro es *(most stupid)*.
5 Mi falda es *(prettiest)*.
6 Mis pantalones son *(ugliest)*.

¡Ya!

3 Translate these sentences into Spanish.

1 Our Spanish teacher is the best!
2 This computer is incredibly cheap.
3 This football match is really really bad.
4 France is much smaller than the USA.
5 This train is the worst.
6 My brothers are my best friends.

Gramática / Hay que saber bien

Adverbs

What are they and when do I use them?
Adverbs are words that describe how an action is done (slowly, quickly, regularly, suddenly, badly, well, very…). You use them to describe how something is done (how often, how quickly, how well…).

Why are they important?
Adverbs help you give useful information and are an easy way to extend your sentences.

Things to watch out for
- Adverbs often end in ***-mente*** (like **-ly** in English).
- Some of the most useful adverbs are irregular!

How do they work?
In English you add **-ly** to the adjective to make them into adverbs. In Spanish you add ***-mente*** to the feminine form of the adjective.

probable *(probable)* → **probablemente** *(probably)* lento/a *(slow)* → **lentamente** *(slowly)*

- Some adverbs are irregular and you just have to learn them.

bastante	*(enough)*	siempre	*(always)*	ahora	*(now)*
a veces	*(sometimes)*	demasiado	*(too/too much)*	ya	*(already)*

- You can learn some in pairs of opposites.

bien	*(well)*	–	mal	*(badly)*	aquí	*(here)*	–	allí	*(there)*
mucho	*(a lot)*	–	poco	*(a little)*	despacio	*(slow)*	–	deprisa	*(fast)*

- Adverbs usually follow the verbs they describe. However, they can come before a verb 'for emphasis'.

Hablamos **rápidamente**. *(We speak quickly.)*
Siempre habla en inglés. *(He always talks English.)*

Preparados

1 Make these adjectives into adverbs and translate them into English.

1 rápido
2 tranquilo
3 franco
4 estúpido
5 severo
6 silencioso
7 claro
8 constante
9 difícil

Listos

2 Fill in the blanks with the correct adverb according to the English.

1 Ana come *(too much)*.
2 Bebemos *(slowly)*.
3 Mis amigos y yo hablamos *(constantly)*.
4 Bajan la escalera *(silently)*.
5 Mi profe siempre habla *(calmly)*.
6 Viajas en avión *(a little)*.
7 Habla francés *(badly)*.
8 Monta a caballo *(frequently)*.

¡Ya!

3 Translate these sentences into Spanish.

1 My brother always eats sandwiches.
2 My girlfriend talks quickly.
3 They study a little.
4 We play tennis sometimes.
5 Pablo does athletics badly.
6 The child eats enough.
7 I spend money easily.
8 I go to the park frequently.

Gramática / Hay que saber bien

Negatives

Which ones do I need to know?

no …	*(not)*	**no** … **ni** … **ni**…	*(either … nor…)*
no … **nada**	*(nothing/not anything)*	**no** … **tampoco**	*(not … either)*
no … **nunca**	*(never)*	**no** … **ningún/ninguna**	*(no, not any)*
no … **jamás**	*(never (stronger than nunca)*	**no** … **nadie**	*(no … nobody/not anybody)*

When do I use them?

When you want to say not, nothing, never, nobody, etc.

Why are they important?

If you use a range of different negatives your sentences will be more complex and more interesting.

How do they work?

In Spanish the simple negative is ***no*** and it goes immediately before a verb (or before a reflexive pronoun or object pronoun).

No como. *(I don't eat.)*
No me levanto temprano. *(I don't get up early.)*
No me dan mucho dinero. *(They don't give me much money.)*

- These negative expressions go either side of the verb, forming a sandwich around it.
  - **No** bebo **nada**. *(I **don't** drink **anything**.)*
  - **No** hacemos **nunca** deporte. *(We **never** do sport.)*
  - **No** fumo **jamás**. *(I **never** smoke.)*
  - **No** tengo **ni** casa **ni** coche. *(I **don't** have **either** a house **or** a car.)*
  - Él **no** es de aquí **tampoco**. *(He is **not** from here **either**.)*
  - Ella **no** tiene **ningún** libro. *(She **doesn't** have **any** books.)*
  - **No** hablo con **nadie**. *(I **don't** speak to **anybody**.)*
- Sometimes, for emphasis, the negative expression can be placed before the verb and in this case 'no' is not used.
  - **Nadie** está aquí. *(**Nobody** is here.)*
  - **Nunca** vamos a ir allí. *(We are **never** going to go there.)*
- ***Sino*** means 'but' (with the meaning 'rather' or 'instead'). ***Sino*** is used to connect a negative first statement with a second statement that is expressing a different opinion.
  - **No** bebo agua, **sino** zumo de naranja. *(I **don't** drink water **but** orange juice.)*
- ***Todavía*** means 'still' or 'not yet'.
  - **Todavía** no ha hecho esquí. *(He **still** hasn't skiied.)*
  - ¿Has estudiado mucho? **Todavía no**. *(Have you studied a lot? **Not yet**.)*
- To express a negative opinion you need to use **que no**.
  - Espero **que no**. *(I hope **not**.)*
  - Creo **que no**. *(I think **not – I don't** think so.)*
  - Claro **que no**. *(Of course **not**.)*

Preparados

1 Make each statement negative and then translate it into English.

1. Vivimos en el norte del país.
2. Tienen muchos problemas.
3. Mi hermana come mucha fruta y verdura.
4. Mis amigos del colegio juegan al baloncesto los viernes.
5. Jaime se levanta a las ocho y media.
6. Mi madre me compró unas botas nuevas.
7. Nos despertamos tarde.
8. Es una buena idea.
9. Mañana vamos a la peluquería.
10. Hablas inglés.

Listos

2 Put the words in the correct order to form a negative sentence.

1. come / Elena / nunca / carne *Elena nunca come carne.*
2. nunca / equitación / no / hacemos
3. mañana / no / por / desayuno / la / nada
4. ni / cole / el / hay / no / ni / en / biblioteca / piscina
5. sábados / me / nunca / temprano / levanto / los
6. a / la / chica / escucha / no / nadie
7. café / jamás / beben / no
8. hay / hacer / nada / no / que
9. profesores / tampoco / escuchan / no / los
10. madre / ninguna / tiene / mi / no / joya

¡Ya!

3 Match up the correct sentence halves. Then write down what each sentence means in English.

1	Juan no lleva…	**a**	…nada para estar en forma.
2	María no tiene…	**b**	…jamás en avión porque tiene miedo.
3	Ana no hace…	**c**	…cuaderno, ni bolígrafo, ni regla.
4	Miguel tampoco…	**d**	…trabajo todavía.
5	Gabriela no escucha…	**e**	…uniforme.
6	Antonia no escribe…	**f**	…ninguna lengua extranjera.
7	Javier no viaja…	**g**	…a nadie y hace lo que quiere.
8	Roberto no habla…	**h**	…hace ejercicio.
9	Mis padres no cocinan…	**i**	…, sino que compran bocadillos en el supermercado.
10	Mi hermano no ha encontrado…	**j**	…nunca correos electrónicos, sino cartas.

Gramática / Hay que saber bien

Questions and exclamations

Asking questions

Why is it important?

You can't get far in any language without being able to understand and ask questions!

Things to watch out for

In Spanish all questions start with an upside down question mark (¿) and end with a normal question mark (?).

How do questions work in Spanish?

There are two ways to form questions in Spanish.

- You can form straightforward yes/no questions by changing a statement into a question and using rising intonation (i.e. making your voice go up) at the end of the question.

  Hablas español. → ¿Hablas español? *(Do you speak Spanish?)*

- Some questions need question words. They always have an accent and come at the beginning of a question.

¿Qué?	*(What?/How?)*	**¿Con quién?**	*(With whom…?)*
¿Cómo?	*(What?/How?)*	**¿Cuándo?**	*(When?)*
¿Cuál/Cuáles?	*(What?/Which?)*	**¿Por qué?**	*(Why?)*
¿Dónde?	*(Where?)*	**¿Cuánto/a?**	*(How much?)*
¿Adónde?	*(Where…to?)*	**¿Cuántos/as?**	*(How many?)*
¿Quién?	*(Who?)*	**¿A qué hora?**	*(At what time?)*

- In Spanish ***qué*** is always used to translate 'which' or 'what' when it comes directly before a noun or verb.

  ¿Qué haces? *(What are you doing?)*
  ¿Qué deporte prefieres? *(Which sport do you prefer?)*

- ***Cuál*** is used to translate 'which one' when it comes before a verb. It can also be translated as 'which of' when used before ***de***.

  ¿Cuál prefieres? *(Which one do you prefer?)*
  ¿Cuáles de estas te gustan más? *(Which of these do you like most?)*

Using exclamations

Why are they important?

Exclamations allow you to express yourself and make your communication more interesting and natural.

Things to watch out for

Remember to use two exclamation marks when writing an exclamation. One upside down (¡) at the start and a normal one at the end (!).

How do exclamations work in Spanish?

Qué always takes an accent when used as an exclamation.

¡Qué lástima! *(What a shame!)* ¡Qué rollo! *(How boring! How annoying!)*
¡Qué va! *(No way!)* ¡Qué raro! *(How strange!)*

Preparados

1 Complete the question with the appropriate question word. Then answer each question in Spanish.

1 ¿*Cómo* te llamas?
2 ¿_____ vives?
3 ¿_____ años tienes?
4 ¿Con _____ vives?
5 ¿_____ asignaturas estudias?
6 ¿_____ hora vuelves a casa?
7 ¿_____ te acuestas?
8 ¿_____ vas de vacaciones este año?
9 ¿_____ te gusta hacer esquí?
10 ¿_____ tiene mi libro?
11 ¿_____ prefieres: la camiseta con agujero o sin agujero?

Listos

2 The computer has printed a list of questions in the *'tú'* form but the questions are needed for a formal interview. Can you help the interviewer by writing out the questions in the *'usted'* form? Then translate each question into English.

1 ¿Cómo te llamas? → *¿Cómo se llama usted?*
2 ¿Tienes experiencia en este tipo de trabajo?
3 ¿Cuántas horas trabajas al día?
4 ¿Vives cerca de aquí?
5 ¿Cuál es tu número de teléfono?
6 ¿Hablas otros idiomas?
7 ¿Sabes mandar correos electrónicos?
8 ¿Dónde has trabajado antes?
9 ¿Cuántos años tienes?
10 ¿Por qué quieres trabajar aquí?

¡Ya!

3 Translate the following questions into Spanish. You can use either the *'tú'* form or the *'usted'* form.

1 Do you like football? *¿Te gusta el fútbol?*
2 At what time do you get up?
3 When do you have photography club?
4 What do you do at the weekend?
5 Where is your school?
6 Where will you go to next week?
7 How much does the necklace cost?
8 Which ones are most expensive?
9 Who wants to play tennis?
10 Who are you going on holiday with?
11 How do you go to school?

Gramática

Hay que saber bien

Connectives

Which ones do I need to know?

a pesar de	*(despite/in spite of)*	**entonces**	*(then)*	**porque**	*(because)*
además	*(also/as well)*	**incluso**	*(even)*	**pues**	*(then)*
antes (de)	*(before)*	**lo primero**	*(first)*	**si**	*(if)*
así que	*(so/therefore)*	**lo primero de todo**	*(first of all)*	**sin embargo**	*(however)*
aún	*(even)*	**mientras**	*(while/meanwhile)*	**tal vez**	*(maybe)*
aún si	*(even if)*	**o/u**	*(or)*	**también**	*(also)*
aunque	*(although)*	**pero**	*(but)*	**y/e**	*(and)*
después (de)	*(after)*	**por eso/por lo tanto**	*(therefore)*	**ya que**	*(since)*

Why are they important?

Using connectives to make extended sentences makes your speaking and writing sound more natural.

How do they work?

- Connectives link together two sentences or two parts of a sentence.
  Mi profesor es simpático **y** nunca grita. *(My teacher is nice **and** never shouts.)*
  Voy en autobús **o** en tren. *(I go by bus **or** by train.)*
  Vivimos en un piso pequeño, **pero** es bastante cómodo. *(We live in a small flat **but** it is quite comfortable.)*
  Me gusta descargar música **porque** es muy fácil. *(I like to download music **because** it is very easy.)*
  Juego al tenis y **también** hago natación. *(I play tennis and I **also** do swimming.)*
- ***Y*** changes to ***e*** if it comes before words beginning with 'i' or 'hi'.
  Estudio matemáticas e inglés. *(I study Maths and English.)*
  Aprendemos francés e historia. *(We learn French and History.)*
- ***O*** changes to ***u*** if it comes before words beginning with 'o' or 'ho'.
  Cenamos a las siete u ocho. *(We have dinner at seven or eight.)*
  Puede ser un problema para mujeres u hombres. *(It can be a problem for women or men.)*
- Another way to extend sentences is to use clauses:
  que *(that/who)*
  donde *(where)*
  cuando *(when)*
  como (like/as)
  cuyo (whose)
- Unlike the question words these do not have accents.
  Vivo en una ciudad **que** se llama Bristol. *(I live in a city **that** is called Bristol.)*
  Mi amigo, **que** trabaja en un banco, gana mucho. *(My friend **who** works in a bank earns a lot.)*
  Fui a Francia, **donde** aprendí a hacer vela. *(I went to France **where** I learnt how to do sailing.)*
  Hacía natación en la piscina, **cuando** tuve un accidente. *(I was swimming in the pool **when** I had an accident.)*
  Mi instituto tiene buenas instalaciones, **como** una gran biblioteca. *(My school has good facilities **like** a big library.)*
  Tengo un amigo **cuyo** perro es muy bonito. *(I have a friend **whose** dog is very attractive.)*

Preparados

1 Complete each sentence with an appropriate connective. Try to use as many different connectives from the box as possible. You can use each one more than once!

o y entonces porque también pero
además aunque después sin embargo por eso

1 Mi hermano estudia inglés, matemáticas *y* geografía.
2 A mi amigo le encanta jugar con su ordenador _____ es divertido.
3 Prefiero comer bocadillos _____ hamburguesas en la cafetería.
4 Compré unos pendientes y _____ fui al cine con mis amigos.
5 Practico deportes, _____ no juego en ningún equipo.
6 Siempre voy al club de ajedrez, _____ a veces no gano.
7 Mi hermano es muy alto y _____ es muy guapo.
8 Me gusta el español, _____ no lo hablo bien.
9 Mi amigo tiene un buen trabajo y _____ tiene más dinero que yo.
10 Fui a ver a mi amiga y _____ fuimos al centro comercial.

Listos

2 Match up the sentence halves and translate the sentences.

1 *Mi amigo nunca va al parque aunque tiene dos perros.*
My friend never goes to the park even though he has two dogs.

1 Mi amigo nunca va al parque…
2 Vivimos en el centro, y…
3 Me gusta mucho mi trabajo porque…
4 José juega al baloncesto…
5 Fui al cine con Emily mientras…
6 Mi madre no cocina nunca, y…
7 Quiero ser medico o…
8 Iré al campo el sábado…
9 No me gusta mi uniforme…
10 El libro es muy interesante, además…

a …por eso hay muchas tiendas.
b …Sophie fue al centro comercial.
c …aunque tiene dos perros.
d …a pesar de ser muy bajo.
e …porque es muy feo.
f …es muy divertido.
g …si hace buen tiempo.
h …tal vez seré abogado.
i …por lo tanto comemos mucha comida basura.
j …me pagan bien.

¡Ya!

3 Complete the sentence with the correct connective.

1 El lugar _____ trabajo está sucio y es muy pequeño.
El lugar donde trabajo está sucio y es muy pequeño.
2 Quiero perder peso, _____ hago mucho deporte.
3 Tengo una prima _____ habla italiano perfectamente.
4 Las manzanas _____ compraron en el mercado estaban muy ricas.
5 Me encanta salir con los perros _____ está lloviendo.
6 Imagino _____ el tren sale a las tres.
7 Se debería usar el transporte público _____ los autobuses o el metro.
8 Le dio muchos regalos, _____ le compró un coche.
9 Estaba en el supermercado _____ vi a Manuel.
10 Conozco a una persona _____ hermano es actor.

Gramática

Para impresionar

The gerund

What are they and when do I use them?

Gerunds are 'ing' words like 'walking', 'buying' and 'living'. You use the gerund:

- To give more information about how something is or was being done.
  Voy **andando** al instituto. *(I go to school on foot.)*
- After the verbs ir *(to go)*, seguir *(to keep on)* and continuar *(to continue)*.
  Sigo **estudiando** español porque me encanta. *(I continue learning Spanish because I love it.)*
- To form the present continuous tense which describes what is happening at this moment.
  ¿Qué estás **haciendo**? *(What are you doing?)*
- To form the imperfect continuous tense which describes what was happening at a moment in the past.
  Estaba **cocinando** cuando llegó mi madre. *(I was cooking when my mother arrived.)*

Why are they important?

Understanding the gerund allows you to use different and more varied tenses.

Things to watch out for

Sometimes English uses a gerund when in Spanish you use an infinitive.

Cantar es divertido. *(**Singing** is fun.)* Le gusta **nadar**. *(She likes **swimming**.)*

How does it work?

To form the gerund in Spanish, take the infinitive of the verb, remove the *-ar*, *-er* or *-ir* ending and add ***-ando*** to *-ar* verbs and ***-iendo*** to *-er* and *-ir* verbs.

- Stem changing *-ir* verbs (but not *-ar* or *-er* verbs) change their spellings for the gerund:
  o → e d**o**rmir *(to sleep)* → d**u**rmiendo *(sleeping)*
  e → i p**e**dir *(to ask)* → p**i**diendo *(asking)*
- Some **irregular gerunds** include:
  caer → cayendo *(falling)*
  leer → leyendo *(reading)*
  oír → oyendo *(hearing)*
  poder → pudiendo *(being able to)*
  reír → riendo *(laughing)*
- The gerund is used with the present tense form of ***estar*** to form the present continuous.

(yo)	estoy		
(tú)	estás		hablando
(él/ella/usted)	está	+	comiendo
(nosotros/as)	estamos		saliendo
(vosotros/as)	estáis		
(ellos/ellas/ustedes)	están		

Estoy haciendo mis deberes. *(I **am doing** my homework.)*
Están preparando la cena. *(They **are preparing** supper.)*

- The gerund is used with the imperfect tense form of ***estar*** to form the imperfect continuous.

(yo)	estaba		
(tú)	estabas		hablando
(él/ella/usted)	estaba	+	comiendo
(nosotros/as)	estábamos		saliendo
(vosotros/as)	estabais		
(ellos/ellas/ustedes)	estaban		

Estaban comiendo pasteles. *(They **were eating** cakes.)*

Preparados

1 What is the poodle *(el caniche)* doing in each picture? Write captions for numbers 2–6. Then write each of these phrases in the first person *(yo)* as if the poodle were speaking.

1 
2 
3 
4 
5 
6 

El caniche está viendo la tele en el salón. → Estoy viendo la tele en el salón.

ver la tele   comer   lavarse los dientes   dormir   ducharse   peinarse   vestirse

Listos

2 Look at the pictures and answer the questions.

1 
2 
3 
4 

5 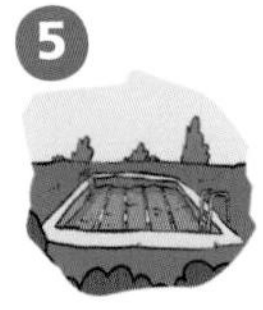
6 

1 ¿Qué está haciendo la chica? *Está leyendo un libro.*
2 ¿Qué está haciendo Carlos?
3 ¿Qué están haciendo?
4 ¿Qué estás haciendo?
5 ¿Qué estamos haciendo?
6 ¿Qué está haciendo Juan?

comer
dormir
jugar
nadar
navegar
leer

¡Ya!

3 Fill in the background to each situation. Use your imagination and the imperfect continuous tense.

andar   comer   correr   dormir   escribir   hablar   jugar   leer   pedir   tomar

1 *José estaba corriendo cuando se cayó en la calle y se rompió la pierna.*

1 José ____ cuando se cayó en la calle y se rompió la pierna.
2 Mis hermanas ____ cuando nuestra madre entró en su dormitorio.
3 Mi padre ____ el periódico cuando llamé a la puerta.
4 Mi profe de música ____ en la pizarra cuando empezó a llover.
5 Cuando Fernando llegó, yo ____ el sol en la playa.
6 Nosotros ____ al fútbol cuando Sergio se cayó.
7 La profe de inglés ____ cuando María gritó.
8 Cuando volví a casa, mi familia ____.
9 Yo ____ cuando Carlos me interrumpió.
10 Miguel ____ información en la estación cuando salió el tren.

Gramática Para impresionar

The perfect and pluperfect tenses

What are they and when do I use them?

- The **perfect tense** describes what someone 'has done' or 'what has happened'.
  He estado dos semanas en Madrid. *(I **have been** in Madrid for two weeks.)*
- The **pluperfect tense** describes what someone 'had done' or 'what had happened' at a particular moment in the past.
  Cuando llegué a casa, María ya **había comido**. (When I arrived home María **had** already **eaten**.)

Why are they important?

Using the perfect and pluperfect tenses means that you can talk about events in the past in more detail.

How do they work?

Both the perfect and the pluperfect tenses are formed using the past participle of the verb.

- The **past participle** is formed by taking the infinitive, removing the *-ar, -er* or *-ir* and adding ***-ado*** for *-ar* verbs *(hablado, comprado…)* and ***-ido*** for *-er* and *-ir* verbs *(bebido, vivido…)*.
- Some common **irregular past participles** are:

Verb		Past participle	
abrir	*(to open)*	abierto	*(open)*
decir	*(to say)*	dicho	*(said)*
escribir	*(to write)*	escrito	*(written)*
hacer	*(to do/make)*	hecho	*(done)*
poner	*(to put)*	puesto	*(put)*
romper	*(to break)*	roto	*(broken)*
ver	*(to see)*	visto	*(seen)*
volver	*(to return)*	vuelto	*(returned)*

- The **perfect tense** is formed by using the verb ***haber*** in the present tense and the **past participle** of the verb.

(yo)	he		
(tú)	has		hablado
(él/ella/usted)	ha	+	comido
(nosotros/as)	hemos		salido
(vosotros/as)	habéis		
(ellos/ellas/ustedes)	han		

Hemos escrito una carta.
*(We **have written** a letter.)*
¿**Has hecho** tus deberes?
*(**Have** you **done** your homework?)*

- The **pluperfect tense** is formed by using the verb ***haber*** in the imperfect tense and the **past participle** of the verb.

(yo)	había		
(tú)	habías		hablado
(él/ella/usted)	había	+	comido
(nosotros/as)	habíamos		salido
(vosotros/as)	habíais		
(ellos/ellas/ustedes)	habían		

¿**Había salido** Juan cuando llegaste? (***Had** Juan **left** when you arrived?)*

- Nothing comes between the verb **haber** and the **past participle**. All negatives and pronouns (reflexive, object, etc.) come before **haber**.

No he comido.	*(I haven't eaten.)*
Me he vestido rápidamente.	*(I have got dressed quickly.)*
No me habían dado los billetes.	*(They hadn't given me the tickets.)*

Acabar de

- When you want to say that someone **has just done** something you do not use the perfect tense. You use the present tense of the verb ***acabar*** (a regular *-ar* verb) followed by the preposition ***de***.

Acabo de pasar la aspiradora.	*(I **have just done** the hoovering.)*
Acabamos de comer pizza.	*(We **have just eaten** pizza.)*

Preparados

1 Put the words in the correct order for each sentence.

1 Delia / la / lavado / ha / ropa *Delia ha lavado la ropa.*
2 la / he / mesa / puesto
3 ha / Pablo / compra / hecho / la
4 hemos / patatas / comido / muchas / fritas
5 dinero / todo / gastado / he / el
6 un / electrónico / escrito / he / correo
7 comprado / medio / zanahorias / de / kilo / ha
8 en / madre / ha / mi / cocina / desayunado / la
9 no / leído / he / libros / muchos
10 he / tarde / me / muy / despertado
11 duchado / he / me / no / todavía

Listos

2 Write about what you have done and what you have never done and then compare this statement to your best friend.

1 …frecuentemente. *He navegado por Internet frecuentemente.*
2 …recientemente
3 …muchas veces.
4 …pocas veces.
5 …una vez
6 No … nunca.

navegar por Internet
hacer esquí
despertarse muy tarde
montar a caballo
comer paella
viajar en helicóptero
hacer submarinismo
romperse el brazo
beber Coca-Cola

¡Ya!

3 Write about what Pedro has done today. Change the verbs in brackets into the perfect tense.

Me llamo Pedro y soy camarero. Acabo de tener un accidente después de un día muy intenso. (1) *(lavar)* los platos y (2) *(preparar)* varios platos típicos como paella y gazpacho. No (3) *(fregar)* el suelo, ni (4) *(limpiar)* la terraza porque no tenía tiempo. Mi jefe (5) *(hablar)* con los clientes, (6) *(contestar)* el teléfono y (7) *(hacer)* las reservas para el fin de semana. Los clientes (8) *(comer)* platos típicos de Andalucía y muchos de ellos (9) *(beber)* vino tinto o rosado. Claro que los clientes (10) *(hablar)* mucho con sus compañeros como siempre. Sobre todo, mi jefe y yo (11) *(disfrutar)* de nuestro trabajo y también (12) *(ganar)* un buen sueldo.

Gramática Para impresionar

The present subjunctive and imperatives

The present subjunctive

What is it and when do I use it?

The present subjunctive is not really used anymore in English but is used a lot in Spanish.
The subjunctive is used:

- To express doubt or uncertainty. When you express a negative opinion the present subjunctive must be used.
  No creo que **existan** problemas. *(I don't think any problems exist.)*
  No es verdad que **fumemos** mucho. *(It's not true that we smoke a lot.)*
- After the word **cuando** when talking about the future.
  Cuando **vayas** a Madrid, debes ir a Lavapiés. *(When you go to Madrid, you should go to Lavapiés.)*
- After the expression **ojalá**.
  Ojalá **haga** sol. *(Let's hope it is sunny.)*

Why is it important?

Knowing some of the situations in which you use the subjunctive will allow you to be more accurate in your communication in Spanish.
If you use it correctly in your GCSE, it will impress your examiner and help you achieve an A or A* grade.

Things to watch out for

As English no longer uses the subjunctive, it won't come naturally to you. If you want to use it successfully you must learn by heart the situations when you will need it.

How does it work?

To form the present subjunctive, take the first person singular (*yo*), remove the final **o** and add these endings.

	hablar *(to talk)*	**com**er *(to eat)*	**viv**ir *(to live)*
(yo)	habl**e**	com**a**	viv**a**
(tú)	habl**es**	com**as**	viv**as**
(él/ella/usted)	habl**e**	com**a**	viv**a**
(nosotros/as)	habl**emos**	com**amos**	viv**amos**
(vosotros/as)	habl**éis**	com**áis**	viv**áis**
(ellos/ellas/ustedes)	habl**en**	com**an**	viv**an**

- If the first person singular (*yo*) is irregular, the subjunctive will take the same form, for example, **hacer** – **hago** – **haga**. There are some **irregular present subjunctive** verbs:
  ir → vaya, vayas, vaya… **ser** → sea, seas, sea…

The imperative

What is it and when do I use it?

The imperative is used to give commands and instructions (Go to sleep. Don't do that.).

Why is it important?

Knowing how to use the imperative will allow you to use a wider variety of structures in your communication.

Things to watch out for

The imperative is generally used in spoken language, so you may hear these verbs in listening exams even if you only use them rarely in your speaking work.

How does it work?

The imperative has a different form depending on whether the command is positive (Sit down.) or negative (Don't sit down.) and who is receiving it.

Positive imperatives

- The positive imperative for one person (**tú**) is formed by removing the **s** from the **tú** form of the verb.

  hablar *(to talk)* → (tú) habl**as** *(you talk)* → ¡Habl**a**! *(Talk! – you)*
  comer *(to eat)* → (tú) com**es** *(you eat)* → ¡Com**e**! *(Eat! – you)*

- These verbs have irregular imperatives in the tú form:

  decir → **di** *(say)*
  hacer → **haz** *(do/make)*
  ir → **ve** *(go)*
  dar → **da** *(give)*
  salir → **sal** *(go/get out)*
  tener → **ten** *(have)*

- The positive imperative for more than one person (**vosotros**) is formed by taking the infinitive and changing the **r** to a **d**.

  bebe**r** *(to drink)* → (vosotros/as) ¡Bebe**d**! *(Drink!* – plural *you)*

- A formal command is given using the present subjunctive.

  tomar *(to take)* → (usted) ¡Tom**e**! *(Take!* – formal *you)*
  comer *(to eat)* → (ustedes) ¡Com**an**! *(Eat!* – formal plural *you)*

Negative imperatives

- You use the present subjunctive form for all negative commands.

  hablar *(to talk)* → (tú) ¡No habl**es**! *(Don't talk! – you)*
  tomar *(to take)* → (usted) ¡No tom**e**! *(Don't take!* – formal *you)*
  comer *(to eat)* → (vosotros/as) ¡No com**áis**! *(Don't eat!* – plural *you)*
  beber *(to drink)* → (ustedes) ¡No beb**an**! *(Don't drink!* – formal plural *you)*

Preparados

1 Make these statements into '*tú*' or '*vosotros/as*' commands.

1 *(tomar – tú)* la primera calle a la derecha.
2 *(doblar – vosotros)* a la izquierda.
3 *(pasar – vosotras)* el puente.
4 *(escribir – tú)* un párrafo.
5 *(hablar – tú)* más despacio, por favor.
6 *(poner – vosotros)* la mesa.
7 *(decir – tú)* algo.
8 *(salir – tú)* a las nueve y media.

Listos

2 Use the present subjunctive to make '*usted*' commands.

1 *(comer)* más. Coma más.
2 *(escuchar)* la radio.
3 *(hablar)* conmigo.
4 *(poner)* la mesa.
5 *(seguir)* todo recto.
6 *(cruzar)* la plaza.

3 Use the present subjunctive to make negative commands.

1 No *(entrar – vosotros)* ahora. No entréis ahora.
2 No *(hacer – usted)* nada.
3 No *(beber – tú)* nada.
4 No *(comer – vosotras)* nada.
5 No *(bailar – tú)* demasiado.
6 No *(levantarse – usted)* temprano.

¡Ya!

4 Complete each of the sentences with the correct present subjunctive verb.

1 No creo que mi amigo *(fumar)*. No creo que mi amigo fume.
2 Cuando *(ir)* a España, compraré un abanico.
3 No pienso que mis profesores *(ser)* antipáticos.
4 Ojalá tú *(poder)* venir conmigo a la disco.
5 No es verdad que mi barrio *(tener)* un polideportivo bueno.
6 Cuando *(tener)* dieciocho años, iré a la universidad.
7 Ojalá *(hacer)* buen tiempo mañana.

Gramática Verb tables

Irregular verbs

Infinitive			Present	Future	Preterite	Imperfect	Gerund / Past participle
dar	I	(yo)	**doy**	daré	**di**	daba	dando
(to give)	you	(tú)	das	darás	**diste**	dabas	dado
	he/she/it	(él/ella/usted)	da	dará	**dio**	daba	
	we	(nosotros/as)	damos	daremos	**dimos**	dábamos	
	you (pl.)	(vosotros/as)	dais	daréis	**disteis**	dabais	
	they	(ellos/as/ustedes)	dan	darán	**dieron**	daban	
decir	I	(yo)	**digo**	**diré**	**dije**	decía	**diciendo**
(to say/tell)	you	(tú)	**dices**	**dirás**	**dijiste**	decías	**dicho**
	he/she/it	(él/ella/usted)	**dice**	**dirá**	**dijo**	decía	
	we	(nosotros/as)	decimos	**diremos**	**dijimos**	decíamos	
	you (pl.)	(vosotros/as)	decís	**diréis**	**dijisteis**	decíais	
	they	(ellos/as/ustedes)	**dicen**	**dirán**	**dijeron**	decían	
estar	I	(yo)	**estoy**	estaré	**estuve**	estaba	estando
(to be)	you	(tú)	**estás**	estarás	**estuviste**	estabas	estado
	he/she/it	(él/ella/usted)	**está**	estará	**estuvo**	estaba	
	we	(nosotros/as)	estamos	estaremos	**estuvimos**	estábamos	
	you (pl.)	(vosotros/as)	estáis	estaréis	**estuvisteis**	estabais	
	they	(ellos/as/ustedes)	**están**	estarán	**estuvieron**	estaban	
hacer	I	(yo)	**hago**	**haré**	**hice**	hacía	haciendo
(to do/make)	you	(tú)	haces	**harás**	**hiciste**	hacías	**hecho**
	he/she/it	(él/ella/usted)	hace	**hará**	**hizo**	hacía	
	we	(nosotros/as)	hacemos	**haremos**	**hicimos**	hacíamos	
	you (pl.)	(vosotros/as)	hacéis	**haréis**	**hicisteis**	hacíais	
	they	(ellos/as/ustedes)	hacen	**harán**	**hicieron**	hacían	
ir	I	(yo)	**voy**	iré	**fui**	**iba**	**yendo**
(to go)	you	(tú)	**vas**	irás	**fuiste**	**ibas**	ido
	he/she/it	(él/ella/usted)	**va**	irá	**fue**	**iba**	
	we	(nosotros/as)	**vamos**	iremos	**fuimos**	**íbamos**	
	you (pl.)	(vosotros/as)	**vais**	iréis	**fuisteis**	**ibais**	
	they	(ellos/as/ustedes)	**van**	irán	**fueron**	**iban**	
oír	I	(yo)	**oigo**	oiré	**oí**	oía	**oyendo**
(to hear)	you	(tú)	**oyes**	oirás	**oíste**	oías	**oído**
	he/she/it	(él/ella/usted)	**oye**	oirá	**oyó**	oía	
	we	(nosotros/as)	**oímos**	oiremos	**oímos**	oíamos	
	you (pl.)	(vosotros/as)	oís	oiréis	**oísteis**	oíais	
	they	(ellos/as/ustedes)	**oyen**	oirán	**oyeron**	oían	
poder	I	(yo)	**puedo**	**podré**	**pude**	podía	**pudiendo**
(to be able to)	you	(tú)	**puedes**	**podrás**	**pudiste**	podías	podido
	he/she/it	(él/ella/usted)	**puede**	**podrá**	**pudo**	podía	
	we	(nosotros/as)	podemos	**podremos**	**pudimos**	podíamos	
	you (pl.)	(vosotros/as)	podéis	**podréis**	**pudisteis**	podíais	
	they	(ellos/as/ustedes)	**pueden**	**podrán**	**pudieron**	podían	

Infinitive			Present	Future	Preterite	Imperfect	Gerund / Past participle
poner	I	(yo)	**pongo**	**pondré**	**puse**	ponía	poniendo
(to put)	you	(tú)	pones	**pondrás**	**pusiste**	ponías	**puesto**
	he/she/it	(él/ella/usted)	pone	**pondrá**	**puso**	ponía	
	we	(nosotros/as)	ponemos	**pondremos**	**pusimos**	poníamos	
	you (pl.)	(vosotros/as)	ponéis	**pondréis**	**pusisteis**	poníais	
	they	(ellos/as/ustedes)	ponen	**pondrán**	**pusieron**	ponían	
querer	I	(yo)	**quiero**	**querré**	**quise**	quería	queriendo
(to want/	you	(tú)	**quieres**	**querrás**	**quisiste**	querías	querido
wish)	he/she/it	(él/ella/usted)	**quiere**	**querrá**	**quiso**	quería	
	we	(nosotros/as)	queremos	**querremos**	**quisimos**	queríamos	
	you (pl.)	(vosotros/as)	queréis	**querréis**	**quisisteis**	queríais	
	they	(ellos/as/ustedes)	**quieren**	**querrán**	**quisieron**	querían	
saber	I	(yo)	**sé**	**sabré**	**supe**	sabía	sabiendo
(to know)	you	(tú)	sabes	**sabrás**	**supiste**	sabías	sabido
	he/she/it	(él/ella/usted)	sabe	**sabrá**	**supo**	sabía	
	we	(nosotros/as)	sabemos	**sabremos**	**supimos**	sabíamos	
	you (pl.)	(vosotros/as)	sabéis	**sabréis**	**supisteis**	sabíais	
	they	(ellos/as/ustedes)	saben	**sabrán**	**supieron**	sabían	
salir	I	(yo)	**salgo**	**saldré**	salí	salía	saliendo
(to go out)	you	(tú)	sales	**saldrás**	saliste	salías	salido
	he/she/it	(él/ella/usted)	sale	**saldrá**	salió	salía	
	we	(nosotros/as)	salimos	**saldremos**	salimos	salíamos	
	you (pl.)	(vosotros/as)	salís	**saldréis**	salisteis	salíais	
	they	(ellos/as/ustedes)	salen	**saldrán**	salieron	salían	
ser	I	(yo)	**soy**	seré	**fui**	**era**	siendo
(to be)	you	(tú)	**eres**	serás	**fuiste**	**eras**	sido
	he/she/it	(él/ella/usted)	**es**	será	**fue**	**era**	
	we	(nosotros/as)	**somos**	seremos	**fuimos**	**éramos**	
	you (pl.)	(vosotros/as)	**sois**	seréis	**fuisteis**	**erais**	
	they	(ellos/as/ustedes)	**son**	serán	**fueron**	**eran**	
tener	I	(yo)	**tengo**	**tendré**	**tuve**	tenía	teniendo
(to have)	you	(tú)	**tienes**	**tendrás**	**tuviste**	tenías	tenido
	he/she/it	(él/ella/usted)	**tiene**	**tendrá**	**tuvo**	tenía	
	we	(nosotros/as)	tenemos	**tendremos**	**tuvimos**	teníamos	
	you (pl.)	(vosotros/as)	tenéis	**tendréis**	**tuvisteis**	teníais	
	they	(ellos/as/ustedes)	**tienen**	**tendrán**	**tuvieron**	tenían	
venir	I	(yo)	**vengo**	**vendré**	**vine**	venía	**viniendo**
(to come)	you	(tú)	**vienes**	**vendrás**	**viniste**	venías	venido
	he/she/it	(él/ella/usted)	**viene**	**vendrá**	**vino**	venía	
	we	(nosotros/as)	venimos	**vendremos**	**vinimos**	veníamos	
	you (pl.)	(vosotros/as)	venís	**vendréis**	**vinisteis**	veníais	
	they	(ellos/as/ustedes)	**vienen**	**vendrán**	**vinieron**	venían	
ver	I	(yo)	**veo**	veré	**vi**	**veía**	viendo
(to see)	you	(tú)	ves	verás	viste	**veías**	**visto**
	he/she/it	(él/ella/usted)	ve	verá	**vio**	**veía**	
	we	(nosotros/as)	vemos	veremos	vimos	**veíamos**	
	you (pl.)	(vosotros/as)	veis	veréis	visteis	**veíais**	
	they	(ellos/as/ustedes)	ven	verán	vieron	**veían**	

Vocabulario

español–inglés

A

el abanico *fan*
el aceite *oil*
ácido/a *acid*
acogedor(a) *cozy*
el acoso *harassment*
acostarse *to go to sleep*
actualmente *currently*
actuar *to act*
acuático/a *aquatic*
adelgazar *to lose weight*
además *moreover*
adjunto/a *enclosed/attached*
admirar *to admire*
adorar *to worship*
adquirido/a *acquired*
la adrenalina *adrenaline*
la advertencia *warning*
aeróbico/a *aerobic*
la aerolínea *airline*
aficionado/a *fan*
el agujero *hole*
el ajedrez *chess*
el ala *wing*
el albergue *hostel*
alejarse *to go away*
el algodón *cotton*
alterado/a *altered*
la alternativa *alternative*
el aluminio *aluminum*
el/la amante *lover*
amar *to love*
la amenaza *threat*
la amistad *friendship*
el amor *love*
amplio/a *wide*
anteayer *the day before yesterday*
la antena *antenna*
anteriormente *previously*
anti-corridas *anti-bullfighting*
el anuncio *advertisement*
apagar *to switch off*
aparcar *park*
aparecer *to appear*
el apartamento *apartment*
apasionado/a *passionate*
apasionante *exciting*
apellidarse *to have as a surname*
apellido *surname*
apetecer *to fancy*
aportar *to provide*
apoyar *to support*
aprovechar *to make the most of*
la aptitud *aptitude*
apto/a *suitable*
las armas *weapons*
arreglar *to fix*
arrojar *to throw*
el arroz *rice*
el artículo *item*
el ascensor *lift*
¡qué asco! *how disgusting!*
el asiento *seat*
asistir *to attend*
el asma *asthma*
el asunto *matter*
los asuntos de negocios *business affairs*
el atasco *jam*
atentamente *sincerely*
la atmósfera *atmosphere*
las atracciones *attractions*
atreverse *to dare*
el aumento *increase*
aunque *although*
la autopista *highway*
avanzado/a *advanced*
el ayuno *fasting*
el ayuntamiento *City Hall*
la azafata *stewardess*
el azafato *flight attendant (male)*

B

el bachillerato *A-level equivalent*
el baile *dance*
el banco *bank*
la banda *band*
la bandera *flag*
la barbaridad *piece of nonsense*
la barra *bar*
barrer *to sweep*
el barrio *neighborhood/district*
la batalla *battle*
la belleza *beauty*
el beneficio *benefit*
el beso *kiss*
la biblioteca *library*
bienvenido/a *welcome*
bilingüe *bilingual*
blando/a *soft*
la bolera *bowling alley*
el bollo *bun, bread roll*
la bolsa *bag*
el bolso *handbag*
los bombones *chocolates*
borracho/a *drunk*
el bosque *forest*
la botella *bottle*
el buceo *diving*
la burbuja *bubble*

C

el caballo *horse*
la cabaña *hut*
la cadena *chain*
caer *fall*
la caída *fall*
la caja *box*
la cajera *female cashier*
el cajero *male cashier, cash point*
el calentamiento *warming*
callado/a *silent*
el callejero *city map*
el calor *heat*
calórico/a *caloric*
cambiar *to change*
caminar *to walk*
el campeonato *championship*
el campo *countryside*
la cancha *sports court*
cansado/a *tired*
la cantidad *amount*
el canto *singing*
la capa de ozono *ozone layer*
la capacidad *capacity, ability*
el carbón *coal*
el Caribe *Caribbean*
el/la carnicero/a *butcher*
caro/a *expensive*
la carrera *race*
la carta *letter*
el cartón *cardboard*
casarse *to get married*
la caseta *stand, stall*
casi *almost*
el castillo *castle*
la cena *dinner*
cerca *close*
el cerdo *pig*
cerrado *closed*
la cerveza *beer*
charlar *to chat*
el chicle *chewing gum*
chulo/a *cool*
el churro *Spanish fritter*
el cinturón *belt*
el circuito *circuit*
el cirio *candle*
el/la ciudadano/a *citizen*
civil *civil*
claro/a *clear*
el/la colega *colleague*
la colilla *butt*
el combustible *fuel*
comenzar *to begin*
comercial *commercial*
el comercio *trade*
la comida basura *junk food*
la compañía *company*
compartir *to share*
el comportamiento *behaviour*
la comunidad *community*
concluir *to conclude*
el concurso *contest*
conducir *to drive*
el conejo *rabbit*
conmigo *with me*
conocido/a *known*
el/la consejero/a *counselor, adviser*
el consejo *advice*
constar de *to consist of*
construir *to build*
la consulta *query*
el/la contable *accountant*
contribuir *to contribute*
conveniente *desirable, convenient*
convertido/a *converted*
la copa *cup*

el corazón *heart*
la corbata *tie*
el cordero *lamb*
el correo *mail*
la correspondencia *correspondence*
la corrida *bull fighting*
cortado/a *cut*
cortar *to cut*
un crack *an ace (slang)*
el crucero *cruise*
el cuadriciclo *quadricycle*
cuál/es *which one/ones*
la cualidad *quality*
cualquier *any*
la cuaresma *Lent*
el cuero *leather*
cuidado *care*
la culpa *fault*
cultivar *to grow*
curioso/a *curious*

D

dañar *to damage*
dar *to give*
decidir *to decide*
decir *say*
la decisión *decision*
declarar *to declare*
la defensa *defense*
la deforestación *deforestation*
dejar *to let*
delante *in front of*
el delantero *forward*
el delfín *dolphin*
los/las demás *other*
demasiado/a *too/too much…*
dentro *inside*
dentro de… años *within… years*
deprimido/a *depressed*
el derecho *right*
desafortunadamente *unfortunately*
desaparecer *to disappear*
el desarrollo *development*
el descanso *rest*
descargar *to download*
describir *to describe*
descubrir *to discover*
el descuento *discount*
desde *from*
desear *to wish*
el desempleo *unemployment*
desenchufar *to unplug*
desgraciadamente *unfortunately*
el desierto *desert*
deslizar *to slide*
desobediente *disobedient*
despacio *slowly*
destacar *to stress*
destruir *to destroy*
la desventaja *disadvantage*
el detalle *detail*
el detergente *detergent*
diario/a *daily*
el dibujo *art*
la dificultad *difficulty*
la dignidad *dignity*
dinámico/a *dynamic*
el dióxido *dioxide*
la dirección *address*
el/la director/a *manager*
dirigirse a *to write to (formal)*
discreto/a *discreet*
la discriminación *discrimination*
disfrutar *to enjoy*
disponer *to have*
distinto/a *different*
la diversión *fun*
el dolor *pain*
el domicilio *home*
el dominio *domain*
el/la drogadicto/a *drug addict*
la duda *doubt*
el dulce *sweet*
durante *during*
durar *to last*

E

echar *to throw away*
el edificio *building*
la editorial *publishing company*
egoísta *selfish*
el electrodoméstico *appliance*
elegir *to choose*
eliminar *to remove*
la embarcación *boat*
sin embargo *but*
emborracharse *to get drunk*
emisión *emission*
la emoción *excitement*
emocionante *exciting*
emparejar *to match*
empezar *to begin*
el/la empleado/a *employee*
emprendedor(a) *enterprising*
la empresa *company*
en seguida *immediately*
en vez de *instead*
enamorado/a *in love*
encantar *to love*
el encargo *order*
encender *to turn on*
enchufar *to plug in*
encontrar *to find/meet*
enfadarse *to get angry*
la enfermedad *disease*
la enfermería *nursing*
enfermo/a *sick*
engordar *to fatten*
el enlace *link*
la enseñanza *education, teaching*
enseñar *to teach*
ensuciar *to get/make dirty*
entender *to understand*
entero/a *whole*
entonces *then*
el entorno *environment*
la entrada *ticket*
entrar *to enter*
entre *between*
entrenar *to train*
entretenido/a *entertaining*
equilibrado/a *balanced*
equipado/a *equipped*
el equipo *team*
la equitación *horseriding*
ese/esa *that …*
esos/esas *those …*
la escalera *stairs*
la escena *scene*
escolar *school*
escuchar *to listen*
la ESO *Obligatory Secondary Education*
el espacio *space*
esperar *to wait*
el estadio *stadium*
estadounidense *Northamerican*
la estancia *stay*
el estilo *style*
estimado/a *dear (formal)*
la estrella *star*
estresado/a *stressed out*
el evento *event*
evidente *clear, obvious*
evitar *to avoid*
la exclusión *exclusion*
la excursión *trip*
la explicación *explanation*
explicar *to explain*
explotar *to exploit*
el exterior *outside*
la extinción *extinction*
extranjero/a *foreign*
extraño/a *strange*
extremo/a *extreme*
extrovertido/a *extrovert*

F

la fábrica *factory*
familiar *familiar*
la fauna *fauna*
la fecha *date*
la felicidad *happiness*
la feria *fair*
el filete *steak*
la finca *state*
fino/a *thin*
la firma *signature*
la flora *flora*
la floristería *florist*
el folleto *brochure*
el formulario *form*
el fósil *fossil*
los fuegos artificiales *fireworks*
la fuerza *strength*

G

gallego *Galician*
la galleta *cookie*
la gallina *hen*
la ganga *bargain*
el garaje *garage*
garantizar *to ensure*
la gasolina *petrol*

la gestión *management*
el gesto *gesture*
gigante *huge*
golpear *to hit*
gordísimo/a *very fat*
la gorra *cap*
la grabación *recording*
gracioso/a *funny*
gráfico/a *graphic*
la granja *farm*
la grasa *fat*
gratis *free*
gratuito/a *free*
grave *serious*
grosero/a *rude*
el guante *glove*
la guerra *war*
el/la guía *guide*
la guirnalda *garland*
gustar *to like*

H

el habitante *inhabitant*
habitualmente *usually*
hablar *to talk*
hacer *to do, to make*
hambre *hunger*
harto/a *sick of*
el hecho *fact*
la herencia *inheritance*
la hermanastra *stepsister*
el hermanastro *stepbrother*
la heroína *heroin*
híbrido/a *hybrid*
la hidroeléctrica *hydropower*
el hielo *ice*
la hierba *grass*
higiénico/a *higienic*
el/la hincha *fan, supporter*
hindú *hindu*
el hipermercado *supermarket*
la hipoteca *mortgage*
el horario *timetable*
horroroso/a *horrible*
el huevo *egg*
humanitario/a *humanitarian*

I

la igualdad *equality*
iluminado/a *lit*
la ilusión *illusion*
ilustrar *to illustrate*
importar *to import*
imprescindible *essential*
impresionar *to impress*
imprimir *to print*
incluso *even*
la incorporación *incorporation*
increíble *amazing/unbelievable*
independiente *independent*
la indignidad *indignity*
individual *single*
individualizado/a *individualised*
la industria *industry*
industrial *industrial*
infantil *infant*
influir *to influence*
ingerir *ingest*
inmerso/a *immersed*
inolvidable *unforgettable*
el insecticida *insecticide*
inseguro/a *insecure*
la instalación *installation*
la institución *institution*
intensivo/a *intensive*
intentar *to try*
el interés *interest*
interesar *to interest*
interior *inside*
introvertido/a *introvert*
el invernadero *greenhouse*
la invitación *invitation*
el/la invitado/a *guest*
ir *to go*
la isla *island*

J

el jabón *soap*
el jamón *ham*
japonés *Japanese*
el/la jefe/a *boss*
el jersey *jumper*
la jornada *working day*
el/la joven *young person*
las joyas *jewelry*
la joyería *jewelry shop*
el/la jubilado/a *retired*
el/la jugador(a) *player*
el juguete *toy*
junto *together*
justo/a *fair*
juvenil *youthful*
la juventud *youth*
laboral *working*
el lado *side*
la lana *wool*
largo/a *long*
la lástima *pity*
la lata *tin, can*
la lavadora *washing machine*
la lavandería *laundry*

L

el lavaplatos *dishwasher*
lavar *to wash*
la lectura *reading*
legar *to bequeath*
lejano/a *distant*
la lenteja *lentil*
lento/a *slow*
levantarse *to get up*
la ley *law*
la libertad *freedom*
libre *free*
llamar *to call*
la llegada *arrival*
llegar *to arrive*
llenar *to fill*
llevar *to carry*
llover *to rain*
la lluvia *rain*
loco/a *crazy*
lograr *to achieve*
la loncha *slice*
la lucha *fight*
el lugar *place*
el lujo *luxury*
lujoso/a *luxurious*
la luz *light*

M

maduro/a *mature*
el maíz *corn*
la maleta *suitcase*
el maletín *briefcase*
malgastar *to waste*
el maltrato *abuse*
mandar *to order, to send*
el manejo *use*
la manera *way*
la mano *hand*
mantener *to hold, to support*
la mantequilla *butter*
el manzano *apple tree*
el mar *sea*
maravilloso/a *wonderful*
el marinero *sailor*
el marisco *seafood*
la mascota *pet*
matar *to kill*
el matrimonio *marriage*
mayor *bigger, older*
la media *average*
el medio ambiente *environment*
la meditación *meditation*
meditar *to meditate*
mejor *better, best*
mejorar *to improve*
memorizar *to memorise*
el menaje *kitchenware*
el/la mendigo *beggar*
menor *minor*
el mensaje (de texto) *(text) message*
la menta *mint*
a menudo *often*
merecer *to deserve*
la merluza *hake*
el metal *metal*
el metro *metre*
la mezquita *mosque*
el miedo *fear*
el miembro *member*
mientras *while*
mil *one thousand*
la milla *mile*
la misa *mass (church)*
mismo/a *same*
el misterio *mystery*
la mitad *half*
mixto/a *mixed*
la moda *fashion*
modificar *to change*
el modo *way*

molestar *to bother*
el monasterio *monastery*
el monopatín *skateboard*
montar *ride*
el monte *mount*
el montón *pile*
el monumento *monument*
morado/a *purple*
morir *to die*
la motocicleta *motorcycle*
el motor *engine*
mover *to move*
el móvil *mobile*
la mudanza *moving*
mudarse *to move*
el mueble *piece of furniture*
la muerte *death*
muerto/a *dead*
el mundo *world*
musulmán/musulmana *Muslim/Moslem*

N

nacer *to be born*
el nacimiento *birth*
nativo/a *native*
la naturaleza *nature*
navegar por Internet *to surf the net*
la Navidad *Christmas*
nazareno/a *from Nazareth*
necesario/a *necessary*
la necesidad *need*
el negocio *business*
nevar *to snow*
la nevera *fridge*
la niebla *fog*
la nieta *granddaughter*
el nieto *grandson*
la nieve *snow*
ningún/ninguna… *no…*
ninguno/a *none*
la noche *night*
el norte *north*
las noticias *news*
la novela *novel*
la novia *girlfriend*
el novio *boyfriend*
nuestro/a *our*
de nuevo *again*
numeroso/a *numerous*
nunca *never*

O

la obesidad *obesity*
obligatorio/a *compulsory*
la obra *work*
obtener *to obtain*
el ocio *leisure*
ocupado/a *busy*
ofrecer *to offer*
oír *to hear*
oler *to smell*
olvidar *to forget*
la oportunidad *opportunity*
la oscuridad *darkness*
oscuro/a *dark*
el otoño *autumn*
otro/a *other (sing.)*
otros/as *other (pl.)*

P

pachucho/a *under the weather*
el padre *father*
los padres *parents*
pagar *to pay*
el pájaro *bird*
la paliza *beating*
las palomitas *popcorn*
el/la panadero/a *baker*
la pandilla *gang*
panorámico/a *panoramic*
la pantalla *screen*
la papelería *stationary*
el paquete *package*
paralelo/a *parallel*
parcial *partial*
parecer *to seem*
la pared *wall*
el paro *unemployment*
el partido *game*
el/la pasajero/a *passenger*
el pasatiempo *pastime*
pasear *to walk*
el paseo *walk*
el pasillo *corridor*
el pastel *cake*
la pastilla *pill*
la patria *homeland*
el pavo *turkey*
peatonal *pedestrian*
el pez *fish*
el pedal *pedal*
el pedazo *piece*
pedir *to request*
la pelea *fight*
la pelota *ball*
la pena *sorrow*
el pensamiento *thought*
pensar *to think*
la pensión *pension*
peor *worse*
la pepita *seed*
perder *to lose*
perder peso/adelgazar *to lose weight*
la pérdida *loss*
perdido/a *missed, lost*
perezoso/a *lazy*
perfectamente *perfectly*
el periódico *newspaper*
perjudicial *harmful*
el permiso *permit, permission*
permitir *to allow*
la persona *person*
el personaje *character*
personalmente *personally*
pertenecer *to belong*
peruano/a *Peruvian*
pesado/a *heavy, tedious*
a pesar de *although*
pescar *to fish*
el peso *weight*
el petardo *firecracker*
la pieza *piece*
pintado/a *painted*
la pintura *painting*
el piso *floor, flat*
la pista *track*
la pizarra *blackboard*
el placer *pleasure*
el plan *plan*
planchar *to iron*
el planeta *planet*
la planta *plant*
plantar *to plantar*
el plátano *banana*
el plato *dish*
pleno/a *full*
la población *population*
pobre *poor*
pobrecillo/a *poor (diminutive)*
la pobreza *poverty*
poner *to put*
porque *because*
el porro *spliff*
el portátil *laptop*
la postal *postcard*
el postre *dessert*
potable *drinking*
potenciar *to enhance*
practicar *to practice*
practico/a *practical*
precioso/a *precious*
preferentemente *preferably*
el premio *prize*
la prenda *garment*
preocuparse *to worry*
la presencia *presence*
la presentación *presentation*
presentar a *to introduce to*
prestar *to provide, to lend*
la prevención *prevention*
principalmente *mainly*
el príncipe *prince*
el principio *beginning*
privado/a *private*
probar *to test, to try*
la procesión *procession*
prohibido/a *prohibited*
pronto *soon, early*
propio/a *own*
el/la protagonista *protagonist*
proteger *to protect*
provocar *to cause*
próximo/a *next*
publicado/a *published*
publicidad *advertisement*
pues *so*
el puesto *post, job*
el pulmón *lung*
la pulsera *bracelet*
el punto de vista *point of view*
puntual *punctual*

Q

quedar *to meet up*
quedarse *to stay*
quejarse *to complain*

Vocabulario

quemar *to burn*
quemarse *to get burnt*
querido/a *dear*
la química *chemistry*
quitar *to remove*
quizás *maybe*

R

¡Qué rabia! *How annoying!*
la ración *ration*
la radiografía *radiography*
raro/a *strange, odd*
el rato *while*
la razón *reason*
recibir *to receive*
recientemente *recently*
recomendable *recommended*
reconocer *to recognise*
recordar *to remember*
recorrer *to travel*
el recuerdo *souvenir*
reducir *to reduce*
el refresco *soft drink*
el regalo *gift*
la regata *water race*
la regla *rule*
regular *regular*
la rehabilitación *rehabilitation*
reincorporarse *to return*
la reinserción *reintegration*
reír *to laugh*
la relación *relationship*
relajarse *to relax*
rellenar *to fill in*
renovable *renewable*
renovar *to renew*
repartir *to spread*
de repente *suddenly*
el/la reportero/a *reporter*
el residuo *waste*
respetuoso/a *respectful*
respirar *to breath*
el resumen *summary*
la resurrección *resurrection*
retirarse *to retire*
reunir *to gather*
reutilizar *to reuse*
el rey *king*
rico/a *rich, tasty*
el riesgo *risk*
el río *river*
la riqueza *wealth*
riquísimo/a *very rich, tasty*
rizado/a *curly*
la roca *rock*
un rollo *a drag*
romper *to break*
roto/a *broken*
la rueda *wheel*
el ruido *noise*

S

saber *to know*
el sabor *taste*
la sala de juntas *boardroom*
el salario *wage*
la salida *departure, exit*
salir *to leave, to go out*
saludable *healthy*
el saludo *greeting*
salvar *to save*
el salvavidas *lifesaver*
las sandalias *sandals*
sano/a *healthy*
la sardina *sardine*
secar *to dry*
la sed *thirst*
seguido/a *followed*
seguir *to follow*
según *according to*
segundo/a *second*
la seguridad *security*
seguro/a *sure, safe*
la selva *jungle*
sencillo/a *simple*
el senderismo *hiking*
sentado/a *sitting*
sentarse *to sit*
sentir *to feel*
la sequía *drought*
el servicio *service, toilet*
la sevillanas *spanish dance*
el siglo *century*
el silencio *silence*
simbolizar *to symbolise*
sin *without*
sino *but*
sin techo *homeless*
el sistema *system*
el sitio *site, place*
sobre *about, on*
la sobredosis *overdose*
de sobremesa (ordenador) *desktop*
sobrevivir *to survive*
la sobrina *niece*
el sobrino *nephew*
la sociedad *society*
solamente *only*
solar *solar*
solicitar *to request*
la solidaridad *solidarity*
soltero/a *single*

T

la temporada *season*
titular *leading*
la tortuga *turtle*
la tostada *toast*
traducido/a *translated*
el/la traductor(a) *translator*
traer *to bring*
el traje *suit*
el tratamiento *treatment*
tratar *to treat*
el traumatismo *trauma*
a través de *through*
la travesía *voyage*
el triciclo *tricycle*
la tristeza *sadness*
la trucha *trout*
el/la tutor(a) *tutor*
tuyo/a *yours*

U

ubicado/a *located*
usted/Ud. *you (formal)*
últimamente *lately*
último/a *last*
único/a *only, unique*
urgentemente *urgently*
usado/a *used*
usar *to use*
el uso *use*
útil *useful*
la utilización *use*
utilizar *to use*

V

vacío/a *empty*
vago/a *lazy*
el vampiro *vampire*
los vaqueros *jeans*
variado/a *varied*
el vaso *glass*
veces *times*
el/la vecino/a *neighbor*
vela *sailing*
el velero *sailing boat*
vender *to sell*
venir *to come*
la ventaja *advantage*
ver *to see, to watch*
la vergüenza *shame*
el vestuario *changing-room*
la vez *time*
una vez *once*
la victoria *victory*
la vida *life*
el vidrio *glass*
el viento *wind*
vigilar *to watch*
vigoroso/a *vigorous*
el VIH / SIDA *HIV / AIDS*
la vista *sight, view*
volar *fly*
el/la voluntario/a *volunteer*
volver *to return*
la vuelta *back*

Y

el yogur *yogurt*

Z

la zanahoria *carrot*
la zona *area*

inglés—español

A

a lot of *mucho/a/os/as*
about, of *de*
active *activo/a*
afterwards *después*
all the time *todo el tiempo*
also *también*
always *siempre*
almost *casi*
and *y*
anything, something *algo*
as well *también*
at the end of *al final de*

B

bad *malo/a*
because *porque*
to become *convertirse*
behind *detrás de*
best *el/la mejor*
better, best *mejor*
black *negro/a*
blue *azul*
book *el libro*
boring *aburrido/a*
brilliant *genial*
brother *el hermano*
brown *marrón, castaño/a*
but *pero*
to buy *comprar*

C

can, to be able *poder*
car *el coche*
to change *cambiar*
to charge a mobile *cargar un móvil*
to chat *chatear*
cheap *barato/a*
chess club *el club de ajedrez*
chicken *el pollo*
choir *el coro*
cigarette *el cigarrillo*
cinema *el cine*
to clean *limpiar*
customer *el cliente/la clienta*
clothes *la ropa*
coffee *el café*
to comb *peinarse*
comfortable *cómodo/a*
concert *el concierto*
cool *guay*
creative *creativo/a*
to cross the square *cruzar la plaza*

D

daily routine *la rutina diaria*
to dance *bailar*
day *el día*
the day after tomorrow *pasado mañana*
the day before yesterday *anteayer*
delicious *rico/a*
design *el diseño*
difficult *difícil*
to do my homework *hacer mis deberes*
to download *descargar*
a drag *un rollo*
during *durante*
dynamic *dinámico/a*

E

to earn money *ganar dinero*
easy *fácil*
egg *el huevo*
energy *la energía*
England *Inglaterra*
English *(el) inglés*
entertaining *divertido/a*
environment *el medio ambiente*
every day *todos los días*
Excuse me… *Perdón…*
expensive *caro/a*

F

few *poco/a*
fair *justo/a*
fair, blond *rubio/a*
fantastic *estupendo/a*
film *la película*
finally *por último*
first *primero*
flu *la gripe*
food *la comida*
football *el fútbol*
for… *desde…*
For how long? *¿Desde hace cuánto tiempo?*
for, (in order) to *para*
free time *(el) tiempo libre*
French *(el) francés*
Friday *el viernes*
from time to time *de vez en cuando*
fruit *la fruta*
fun *divertido/a*

G

great! *¡qué bien!*
German *(el) alemán*
Germany *Alemania*
to get dressed *vestirse*
to get up *levantarse*
to go on an outing *ir de excursión*
to go out *salir*
to go to *ir a*
to go to bed *ir a dormir*
to go to the park *ir al parque*
good luck *buena suerte*
good-looking *guapo/a*
great *genial*
green *verde*
grey *gris*
gym *el gimnasio*

H

half a kilo of *medio kilo de*
hand *la mano*
hardly ever *casi nunca*
hard-working *trabajador(a)*
to hate *odiar*
to have a cold *tener un resfriado*
to have a fantastic time *pasarlo bomba*
to have a wonderful time *pasarlo fenomenal*
to have breakfast *desayunar*
to have dinner/supper *cenar*
he *él*
healthy *sano/a*
here *aquí*
daughter *la hija*
his/her *su(s)*
history *la historia*
holidays *las vacaciones*
how often? *¿con qué frecuencia?*
to be hungry *tener hambre*
to hurt *doler*

I

I *yo*
ICT *la informática*
ill *enfermo/a*
in *en*
in front of *delante de*
in order to *para*
in the evening *por la tarde*
in the morning *por la mañana*

L

language club *el club de idiomas*
last Friday *el viernes pasado*
last summer *el verano pasado*
last winter *el invierno pasado*
last year *el año pasado*
later *más tarde*
lawyer *el/la abogado/a*
lazy *perezoso/a*
least *el/la menos*
leather *de cuero*
left *izquierda*
less… than *menos… que*
lesson *la clase*
Let's see… *A ver…*
library *la biblioteca*
life *la vida*
like *gustar*
to listen to music *escuchar música*
arrive *llegar*

long *largo/a*
to lose weight *adelgazar*
lunch hour *la hora de comer*

M

main course *el segundo plato*
market *el mercado*
to marry *casarse*
martial arts *las artes marciales*
match (football) *el partido de fútbol*
Monday *el lunes*
month *el mes*
monument *el monumento*
more *más*
more… than *más… que*
more or less *más o menos*
the most/ the -est *el más…*
moving *emocionante*
to must *deber*
my *mi(s)*

N

nationality *la nacionalidad*
to need *necesitar*
neither *tampoco*
never *nunca*
next year *el año que viene*
nice, pretty *bonito/a*
night *la noche*
no mucho *not a lot*
noise *el ruido*
normally *normalmente*
nothing *nada*
nothing else *nada más*
now *ahora*
now and then *de vez en cuando*

O

o'clock *en punto*
of course *claro que sí*
often *a menudo*
old-fashioned *anticuado/a*
on foot *a pie*
on time *a tiempo*
or *o*
our *nuestro/a*
organised *organizado/a*

P

patient *paciente*
to pay *pagar*
to phone *llamar por teléfono*
pink *rosa*
to play *jugar*
to play football *jugar al fútbol*
please *por favor*
por eso *so, therefore*
practical *práctico/a*
professional *profesional*
to protect *proteger*
public transport *el transporte público*
pupil *el/la alumno/a*

R

to read *leer*
to recycle *reciclar*
red *rojo/a*
red haired *pelirrojo/a*
responsible *responsable*
to rest *descansar*
restaurant *el restaurante*
return (ticket) *(el billete) de ida y vuelta*
to ride a bike *montar en bicicleta*
to run *correr*

S

sandwich *el bocadillo*
Saturday *el sábado*
to save *ahorrar*
school *el instituto/colegio*
to send an email *mandar un correo electrónico*
serious *serio/a*
she *ella*
shop *la tienda*
shopping centre *el centro comercial*
short *bajo/a, corto/a*
to shower *ducharse*
shy *tímido/a*
to sing *cantar*
single ticket *el billete de ida*
sister *la hermana*
slim *delgado/a*
to smoke *fumar*
sometimes *a veces*
sort of… *tipo de…*
Spanish *(el) español*
to speak *hablar*
sport *el deporte*
to start *empezar*
starter *el primer plato*
straight on *todo recto*
strict *estricto/a*
striped *de rayas*
strong *fuerte*
to study *estudiar*
stupid *estúpido/a*
to sunbathe *tomar el sol*
Sunday *el domingo*

T

take *tomar*
to take photos *sacar fotos*
talkative *hablador(a)*
tall *alto/a*
text message *el mensaje de texto*
they *ellos/as*
their *su/s*
theirs *suyo/a*
then *luego*
these *estos, estas*
thirst *sed*
this *este, esta*
Thursday *el jueves*
ticket *el billete/la entrada*
to tidy up *ordenar*
tired *cansado/a*
to *a*
to feel well *sentirse bien*
toast *la tostada*
today *hoy*
tomorrow *mañana*
to travel *viajar*
tree *el árbol*
Tuesday *el martes*
to turn right *girar a la derecha*
twice a week *dos veces a la semana*

U

ugly *feo/a*
uncomfortable *incómodo/a*
useful *útil*
usually *generalmente*

W

to wake up *despertarse*
Wales *Gales*
to wash *lavar*
to waste *malgastar*
water *el agua*
wavy *ondulado/a*
to wear/to carry *llevar*
the weather *el tiempo*
Wednesday *el miércoles*
week *la semana*
weekend *el fin de semana*
Well… *Pues/Bueno…*
what's more *además*
with *con*
to work *trabajar*
worst *peor*
to write *escribir*

Y

yellow *amarillo/a*
yesterday *ayer*
yesterday evening *ayer por la tarde*
you (sing.) *tú*
you (plural) *vosotros/as*
yours (sing.) *tuyo/a*
yours (plural) *vuestro/a*